Strangers in the Land

Strangers in the Land

PATTERNS OF AMERICAN NATIVISM
1860-1925

JOHN HIGHAM

RUTGERS UNIVERSITY PRESS
New Brunswick, New Jersey

Third paperback printing, 1994

Library of Congress Cataloging-in-Publication Data

Higham, John.
 Strangers in the land.

 Bibliography: p.
 Includes index.
 1. Minorities—United States. 2. Prejudices—
United States. 3. Nativism. 4. United States—
Emigration and immigration. 5. United States—Race
relations. 6. United States—Ethnic relations.
I. Title.
E184.A1I15 1988   305.8'00973   87-32336
ISBN 0-8135-1317-0
ISBN 0-8135-1308-1 (pbk.)

British Cataloging-in-Publication Information Available

Permission has been granted by the *New Republic* to quote from their issue
of June 4, 1924, and by Grosset and Dunlap for a quotation from Peter B.
Kyne's *Never the Twain Shall Meet*.

To the Memory of

MY FATHER AND MOTHER

And if a stranger sojourn with thee in your land, ye shall not vex him. But the stranger that dwelleth with you shall be unto you as one born among you, and thou shalt love him as thyself; for ye were strangers in the land of Egypt. . . .

—Leviticus, xix, 33-34

Preface to the Second Edition

The occasion for this new edition of *Strangers in the Land* was provided by a scholarly quarterly, *American Jewish History*, which devoted the entire issue of December 1986 to a reexamination of the book and the topic it treats. My publisher and I had grown accustomed over the years to letting the book take care of itself. Now the obligation to respond to the stimulating essays that the editor of *American Jewish History*, Marc Lee Raphael, had gathered forced me to think afresh about the meanings the work had for me when I conceived it and the meanings it retains today. The present edition includes a modified version of the comment I wrote for that recent symposium. In order not to intrude unduly on the book itself, I have placed these personal reflections at the end, as an afterword, and have dispensed with the preface carried in earlier editions. I am grateful to *American Jewish History*, its editor, and its contributors for helping me to understand my own book in the context of more recent history.

The text used here adds a few more corrections (only one of them substantive) to those that were made for Atheneum's paperback edition in 1963. Reviewing for the last time these small improvements on the text that Rutgers University Press published in 1955 has brought to mind certain obligations unacknowledged heretofore. In addition to the mentors, friends, and librarians thanked in the first edition, I want to record an enduring obligation to the then director of Rutgers Press, William Sloane, who gave the book its title and its handsome appearance; to Katherine Morgan, my deft copy editor; to Richard Hofstadter and Ray Billington, two superlative historians who were (outside of my own circle) my earliest and most sustaining readers; and, closest at hand, to my wife, Eileen.

Contents

Strangers in the Land

Chapter One

Patterns in the Making

> Providence has been pleased to give this one connected country to one united people—a people descended from the same ancestors, speaking the same language, professing the same religion, attached to the same principles of government, very similar in their manners and customs. . . .
> —*The Federalist*

Nativism has been hard for historians to define. The word is distinctively American, a product of a specific chain of events in eastern American cities in the late 1830's and early 1840's. Yet it has a penumbra of meaning so broad and indefinite that sometimes it seems to refer to a perennial human experience. Does nativism consist only of the particular complex of attitudes dominant in the anti-foreign crusade of the mid-nineteenth century? Or does it extend to every occasion when native inhabitants of a country turn their faces or raise their hands against strangers in their midst?

From the Garden of Eden to 1984, no age or society seems wholly free from unfavorable opinions on outsiders. Understood in such general terms, nativism would include every type and level of antipathy toward aliens, their institutions, and their ideas. Its beginnings in American history would date from the first Indian resistance to white intruders. This view, by reducing nativism to little more than a general ethnocentric habit of mind, blurs its historical significance. On the other hand, confining nativism to the special sort of movement prominent for a couple of decades in the middle of the nineteenth century is too narrow; the inner spirit of that movement has taken quite different guises at other times and places. The spirit of American nativism appeared long before the

3

word was coined about 1840 and had its deepest impact long after the word had largely dropped out of common parlance.

Not the nativists themselves, apparently, but rather their critics attached the label to them. When anti-foreign parties arose in New York and other cities after 1835 and evolved gradually into the powerful "Know-Nothing" agitation of the 1850's, opponents denounced the movement as bigoted nativism. Its champions, however, preferred another designation. At first they called their organizations Native American parties, then simply the American party. Their philosophy they described as Americanism. "The grand work of the American party," proclaimed one of the Know-Nothing journals in 1855, "is the principle of nationality . . . we must do something to protect and vindicate it. If we do not it will be destroyed." [1]

Here was the ideological core of nativism in every form. Whether the nativist was a workingman or a Protestant evangelist, a southern conservative or a northern reformer, he stood for a certain kind of nationalism. He believed—whether he was trembling at a Catholic menace to American liberty, fearing an invasion of pauper labor, or simply rioting against the great English actor William Macready—that some influence originating abroad threatened the very life of the nation from within. Nativism, therefore, should be defined as intense opposition to an internal minority on the ground of its foreign (i.e., "un-American") connections. Specific nativistic antagonisms may, and do, vary widely in response to the changing character of minority irritants and the shifting conditions of the day; but through each separate hostility runs the connecting, energizing force of modern nationalism. While drawing on much broader cultural antipathies and ethnocentric judgments, nativism translates them into a zeal to destroy the enemies of a distinctively American way of life.

Continuous involvement in larger movements of American nationalism has meant that nativism usually rises and falls in some relation to other intense kinds of national feeling. The nationalist nexus has also meant that the nativist's most characteristic complaint runs against the loyalty of some foreign (or allegedly foreign) group. Seeing or suspecting a failure of assimilation, he fears disloyalty. Occasionally the charge of disloyalty may stand forth naked and unadorned, but usually it is colored and focused by a persistent conception about what is un-American. In other words, nativistic agitation had tended to follow certain stylized themes. Three of these themes stand out as main currents in American nativism, each with a separate history reaching back before the Civil War.

By far the oldest and—in early America—the most powerful of the anti-foreign traditions came out of the shock of the Reformation. Protestant hatred of Rome played so large a part in pre-Civil War nativist thinking that historians have sometimes regarded nativism and anti-Catholicism as more or less synonymous.[2] This identification, by oversimplifying two complex ideas, does little justice to either. Many social and religious factors, some of them nativistic only in a very indirect sense, have contributed powerfully to anti-Catholic feeling. It has drawn heavily, for example, from the very beginning of the Reformation on a conception of popery as steeped in moral depravity. Generation after generation of Protestant zealots have repeated the apocalyptic references of the early religious reformers to the Whore of Babylon, the Scarlet Woman, the Man of Sin, to which they have added tales of lascivious priests and debauched nuns. On a rational level, too, the clash of faiths has cut deeply. One must expect some measure of tension to survive all adjustments between them, increasing or diminishing in proportion to the force with which Protestant and Catholic assert historic claims. Anti-Catholicism has become truly nativistic, however, and has reached maximum intensity, only when the Church's adherents seemed dangerously foreign agents in the national life.

Although modern nationalism was in its infancy in the sixteenth century, the Protestant revolt exhibited a vaguely patriotic tinge from the time Martin Luther first rallied the German princes against the Church of Rome. In England, particularly, hatred of Catholicism entered into an emerging national consciousness. The English in the sixteenth and seventeenth centuries were struggling more or less continuously against rival Catholic powers or their own pro-Catholic monarchs. The Roman pontiff loomed in English eyes as the great foreign tyrant, menacing the nation and its constitution; his followers had the aspect of a fifth column. By 1679 Titus Oates could plunge the whole kingdom into hysteria with crazy charges of a subversive Catholic conspiracy.

Carried across the Atlantic, the anti-Catholic heritage formed an important element in colonial loyalties and, with the rise of an American nationalism, affected that in turn. The tradition acquired a very real local significance in the New World, for the English colonies were wedged between two hostile Catholic empires, France and Spain. Consequently a militant Protestantism deeply colored the American national feeling stimulated by the French and Indian War. Then the American Revolution, accompanied by a growing religious toleration and secular democracy, largely suspended the wars of the godly.[3] But anti-Catholic xenophobia by no means disappeared. Although recessive, it remained an important counterpoise to more generous ideals of nationality.

For two principal reasons an undercurrent of Protestant nativism persisted into the new democratic America and revived in the second quarter of the nineteenth century. One reason lay in the character of American institutions. Catholic traditions continued to look dangerously un-American partly because they did not harmonize easily with the concept of individual freedom imbedded in the national culture. Americans regarded political liberty as their chief national attribute and supreme achievement. Observing the authoritarian organization of the Catholic Church and its customary association with feudal or monarchical governments, they were tempted to view American liberty and European popery as irreconcilable.

Secondly, a fresh Catholic challenge to American institutions emerged. The Catholic empires that had seemed to block national aspirations in the eighteenth century had given way; but in their place the nineteenth century brought a flood of Catholic immigrants. Nativists, charged with the Protestant evangelical fervor of the day, considered the immigrants minions of the Roman despot, dispatched here to subvert American institutions. (Indeed, the most excited patriots detected a vast European plot headed by the Pope.) Surely such creatures were unfit for citizenship. Anti-Catholic nativism, aiming at stiff naturalization laws and exclusion of Catholics and foreigners from public office, completely overshadowed every other nativist tradition.

By themselves, however, these factors were apparently not enough to make the "No-Popery" agitation a major force in national affairs. It became such only when sectional strife produced a general crisis in American society in the 1850's. With the old parties dissolving and the bonds of national unity strained to the breaking-point, the American party offered a way of championing national homogeneity. Its strength reached a climax in 1855, when it elected six governors on a platform that subordinated the foreign peril to a simple appeal for maintaining the Union by developing "a sentiment of profoundly intense American feeling." [4] But the division between North and South, which nativists endeavored to submerge, soon submerged nativism. The anti-foreign crusade could not prevail against sectional forces which were themselves evolving into overriding loyalties. Northern nativists rallied to the northern nationalism of Abraham Lincoln; southern nativists submitted to a new southern nationalism.

A second nativist tradition, much less prominent in the 1850's than anti-Catholicism, went back a half-century before. From the 1790's, a fear of foreign radicals had lurked in the corners of the American mind. While agitated Protestants regarded the immigrant as yoked to religious despotism, timid conservatives sometimes found him prone to political revolution. Despite inconsistencies between the two charges of submissiveness to tyranny and abandonment to discontent, anti-Catholic and anti-radical nativism agreed in a cardinal assumption: the European's disloyalty strikes directly at republican freedom.

For a long time it was hard for Americans to view revolution in a very ominous light. Their own origins as a nation rested in it; their Declaration of Independence celebrated it. On the whole, American opinion applauded the liberal revolutions occurring in Europe and Latin America in the eighteenth and nineteenth centuries. Refugee radicals not infrequently received a hero's welcome in the home of the oppressed. Still, another attitude toward revolutionists was possible, even at an early date. In contrast to similar upheavals in other lands, the American Revolution had involved relatively little political or social transformation; its leaders aimed at perfecting an existing society, not at building a new one on its ruins.[5] In retrospect, the spirit of '76 could appear even more sober than it was, and vastly different from the temper of *foreign* revolutions. And since the flexibility of American institutions has continued to discourage extreme dissent, America's most uncompromising radicals have in fact come from abroad. This persistent contrast between a generally hopeful psychology of mobility in America and the more desperate politics born in class-ridden Europe has fostered the belief that violent and sweeping opposition to the status quo is characteristically European and profoundly un-American. Thus, anti-radical movements in America, like anti-Catholic ones, have had a singular propensity to assume a nationalistic form.

Anti-radical nativism crystallized at the end of the eighteenth century under the impact of the French Revolution. In 1798 the United States faced both an internal and an external crisis comparable in some ways to the sectional split of the 1850's. Internationally the country was heading toward war with revolutionary France. At home a "factious" opposition, brandishing French slogans, was organizing against the Federalist gentlemen who had unified the new nation. Sober Federalists quailed at the ardent sympathy the Jeffersonian party showed toward French democracy; for the intellectual ties between Jeffersonian and Jacobin simply confirmed a fundamental Federalist conviction that democracy was a subversive, revolutionary idea. Furthermore, the ruling gentlemen noted grimly the internal support their opponents received from English, French, and Irish immigrants. Pessimists at heart, the Federalists concluded that Europe's disorders might swiftly overwhelm the new world.[6] In their hysterical determination to check foreign radicalism and native dissent, they proceeded to enact the notorious Alien and Sedition Acts.

By 1800 the war crisis had passed; and at home the triumph of Jeffersonian democracy largely dispelled both conservative pessimism and anti-radical nativism. The passing of Federalist gloom left the American people convinced of their invulnerability to the social ills of the Old World. For many decades confidence in the stability of American institutions and in their appeal to all mankind quieted nationalistic fears of revolution. But occasional doubts lingered in conservative circles. Perhaps people bred under oppression lack self-reliance and self-restraint; in America they may confuse equal rights with "voluptuous license." Perhaps a man discontented in his own country will have no settled principles or loyalty at all.[7] The coming of the German Forty-Eighters rekindled the flickering suspicions. These refugees from revolution, among them the founders of a Marxist movement in America, brought a whole grab-bag of unorthodox ideas. Especially in the

South, where German opposition to slavery caused alarm, and in the Midwest, where German settlement concentrated, the xenophobia of the 1850's included anxiety over the threat of immigrant radicals to American institutions.[8]

The anti-radical and anti-Catholic traditions had, on the surface, a negative character that sets them apart from a third and more recent style of nativist thinking. The first two traditions declared what America was not, more clearly than what it was or should be; they aimed from the outset to define the nation's enemies rather than its essence. Racial nativism, on the other hand, began the other way around. Originally and basically, what may be called the Anglo-Saxon tradition characterized the in-group directly, the alien forces only by implication. The concept that the United States belongs in some special sense to the Anglo-Saxon "race" offered an interpretation of the source of national greatness. The idea crystallized in the early nineteenth century as a way of defining American nationality in a positive sense, not as a formula of attack on outsiders. Thus it affected American nationalism long before it became a factor in American nativism. Despite the inherently parochial bias involved in pointing to a single, limited source of nationhood, Anglo-Saxonism gave only the slightest inkling of its nativistic potentialities until the late nineteenth century.

By one of the manifold ironies of intellectual history, the Anglo-Saxon tradition began as a liberal doctrine: an idea that ended as a slogan for reaction arose as a call for freedom. By another irony, the Americans who attributed the uniqueness and distinction of their nation to the Anglo-Saxon race were simply echoing the prior claims of the English. Proud appeals to Anglo-Saxon origins and ancestors came into vogue in England in the seventeenth and eighteenth centuries among the champions of Parliament. In opposition to royal absolutism, the Parliamentarians sought precedents and roots for English liberty in the ancient institutions and temperament of the country before the Norman conquest. Relying on Tacitus' vivid picture of the Germanic barbarians and on other early texts, the Parliamentarians traced England's freedom-loving heritage to the "Goths," a collective designation for Angles, Saxons, Jutes, and the other primitive tribes that invaded the Roman Empire.

Like the parallel exaltation of Frankish and Gallic forebears in

France, the Gothic vogue had little nationalistic significance until inflated by the romantic ferment of the early nineteenth century. Romantic writers and scholars, rebelling against the uniformitarian outlook of the Enlightenment, loved the diversity and the organic inwardness of all forms of life; to them a nation fulfilled itself through the endogenous forces within its own language and history. Thus the romantics sought in the mists of an early medieval (or "Gothic") past the indestructible core not only of their political institutions but of their whole national character.[9] The circle of ancestral distinction tended to narrow to the Anglo-Saxons, who emerged as the finest offshoot of the Teutonic branch of the Goths; and Englishmen discovered that they owed their national genius to this supposedly unitary racial source.

In England the fountainhead of the new racial nationalism was Sharon Turner's very popular *History of the Anglo-Saxons* (1799-1805), and in American thought the idea received its first considerable impetus from the appearance of a Philadelphia edition of Turner's two-volume work in 1841. As the tradition passed into American hands, it preserved its early libertarian emphasis. Although it now ministered to the national ego instead of implementing a constitutional controversy, this romantic cult still stressed, as the supreme Anglo-Saxon virtue, a gift for political freedom. In the Anglo-Saxons, or perhaps the Teutons, had been implanted a unique capacity for self-government and a special mission to spread its blessings.[10]

In popular thought and emotion, this idea found an initial outlet not among nativists but among expansionists. Many an American, during the annexation of Texas and California, saw himself in the role of his conquering ancestors, executing a racial mandate to enlarge the area of freedom. The penny press roared that the Anglo-Saxon impulse would carry the American flag throughout the continent; whereas those who detested the expansionist movement, like James Russell Lowell, excoriated Anglo-Saxonism as a hypocritical mask for aggression.[11] Nativists, on the other hand, touched on this idea only very rarely and very lightly. Horace Bushnell, as early as 1837, had cautioned the Americans to protect their noble Saxon blood against the miscellaneous tide of immigration, and in the 1850's there were occasional suggestions that a Celtic flood might swamp America's distinctive Anglo-Saxon traits.[12] But on the whole, racial nationalists proclaimed an unqualified confidence in the American destiny. Sometimes they explicitly averred that the Anglo-Saxon would always retain predominance over all comers.[13]

It is significant that the very concept of race had not yet attained its later fixity and definiteness. Racial nationalism, having arisen out of political and literary speculation, not out of scientific inquiry, displayed a characteristic vagueness. In the sense in which nationalists used the word, "race" often meant little more than national character. It usually suggested some sort of innate impulse, but, despite the growing biological interests of the nineteenth century, this was understood as an ongoing spirit more than a physiological actuality. At best a minor strain in American thought before the Civil War, Anglo-Saxon nationalism then lacked both the intellectual and emotional pungency essential to a serious, nativistic appeal.

In addition to the special curbs on race-thinking, every nativist tendency in pre-Civil War America operated under powerful limitations. Only during the two great crises of the 1790's and 1850's did fear of foreign minorities strike deeply in many native hearts. Even then, wider, more inclusive ideals of nationality were stubbornly defended and ultimately victorious. In general the American people maintained a cocksure faith in themselves, in their boundless opportunities for improvement and acquisition, and in the self-perpetuating strength of their principles of freedom.

Nevertheless some of the major ideological outlines of American nativism had been established. The anti-Catholic, anti-radical, and Anglo-Saxon traditions had opened channels through which a large part of the xenophobia of the late nineteenth and twentieth centuries would flow. The content and dynamics of that later story would come from social, economic, and intellectual changes unimagined in the days of the Know-Nothings. But the basic patterns were there.

Chapter Two

The Age of Confidence

[She] gathers the chosen of her seed
From the hunted of every crown and creed.
                    *   *   *
Fused in her candid light,
To one strong race all races here unite.
                    —Bayard Taylor, "Centennial Ode"

Faugh a Ballagh! The Gaelic cry rang out through dense fog and gunsmoke as a wave of Union troops surged up the heights behind ruined Fredericksburg. In their midst floated a green flag bearing the golden harp of Ireland. For fifteen minutes Confederate cannon and muskets poured down volley after volley from impregnable positions a few paces away. At the end of the carnage two-thirds of General Thomas Meagher's Irish Brigade were left crumpled on the field.[1]

About the same time, a little band of dispirited men came together in New York City for the last recorded meeting of the Grand Executive Committee of the Order of United Americans. The largest of the nonpolitical nativistic associations, the O.U.A. had spread through sixteen states in the early 1850's, trumpeting a message of hatred and fear of immigrants and Catholics. Now a demoralized remnant could no longer pay its bills or secure a quorum at consolidated meetings.

One ended in glory while the other expired in neglect, but the death of Irishmen at the Battle of Fredericksburg and the death of the O.U.A. on the home front were connected and symptomatic. All over the country foreign-born Americans flocked to the colors.

Five hundred thousand of them served in the Union armies alone, often organized in their own companies, regiments, and even divisions. Everywhere the anti-foreign movement of prewar years melted away. The very heart of Know-Nothingism, the American party, vanished in 1860, its last surviving strength passing into the Constitutional Union party which stood for nothing but the preservation of the nation. The Sons of America, once mighty in Pennsylvania, succumbed when the war began. A mere fragment of the Order of United American Mechanics remained in existence.[2] The war completed the ruin of organized nativism by absorbing xenophobes and immigrants in a common cause. Now the foreigner had a new prestige; he was a comrade-at-arms. The clash that alienated sections reconciled their component nationalities.

While quieting old anxieties, the war raised new ones; but in only two special instances did these concern foreign groups. The fearful draft riots that rocked New York for four days in 1863 arose principally from the discontents of the city's Irish working class. The convulsion was widely interpreted as a disloyal Irish conspiracy inspired by Confederate agents. Out of the horror that the rioting produced, came an effort to revive the Know-Nothing movement, but it passed swiftly and without consequence.[3] Altogether, the nativistic repercussions of the event were slight in comparison to the provocation.

Suspicions of disloyalty also touched the Jews during the war years. Too small a group to contribute noticeably to the armed forces, they had only recently won prominence in America as retail merchants and clothing manufacturers. At a time when war profiteering was rife and traders of all sorts were swarming through Union lines to smuggle and speculate in southern cotton, the Jews were often singled out for exploiting the war effort. In 1862 General U. S. Grant curtly ordered every Jew expelled from his military jurisdiction—an act that may stand as the principal nativistic incident of the war years.[4] Three weeks later, on instructions from Lincoln, the order was revoked.

These ripples of distrust were slight compared to the storm of hatred which lashed anti-war groups of native background. The great fear of an internal menace in the North concerned homespun Copperheads. Mob attacks on anti-war newspapers and even an occasional lynching of a suspected secessionist replaced the nativistic riots of the 1850's. One patriotic citizen of Illinois described her Copperhead neighbors as "worse then the meanest thing a person can think of . . . Threatening what they will Do with Women Murdering Them if They can get a Chance . . . Oh they are to lowlife to let walk on gods Green Earth."[5] While nativism withered, nationalism flourished.

In addition to the psychological bonds of a common enmity, the war forged between American ethnic groups the ties of a common economic need. Foreign-born civilians served the Union cause behind the lines in as important a way as foreign-born soldiers at the front. From the depopulated farms and straining factories of the North came clamorous demands for immigrant labor. In 1864 Congress revived an eighteenth century technique for stimulating the flow of fresh European manpower. A contract labor law authorized employers to pay the passage and bind the services of prospective migrants.[6]

Postwar America Beckons

The statute did not long outlive the war that produced it, but the population hunger behind it grew more imperious than ever in the following years. The immigrant might not have retained his wartime laurels for long if his peacetime services had not loomed so large. As it was, the Civil War inaugurated an era of immense industrial, agricultural, and geographical expansion, in which the hundreds of thousands of annual arrivals from across the Atlantic seemed a national blessing. For two decades after Appomattox the summons to enrichment and opportunity smothered any serious nativist challenge. As the Civil War drew to a close, the Chicago *Tribune* sounded a jubilant keynote for the era ahead: "Europe will open her gates like a conquered city. Her people will come forth to us subdued by admiration of our glory and envy of our perfect peace. On to the Rocky Mountains and still over to the Pacific our mighty populations will spread. . . . Our thirty millions will be tripled in thirty years."[7] If the country did not quite live up to the *Tribune's* grandiose statistics, for twenty of those thirty years it echoed the paper's confident welcome.

Transatlantic migration was resumed in force when the war ended, and the throngs who came found the way prepared and a place awaiting them. Better transportation greatly shortened and tempered the rigors of the Atlantic crossing; for in the 1860's steamships replaced the old sailing vessels as carriers of human cargo.[8] Once arrived, immigrants usually moved into a pattern of settlement created by earlier compatriots. In 1860 the proportion of foreign-born to the total population of the United States was already about what it would remain through 1920, and most of the immigrants were concentrated in urban areas. Indeed, the twenty-five principal cities had a higher percentage of foreign-born residents in 1860 than they have had since.[9]

Nor did very notable changes occur, until the 1880's, in the nationalities involved or in their regional distribution. German immigration held the leading position it had attained in the late fifties, and it continued to pour chiefly into the Middle West, drawing increasing numbers of Bohemians and a scattering of Poles in its wake. British immigration (English, Scotch, and Welsh) rose to second place among the transatlantic currents. As skilled craftsmen, farmers, miners, and white-collar workers, the British diffused themselves more evenly throughout the country than any other group. Irish immigrants, although now less numerous than Germans or British, still came in large numbers. Now, as before the Civil War, Irishmen concentrated in the northeastern states. There they did most of the common labor and found increasing opportunities as industrial workers, though mining attracted many to the Far West.[10] Two other groups also sprang into prominence in the war and postwar years. Scandinavians, having established themselves in the prairies of the upper Mississippi Valley two decades before, began to migrate in great numbers in the 1860's. Unlike other nationalities, they avoided the cities for the most part, spreading instead westward across the plains. Meanwhile French Canadians, pulled southward by the Civil War, flocked to the mill towns of New England to compete with the Irish.[11] Thus, by 1865, each nationality was vaguely familiar in the region that received it, and each had familiar tasks.

The fact that an earlier generation had cleared the paths they trod undoubtedly eased the immigrants' reception, but the basic condition of their popularity was the appetite for material growth and achievement that dominated postwar America. With only marginal dissent, the "Gilded Age" that Mark Twain satirized and adored, the "Chromo Civilization" that E. L. Godkin criticized and defended, gave itself over to avid dreams of wealth. The headlong growth of business made the city, the machine, and the capitalist the controlling forces in American culture. The expansion of the railroad system, particularly, quickened the whole economy, opening up vast natural resources and creating a national market capable of absorbing them. The very real economic exploits of the age underwrote its booster spirit. There seemed no end to what the country could produce with men enough to do the work and to buy the results. The immigrants served both ways. And business leaders, marveling that population growth kept pace with economic opportunities, saw in the flow of immigration the workings of one of the grand laws of nature.[12]

Many businessmen, unwilling to leave matters entirely in the hands of a beneficent fate, actively expedited the immigrant traffic. Here the railroads played a key role, as they did throughout the economy. Railroads that pushed boldly into the empty West had a wilderness to settle. They needed immigrants not just for construction but to buy the great railroad land grants and to insure future revenues. Following the example set by the Illinois Central in the 1850's, the Burlington, the Northern Pacific, and other lines sent agents to blanket northern Europe with alluring propaganda. Other real estate interests sometimes organized similar campaigns. "*The real estate owners,*" said the head of a group of speculators planning to advertise in Europe, "*are the parties who make money out of immigrants immediately on their arrival.*"[13]

Nearly everyone who had something to sell or something to produce hoped to make money out of immigrants. Merchants looked to immigration for a growing supply of customers, and organized in various localities to attract it. In the early eighties, the Immigration Association of California, formed by members of the San Francisco Board of Trade, established hundreds of contacts with agents in Europe.[14] Mining enterprises from Pennsylvania to the Rockies were chiefly dependent on foreign-born labor; manufacturing was only somewhat less so. By 1870 about one out of every three employees in manufacturing and mechanical industries was an immigrant—a proportion which remained constant until the 1920's.[15] New England factory owners actively recruited labor in

French Canada, and others may have done the same in Europe. Even in 1882, when immigration reached its highest point in the nineteenth century, the *Commercial and Financial Chronicle* greeted it as a foundation for unparalleled business expansion.[16]

The general public shared the businessman's inclination to evaluate the newcomers in tangibly economic terms. There were elaborate calculations (how characteristic of the Gilded Age!) putting a price tag on immigrants in order to fix their per capita contribution to national wealth. Statisticians of the United States Treasury Department settled upon $800 as the average monetary value of an immigrant. Amateur mathematicians showed less restraint. One valued immigrants at $1,000 apiece on the ground that each was worth twice as much as an ante-bellum slave. Andrew Carnegie raised the estimate to $1,500.[17] In a generation of exuberant materialism and expansive confidence, the figure of the immigrant seemed truly touched with gold.

The federal government smiled on the transatlantic influx and for a time toyed with schemes to assist it. The Republican party in 1868 and 1872 promised to continue to encourage immigration, as it had done during the Civil War, but after the repeal of the contract labor law in 1868 the customary *laissez faire* policy again prevailed.[18] In 1874 Congress nearly abandoned its traditional opposition to special privileges for immigrant groups when it appeared that thousands of Mennonites might go to Canada instead of the United States unless a great block of public lands was set aside for them. Some Congressmen objected to offering any group "a separate right to compact themselves as an exclusive community," whereupon three western states held out the enticement of exemption from militia service. (Most of the Mennonites came.) [19] Thus, in the end, official promotion of immigration was left to the states.

The demand for immigrants was most widespread and intense outside the densely populated states of the Northeast; in the West and South, virtually every state appointed agents or boards of immigration to lure new settlers from overseas. Michigan began the practice in 1845. By the end of the Civil War the northwestern states were competing with each other for Europeans to people their vacant lands and develop their economies. Then the South joined in, hoping to divert part of the current in its direction in order to restore shattered commonwealths and replace emancipated Negroes. In the 1860's and 1870's, at least twenty-five out of the thirty-eight states took official action to promote immigration. South Carolina, in its desperation, added the inducement of a five-year tax exemption on all real estate bought by immigrants.[20]

Although economic incentives obviously fired the national lust for population, they alone do not explain it. If opportunities for immediate profit had formed a sufficient basis for a receptive attitude toward foreign groups, the long, searing depression of 1873-1877 would surely have killed such sympathies and desires. Actually, the campaign to stimulate European immigration slackened during the depression without by any means dying out. Hard times contributed powerfully to an exclusionist movement against the Chinese but did not substantially affect the status of the European. Two other conditions sustained the reign of confidence when the economy sagged. Of utmost significance was the survival in public opinion of a general, undaunted indifference to America's accumulating social problems. This complacent mood contrasted sharply with the spirit of ferment, unrest, and reform in the Know-Nothing era. Then the slavery crisis had brought to a head a multitude of discontents and dissatisfactions with the status quo. Reformers balked in their purposes had turned upon Catholics and foreigners as the "real" obstacles to progress; frightened conservatives had found in alien influence the "true" explanation of social discord.[21] Now, however, there was no domestic cleavage deep enough to produce comparable anxieties and no nation-wide agitation to awaken the sleeping conscience of society. Untroubled by doubts of the success of their own institutions, Americans saw little reason to fear the influence of foreigners upon them. Confidence in the country's economic vitality extended, by and large, to its whole social order.

Certainly there was much in American life to justify uneasiness: corruption, peculation, undisciplined wealth, rural blight, and urban squalor on perhaps an unprecedented scale. But the only organized, sustained protest—that of farmers in conflict with the railroads—failed to shake the general public or to touch on problems related to immigration. This was a day when complacency ruled college and pulpit, when labor remained largely unorganized and politicians largely undisturbed. An occasional exception may help to prove the rule. At the end of the 1860's, the extortions of the Tweed Ring in New York City, supported to a considerable degree by Irish votes, aroused an outraged middle-class opposition. In the process, leading civic reformers struck a good many nativistic blows at "the rule of the uncultivated Irish Catholics." For a time the crusading cartoonist, Thomas Nast, flayed the Catholic Church, the Irish, and Tweed with equal fury.[22] After the Boss's ouster, however, reform subsided. It was sporadic throughout the period, and in general New Yorkers seemed to accept the increasing power of the Irish in municipal politics with apathy.[23]

If indifference to domestic problems saved the foreign-born from some lines of attack, indifference to international problems saved them from others. Conflict between nations is, of course, a fruitful source of nativism when an internal minority is somehow connected with the hostile power. The first great wave of American nativism, in 1798, grew in large measure out of the internalization of an undeclared war with France; for much of the immigrant population on that occasion appeared pro-French.

In the period after the Civil War, however, the United States probably felt more secure from interference by European powers than it did at any other time. Isolation was a fact more than a theory. "Surrounded as we are, by two mighty oceans," said an ardent nationalist, "our Republic can never fall, as others have, by a foreign foe." [24] Comforted by knowledge of its military security, the country tolerated Irish Fenian activities which would certainly have provoked a good deal of tension in other contexts. With impunity, Americans indulged their own Anglophobia and allowed Irish-Americans to do the same in more violent ways. For five years the Fenians, without arousing significant resentment, attacked Canada from American territory, organized revolts in Ireland, and tried to incite war with Britain.[25] Untroubled by dangerous adversaries abroad, the United States could work out its own group relations in isolated safety.

Cosmopolitan Traditions

There was nothing new about the positive response of postwar America to European-born minorities. The conditions of the period —economic opportunity, social stability, and international security

—did not create but merely sustained and perpetuated a set of broadly tolerant attitudes. Over the centuries, America had developed a fluid, variegated culture by incorporating alien peoples into its midst, and the experience had fixed in American thought a faith in the nation's capacity for assimilation. This faith, carrying with it a sense of the foreigner's essential identification with American life, expressed itself in a type of nationalism that had long offset and outweighed the defensive spirit of nativism. A cosmopolitan and democratic ideal of nationality made assimilation plausible to Americans, and the immediate situation made it possible.

"E pluribus unum" expressed the essence of America's cosmopolitan faith—a conviction that this new land would bring unity out of diversity as a matter of course. Intellectually, this conviction was rooted in Christian and democratic values. Along with the parochialisms, the fanaticisms, and the xenophobias that Christianity has nourished, it has had another, perhaps more important, side. The ancient Christian doctrine of the brotherhood of man proclaimed the ultimate similarities between all peoples and their capacity for dwelling together in unity. The democratic values enshrined in the Declaration of Independence postulated an equal opportunity for all to share in the fullness of American life. Both Christian universalism and democratic equalitarianism had withstood the nativist ferment of the ante-bellum period. Both had vitalized George W. Julian's fiery condemnation: "Know Nothingism . . . tramples down the doctrine of human brotherhood. It judges men by the accidents of their condition, instead of striving to find a common lot for all, with a common access to the blessings of life." [26]

The twin ideals of a common humanity and of equal rights continued in the 1870's and 1880's to foster faith in assimilation. Temporarily the tasks of postwar reconstruction even widened assimilationist ideals; for the Radical Republicans' effort to redeem the southern Negro, to draw him within the pale of the state, and to weld the two races into a homogeneous nationality discouraged emphasis on basic human differences. To James Russell Lowell, for example, just and equal treatment of black men meant simply an enlargement of the Christian mission which the United States had long performed in bringing together the peoples of all nations in a common manhood. And Elisha Mulford, philosopher of Reconstruction, argued that the nation "is inclusive of the whole people. . . . There is no difference of wealth, or race, or physical condition, that can be made the ground of exclusion from it." [27]

Out of such assumptions, Americans fashioned an image of themselves as an inclusive nationality, at once diverse and homogeneous, ever improving as it assimilated many types of men into a unified, superior people. According to this long and widely respected view, the Americans derived some of their very distinctiveness as a nationality from the process of amalgamation. "We are the Romans of the modern world," boasted Oliver Wendell Holmes, "the great assimilating people." [28] The boast went back at least to the Revolutionary period, when the founders of the American nation needed to distinguish their own national character from that of the mother country. The French observer Crèvecoeur phrased the classic definition: the American is a "new man," risen out of a blend of a half-dozen lesser peoples. No exclusive group could possibly combine the many excellences which America received from its varied origins.

In short, American nationality was emerging from a melting pot that functioned automatically. Few in the nineteenth century used the metaphor, but many shared the idea. De Witt Clinton, Ralph Waldo Emerson, and Walt Whitman all glorified the fusion, through immigration, of a mixed and still developing people. Herman Melville gave this cosmopolitan belief its noblest expression: "We are the heirs of all time, and with all nations we divide our inheritance. On this Western Hemisphere all tribes and peoples are forming into one federated whole; and there is a future which shall see the estranged children of Adam restored as to the old hearthstone in [an American] Eden. . . . The seed is sown, and the harvest must come." [29]

By mid-century, the concept of a mixed, assimilating nationality acquired a vaguely "racial" import: a mixed race has physical and moral qualities superior to one inbred, and in the United States the best intermingling has occurred. Thereafter, a host of intellectuals endorsed the nationally invigorating results of racial mixture. The most popular preacher of the day, Henry Ward Beecher, considered the cultural and religious peculiarities of the immigrants inconvenient but also inconsequential in comparison with their enrichment of American blood. [30]

Support came also from new philosophical and scientific enthusiasms. English scientists, including Darwin himself, offered a compelling explanation for the success of the American melting pot, maintaining that migration functions as a process of natural selection, bringing the most energetic men from all parts of Europe to the New World. Herbert Spencer, the great philosopher of evolution, provided direct confirmation. In a celebrated interview in 1882 he predicted from "biological truths" that immigration and intermixture would produce here a finer, more adaptable type of man than the world had yet known.[31]

Spencer's principal opponent, William T. Harris, reasoned from cultural rather than naturalistic grounds to the same conclusion. Hegelian dialectic led him to believe that a new synthesis of nationalities was forming in America, with universal toleration and sympathies. The process, he thought, was farthest advanced in the most cosmopolitan region, the Mississippi Valley. Ultimately, Frederick Jackson Turner's frontier hypothesis would restate the notion in physiographical terms: "In the crucible of the frontier the immigrants were Americanized, liberated, and fused into a mixed race, English in neither nationality nor characteristics." [32] In one way or another, the age of confidence resounded with assertions that America's "cosmopolitan character in the future is assured, [and] the peaceful blending of many nationalities has resulted in the 'survival of the fittest.' " [33]

Together with this ideal of nationality, the Americans embraced a similarly cosmopolitan interpretation of their national mission. One doctrine complemented the other. Patriots who rejoiced in the strength of a universal heritage expected their nation to perform a universal service. Like the theory of nationality, the concept of a national mission fused Christian with democratic values in the heat of the American Revolution. In revolting from British authority, the colonists looked upon their bid for freedom as service to a world-wide cause. They were realizing—so they thought—the free, rational life of which Europe dreamed but which Europe denied. To fulfill their cosmopolitan task it behooved them to provide for others a haven from Europe's oppressions. Thus Americans could enlist in the cause of general human liberty without actively intervening anywhere.

Tom Paine's *Common Sense* struck the keynote in urging a

declaration of independence. Not England, but all of Europe is America's parent, he said, for the New World has sheltered freedom-loving refugees from many countries. Since oppression is triumphing elsewhere, America must prepare an asylum for mankind.[34] Thereafter, the idea of America's mission to provide a home for the oppressed became a cliché and an incantation. Like the theory of mixed nationality, it affirmed the superiority of the United States over Europe and the patriotic significance of a liberal immigration policy.

During the third quarter of the nineteenth century American sympathies for European revolutionists perceptibly diminished, but the theme of refuge from oppression still had a general appeal. An English visitor in 1866, gazing on New York's rickety immigrant depot, commented, "Every true republican has in his heart the notion that his country is pointed out by God as a refuge for the distressed of all the nations." Even the struggling xenophobic society, the United American Mechanics, felt compelled to acknowledge that it did not "forget that our land should be an asylum for the oppressed." Nor did the business interests that profited from immigration fail to refer to America's role in succoring the oppressed.[35]

But it was among the victims of oppression that the dream of an American refuge struck real fire. Significantly, a Jewish-American poet aroused by Russian pogroms to a consciousness of America's mission put the asylum theory more eloquently than anyone else. When Emma Lazarus wrote in aid of a fund-raising campaign for the Statue of Liberty, the old ideal flashed through the condescending humanitarianism of her phrases:

> Give me your tired, your poor,
> Your huddled masses yearning to breathe free,
> The wretched refuse of your teeming shore,
> Send these, the homeless, tempest-tost to me,
> I lift my lamp beside the golden door! [36]

The Ethnocentric Residue

Yet the condescension was there too, along with the cosmopolitanism. Emma Lazarus' image of the immigrants as "tempest-tost" and yearning to breathe free reflected one aspect of the spirit of her age; her picture of them as wretched refuse mirrored another. And the two were not incompatible. They dwelt together in poetry and in public opinion. From one point of view the immigrants symbolized the force of freedom pulling men through a golden door. From another they looked poor and huddled and unattractive. The two judgments could coexist because they were of a very different order from one another. The former image—positive and attractive—referred to the immigrant's impact on the nation. In terms of his relation to national strength and survival, the immigrant appeared a blessing rather than a danger. The second, negative view referred to direct personal and social relations with the immigrant. The distinction is crucially important. It reminds us that unfavorable reactions to the personal and cultural traits of European peoples are not in themselves nativistic. They become so only when integrated with a hostile and fearful nationalism.

In 1884, near the close of the period, a magazine writer made the point very well and in doing so summed up both aspects of his generation's response to the immigrants. "No one," he said, "now accuses any large or influential portion of the foreign element of a set purpose to spread ideas subversive of our political institutions. Such tendencies and ideas as are most deprecated in the foreigners of the United States relate to manners, to mere habits of life and social practices." [37] In other words, the prevailing conditions and the dominant national ideals of the postwar era militated against nativism without dislodging a sense of superiority. An ethnocentrism that applied largely to "mere habits of life," that raised no question of the newcomer's patriotism or his ultimate assimilation, could survive side by side with a generally tolerant and receptive outlook.

Yet we cannot afford to ignore the simpler ethnocentric judgments that persist beneath the ebb and flow of nativism. Although those judgments often exist where nativism does not, they provide the cultural subsoil in which it grows. And, to complicate matters still more, we must recognize that the ethnocentric attitudes displayed toward different outside groups have their own great range of intensity.

In the absence of other disturbing factors, Americans rated lowest the nationalities most conspicuously remote in culture and race.

No variety of anti-European sentiment has ever approached the violent extremes to which anti-Chinese agitation went in the 1870's and 1880's. Lynchings, boycotts, and mass expulsions still harassed the Chinese after the federal government yielded to the clamor for their exclusion in 1882. At a time when the Chinese question had virtually disappeared as a political issue, a labor union could still refer to that patient people as "more slavish and brutish than the beasts that roam the fields. They are groveling worms." [38] Americans have never maintained that every European endangers American civilization; attacks have centered on the "scum" or "dregs" of Europe, thereby allowing for at least some implicit exceptions. But opponents of Oriental folk have tended to reject them one and all.

At the opposite end of the cultural spectrum, as Americans saw it, were the peoples of Britain and the Anglo-Canadians. These met so ready an acceptance that contemporary observers scarcely noticed their coming. Despite a persistent American hostility toward the English government and aristocracy, despite also the British immigrants' tendency to remain loyal subjects of the Queen, they did not really seem foreigners at all. A sense of cultural identity exempted them from Anglophobia, and even recurrent international tensions between the two countries never disturbed the British immigrants' status.[39]

The Germans fared nearly but not quite so well. They insisted belligerently on their right to amusements that shocked the censorious—to card-playing, to beer gardens, to Sunday frolics; and when the temperance issue revived in the seventies the Chicago *Tribune* thought enforcement of a Sunday-closing law necessary to prevent "the German conquest" of the city. Then, too, the great German quarters of midwestern cities, full of saloons, foreign signboards, and German-language schools, seemed disturbingly self-contained. On the other hand, the Germans had a reputation for thrifty, honest, industrious, and orderly living.[40] As for their recreational gusto, an increasingly urban world was pulling more and more Americans in the same direction. Indeed, the German example popularized beer-drinking and helped to relax America's Sunday habits. In testifying to easy assimilation, an observer remarked in 1883, "The German notion that it is a good thing to have a good time has found a lodgment in the American mind." [41]

Distrust of Irish and Jews went deeper. As the pillars of an alien faith, the Irish attracted a good measure of any anti-Catholic sentiment that might be in the air; an Irishman's loyalty to his priest was too firm for anxious Protestants to rest easily. And along with religious distrust went a social criticism. Americans pictured the Irish as rowdy ne'er-do-wells, impulsive, quarrelsome, drunken, and threadbare.[42] Childhood conflicts gave these attitudes deep and early roots in many minds, for middle-class boys growing up in the American town of the late nineteenth century battled incessantly with roughneck Irish gangs from the other side of the tracks. "No relations except combat," Henry Seidel Canby recalls, "were possible or thought of between our gangs and the 'micks.' . . . They were still the alien, and had to be shown their place."[43] If this sense of social distance related partly to the unruly behavior of the Irish, it also pertained to their lowly economic status. In middle-class American eyes, the Irish were inferior not only because they were rowdies but also because they were poor. Impoverished Irish immigrants still squatted in tumble-down, one-room shanties on the fringes of the cities. Indignant property-owners in the vicinity continually petitioned against this "low and squalid class of people, who . . . keep . . . the surroundings in a filthy and disgusting condition."[44]

The Irish stereotype, however, could not help but soften as more and more Irishmen rose out of the ranks of unskilled labor and merged in speech and manner with the older population. By the early eighties, they were generally well regarded. It was almost a proverb to say that a good workman does as much as an Irishman; and even the harshest critics of the Irish looked forward confidently to their assimilation.[45]

The Jews, on the other hand, lost in reputation as they gained in social and economic status. Alone among European immigrant groups, the Jews during this period met a distrust that spread along with their increasing assimilation. The nativistic criticism of Jewish loyalty that had risen during the Civil War vanished as soon as the war ended, but in its place there emerged during the 1870's a far more tenacious pattern of social discrimination.

Smallest of the prominent immigrant groups, American Jewry was largely a by-product of immigration from Germany. At first, native folk had difficulty in differentiating Jews from Germans,[46] but with the dispersion of Jewish peddlers and shopkeepers throughout the country, the European tradition of the Jew as Shylock came to life. To a segment of American opinion, the Jews seemed clothed in greed and deceit. It was this conception that had exposed them to the charge of disloyal profiteering during the war. Thereafter the persistent Shylock image acquired a significant new dimension. It broadened during the Gilded Age into an indictment of Jewish manners for vulgarity and ostentation. The Jew, it now appeared, was not only mercenary and unscrupulous but also clamorously self-assertive—a tasteless barbarian rudely elbowing into genteel company.[47] In line with this impression, society began to exclude Jews from areas of intimate social intercourse, the most celebrated of the initial proscriptions being at eastern summer resorts. Despite public shock and indignation when the leading hotel at Saratoga Springs refused to admit the eminent banker Joseph Seligman in 1877, many smaller establishments soon adopted the same policy.

Friendly observers conceded a grain of truth in the new indictment. By the 1870's many German Jews were prospering mightily, and a fair share of them had risen to affluence too rapidly to acquire the discipline of culture.[48] Equally pertinent, however, was the pervasive vulgarity and the general social climbing that were upsetting the stability and simplicity of American society on a grand scale. In an age of parvenus the Jew provided a symbol of the parvenu spirit. Anti-Semitic discriminations subjected him to a discipline that native Americans could not so easily impose on themselves.

Despite their unusual social mobility, the Jews shared significantly in a common immigrant experience. Like the Irish and Germans, they faced criticism applied to "mere habits of life." No one in the age of confidence denounced them as subversive or expressed doubts of their ultimate assimilation. German bons vivants, Irish roughnecks, and Jewish vulgarians might seem discomforting; but the overriding assumptions of the immigrant's economic value and of the American's mixed nationality held anxious speculation firmly in check. In short, there was no pressing sense of the foreigner as a distinctively *national* menace. That could develop only with a loss of faith in the process of assimilation. In the postwar decades, nationalism was complacent and cosmopolitan.

The Nativist Heritage

Nevertheless, beneath the surface of the age of confidence, the traditions of American nativism persisted. Instead of being liquidated, anti-foreign fears were simply contained. In a partial and stunted form each of the nativist themes maintained a peripheral place in American thought. Each of them, in fact, found some new or continuing area of sensitivity where it could fasten and feed.

After the Civil War religious forces never recovered the commanding influence which they had exerted throughout the culture of earlier decades. The Protestant crusade against Rome never again dominated nativist thought as completely as it had in mid-century. But anti-Catholicism was far from dead, and in the 1870's it flared up in several northern states. In contrast to the Know-Nothing movement, the much milder agitation of the seventies was due primarily to Catholic demands for state aid. Although conflicts over public education had arisen between Catholic and non-Catholic groups before the Civil War, the Church had not been strong enough to press its traditional claims on a broad front. Now, however, it comprised a majority or near-majority of the church-going population in some cities. Also, it was probably emboldened by the relaxed and tranquil state of public opinion. About 1869, therefore, Catholics in many parts of the Northeast and Midwest opened a campaign to eliminate the Protestant tinge that Bible-reading gave to the public schools, to secure for their own parochial schools a share of the funds that the states were providing for education, and to get for Catholic charitable institutions public subsidies comparable to those traditionally awarded to Protestant charities. At first, the pressure brought some success in each respect; the Democratic administration in New York proved especially complaisant.[49] But Protestants soon counterattacked, with the result that separation of church and state actually increased.

The controversy spilled over into politics in the mid-seventies, when the Republicans desperately needed a new issue to replace their now discredited Reconstruction policies and to distract the public from the scandals of the Grant régime. Running for governor of Ohio in 1875, Rutherford B. Hayes worked fiercely to smear the Democrats as subservient to Catholic designs. President

Grant struck a similar campaign note at a veterans' reunion that fall by hinting darkly that unless the public schools were kept free from sectarian influence the nation might face a new civil war between the forces of patriotism and intelligence on the one side and superstition and ignorance on the other.[50] One Democratic Senator wryly commented that the Republican matadors were looking for another beast to slay now that Jeff Davis and the "bloody shirt" were losing their popular appeal. "The Pope, the old Pope of Rome, is to be the great bull that we are all to attack." [51]

In a few areas, notably New Jersey and Ohio, the Republicans reaped some advantage from the religious question in the 1875 elections, but the attempt to inflate it into a major national issue failed miserably. Grant's annual message to Congress in December stressed the importance of a constitutional amendment forbidding the appropriation of public funds for denominational schools. The public received the idea with considerable apathy, however, and the Democratic House of Representatives moved to take the partisan sting out of it by passing a watered-down version almost unanimously.[52] During the election of 1876 occasional Republican charges that the "Romish Church" was using the Democratic party to overthrow the American public school system made little impression. By then Catholic leaders had recognized the dangers of a militant course and had desisted from it.[53]

Inevitably a measure of Protestant nationalism accompanied this anti-Catholic revival. Attacks on the Catholic Church as a foreign despotism reappeared; the suspicion circulated that the priests were trying to subordinate the United States to Rome; there was even some murmuring over immigration. But by and large the controversy swirled around concrete institutional issues, involving relatively little talk of a papal conspiracy to subvert the nation. Above all, anti-Catholics dealt gently with the immigrants. Blame fell instead on the clergy. One foe of Rome contended that the Irish would assimilate if the priests did not keep them separate. Another thought that the priesthood drove the Irish into reluctant hostility to public education. Another acknowledged the innocence of Catholic laymen and held the hierarchy alone disloyal. The anti-Romanist editor of *Harper's Weekly* praised America's role as a refuge for the oppressed and its ability to assimilate all comers.[54]

The mild temper of Protestant nativism in the seventies is best evidenced by the new secret society that it produced. The Order of the American Union took form in New York City about 1870, modeled after the prewar Know-Nothings. Unlike the latter, however, it admitted all Protestants, native and foreign-born, to membership and confined its agitation to anticlerical issues; it called on the American people "of all nationalities" to unite against the political activities of the Catholic Church. The O.A.U. reached a peak in 1875 with about forty councils in New York, a score in Ohio, and a scattered following elsewhere. In spite of high hopes, it had little success in influencing elections, and in 1878, while Edwin Cowles, editor of the Cleveland *Leader*, was president of the order, an exposé published in the New York *Herald* caused its rapid disintegration.[55]

Another set of events in the 1870's, quite different from those on which anti-Catholicism rested, lent some slight encouragement to the anti-radical tradition. Like the fear of popery, the fear of imported discontent barely scratched the armor of national confidence; yet it was in this period that anti-radical nativism assumed a distinctively modern aspect. Because Marxism and allied social-revolutionary doctrines were taking hold among European workingmen, revolution was acquiring a new significance. Henceforth it would mean, for the most part, not the replacement of monarchy by liberal democracy, but rather the uprising of the working class against capitalism. Americans cast dark glances across the Atlantic at the Paris Commune of 1871, and a few observers saw in it a portent of future convulsions between labor and capital.[56] Here and there some conservatives were beginning to associate working-class aspirations with revolutionary violence. Since revolutionary doctrines and organizers, although pathetically weak, came almost entirely from Europe, the old conjunction of immigration and radicalism could assume a new scope and aspect. Class conflict could appear an un-American product of foreign agitators.[57]

The Paris Commune sowed one seed of this suspicion. Another was planted with the formation in the 1870's of the first socialist party in America, a largely immigrant organization. The industrial violence of the Molly Maguires in the Pennsylvania coal fields left a third. But the concept of a labor revolution instigated by foreigners really crystallized during the sudden, wild fury of the

railroad strikes of 1877. Goaded by repeated wage cuts, railroad
workers and others battled with state militia, pillaged trains, and
rioted from Baltimore to San Francisco. This outburst of unorganized, undirected misery was a new phenomenon in America.
To frightened nativists, the light of flaming boxcars revealed the
hand of the foreign "communist." Panic-stricken over the safety of
his family, John Hay cowered at home and believed the government utterly helpless in the face of a rebellion of foreign workingmen. The New York *Herald* asserted that foreign demagogues
"have imported ideas and sentiments which have repeatedly deluged France in blood. . . . The railroad riots . . . were instigated by men incapable of understanding our ideas and principles."
Congressman James A. Garfield assured his constituents that trouble between capital and labor stemmed from foreign radicalism.[58]

In California, Garfield's point seemed particularly evident. There
the unrest of 1877 produced the Workingmen's party, led by a
demagogue of Irish birth, Denis Kearney, who raved against both
the rich and the Chinese. The radical agitation of anti-Chinese
immigrants inspired an anti-radical, anti-European reaction among
old-stock conservatives. Frank Pixley, a former Know-Nothing
now closely associated with Leland Stanford of the Southern Pacific Railroad, sparked the new xenophobia. Pixley's weekly journal, the *Argonaut*, sympathized mildly with the anti-Chinese sentiment among the working people of San Francisco until Kearney's
wild threats filled the air. Then the *Argonaut* forgot the Chinese
and turned on the labor movement as a foreign insurrection. Let us
prepare, Pixley thundered, to meet these aliens "with ball and bay-
onet." Thenceforth the paper was furiously and inveterately anti-
foreign.[59]

As in the case of anti-Catholicism, however, much anti-radical
sentiment in the age of confidence lacked nativistic significance.
Conservatives often linked radical ideas with a discontented lower
class without invoking foreign influence.[60] More important, hardly
anyone seriously believed that insurrectionary immigrants could
endanger American institutions. Except in moments of panic such
as Hay experienced, the peril of revolution seemed too novel to be
genuinely credible. The *Nation* probably expressed a common
conservative judgment on the railroad strikes: "The kindest thing
which can be done for the great multitudes of untaught men who

have been received on these shores, and are daily arriving, and who are torn perhaps even more here than in Europe by wild desires and wilder dreams, is to show them promptly that society as here organized, on individual freedom of thought and action, is impregnable, and can be no more shaken than the order of nature." [61] All in all, the thunderclap of 1877 passed too quickly to damage America's faith in its "impregnable" society. But the events could not be forgotten, and it was by no means certain that confidence would survive serenely another such upheaval.

If confidence inhibited the established nativist traditions, it positively suffused the Anglo-Saxon cult. This too found new sources of support in postwar America, yet it failed completely to register a nativistic impact.

With the decline of expansionist sentiment on the eve of the Civil War, the Anglo-Saxon doctrine lost its popular vogue, but it retained a hold on the cultivated classes. Among them it won increasing intellectual prestige in the seventies and eighties. Undoubtedly the most important reason for the trend lay in the pride of ancestry stimulated by the chaotic social climbing of the Gilded Age. At a time when parvenus were managing practical affairs and clamoring for admission to the choicest circles, there was compensation and a measure of status in associating one's personal lineage with the original fount of national greatness. Thus Anglo-Saxonism became a kind of patrician nationalism. As such it synchronized with the enormous influence which English ideas, English literature, and English social standards were securing among the American elite. England's "scientific" historians offered fresh documentation for the racial doctrine, with support for the Teutonic version from German sources; English lecturers campaigned personally; even the English religious cult of Anglo-Israel carried across the Atlantic the doctrine that the Anglo-Saxons were God's chosen people.[62] These Anglophile currents affected particularly the Brahmin gentry of New England, and New Englanders did much to spread them elsewhere in the country.[63]

Also, in a general way, the rise of Darwinism in the post-Civil War period helped to encourage interest in hereditary and therefore in racial determinants. As early as 1873 a clergyman described the "American race" as "a sprout of the Anglo-Saxon stock, which, all fresh and vigorous, asserts its Darwinian right to exist." [64] All of these factors—the quest for ancestors, the influence of English culture, and the impact of the theory of biological evolution— came to focus in John Fiske. This magnetic publicist of ideas was enormously proud of the New Englander's ancestry and believed himself a lineal descendant of King Alfred. He browsed in English churchyards and drank deeply from England's leading Teutonist, E. A. Freeman. When Fiske shifted in the 1880's from popularizing Darwinian science to popularizing American history, he was well prepared to celebrate the glories of the English race in the New World.[65]

Still the Anglo-Saxonists were pro rather than con. During the age of confidence almost no race-thinker directly challenged a tolerant and eclectic attitude toward other European groups. Instead, Anglo-Saxon and cosmopolitan nationalisms merged in a happy belief that the Anglo-Saxon has a marvelous capacity for assimilating kindred races, absorbing their valuable qualities, yet remaining basically unchanged. John Fiske, for example, acclaimed the American for quickly assimilating other European strains while remaining thoroughly English. If doubts arose of how this paradox could come about, the answer lay in the mixed character of England's early population: European immigration was simply recombining in the United States the strains which had earlier blended in English blood.[66] In short, American race-thinkers harmonized their cultural bias with their traditional ideal of nationality. They retained confidence in assimilation, and in their outlook a certain cosmopolitan flavor remained.

The easy juggling of race concepts, which kept parochial and cosmopolitan ideas revolving in a single orbit, depended partly on the whole structure of national confidence and partly on the continuing vagueness of the race-idea. Whatever palpitations one might feel about a foreigner's political or religious loyalties, the notion that European immigrants might endanger the great inborn spirit of the nation strained credibility. The age was too optimistic to entertain such a fear, and the immigrants' own lineage seemed too closely connected with the great Gothic family to inspire alarm.

Anglo-Saxon nationalism, then, posed even less of an obstacle to the postwar mood of confidence than did the explicitly nativist themes. At least, anti-Catholicism had a flurry in the seventies, and anti-radical nativism promised to be increasingly pertinent to an industrial society. All three traditions of national exclusiveness were tenacious and adaptable. But under the conditions of increasing familiarity with the principal immigrant nationalities, zeal for material progress, and indifference to social and international problems, none of the nativist traditions could blunt the nation's assimilationist and cosmopolitan creed.

Chapter Three

Crisis in the Eighties

> The times are strangely out of joint. . . . Capital piles on capital, in combination reaching alpine heights. . . . The rich grow richer, and the poor become poorer; the nation trembles under the tread of discontented thousands; strikes are the order of the day.
> —Speech in Kentucky legislature, 1890

> . . . the old cry in favor of unrestricted immigration has almost entirely ceased.
> —Franklin B. Sanborn, 1887

In 1882 a writer in the *Atlantic Monthly* predicted in ominous tones the coming of a great struggle for the preservation of the American social and economic order. During the course of various reflections on urban poverty and industrial discontent the author turned aside at one or two points to assail the European immigrant with a bluntness and sweep perhaps unknown in a general magazine for a generation. What was significant was not so much the vague substance of the attack as the conclusion which it supported and to which the whole article pointed: "Our era . . . of happy immunity from those social diseases which are the danger and the humiliation of Europe is passing away . . . every year brings the conditions of American labor into closer likeness to those of the Old World. An American species of socialism is inevitable." [1]

Few observers in 1882 took so gloomy a view of the American future or of the place of the immigrant in it. Except for the Civil War crisis—now largely liquidated—the country had suffered no fundamental schism in all of the nineteenth century. It could look back upon an otherwise uninterrupted process of economic development, westward expansion, and institutional crystallization. Surely only the most fretful of skeptics could doubt the uniqueness and fixity of the nation's destiny. Above all, nineteenth century Americans had grown accustomed to congratulating themselves for having a society *without* basic cleavages. In contrast to Europe, with its more rigid division of classes, its more deeply entrenched inequalities, and its pent-up dissatisfactions, America seemed to have dissolved the external restraints on individual achievement. It was an article of faith that this land of opportunity had leveled all the barriers to individual mobility; and the corollary that a completely free society was an unshakable one appeared hardly less certain. Sheathed in the conviction, public complacency rode out the troubles of the 1870's. But on a few sensitive minds the stresses of the decade left unhealed scars, and by the early eighties voices of doubt were beginning to be heard. Were classes congealing, and did this sharpening alignment portend a relapse into the internal strife of Europe? Were American horizons really and permanently open, or were they contracting? Some who wondered took the first long, hard, new look at the immigrants.

Social Chasms and Anxious Reformers

Although the bustling American scene in the early eighties wore a generally tranquil air, indications abounded that the issues thrust forward in the previous decade had not vanished in the first flush of renewed prosperity. The sodden wretchedness of the slums settled more deeply into the heart of great cities every year. The grip of vice and lawlessness on chaotic municipal governments kept the growing urban problem as far as ever from solution, until at last a régime of crime in Cincinnati goaded the populace to three terrible days of fire and riot in 1884. ("The dangerous tendencies of the population in large cities must be distinctly recognized," the shocked New York *Tribune* editorialized.[2]) Meanwhile a relentlessly advancing factory system cut off more and more employees from direct relations with their employers. In reaction, the first mass movement of American workingmen was in the making. Skilled and unskilled workers alike flocked to the mushrooming Knights of Labor, which cast off its early cloak of secrecy in 1881 and started to climb to national significance. This to many was the most startling portent of all, for the Knights' gusty enthusiasm spilled into a dozen reformist proposals, while Master Workman Terence Powderley thundered vague preachments on abolishing the "wage system."

At the other end of the scale, power and arrogance accumulated no less swiftly. Business combinations sprouted on all sides, many of them pressing toward monopoly. Henry Demarest Lloyd's pioneering exposé of the Standard Oil Company in 1881 supplied a dramatically documented illustration of a trend which was becoming increasingly hard to ignore. Many of the new tycoons did nothing to disguise it. This was the uninhibited period when William Vanderbilt rapped out his famous "The public be damned," when the United States Senate became known as a millionaire's club, when another business leader is supposed to have said that the rich own America and intend to keep it. With something of the same spirit the money-kings thrust upward in the social world, flaunting unheard-of riches with a fine abandon. A public which followed in the daily newspapers the doings of syndicates and rings and trusts was beginning to read in the comic magazines of Mrs. Astor's gilded balls and of Ward McAllister's pretentious attempts to define the "Four Hundred." These yawning social and economic contrasts became more evident still when the economy slid downhill in 1883, 1884, and 1885. Corporations cut wages savagely, sometimes as much as 20 per cent; unemployment mounted to a million or more; and though the slump was less severe than that of the seventies, poverty stared with fiercer eyes on wealth unshaken and untamed.[3]

A parallel crisis impended in the rural West and South. It did not affect the immigrant's status as obviously or as directly as the urban cleavage did, but indirectly the farmers' anxieties heightened every tension in the cities. Ever since the Civil War the old sense of equality and opportunity had been slipping from the farmers' grasp. Monopoly touched the rural producer first and touched him hardest. Declining farm prices and rising debts made the middleman's grip all the more onerous, while the processes which piled up wealth in the cities ate away at the prestige of rural life.

Although good weather and good times hushed the farmers' complaints in the early eighties, urban America was not unaware that the countryside no longer promised a living to anyone willing to work for it. Geographic as well as economic facts compelled attention in this regard. Homesteaders in the early eighties were swarming into the last great area of unsettled grasslands in the United States, peopling western Kansas and Nebraska, overrunning the Dakotas, and colliding with cattlemen on the high plains of Montana, Wyoming, and Colorado. Despite the vast self-assurance with which the decade opened, those few who wondered about the hardening of class lines sometimes pondered also the shrinking promise of the frontier. In American thought an ingenuous faith in the open road westward had long supported belief in an open road upward. The eighties cast a shadow over both ideas at the same time. A new sense of "closed space" compounded the emerging fears of a closed society. As early as 1881 a letter writer in the New York *Tribune* averred that the next generation would find America's resources and opportunities all parceled out. "The nation," he wrote, "has reached a point in its growth where its policy should be to preserve its heritage for coming generations, not to donate it to all the strangers we can induce to come among us." [4]

During the first half of the decade only a handful of Cassandras took so troubled a view of the American future that their conception of the immigrants soured. Wherever an optimistic indifference toward social problems prevailed, the tradition persisted of the immigrant as an economic blessing easily assimilated into America's mixed nationality. On the whole, therefore, reformers and humanitarians discovered an immigration problem somewhat sooner than did conservative spokesmen. The latter had a vested interest in complacency; the former faced the crisis of the eighties early and with alarm.

One important effect of the crisis, in fact, was to awaken a torpid social conscience and to call forth a new body of middle-class reform opinion. Tugging in a dozen different directions at once, often intellectually vague and usually ineffective in practice, the reformers inaugurated a many-pronged criticism of the urban, industrial scene. Whatever the specific ills that caught their eye, the more anxious reform thinkers came back time and again to the great issue: the polarization of American society. They believed passionately in the traditional ideal of a fluid, homogeneous culture; yet they saw it threatened everywhere. Most of them, urbanites themselves, located the heart of the trouble in the recklessly expanding cities. And there, in teeming concentration, were the immigrants, linked in one way or another to every festering problem. It was not difficult for this early generation of urbanized reformers—full of dark forebodings and ill-experienced in realistic social analysis—to fix upon the immigrants as a major source of current disorders. Nor was it entirely unreasonable for men who feared a decline of opportunity and mobility to lose confidence in the process of assimilation. In discovering an immigration *problem*, the social critics of the eighties might not indulge in the characteristically nativist assault on the newcomer as a foreign enemy of the American way of life; they might not speak in the accents of nationalism. But they raised the question of assimilation in a broadly significant way by connecting it with the central issues of the day. They gave intellectual respectability to anti-immigrant feelings.

A restless Congregational clergyman sounded the great opening blast. Josiah Strong stood in the vanguard of the small company of religious thinkers who were bringing an ethical, evangelical imperative to the pattern of reform. Among the pioneering appeals to a new Christian conscience, Strong's *Our Country* was the most apocalyptic. Published in 1885, this tremendously popular appeal for support of home missions radiated a sense of imminent crisis. It proclaimed great dangers focalizing in the cities, to religion, to morality, to politics. Above all it pointed to the danger of class strife and predicted eventually an open struggle between selfish rich and degraded poor. All these perils, Strong believed, were enhanced by immigration. He cast his anti-foreign complaints in a traditional mold, accusing the immigrants of crime and immorality, of corrupting municipal government, of furnishing recruits for Catholicism and socialism. But what made the words urgent and significant was a conviction that in each of these respects the foreign influx was hastening the onset of a terrible upheaval in American society. Although he neither hated immigrants as such nor preached the complete failure of assimilation, he delivered the first sweeping indictment of immigrant influence since the 1850's.[5]

The next year, in a series of lectures that attracted a good deal of attention, another clergyman stated Strong's fears more explicitly. In the cities, said Samuel Loomis, men have become divided into two widely separated classes. On one side of the gulf are the business and professional people, mostly native-born and

Protestant. On the other is the working class, nearly all of it foreign in background, much of it Catholic, and the rest convinced that Protestantism serves only the well-to-do.[6]

It remained for a newspaper reporter to demonstrate at the end of the decade the appalling width of the chasm. Jacob Riis's *How the Other Half Lives* (the title itself was significant) dramatized as nothing else did the full degradation and misery of immigrant lives in the slums. The conditions Riis described were not new, but his reaction to them was part of the new "Social Gospel." Passionately, he warned that only a Christian sense of justice could stop the dreadful wedge that greed was driving between the tenement dwellers and the upper classes. Since the slums and the foreign quarters coincided, Riis treated them as synonymous. In exposing the slums he was revealing the disorganization and squalor of their foreign residents. Although he generally wrote of the immigrants with sympathetic warmth and blamed "the evil they breed" on the conditions surrounding them, his book aroused anti-foreign as well as anti-tenement attitudes.[7]

Other voices spoke from the colleges and universities. A new generation of economists, trained in the nationalist presumptions of German economics at such places as Halle and Heidelberg, was unseating the academic champions of *laissez faire*. More than many reform thinkers of the day, leading economists of the "historical school" believed in big government and in organized labor as instruments for promoting human welfare. Sympathizing with labor's aspirations, they contended particularly that immigrant competitors were undermining the workingman's standard of living. And as proponents of governmental intervention, the economists were pioneering advocates of immigration restriction: it offered a relatively easy and painless way of invoking national authority to combat corruption, squalor, and injustice.

Beneath these special emphases, the academic reformers shared the ethical zeal and the fears of social disintegration that motivated their Social Gospel allies. Richard T. Ely's first books called upon a collective, Christian ethic to prevent an impending war between capital and labor. His German-trained friend, Edmund J. James, warned as early as 1883 that foreign elements were disturbing the homogeneity on which free government must rest.[8] Ely's student, Edward W. Bemis, published a brilliant article in a religious journal on the need for sharp restriction of immigration, while another of the same group, Richmond Mayo-Smith, wrote the first scholarly book on the subject. *Emigration and Immigration* throughout showed Mayo-Smith's concern with national homogeneity and the discord threatening it. At a time when social and economic problems are pressing acutely upon us, is immigration, he asked, endangering America's free, self-reliant, orderly culture, the unique economic well-being of its working people, and the prestige of industrial pursuits? His answer, though measured and good-tempered, was emphatically yes. Meanwhile, in 1888, the American Economic Association, which these men founded, offered a prize of $150 for the best essay on "The Evil Effects of Unrestricted Immigration." [9]

A similar outlook permeated many of the separate, middle-class reform movements that were fixing on particular social problems. Taking a new lease on life, crusaders for temperance and for women's rights assailed the immigrant's subversive, European attitudes on these questions. "Every reformatory movement of the day," declared a prohibitionist, "finds here its most persistent and indefatigible foe." [10] None agreed more loudly than the apostles of clean city government. The immigrants' votes did in fact go chiefly to the bosses, and during the Tweed régime civic reformers had already vented their wrath on both. In the mid-eighties, as the movement to redeem the cities became an organized crusade capable of more than fitful protest, it displayed an unabashed nativism. George W. Curtis, a veteran of Tweed days, talked about the lack of patriotism in "the ignorant, lawless, idle and dangerous overflow of all other countries." New York's reform mayor, Abram S. Hewitt, although elected by Tammany, launched into pointblank attacks on the immigrant menace, ultimately picking a celebrated quarrel with his Irish Board of Aldermen over the propriety of flying the shamrock flag at City Hall on St. Patrick's Day. "America should be governed by Americans," he told the irate city fathers in 1888, and his supporters demanded that those who prefer another flag should go back where they came from. [11]

While all of these overlapping agitations centered on the stresses in urban America, another emerging reform group put the immigration issue in a rural context also. Opponents of land monopoly were quick to sense a relation between contracting horizons in the

West and unchecked immigration. Alarm over corporate exploitation of the public domain and an accompanying growth of tenancy was just beginning in the 1880's. Protests arose hand in hand with a new consciousness that the supply of good vacant land was dwindling, that it might soon give out. Once gone, where would the United States find room for its immigrant-inflated population? Henry George, the greatest of all of the land reformers and one of the first Americans to rage at the country's reversion toward European conditions, connected the closing of the safety valve of western land with the danger of immigration, as early as 1883. "What," he queried, "in a few years more, are we to do for a dumping-ground? Will it make our difficulty the less that our human garbage can vote?" [12] Like George, Josiah Strong predicted that when the public lands were gone, the immigrants would crowd the cities more and more, and the next year, 1886, a special investigator for the staid *North American Review* announced that the evil day had arrived: at a time of growing immigration and land monopoly, "the public domain of the United States is now exhausted." [13]

With such considerations in mind, Congress enacted a law in 1887 prohibiting nondeclarant aliens (those who had not declared their intention to become citizens) from owning real estate in the federal territories. Although aimed chiefly at nonresident landlords, the law reflected concern about immigration and overpopulation as well.[14] In the same year an agricultural collapse sent thousands reeling backward from the Great Plains. If the farmers themselves took little heed of the immigration issue as yet, their distresses lent weight to the incipient claustrophobia in the urban world.[15]

Behind many of the miscellaneous complaints which reformers were bringing against the immigrants lay solid reality, although the critics generally exaggerated and misconstrued it. The day of the pioneer *was* passing, and it *was* becoming more difficult and costly to establish an independent farm. Immigration was flowing more than ever toward the cities, and there it did complicate the slum problem, strain the old moralities, strengthen boss rule, and accentuate the rift of classes. In these and other respects, however, the foreign-born played a relatively constant role in a rapidly changing situation. For a long time they had suffered from and added to the cultural dislocations inherent in the rise of an unregulated industrial economy. Yet the immigrants' part excited slight alarm as long as the problems themselves did not seem pressing. The 1880's brought these long-germinating problems into a sharp focus and, by awakening a body of sensitive reform opinion, summoned forth the immigrant's first cogent critics.

Meanwhile, one group of reformers in particular broke the way toward a new immigration policy. To the directors of urban charities, perhaps the most conservative of all of the forces enlisted for social improvement, the immigrant had presented something of a problem even during the years of his highest repute. More or less constantly, relief agencies in the large cities had worried over the strain that immigrants imposed on their financial resources and on the life of the community.[16] Although at the opening of the 1880's the general mood of crisis which was to develop during the decade barely flecked the horizon, philanthropists were deep in a miniature crisis of their own. To solve it they precipitated the first national controls over immigration. The immigration act of 1882, despite a limited scope and a tentative approach, laid the foundations for federal immigration restriction.

Previously, the federal government had taken notice of European immigrants in only two respects. It counted the number of entrants for statistical purposes, and it decreed certain minimum living conditions aboard ship. In default of other federal action, immigration remained a concern of the individual seaboard states. The states placed administration of their own feeble regulations in the hands of boards of unpaid charity leaders. The whole program aimed merely at an orderly reception, at helping those in temporary difficulty, and at discouraging the entry of the permanently incapacitated. New York, which received three-fourths of all newcomers, bore the main load. There the state Board of Commissioners of Emigration maintained a fund for supporting needy and distressed immigrants by collecting from shipowners a small fee in lieu of a bond for each alien landed. The state also hoped to forestall the most serious burdens by requiring a special bond for each immigrant who seemed likely to become a permanent charity case.

This loose system broke down under judicial attack. In 1876 the Supreme Court, in a nationalist mood, declared that the states' practices unconstitutionally infringed on Congress's exclusive power to regulate foreign commerce. Henceforth New Yorkers would have to pay out of their own pockets for the supervision and care of immigrants unless the federal government assumed responsibility.[17] Charity leaders were appalled. The burden now thrust upon them seemed especially heavy because under the impact of Darwinian ideas they were beginning to regard poverty—previously attributed to moral weakness—as an inherited tendency. "The hereditary character of pauperism and crime," said a leading welfare worker, "is the most fearful element with which society has to contend." [18]

The New York Board of Emigration Commissioners and the New York Board of Charities immediately joined with similar agencies in other eastern states to press for federal regulation of immigration. Their proposals went beyond the old state system in two respects: they urged Congress to levy a small head tax directly on the immigrant to pay for administration and relief; and they wanted convicts and immigrants unable to support themselves positively excluded. This, they thought, would stop the influx of "confirmed paupers."

For six years Congress was unmoved. Business interests, particularly, resisted any action that might diminish immigration in the slightest. Finally, when conditions were becoming chaotic at New York's immigrant depot, the pressure of charity groups and of New York politicians succeeded. Pleading that hereditary European pauperism was incurable, they drove the federal government to assume partial jurisdiction. The immigration law of 1882 gave the Secretary of the Treasury executive authority over immigration but cautiously delegated the actual inspection of immigrants to existing state agencies. The United States was to accumulate an immigrant welfare fund by taxing each entrant the modest sum of fifty cents (New York had collected $1.50 from shipowners for each passenger). Also, convicts, lunatics, idiots, and persons likely to become a public charge were denied admission.[19] Thus, without intending to restrict immigration, the United States took a hesitant but decisive step to control it.

Later in the decade, charity workers voiced a rising alarm at the whole foreign tide, and began to talk about general restrictions. So did other reformers; after 1885 their complaints about foreign influence frequently included demands for limiting it. But middle-class reform never again played a determining role in making immigration policy, and the more popular the anti-foreign sentiment of the late nineteenth century became, the less the reformers contributed to its shaping. If broader segments of American society and thought had not also succumbed to a crisis mood, the nativist drift of the eighties would have been far less pronounced. In the middle years of the decade, men with all sorts of opinions and backgrounds were shaken loose from complacency, and turned fearfully against the stranger.

Militant Labor and Adamant Capital

In industrial society no other group comes into closer, more continuous contact with the immigrant population than the native workingmen. If anyone had cause for complaint against the foreign-born on grounds of substantial self-interest, it was the American hand who did much the same work, served the same boss, and often lived in the same neighborhood. Relations between the two, though frequently good-natured, were seldom entirely free from strain. The immigrant derived not only from a more or less alien culture but also from mean, impoverished circumstances. Entering the American economy on its lowest rungs, he commonly began by accepting wages and enduring conditions which Americanized employees scorned. In time the immigrants learned to demand more, and in the long run their manpower actually created more opportunities than it absorbed in the dynamic American economy of the nineteenth century.[20]

American wage-earners, however, were impatient of long-run views during periods of hardship and stress. They eyed the foreigner for what he was at the moment—a cheap competitor, whose presence undoubtedly held down wages and bred unemployment in temporary local situations. And in a more general sense, workingmen could reasonably anticipate greater economic security through anti-foreign discriminations, just as industrialists could reasonably expect advantages from protective tariffs. Consequently, every anti-immigrant agitation in the nineteenth century had drawn support from the urban laboring class. It contributed a rowdy element to the Know-Nothing movement, gave birth to societies like the Order of United American Mechanics, and sparked the repeal in 1868 of the Civil War statute encouraging the importation of contract labor.[21]

The tremendous immigrant influx of 1882, followed by the industrial depression of 1883-1886, persuaded many wage-earners that the whole incoming stream directly threatened their own livelihood. In New York City an Independent Labor party petitioned Congress to impose a head tax of $100 on each entrant. Philadelphia saw the appearance of a National Home Labor League, aiming "to preserve the American labor market for American workingmen." About 1887 a poll of 869 Wisconsin workers in varied occupations showed approximately half of them convinced that immigration was injuring their trade.[22]

In the late eighties, workingmen of several states secured direct discriminatory legislation against foreign labor. Virtually for the first time, American legislatures excluded unnaturalized immigrants of all nationalities from certain types of common employments. These statutes, though slight in their immediate effects, marked the beginning of a general departure from the old common law tradition. Under the common law, aliens from friendly countries suffered no general disqualifications in job-holding; except for positions requiring allegiance to the sovereign, they could work and trade as freely as citizens.[23] Several Pacific Coast states had excluded the Chinese from some occupations at an early date, and California in 1850 had instituted an oppressive tax on all foreign miners, but otherwise European immigrants apparently retained full employment rights everywhere until the 1880's.[24] Then, the initial restrictions applied to the construction of public works—a type of activity to which unskilled immigrant labor traditionally flocked. Under the spur of widespread unemployment the United States House of Representatives passed a bill in 1886 prohibiting the employment on public works of any alien who had not declared his intention to become a citizen. The Senate failed to act on the proposal, but some of the states proceeded to adopt regulations to the same effect. In 1889, Illinois, Wyoming, and Idaho banned nondeclarant aliens from both state and municipal projects.[25]

Petty though the enactments and the feelings behind them were, one may wonder why they did not materialize before this time. Granted that economic stresses in the mid-eighties encouraged a fear of immigrant competition, the question remains: Why did the issue arise during *and after* so short-lived a depression, having remained dormant through the much longer and more severe depression of the 1870's? Were workingmen responding in their own terms to misgivings that really transcended job consciousness, that flowed out of the whole encompassing social crisis? Was there something more than personal, economic resentment in a midwestern carpenter's outburst in 1886: "We poor, native-born citizens are just pulled around same as dogs by foreign people. We do not stand any show, and it seems as though everything is coming to the very worst in the near future unless free immigration is stopped." [26]

An answer is suggested by events in the coal fields of Pennsylvania, the region where militant anti-foreign sentiment gripped the native working class earliest and most fiercely. In the seventies and eighties the coal mining country was rapidly becoming the industrial hell of the northeastern United States. More than anywhere else perhaps, in those grimy company towns set in a ravaged landscape, class cleavage mocked the historic American promise of an open society. Nowhere did labor unrest cut more deeply. For a decade after 1865, strikes, lockouts, and suspensions prevailed everywhere in the region, punctuated by the industrial violence of the Molly Maguires.

The coal operators, already harried by chaotic overproduction, pitilessly counterattacked. Some of them began in the 1870's to bring in more docile laborers from Hungary and Italy.[27] The New York *Times* greeted these latter effusively, promising that the United States would gladly transform a million Italian beggars into prosperous citizens; but Pennsylvania miners took another view of the matter. Since the new groups entered into an already tense situation as creatures of the employers, they encountered resentments that were more than ethnocentric and went beyond economic competition. The immigrants seemed both symbols and agents of the widening gulf between capital and labor. The hatred of them was a hatred of the corporations for trying "to degrade native labor by the introduction of a class who, in following the customs of their ancestors, live more like brutes than human beings." [28]

From the outset the Slavic and Italian immigrants ran a gamut

of indignities and ostracisms. They were abused in public and isolated in private, cuffed in the works and pelted on the streets, fined
and imprisoned on the smallest pretext, cheated of their wages,
and crowded by the score into converted barns and tumble-down
shanties that served as boarding houses. The first of them to arrive in western Pennsylvania, a group of Italian strikebreakers
hired by the Armstrong Coal Works in 1874, were met by riots
and armed attacks in which several of the newcomers were killed.[29]
The problem remained a local one through the seventies, a period
in which Pennsylvania's total immigrant population from Poland,
Italy, and Hungary never exceeded some seven thousand. In the
next decade their numbers grew tenfold, and the issue of "contract
labor" flared into prominence across the whole region. Apparently,
relatively few of the new arrivals—who were now pre-empting
most branches of common labor throughout industrial Pennsylvania—were actually imported from Europe under contractual arrangements with their prospective employers. But corporate power
seemed so great and so menacing to American workers that they
uniformly attributed a captive status to the new nationalities.
Every time that employers brought a carload of eastern Europeans under armed guard from Pittsburgh or New York to work a
struck mine (great numbers arrived this way during the bloody
Hocking Valley strike of 1884), the impression seemed confirmed.[30] This first workingmen's anti-foreign movement in the
postwar era took form, therefore, as an attack on a supposedly
servile class.

The mounting discontent of the early eighties stimulated the
Knights of Labor, and as they spread swiftly from their early base
in eastern Pennsylvania, the Knights carried far and wide the agitation against contract labor. In 1884 Powderley's supporters
brought the question before Congress, where sympathetic legislators repeated the charge that monopolists were shipping from
Hungary and Italy, "as so many cattle, large numbers of degraded,
ignorant, brutal . . . foreign serfs" to replace American citizens.[31]
Both major parties and several small ones endorsed the Knights'
plea for a ban on contract labor, while the Democrats blamed the
Republicans for subjecting American workingmen to imported
competition. The next year Congress fulfilled platform promises
with a law forbidding anyone to prepay the transportation of an

immigrant to the United States in return for a promise of his services. One Congressman asserted that exclusion of the small number of such cases would make no difference but that he would vote for the measure because of the universal labor demand for it. Two years later an administrative act brought into existence a new type of federal official, the contract labor inspector, who quizzed arriving immigrants on their plans for employment.[32] To have a job before entering the country was becoming more reprehensible than to be unemployed afterward.

Although a good deal of unqualified anti-foreign sentiment was circulating among American workingmen by this time, the campaign against contract labor rested on a sharp distinction between voluntary immigration and that induced or controlled by capitalists. With remarkable unanimity, union leaders clung to this distinction through the late eighties and into the beginning of the next decade. Blaming their troubles either on contracts or on more subtle business techniques for stimulating immigration, the principal labor spokesmen refused to acknowledge that a normal, unencouraged, transatlantic movement harmed American workers. Powderley in 1888 insisted that few southeastern Europeans would come to the United States without employers' inducements. The organ of the Knights of Labor cursed "the stupendous folly of an industrial system which makes so naturally beneficent a thing as an increase of population a menace to the welfare of the wealth producers." Samuel Gompers, head of the rising American Federation of Labor, agreed that voluntary immigration was easily assimilated. The native-born editor of *The Rights of Labor* explicitly opposed any restrictions beyond the law of 1885, and as late as 1892 the president of the Amalgamated Association of Iron and Steel Workers told Congressmen: "We are not objecting to immigration that is voluntary." [33] *Organized* labor was clearly reluctant to convert its vaguely class-conscious position into a thoroughly nativistic one. The unions played a surprisingly limited role, after the passage of the contract labor law, in initiating a broader restriction movement.

Two factors explain the unions' unwillingness to support a general limitation on immigration, the chief being their own ethnic composition. Partly because old-stock American workers tended to cherish an individualistic psychology, an extremely large proportion of union members were themselves foreign-born. In Illinois, for example, four-fifths of the trade union membership in the eighties came from overseas, and everywhere Englishmen and Irishmen stood out as labor leaders.[34] Along with its international background, much of organized labor had an international faith. The concept of the solidarity of workingmen in all countries was by no means an exclusively Marxist idea. In 1878 the Knights of Labor had resolved that "nothing should be said opposing any portion of humanity." Many trade unions incorporated the word "international" into their names. The early leaders of the A.F.L. adopted peculiarly American tactics but preserved an internationalist spirit.[35] As long as labor leaders identified the new immigrants with contract labor, they evaded inner conflict, but outright opposition to immigration involved a fuller commitment to nationalism than they yet could make.

In point of fact the unions underwent less of a change of heart toward the immigrant than did their capitalistic adversaries. While labor leaders centered their fire on a special kind of immigration, business leaders were becoming broadly critical of the whole immigrant stream. They did not, of course, share the malice which some workingmen felt toward foreign-born competitors, but the revolution in their attitudes was greater and in terms of policy more significant. After leading the chorus of praise for immigration in the age of confidence, the businessman was now turning almost full circle. This shift, instead of bringing capital into some accord with labor, actually reflected the widening breach between them. Where one saw the foreigner as a tool of oppression, the other discerned an agent of unrest. The two lines of attack had little in common except their origin in a common situation: both reacted to the immigrant as a disruptive wedge in a dividing society.

Far from concentrating on the purely economic aspects of immigration, businessmen fretted about its consequences for social stability. The depression of the seventies had caused a few to ponder the danger of further additions to the army of jobless, and renewed unemployment in the mid-eighties heightened this concern. Each of the urban problems to which reformers pointed, from overpopulation to intemperance, multiplied business anxieties. The *Commercial and Financial Chronicle* worried because almost every "danger to the organization of society" originated among immigrants. Every disturbance of the social order, the journal warned, diminishes the courage and enterprise of capital.[36]

The disturbances which particularly alarmed business opinion issued from the ranks of labor. By 1885 the mounting tempo of strikes and the sudden, furious growth of the Knights of Labor demonstrated to employers that a crisis indeed impended in the industrial world. Their reaction, on the whole, was unyielding and uncomprehending. American business found the whole tide of unrest baffling, except on the theory that foreign influence lay behind it. Two aspects of affairs impressed employers very forcibly: the prominence of foreigners both as leaders and as members of the unions; and the presence of proletarian radicals here and there among the immigrant throngs. Perhaps cheap foreign labor was proving exorbitantly expensive in its social costs.

The Slavic newcomers in Pennsylvania, supposedly the most docile of immigrants, soon provided a dramatic confirmation of businessmen's fears. Driven to desperation, several thousand Hungarian coke miners displayed a belligerence and solidarity that confounded the anticipations of unions and operators alike. In January 1886, a state law went into effect forbidding women to work in the mines. The immigrant coke workers, paid on piecework, had depended on their wives' assistance to eke out a living. When the coke syndicate, headed by Henry Clay Frick, refused to raise the rate of pay, the Hungarians threw down their tools. There were riots and arrests. The strike extended to native-born and northern European miners. The syndicate tried to intimidate the Hungarians by threatening to evict them from their company houses in the dead of winter; they replied that they would resist with their lives. Instead of risking a blood-bath, the syndicate resorted to another tactic—a general lockout. This too failed to daunt the strikers, and in the end they won a small advance.[37]

These events provoked the organ of Pittsburgh's industrialists to indignant reflections on "furious Huns" and their lack of sympathy with American institutions. The journal concluded that immigration was hastening the social ills of overcrowded Europe. The American Iron and Steel Association spoke for restriction more bluntly: "It is impossible to deal intelligently and thoroughly with the labor question without dealing with the immigration question." [38]

By this time the anti-immigrant trend in business circles was well advanced. A survey of the opinions of 795 employers in Wisconsin—mostly with medium-size or small businesses—showed a big majority in favor of restriction, the proportion hostile to immigration being much larger than that in the somewhat similar poll of workingmen's attitudes taken a year later. And in 1888 the National Board of Trade, forerunner of the United States Chamber of Commerce, for the first time came out for protection against "the scourings of foreign disease, pauperism and crime." [39]

The change in business opinion, remarkable as it was, did not come without misgivings and qualifications. Like the unions, the corporations could not in a single decade wholly sever the ties that bound them to the immigrants. Some businessmen remained complacent, continuing to celebrate the economic value of immigration, the operation of the law of supply and demand in regulating it, and the power of a homogeneous society to assimilate it. More commonly, business spokesmen reacted against immigration without reaching specific conclusions on how to cope with the problem. Caught between growing trepidations and a lingering appreciation of the immigrant's usefulness, employers often sounded querulous, uncertain, unready to espouse a definite line of action.[40]

Above all, neither industrialists nor labor chieftains were in the full sense of the word nativist. Neither displayed much of a quality essential to a thoroughgoing xenophobia: an aroused and defensive nationalism. They approached immigration problems primarily in the guise of interested parties, and though their concern embraced the whole structure and future of American society, they indulged very little in florid appeals to national loyalty or survival. It was a short step from concrete anxieties about the social order to vaster beliefs that the nation itself stood in peril, but neither of the organized interests most directly affected by immigration blazed the way.

Beginning of Hysteria

Yet elsewhere in public opinion it was perhaps inevitable that the disturbing implications of the social problems heading up in the 1880's should awaken a strident nationalism. Nationalism has functioned as the most powerful unifying force in modern society, and its intensity has increased enormously in times of serious disruptive pressures. The fiery nationalisms of the fifties grew out of sectional cleavage; by the same centripetal principle, class cleavage could hardly fail in the eighties to produce a resurgence of nationalism. In both cases a baffled need for unity asserted itself in nativistic aggression.

Perhaps this explanation of the function of the new nationalist ferment may also help to locate its most active sources. At least it is suggestive that the pioneers of the nativist revival were not the appointed representatives of militant labor or the conscious spokesmen of adamant capital—not men securely attached to the congealing power groups that were straining the social fabric. Instead, a full-blown xenophobia dawned diffusely in the amorphous, urban and semi-urban public which lay in between. May not the very "in-betweenness" of petty businessmen, nonunionized workers, and white-collar folk have left them easy victims of demoralization? In a conservative era that was unable to ignore yet unwilling to face up to its inner schisms, the rootless "in-betweeners" had few resources to resist the loss of homogeneity. But they knew, at least, that they belonged to the nation and it to them. They could understand the discord in their Eden, and combat it, as an alien intrusion.

The sense of danger pressing on reformers, business leaders, and organized labor burst forth before this larger public about 1886, when an unprecedented eruption of strikes and mass boycotts opened an era of massive and recurrent discontent. Nativism, as a significant force in modern America, dates from that labor upheaval. At a time when monopoly and plutocracy cast darkening shadows over the summits of American society and when opportunity to escape westward seemed to be diminishing, unrest in the depths took on redoubled meaning. Each of the historic traditions of American nativism—submerged for a generation—came to life. Among the three fears, of European radicals, European religion, and European races, the last enjoyed the smallest vogue. Still the stepchild among American nativisms, the Anglo-Saxon tradition evolved within an intellectual elite whose separate story belongs in a later chapter. Anti-radical and anti-Catholic ideas were already integrated into American popular culture; they contain the essence of the nativist revival. And since a labor convulsion precipitated that revival, anti-radical nationalism was initially its most suitable vehicle.

The belief that revolutionary immigrants imported the seeds of labor unrest had already proved relevant to industrial America in the 1870's. The new swell of discontent seemed to confirm the worst suspicions of 1877. If one needed objective evidence that the tumult was foreign-inspired, the prominence of immigrants in the labor movement gave specious credibility to the charge. Furthermore, a tiny group of noisy anarchists, almost all of them immigrants, was becoming more active. In Chicago, almost the only place where the anarchist movement showed vitality, English- and German-language newspapers gleefully instructed readers on how to manufacture dynamite.[41]

There the event that catalyzed nationalistic fears of immigrant radicalism occurred. Industrial discontent was reaching its height in May 1886, culminating in a loose attempt at a nation-wide general strike for an eight-hour day. In the thick of the "eight-hour" strikes, the Chicago anarchists called a meeting in Haymarket Square. Nervous police closed in on the peaceful throng; a bomb exploded in their midst. In itself, the occurrence was slight compared to the railroad violence of 1877. But because of the doubts and anxieties of the decade following, the Haymarket Affair was to go down as the most important single incident in late nineteenth century nativism.

Instantly, a torrent of nationalist hysteria coursed through the cities of the Northeast and Midwest. Unable to discover the bomb-thrower's identity, Chicago authorities nevertheless sentenced six immigrants (five of them German) and one native American to death, and another German to a long prison term. In the big daily newspapers the stereotype of the immigrant glowed bright red, restriction sentiment suddenly coalesced, and editorial writers brayed:

The enemy forces are not American [but] rag-tag and bob-tail cutthroats of Beelzebub from the Rhine, the Danube, the Vistula and the Elbe.

These people are not Americans, but the very scum and offal of Europe.

. . . an invasion of venomous reptiles.

. . . long-haired, wild-eyed, bad-smelling, atheistic, reckless foreign wretches, who never did an honest hour's work in their lives . . . crush such snakes . . . before they have time to bite.

There is no such thing as an American anarchist. . . . The American character has in it no element which can under any circumstances be won to uses so mistaken and pernicious . . . a firm stand in favor of the right of Americans to govern America. . . .

. . . a danger that threatens the destruction of our national edifice by the erosion of its moral foundations.

. . . Europe's human and inhuman rubbish.

Our National existence, and, as well, our National and social institutions are at stake.[42]

For years the memory of Haymarket and the dread of imported anarchy haunted the American consciousness. No nativist image prevailed more widely than that of the immigrant as a lawless creature, given over to violence and disorder. Ripples spread out from Haymarket in a dozen directions, mingling more and more subtly with almost every current of xenophobia. Nativistic reformers joined in denouncing the immigrant as an author of revolution as well as an agent of reaction; and for the wide public which associated Haymarket with labor militancy, the stain of foreign turbulence tainted the entire labor movement.[43] Of course the unions on the whole repudiated the charge and kept their own limited attack on immigration free from nationalist themes. Only the most bourgeois of unions reflected the nativist spirit—a fact which tells something of its basis and appeal. The Order of Railway Conductors was exceptional both for its horror of strikes and for its unabashed, anti-radical nativism. After Haymarket, the order insisted that lawless foreigners were behind most of the current "labor troubles" and that complete suspension of immigration might be necessary to keep the United States from becoming a foreign nation. At the same time the Railway Conductors stood for a partnership of labor and capital "working side by side for the permanent advantage of all our honest business ventures in this boasted land of equality. . . ." [44]

Most concretely, nativist agitation manifested itself through the rebirth in the late eighties of an organized movement. Little nativist societies sprang to life, attracting lower-middle-class and working people to the search for unity through national conflict. At first some of them organized politically on the pattern of the prewar Know-Nothings. Three weeks after the Haymarket Affair, Peter D. Wigginton, a railroad attorney in California, founded the American party, declaring that the time had come for the American people to take full charge of their government "to the exclusion of the restless revolutionary horde of foreigners who are now seeking our shores from every part of the world." [45] This single-purpose party, while failing miserably to achieve national significance, made an impression for a time on politics in the San Francisco area. It found recruits chiefly among young workingmen and white-collar employees. It posed as "the real law and order party," contending that foreigners incited all strikes, riots, and disorders. Indeed, it regarded the strike as a foreign importation. In the same breath, the party denounced organized capital: "Thirty years ago the wealth of the nation was largely distributed among the masses; to-day it is largely owned or controlled by comparatively few men. Class legislation, monopolies, syndicates, rings . . . are written with an iron hand in the history of this increase of millionaires." [46]

By the 1880's the two-party system had become too deeply entrenched for a distinctively nativist party to repeat even the brief success of the Know-Nothings. Furthermore, a separate trial of strength had little attraction when the Republicans were showing signs of interest in the immigration issue. In 1887 Republican conventions in Pennsylvania and Ohio came out for immigration restriction. The Republican Senator, Justin Morrill, a veteran nationalist in matters of tariffs and education, introduced a bill for general restriction. The next year the California Republican convention spoke its alarm over an increasing influx of foreign radicals.[47] Aside from the short-lived American party, therefore, na-

tivistic associations took the form of "patriotic" societies, operating as pressure groups within the existing party structure.

The most powerful patriotic society of the day was an aggrega-
tion of Civil War veterans, the Grand Army of the Republic, then
climbing toward its peak membership of some four hundred thousand. G.A.R. spokesmen, already long practiced in nationalist attacks on the South, began in the late eighties to splutter over the
immigration of foreign radicals, who were allying with "copperheads and ex-rebels, for venomous warfare against the soldiers." [48]

The societies which cultivated the anti-radical tradition most insistently, however, were three secret fraternal organizations whose
roots went back to the earlier nativist ferment of the 1840's: the
Order of United American Mechanics, the Junior Order United
American Mechanics, and the Patriotic Order Sons of America.
They had started among American workingmen exercised over
immigrant competition, but by the eighties they were soliciting
members from all walks of life and actually attracting, along with
skilled workers, such people as clerks, small merchants, and minor
public functionaries. They admitted only native whites and required "that in all business transactions we shall remember our
own nationality." The secret of their feeble survival through the
age of confidence lay not so much, however, in an anti-foreign
appeal as in the insurance benefits which they provided for their
small memberships. Each maintained a fund to aid members in times
of sickness, death, or other distress.[49]

A new vigor enlivened the three orders in the late eighties. The
Order of United American Mechanics, the only one of the three
with a continuous existence through the Civil War period, established in 1887 a quasi-military rank, the Loyal Legion, which
brought the organization before the public eye by parading. The
Junior Order United American Mechanics, an offspring of the
O.U.A.M., dissolved all ties with the parent society in 1885 and
grew from fifteen thousand members at the end of that year to
sixty thousand in 1889. Its strength centered in Pennsylvania,
where all three groups had been founded.[50] The Patriotic Order
Sons of America, a postwar revival of the older Sons of America,
entered a comparable period of expansion, its star-studded, red-
white-and-blue regalia spreading widely through the North, Midwest, and California. It established a feminine auxiliary, the Patri-

otic Daughters of America (1885), and in 1887 it had the most successful year in its history.[51]

The fraternal orders all espoused an identical program. Their buckshot attacks on immigrants hit particularly at "Anarchists and all that class of heartless and revolutionary agitators" who come "to terrorize the community and to exalt the red flag of the commune above the Stars and Stripes." [52] At the same time, the orders felt wider anxieties and urged a nationalist solution to social problems. Only organized patriotism, they said, can save the country from foreigners interested in nothing but "the almighty dollar." Yet patriotism, they sometimes confessed, was suffering in America—suffering from the selfishness of plutocratic capitalists and striking workers. Perhaps avarice on both sides heralds an approaching war between labor and capital in which "the victory will be with the man from over the sea." [53]

While raging at imported discontent, the fraternal orders played on a second anti-foreign theme. They were anti-Catholic as well as anti-radical, though they usually put the radical issue ahead of the religious one. To another group of nativists, fewer perhaps in numbers but swayed by a matchless fury, the Catholic peril loomed largest. For all the differences between the two traditions of exclusive nationalism, the crisis of the eighties revitalized both, and in many minds they overlapped. One nativist, for example, declared: "Two lines of foreign influence are now at work among us, both of which are fraught with evil portent to our Republic; one tends toward license, agrarianism, anarchy; the other tends toward superstition, ultramontanism, tyranny: both by different roads to one ultimate end, *despotism!*" [54]

The social-economic tensions which activated the anti-radical movement had much to do with its anti-Catholic counterpart also. The sharpest manifestations of anti-Catholic nationalism occurred in the same "in-between" strata which fed the American party and the nativist fraternal orders, and religious xenophobes sometimes evinced the same social anxieties. Occasionally the fear of class war was straightforwardly confessed: in discussing the growth of an arrogant plutocracy and increasing envy among the idle poor, an anti-Catholic journal in 1889 predicted a revolution "unless the vast middling-class will educate the two extremes, check the power of the very rich and elevate the extreme poor." More often, anti-

Catholics imputed the antagonism between capital and labor to Romanist labor leaders, whom they charged with fomenting discontent under priestly instigation.[55]

Along with this common basis in class cleavage, however, Protestant nativism had its own specific roots in religious conflict. The religious factor lit the anti-Catholic movement with the flame of fanaticism. "I believe fully," wrote one zealot, "that the Protestant will win, as God is on our side, and . . . it will be a victory, tho' many a brave warrior may bite the dust. . . . I wish I could with the brave cohorts of Jesus lead on to conquer, or under his blood-stained banner die. Twere a death most gladly to be hailed." [56] Anti-Catholic nativism might have amounted to little if, on top of the general crisis of the eighties, a crisis in Protestant-Catholic relations had not supervened.

On the whole the Catholic hierarchy, under the temperate leadership of Cardinal Gibbons, followed a less militant policy than it had in the early seventies; but some Catholic educators in the late eighties renewed pleas for state aid. In the special field of Indian schools, successful lobbying by the Bureau of Catholic Indian Missions reversed the original distribution of federal funds to church-operated reservation schools, so that by the end of the decade Catholics were receiving a disproportionately large, rather than a disproportionately small, share of federal appropriations for Indian education. More important than these peripheral claims, however, was the tumultuous institutional growth of Catholicism itself. The years immediately following the Third Plenary Council in 1884 witnessed a spectacular expansion in dioceses and especially in parochial schools. At the council's bidding, each parish strove to build a school, and Catholic parents felt increased pressure to send their children there.[57] At the same time non-Catholics were becoming increasingly insistent on a standard, compulsory system of education dominated by the secular state. A sweeping attempt to establish public regulation of parochial schools convulsed Massachusetts from 1887 to 1889. Concurrently Ohio imposed attendance requirements on all schools, and Illinois and Wisconsin (where some Lutheran and Catholic schools used German as the language of instruction) hotly debated legislation requiring all children to be taught in English.[58]

To great numbers of Americans the common school was becoming a potent patriotic symbol. The belief that papists might some-how gain the upper hand over it helped to endow anti-Catholic feeling with nationalistic significance. Thus a propaganda organization formed by an eminently respectable group of New Yorkers in 1889 with the sole aim of guarding public education from Catholic aggressions called itself the National League for the Protection of American Institutions. It revived the movement for a constitutional amendment against sectarian appropriations of public funds and worked to end the system of federal grants to Indian mission schools.[59] Leather-lunged anti-Catholic rabble-rousers took up the cry with considerably less decorum. The Reverend Justin D. Fulton, a veritable fountain of nativist bilge whose weekly tirades in Boston drew enormous crowds, devoted a whole book to the papal plot against the American school system, arguing that Cardinal Gibbons had already made himself the actual master of the United States.[60]

Another link connecting anti-Catholicism with nationalism was forged in the political strife of the cities. The municipal scene presented a spectacle not only of class divisions and civic corruption but also of a sharpening political cleavage. Irish Catholic politicians, having served their apprenticeships as ward bosses and minor officeholders, were taking over the controlling positions in the Democratic machines. As Irish influence over one party grew (New York, Boston, and other cities got their first Irish mayors in the eighties) the old stock solidified more than ever behind the Republican standard. The split became so wide that in one instance the Democratic candidate for mayor of Chicago was opposed by every general English-language newspaper (except one that he owned), but supported by virtually the entire immigrant press and elected by a large majority.[61] This was the half-truth in the Reverend Samuel Burchard's calamitous description of the Democrats as the party of rum and Romanism; and this shift of political power into Irish hands gave many a Protestant Republican such as Burchard all the evidence he wanted that the Romanists were reaching for the vitals of the nation.

Accordingly, the late eighties gave birth to an anti-Catholic movement tinged with more hysteria and suffused with a deeper nativism than the religious friction of the mid-seventies. But what most clearly distinguished the new Protestant nativism from that of the preceding decade was its inclusion of the immigrant along with the priest as an object of attack. In an age relatively untroubled with social problems, anti-Catholics had tended to restrict their ire to the Roman hierarchy. Now they denounced immigration as a complementary national problem. Typically they trembled at the Roman challenge to American freedom, rallied to the defense of the public school system, and urged limitations on immigration and naturalization.

A whole crop of secret, anti-Catholic societies sprang up, none of more than local consequence but scattered in many localities. Regardless of actual size, they usually aspired to become a dominant force in American politics. It is noteworthy that one of the earliest of the new groups arose in Chicago in 1886. Named at first the United Order of Deputies and later the American League, it attracted ten or fifteen thousand from the lower-middle and working classes; it demanded that employers discharge all Romanists, but never realized its grandiose political ambitions.[62] In the same year a New York political adventurer formed the Minute Men of 1886, campaigning for the public school system and against immigration. The next four years saw the appearance of the Red, White and Blue (a super-secret little group formed by an impecunious bookseller to meet the perils described in Josiah Strong's *Our Country*), the United Order of Native Americans, the American Patriotic League, the Get There American Benefit Association, and the Loyal Men of American Liberty.[63]

Some of these groups worked in friendly cooperation with and recruited members from pre-existing anti-Catholic societies organized by British immigrants. Few Americans hated the Catholic Irish more than did the Protestant Irish. They had composed most of the membership of the American Protestant Association ever since its formation in the 1850's, and about 1870 they transplanted the more bellicose Loyal Orange Institution from Great Britain. To these fraternal orders was added the politically conscious British-American Association in 1887. "It is the honor of the Anglo-American and British-American organizations," declared a nativist journal, "that they are the only foreign-born element that can be regarded in any sense as an organized part of this movement."[64] The fact that the foreign societies gave less attention than the native ones to immigration restriction did not stand in the way of an entente between the two types, though the native-born groups sometimes fretted that their allies could not become "wholehearted Americans." [65]

The organization which ultimately developed real power wrapped itself in the deepest secrecy in the eighties and did not, therefore, become generally known. The American Protective Association was born in 1887 in Clinton, Iowa, a railroad junction on the banks of the Mississippi that claimed to be the largest manufacturing center in the state. The A.P.A. came out of the fevered imagination of Henry F. Bowers, who directed it for six years. Bowers, a deeply pious, slightly paranoid, middle-aged widower, saw Catholic conspiracies everywhere. A self-taught lawyer, he blamed his own educational deficiencies on a subversive Jesuit conspiracy against the public schools of Baltimore during his youth. Consequently he had the school question uppermost in mind.[66]

The immediate circumstances from which the order arose were, however, political and social; its origin reflected in miniature the general crisis of the eighties. Bowers was a close associate and adviser of Clinton's mayor, Arnold Walliker, who had come into office with the combined support of local businessmen and the Knights of Labor. Walliker soon alienated the biggest corporation in town and also lost the backing of the Knights. His defeat for reelection in 1887 was due chiefly to the Irish mill workers who comprised a large part of the union's strength in Clinton. Convinced that Catholic influence had undone Walliker, Bowers and he organized the A.P.A. within a week after the election. The small group that met in Bowers' office to found the secret order included several businessmen and dissident members of the Knights of Labor who shared a bitter determination to thwart the growing power of Romanism in local politics and labor.[67]

Bowers' fanaticism gave the A.P.A. its initial impetus, and the social tensions of the day provided recruits. He traveled widely through Iowa and into adjacent states, lecturing publicly on the Roman peril and secretly founding A.P.A. councils. Every recruit took an oath never to vote for a Catholic, never to employ one when a Protestant was available, and never to go out on strike with Catholics. Much of this early support came from disaffected union members, especially from the Knights of Labor, which was falling apart due to the anti-labor reaction after the Haymarket

Affair. In some places Bowers drew mostly from railroad trainmen, switchmen, and clerks, who felt dissatisfied with unions and threatened with Irish competition. By 1890, when the National Council of the A.P.A. convened for the first time in Chicago rather than in Iowa, its local councils were flourishing in communities scattered from Detroit to Omaha.[68]

Limits of the New Nativism

For the A.P.A., and also for the whole modern nativist movement, the 1880's were formative years; they brought nothing to fruition. As an organized force, xenophobia remained fragmentary. As a legislative program, it achieved nothing beyond the contract labor law. Even as a point of view, it was incomplete. Long-submerged fears of European threats to American freedom had, to be sure, reawakened, but the sense of danger had only begun to press against America's cosmopolitan traditions. Confidence in the process of assimilation and in the resulting fusion of a superior nationality was still widespread. For all of the talk of foreign dangers, hardly anyone denied the ultimate success of assimilation. The most advanced restrictionists still boasted of America's absorptive powers, contending only that the process was becoming too slow for safety. Significantly, the pro-restrictionist Philadelphia *Press* commented in 1888: "The strong stomach of American civilization may, and doubtless will, digest and assimilate ultimately this unsavory and repellent throng. . . . In time they catch the spirit of the country and form an element of decided worth." [69]

The old pride in America as a home of the oppressed survived more feebly than the melting-pot idea. The concept of an American haven for people discontented with their own governments exerted little fascination for an age that feared revolution. But though the idea was not often invoked, it was rarely repudiated. The grand dedication ceremonies for the Statue of Liberty in October 1886 passed off without a single reference to the poetic welcome that Emma Lazarus had penned three years before to "huddled masses yearning to breathe free." Orators expatiated far more on liberty radiating outward into the world than on oppression seeking refuge here.[70]

Along with the force of inherited beliefs, other factors curbed the fledgling nativism of the eighties. Xenophobia had geographical as well as intellectual limits. Despite some western concern over a diminishing land supply, anti-foreign and anti-Catholic sentiment thrived chiefly in the urban areas of the Northeast and the older Middle West. Newspapers west of the Mississippi and south of the Mason and Dixon Line still favored immigration, in contrast to the critical tone developing in the press of more thickly settled areas.[71] In the South, particularly, the dominant groups clamored for a larger white population and met no opposition in doing so. Although few immigrants actually materialized, the "New South" clung through the 1880's to the business dream of industrial progress and population growth. Likewise, the Catholic issue failed to arouse interest there. Accordingly, none of the nativist societies penetrated south of Virginia. A member of the Order of United American Mechanics tried to establish a council in Florida but had to disband it. Those who joined soon lost interest, while outsiders considered the order dangerously akin to a labor union.[72] The immigrants were urban people, their church was an urban institution, and the initial attacks on them were related to problems that centered in the cities of the North.

A final limitation remains to be mentioned. The authentic nativism of the eighties contained no assertion of—much less any emphasis upon—a broad, fundamental distinction between immigrant types. In its anti-immigrant aspect, the hatred struck at foreigners indiscriminately. Particular targets, such as German anarchists, Irish Catholics, and Slavic contract labor, might receive the brunt of the attack, but in each case the xenophobe interpreted his particular enemy as symbolic of a generalized foreign danger. He made no effort to select any part of the immigrant stream as the bearer of all of its vice. The point is important, for historians have usually traced the beginnings of modern nativism to a shift in the sources of immigration, a shift from an "old immigration" of northwestern Europeans to a "new immigration" from southern and eastern Europe. A turn in the immigrant tide was indeed under way in the eighties, but later observers saw it more clearly and took it more seriously than anyone could at the time. Nobody yet understood that a deep and permanent change in the whole course of immigration was under way. As late as 1891 journalists dismissed "the increase from undesirable sources" as a temporary phe-nomenon.[73]

Although the differences between "old" and "new" immigrants were much less sharp and the shift occurred much less abruptly than twentieth century nativists have taught us to believe, those abstractions do summarize a significant transition. In the late nine-teenth century the impulse to emigrate reached progressively deeper into Europe, uprooting more and more remote peoples. The Slavic and Italian influx to Pennsylvania began in the seven-ties, and by 1880 the Great Lakes region also had substantial clus-ters of Poles, while New York's Lower East Side contained crowded districts of Italians and Russo-Polish Jews.[74] That year saw a sudden jump in immigration from Italy and Hungary; in the next, pogroms hurried a mass exodus of Jews from the Russian Empire. Throughout the eighties, Italian, Slavic, and Yiddish im-migration increased. The peasants from these lands beyond the Alps lived much closer to serfdom than did the folk of western Europe, who were still pouring into the United States in undi-minished numbers; and the eastern European Jews were seeing a world outside of the ghetto for the first time. By western Euro-pean standards, the masses of southern and eastern Europe were educationally deficient, socially backward, and bizarre in appear-ance.

Long before the coming of the new immigration, the common people of eastern Europe had excited in Americans a simple, ethno-centric repugnance which marked the great social distance between them. The few Americans who had any firsthand contact with the eastern European masses in the early and mid-nineteenth century often judged them more personally distasteful than the immigrant groups which were presenting an immediate issue. An old-fash-ioned New York gentleman in the 1830's burst out: "A dirty Irish-man is bad enough, but he's nothing comparable to a nasty . . . Italian loafer." American travelers in Europe felt a similar con-tempt. "The lowest Irish are far above the level of these crea-tures," John Fiske observed in Italy. Even Emerson had been thankful that immigration brought "the light complexion, the blue eyes of Europe," that "the black eyes, the black drop, the Europe of Europe, is left." And in the early seventies, at the peak of America's receptiveness to immigrants, native settlers refused to move into the same vicinity with a Polish colony in Illinois, the land nearby long remaining vacant.[75]

That the arrival of the new immigrants in large numbers would generate instant dislike was, therefore, only to be expected. But the initial hostility they suffered consisted almost wholly of the conventional reaction against their culture and appearance. Except perhaps where they were caught up in domestic tensions such as those in the Pennsylvania coal fields, the southern and eastern Europeans did not as yet seem a distinctive threat to national unity or survival. Thus the criticism of the Italians and of the Jews—the groups which fared worst in most places—fastened on stereotyped traits, not on imputations of subversive activity or total unassimilability.

The Italians were often thought to be the most degraded of the European newcomers. They were swarthy, more than half of them were illiterate, and almost all were victims of a standard of living lower than that of any of the other prominent nationalities. They were the ragpickers and the poorest of common laborers; in one large city their earnings averaged 40 per cent less than those of the general slum-dweller.[76] Wherever they went, a distinctive sobriquet followed them. "You don't call . . . an Italian a white man?" a West Coast construction boss was asked. "No, sir," he answered, "an Italian is a Dago." [77] Also, they soon acquired a reputation as bloodthirsty criminals. Since southern Italians had never learned to fight with their fists, knives flashed when they brawled among themselves or jostled with other immigrants. Soon a penologist was wondering how the country could build prisons which Italians would not prefer to their own slum quarters. On the typical Italian the prison expert commented: "The knife with which he cuts his bread he also uses to lop off another 'dago's' finger or ear. . . . He is quite as familiar with the sight of human blood as with the sight of the food he eats." [78]

The reception of eastern European Jews in the few great cities where they first settled was hardly less adverse. Almost as strange to the German Jews who had preceded them as to the native Americans, these impoverished, undernourished refugees wore long black coats and untamed beards, practiced a distinctive religious ritual, and spoke their own language—Yiddish—with vivid gesticulations. Doubtless they were dirty; such at least was the initial and contemptuous image their presence inspired. The New York *Tribune* in 1882 noted blandly: "Numerous complaints have been made in regard to the Hebrew immigrants who lounge about Battery Park, obstructing the walks and sitting on the chains. Their filthy condition has caused many of the people who are accustomed to go to the park to seek a little recreation and fresh air to give up this practice. The immigrants also greatly annoy the persons who cross the park to take the boats to Coney Island, Staten Island and Brooklyn. The police have had many battles with these newcomers, who seem determined to have their own way." [79] To this first impression unfriendly observers soon added the traditional Shylock stereotype. Many of the Jewish immigrants started out in America with a peddler's pack. Since the railroads and the mail order houses had deprived peddlers of a useful function as rural distributors, however, they competed raucously in the city streets. Here, to many Americans, was the very personification of avarice and cunning. "Money is their God," wrote Jacob Riis of the Russian Jews as a whole. [80]

Painful though these epithets were, they failed to touch the springs of nationalism. Nativists in the eighties almost wholly ignored the rising new immigration. The points of departure for modern American nativism lay not in external stimuli but in internal conditions, not in new peoples or ideas but in new problems reacting upon the recessive traditions of American nationalism. The problems, to be sure, were not completely novel. They included such recurrent issues as religious conflict and economic competition, but these functioned within a larger context both startling and unfamiliar. For the first time in American history (with the partial exception of the Federalist era) a sizeable section of opinion made the momentous and troubling discovery that the United States confronted the social ills of the Old World.

Chapter Four

The Nationalist Nineties

Still I think that . . . the one last surviving popular ideal of
patriotism will save us from tumbling to pieces this time.
—Henry Adams, 1896

The crisis of the eighties passed imperceptibly into the deeper
strain and anguish of the nineties. No clear division separated the
two decades, either in the history of nativism or in the general
course of American civilization. The period from about 1885 to
1897 was one of recurring calamities and almost unrelieved discontent, culminating in the savage depression of 1893-1897. In the industrial North and in the farming regions west and south of it,
masses of Americans groped to escape the dominance of an uncompromising plutocracy—and groped in vain. Meanwhile, fear of
the stranger accumulated on all sides, mounting into hatred, burst-
ing into violence, and intruding into politics. Nativist movements
occupied a significant place among the rising currents of national
feeling that swept the decade. None of these chauvinistic enthusiasms quite overcame America's optimistic and cosmopolitan heritage, just as the underlying fears of a closed society were never
fully realized. But the unsolved problems of an industrial, urban
culture grew steadily more vexing; and the nativist response became more general, more insistent, and more explicitly nationalist.

Unrest in an Age of Depression

Industrial warfare sputtered on during the early and mid-nineties, as rebellious employees continued to clash with unyielding

employers. The governors of at least five states called out National Guard units in the summer of 1892 on occasions of industrial violence, and at Homestead, Pennsylvania, steel workers fought head on with an army of private detectives. Two years later, during another crescendo of discontent, the tremendous Pullman strike unleashed idle mobs in the Chicago railroad yards and brought United States courts and soldiers into the battle on the company side. The spirit of rebellion was abroad in rural America too; southern and western farmers were defying the reigning economic orthodoxies and the existing party structure alike in the angriest political crusade of their lives. Their determination to redeem from government what seemed lost to monopoly heightened year by year, leading through Populism into Bryanism and the election of 1896. Privileged groups resisted every challenge as doggedly as the federal government clung to a gold standard, but the protests could no more be stopped than could the steady drain on the Treasury's gold reserve.

If public finances were bad, private ones were often worse. A wave of business failures in 1893 ushered in four years of depression. Soon, millions were out of work, many to become tramps, some to collect in little bands marching on Washington as "petitions on boots." This national economic breakdown may not, in itself, have wrought more suffering than the depression of the seventies, but it came at a more anxious moment and afflicted a society less confident of its general state of health. The "panic of '93" gave an important impetus to nativism because it climaxed several years of baffled discontent.

In pondering the practical issue of immigration restriction, both capital and organized labor moved gradually and steadily in the anti-foreign direction they had begun to take during the preceding decade. The conditions that engendered mutual hostility between employers and unionists subjected to mounting strain the ties that linked them to the immigrants. Evidence of foreign participation in strikes continued to work on business opinion. The *Commercial and Financial Chronicle* felt a new zeal for restriction after a Russian-born anarchist tried to kill Henry Clay Frick, Pittsburgh industrialist, in 1892. The same year the National Board of Trade, prompted by its Chicago and New York affiliates, came out overwhelmingly for a plan to admit only immigrants passing an inspection by American consuls overseas.[1] Thus some of the confusion in business thinking was becoming resolved, even before the panic, in favor of a moderate degree of restriction. On the other hand, many business leaders hesitated before decisive action, fearful of complicating production problems in an effort to solve social problems. The New York *Journal of Commerce* held defiantly to the traditional position, arguing for free immigration on the ground that men, like cows, are expensive to raise and a gift of either should be gladly received. "A man," the paper added, "can be put to more valuable use than a cow." [2]

The long downward plunge of the depression stopped this line of argument. The happy pastime of calculating the dollar value of each new arrival passed into neglect. Instead, businessmen reflected on how unemployed aliens burdened the community and enlarged the stagnant pool of unused manpower. Seen in a context of hunger and want, the newcomer appeared more than ever a danger to society. In 1894 the National Board of Trade deliberated, though it did not adopt, a new and advanced proposal to restrict immigration by a test of literacy. Other groups did take a determined stand. Arguing for thoroughgoing restriction, the general manager of the American Iron and Steel Association maintained that the depression was greatly aggravated by "the presence among us of thousands of idle and vicious foreigners who have not come here to work for a living but to stir up strife and to commit crime." [3] These sentiments became sufficiently popular by the mid-nineties to win support for a strict literacy test of immigration from a number of business organizations: the Boston Merchants Association, the Boston Chamber of Commerce, the Seattle Chamber of Commerce, The Chicago Board of Trade, and the Commercial Travellers of the United States.[4]

Like the economic ties binding industrialists to immigrants, the ethnic and idealistic bonds between American- and European-born workers were weakening. The distinction between voluntary and induced immigration, which organized labor cultivated so assiduously through the eighties, was now wearing thin. As the new immigration continued to expand in the early nineties, the unions had to face the fact that this was no mere conspiracy on the part of employers. Organized labor confronted a clear choice between national and international loyalties. Painfully, it adjusted itself to nationalism.

The declining Knights of Labor, which was fast losing its character as a workers' movement, came out for a general restriction of immigration in 1892. At Powderley's warning that American liberty was slipping away, the Knights proposed the exclusion of all immigrants who lacked sufficient resources to support themselves for a year after landing.[5]

The American Federation of Labor and its member unions yielded less easily. They still had great numbers of foreign-born members and strong international sympathies. A.F.L. President Samuel Gompers was well in advance of the rank and file. This rough-hewn, pugnacious man was himself a Jewish immigrant boy from England, and he had risen to labor leadership through a New York industry—cigar-making—which was exposed to wave after wave of immigrants. Around 1890, when Gompers was first adopting a restrictionist position, cigar-making was receiving a new influx of immigrant labor, a flood of Russian Jews. This was a group whose arrival many older Jewish immigrants feared and resented. Gompers brought the immigration issue before the A.F.L. convention in 1891 with a plea for "relief from this pressing evil." The convention replied that further restriction was unnecessary.[6] Only after 1893 did nativist agitation become widespread among the unions; then three more years passed before it bore much fruit.

With the coming of the depression, want embittered all of the unsatisfied resentments of preceding years. Now labor papers teemed with discussion of immigration, and editors strove to convince their members of its danger. John Swinton, a prominent labor editor, put the case with crystal clearness: the supply of labor has far outstripped the demand, immigrants add to the crowds of unemployed in the cities, capitalists exploit the situation by hiring workers on their own terms, and there is no escape to the West now that the "free lands of other years are fenced in." Other labor spokesmen branded cosmopolitan ideas as sentimental and erected self-preservation as a patriotic alternative: "We sympathize with the oppressed of the Old World, but we . . . are as a country . . . in the position of any other asylum whose dormitories are full up. . . . The American movement is strictly American. . . . We cannot go abroad and hope to lift up the labor of the world. . . . The selfishness that provides for the home and protection of the family from want or danger is the only spirit in which this question may be considered successfully." [7]

Foreign-born and internationalist workers replied by appealing to the brotherhood of man and by blaming the capitalists rather than the immigrants for labor's troubles. The Boston Central Labor Union thought it detected a revival of the principle of the Fugitive Slave Laws in immigration restriction.[8] This opposition prevented action at the A.F.L. conventions in 1894 and 1896, but the next year restrictionists finally secured official endorsement of the literacy test. By then several other labor organizations had already done so—no great number. A few unions were also beginning to exclude from membership aliens who had not declared their intention to become citizens.[9] Organized labor moved with the nativist tide in the nineties, but certainly not in advance of it, or with full assurance.

While the leading interest groups concerned with immigration struggled to define their point of view, nativist tendencies functioned much more powerfully beyond their ranks. Even the workingman's economic jealousy had freer play outside of the confines of official union policy. The fear of job competition from foreigners contributed to a host of incidents and movements; most tangibly, it appeared in restrictions on employment. Under the pressure of intense and prolonged unemployment, several state legislatures went far beyond the pinprick discriminations of the previous decade. In 1894 and 1895 New York and Pennsylvania excluded all aliens (not just those who had not yet declared their intention to become citizens) from jobs on state and local public works.[10] Since immigrants traditionally did most of the common labor in the North, the new laws threatened to close a large opportunity to them. Idaho, where mining was suffering from the slump, also prohibited private corporations from hiring aliens who had not declared their intention to become citizens.

Economic discrimination reached a peak in two Pennsylvania statutes sponsored by coal miners in 1897. One set up residence and language requirements for certification as a miner. The other required employers to deduct a special state tax from the wages of all alien laborers.[11] This levy on the most poorly paid and underprivileged group in the state—"a vicious species of class legislation" in the words of the highest Pennsylvania court—did not survive a legal test. In general the courts in the late nineteenth century took an old-fashioned view of the civil rights of aliens and held such statutes contrary to the Fourteenth Amendment.[12] Their enactment, however, reveals vividly the impact of depression on nativism.

Yet, discriminatory legislation was far from common, and fear of direct economic competition from immigrants must have affected only limited groups and regions. A depression environment exacerbated anti-foreign sentiment in much broader, though less obvious, ways. In accounting for the main trends of xenophobia in the nineties one can never wholly separate the economic collapse from the social turmoil that accompanied it.

One of the outstanding nativist consequences of this combined social and economic breakdown was a nation-wide extension of the attack on immigration. Before the blighted nineties, anti-immigrant agitation had made little headway outside of the industrial North. Although the issue of land monopoly had already provoked some xenophobia in the South and in the trans-Mississippi West, it was scattered and sporadic. The Northeast and Old Northwest still remained the centers of nativism, but the fever now spread throughout the land, infecting all sections and every class.

The farmers' economic status deteriorated rapidly from 1890 on, and in the accumulating agrarian protest movements a distrust of foreign influence grew more marked.[13] But until the depression, important western newspapers welcomed European settlers and denounced the restrictionist clamor in the East. The South was wedded still more firmly to the traditional business gospel of immigration as a key to material development. Southern Congressmen put up the only vigorous opposition to a mild strengthening of immigration laws in 1891. As late as the spring of 1893, an official British investigator concluded that stringent immigration restriction was unlikely in the United States because of the resistance of the South and West.[14]

Just at that time, however, nativism was becoming nation-wide under the pressure of nation-wide distress. In the West conservative and radical spokesmen alike cried out against a European invasion. Three legislatures petitioned Congress to check it. Indiscriminate immigration, said Wyoming, "now threatens to overwhelm this nation." It "threaten[s] the perpetuity of our institutions," echoed California. The state of Washington wanted Congress to prohibit all immigration for ten years.[15] In several northwestern states, societies to promote immigration maintained a feeble existence but endorsed the principle of restriction.[16] When a showdown came in Congress in 1896-97, the area west of the Missouri River voted almost unanimously for general immigration restriction.

Xenophobia rapidly gained ground in the South as well. The most various types—businessmen, lawyers, educators, Populists—raised their voices against "this mass of European corruption." [17] By 1896, a good majority of southern Senators and Representatives had swung over to restriction. On the other hand, the South, the section with the fewest immigrants, still had the greatest lust for them. Regional and state immigration associations, though much less active than in earlier years, continued to meet at the behest of the railroads and their political and economic allies. And in Congress every other part of the country cast a heavier vote for restriction. On one key vote in the House of Representatives the pro-restrictionist majority of 193 included thirty-nine southerners, but of the thirty-seven Congressmen who voted against restriction, twenty-four came from the South as against seven from the Mid-Atlantic states, three from the Midwest, two from New England, and one from the trans-Missouri West.[18] Thus the economic tempests of the nineties swept West and South into nativist ranks but left a powerful opposition still entrenched in the latter.

Aside from this expansion of appeal, perhaps the commonest difference between the nativisms of the eighties and the nineties was one of intensity. The general temperature was hotter in the latter decade. We may read it by various gauges, for the intensification of nativism was apparent in action and legislation as well as in sentiment. Much of the evidence of this new intensity concerns the specific foci of agitation and is reserved for later pages. One overall aspect is relevant here as a keynote to the whole decade. Nativists in the 1890's repeatedly championed the values of nationalism in a very conscious, explicit way. They discovered that American patriotism was undergoing a decline, a decline due partly to the immigrant's disruptive and disloyal tendencies. They pleaded for a reawakened sense of nationality. Sometimes, in place of any specific accusation against the newcomers, they argued simply that a great nation requires a homogeneous people.[19] Nativists now were not just reflecting a revival of nationalism; they were its conscious apostles.

In this respect nativism formed but one part—though an important part—of the tide of national feeling that beat upon the American public during the last decade of the century. The period resounded with organized campaigns to arouse a vigorous "Americanism." Flag exercises, replete with special salutes and pledges, spread throughout the public schools along with agitation for inculcating patriotism. Among well-to-do, status-conscious circles, over a dozen hereditary patriotic societies sprang up in the early nineties to cultivate a keener, more exclusive sense of nationality. Beginning with the Sons of the American Revolution in 1889, these prestige organizations embarked on a round of banquets, receptions, and celebrations. Their principal theme was always the dire importance of perpetuating the pure American spirit of one's ancestors.[20] Meanwhile a tempest raged within the ranks of the Roman Catholic hierarchy in the United States, as a group of nationalistic clerics, largely Irish in background, denounced many of their German-American brethren for resisting Americanization and clinging to a divided loyalty. The chief socialist movement of the day called itself Nationalism and proposed "to realize the idea of the nation with a grandeur and completeness never before conceived." [21] Above all, these sentiments manifested themselves in astonishingly belligerent attitudes toward foreign governments. Jingoism was the most aggressive expression of late nineteenth century nationalism.

As early as 1889, when the United States asserted sweeping rights over the Bering Sea, public opinion was becoming sensitive to minor international controversies. Two years later there was talk of war with Italy and, because of a sailors' brawl in a Valparaiso saloon, a more serious threat of conflict with Chile. In 1895 jingoist frenzy brought the United States close to war with Britain for the odd reason that Venezuela disputed her boundary with British Guiana. At that point the Cuban Revolution absorbed the jingoes in a crescendo of excitement culminating in the Spanish-American War. It is hard to doubt that these bellicose outbursts flowed from the same domestic frustrations that generated nativism. The first important harbinger of both jingoism and nativism was Josiah Strong, whose attack on immigration accompanied a grandiose vision of global conquest. Not all jingoes were nativists or all nativists jingoes, but both the aggressive psychology of the one and the defensive reaction of the other provided instinctive rallying points for a society dubious of its capacity to compose its conflicts.[22]

To put the matter another way, when the troubles of the late nineteenth century raised doubts of the nation's stamina, two short cuts for restoring confidence presented themselves: disunity might be rationalized as a product of foreign influence, or denied by a compensatory demonstration of national virility. One response led toward protective measures at home, such as immigration restriction; the other encouraged an offensive posture abroad. Of the two, the jingoist tactic was more exhilarating than the nativist and closer to the habitual strut and swagger of the American spirit. It had, therefore, a greater immediate impact. Nativism fell short of its major objectives in the nineties, while jingoism carried the day.

As early as the late eighties, according to a scholarly observer at the time, Fourth of July orators were boasting of American national power instead of America's freedom from the social ills of Europe. And in 1896 a leading magazine described the public mood as follows:

This uncertainty and difference of opinion within party ranks have bred general suspicion and universal irritability. Moreover, the loose . . . talk about American principles and the American flag which has been in the air for the last two or three years has borne its fruit in what might be called an explosive condition of opinion in some sections of the country. . . . newspapers . . . have formed the habit of talking about foreign countries as if they were all the enemies of the United States, and as if to be a true American involved hatred of everything French, English, German, Italian, or Spanish. . . . In the general uncertainty about domestic questions, the confessed inability to deal with the currency question . . . and the hopeless groping about for something definite to stand on, the members of Congress have rushed pell-mell through any door of escape into a foreign field. The result has been that both parties have outdone each other in an attempt to take the most extreme positions and use the most violent language. . . .[23]

But if jingoism outdistanced nativism, it also aggravated it. The two anti-foreign movements—one international, the other internal—complemented each other, so that the jingoist atmosphere of the decade helps to explain the depth and intensity of its nativism. A public opinion chafing for conquest abroad was not likely to forego similar satisfactions at home. Furthermore, the jingo spirit jeopardized immigrant minorities very directly by creating a new sense of insecurity. After 1890 at least a flickering consciousness of global dangers and rivalries intruded upon the American public's complacent aloofness toward foreign relations; and a series of diplomatic crises shook the feeling of military security, which was one of the last bulwarks against nativism still intact. Consequently, the immigrants' national loyalties became a matter of greater moment, and suspicions that they harbored disloyal attachments to some threatening world power were more easily aroused.

Most of the foundations of the age of confidence had already been rudely shaken. One of them, indifference to social problems, had cracked in the eighties. A second basis of confidence, easy expectations of endless material expansion, was challenged by the restrictions of monopoly, the passing of the frontier, and the experience of grinding depression. When a wave of jingoism swept over the old indifference to international problems, the principal conditions upholding the assimilationist faith of the post-Civil War period were all in peril.

Anti-Catholicism Rampant

If nativism burst some of the limits that had previously confined it, its over-all ideological structure nevertheless remained for the most part unchanged. Grounded in social circumstances similar to those of the eighties, the nativism of the 1890's perpetuated all of the anti-foreign complaints that had circulated during the earlier decade. To reformers, the immigrants were the source of municipal squalor and corruption,[24] to workingmen a drag on wages, to militant Protestants the tools of Rome; and to nearly all their critics the newcomers were agents of discord and strife. Thomas Nixon

Carver, a conservative economist, blamed them for precipitating a labor problem by widening the class gulf between capital and labor; the *Nation* on one occasion attributed the deep agrarian unrest in the West to "peasants fresh from Europe"; and the major strikes of the decade evoked repeated references to dangerous foreign rabbles. Consequently, the anti-radical tradition remained a major nativist attitude, picturing the foreigner as steeped in anarchism or at least as an incendiary menace to that orderly freedom which Americans alone could supposedly preserve.[25] And anti-Catholicism, in continuing to provide an alternative theme, blossomed spectacularly.

The vitality of both traditions is striking in view of the fact that both targets, the anarchist and the Pope, were less vulnerable to attack after 1890 than they had been before. Judged objectively, these nativist symbols should have seemed progressively less menacing, for the circumstances of the decade lent diminishing support to conceptions of the immigrant as an agent of either proletarian revolution or papal despotism. The most serious unrest developed among the native-born farmers who composed the Populist party; the most alarming strikes appeared among English-speaking steel workers and railroad employees.[26] The anarchist movement was broken in Chicago, internally divided in New York, and—except for an individual attack on Henry Clay Frick—outside of the public eye. Likewise, the Catholic Church gave less occasion for religious nativism than it had a few years before. After 1890 the specific conflicts of the previous decade over relations between church and state reached a better adjustment, and the leading Catholic prelates went out of their way to demonstrate their attachment to American institutions. Non-Catholic pressure for state regulation of parochial schools abated, the federal government gradually withdrew from collaboration with religious bodies in Indian education, and prominent Catholic spokesmen showed a friendlier attitude toward the public school system. To be sure, a vast public display of Catholic strength at the time of the Chicago World's Fair caused some heartburning, and the appointment in the same year of Archbishop Francis Satolli as the Pope's first permanent delegate to the United States struck a number of Protestants as an act of insidious aggression.[27] But these were minor incidents.

In the case of anti-radicalism the fact that the target was less in evidence did seem to blunt the hostility. Even the most irrational attitudes secure a focus from the objective situation which they represent as well as misrepresent; "prejudices," in distorting reality, still reflect it. Revolutionary immigrants never caused enough real, sustained anxiety in the nineteenth century to rouse Congress to a legislative ban.[28] Although an explicit anti-radical nativism persisted, to a considerable extent the image of foreign radicals became diffuse. It tended to dissolve into vaguer visions of foreign license, lawlessness, and disorder. The adversary usually remained a symbol of unruly discontent, but he assumed a more protean, indefinite shape. Often he seemed to lose almost all distinguishing traits and become simply un-American, so that the anti-radical tradition partially blended with jingoism. Thus the hereditary patriotic societies, while characterizing "the foreign element" as abandoned to anarchy, socialism, and lawlessness, more frequently reduced the newcomer's crime to simpler terms: he "threatens to smother and obliterate American predominance, American influence, and American ideas and institutions." [29]

On the other hand, anti-Catholic nativism retained its piercing directness and redoubled its energy. Catholics, after all, were still prominent on the American scene, their multiplying churches ever more visible in the cities of the North and West, their influence in local politics undiminished. In fact, the general Democratic victories in the elections of 1890 and 1892 inevitably worked to the advantage of Irish politicians and therefore exacerbated anti-Catholic feeling; for Protestant xenophobes interpreted the election results, of course, as further Roman aggression.[30] Perhaps, too, the idea that papal minions posed a subversive threat to national freedom was so deeply entrenched in myth and memory that it needed relatively little objective confirmation.

No other xenophobia functioned in so highly organized a way as anti-Romanism. Its agencies, aside from the Protestant churches themselves, were of three types. The *ad hoc* committees, such as the National League for the Protection of American Institutions or the Citizens' Committee of One Hundred of Cook County, worked in the open, endeavoring to mobilize broad support for specific legislative objectives. The nativist fraternal orders collaborated in such lobbying activities but otherwise held aloof from politics. The orders functioned more as prestige groups than as pressure groups, in that sense resembling the hereditary patriotic societies which served a higher social stratum. The Junior Order United American Mechanics, combining anti-radical with anti-Catholic nativism, emerged in the nineties as the undisputed leader among such organizations. It reached a membership of 160,000 and took a vigorous part in the agitation for immigration restriction.[31]

Neither the *ad hoc* committee nor the old-fashioned fraternal order approached in militancy the political secret society. It alone could satisfy the urge for political power. A struggle to drive the Irish Catholic adversary from his position in American politics offered very real rewards, and the lure of power provided one of the outstanding incentives for anti-Catholic organizations. Among groups of this type, the American Protective Association most effectively exploited both the political ambitions and the broad, national anxieties on which anti-Catholicism throve. It absorbed many of the other nativist societies which had sprouted in the eighties and dominated the gaudiest wave of religious nativism in fifty years.

Until 1893 the A.P.A. grew steadily but unspectacularly in the upper Mississippi Valley from eastern Nebraska to Michigan, taking root in larger towns and cities where Catholics were rising in political and social status. Under Henry F. Bowers' persevering leadership, the organization combined some of the characteristics of a secret fraternal order with a primary interest in politics. Bowers, who was a devoted Mason, presumably borrowed heavily from Masonry in concocting a black and yellow regalia, an elaborate initiation, and a recreational program. More important, Masonic lodges, being tinged by an anti-Catholic heritage, provided a source of membership for the A.P.A., and often a body of political allies.[32] By 1891 the A.P.A. was strongly established in Omaha and helped the Republicans, whom it endorsed, to sweep that usually Democratic city by large majorities. Twelve months later, in Saginaw, Michigan, the A.P.A. elected William S. Linton to Congress, where he remained its chief spokesman. Yet, up to 1893, membership did not exceed seventy thousand.[33]

That year the society flared suddenly into national prominence, first tightening its grip on the Midwest and then spreading eastward and westward. It grew very rapidly throughout the Great Lakes area, crossed into western New York and Pennsylvania, and pushed as far east as Massachusetts. In November 1893, it claimed ten thousand members in Columbus, Ohio, sixteen thousand in Buffalo, and similar strength in Pittsburgh.[34] Meanwhile A.P.A. councils blossomed in Denver and other Rocky Mountain towns, in San Francisco, and in Seattle. During the first half of 1894 the A.P.A. reached its crest. Altogether, it may have enrolled a cumulative total of half a million members. Although it was becoming an important force in a number of East and West Coast cities, the center of its power remained in the Midwest. Michigan, Ohio, and Minnesota were probably the leading A.P.A. states, in approximately that order. An effort to organize the South made little headway below Kentucky. (Southerners were generally apathetic toward anti-Catholicism and viewed the A.P.A. as a Republican tool.) Everywhere the movement got the great bulk of its support in urban communities, although its influence now spread into rural areas of the Midwest also.[35]

Some of this growth resulted from the new leadership which the A.P.A. acquired in 1893. Control passed from Bowers' elderly hands into the more agile ones of William J. Traynor, who had built a strong organization in Michigan as president of the state council. "Whiskey Bill," as the Catholics called him, was a former saloonkeeper, a nativist newspaper publisher, and a veteran of the Order of the American Union, with long experience in promoting anti-Catholic organizations. He had a keener political sense than Bowers and immediately launched an aggressive organizing drive.[36] But the tide of sentiment he manipulated was surely not of his making. The upthrust of the A.P.A. corresponded too closely to the general expansion and intensification of nativism to be due chiefly to internal causes. Only the depression of 1893 can adequately explain the surge of Protestant nativism that year.

A.P.A. organizers hastened to exploit the climate of economic disaster. Wherever men would listen, they blamed the collapse on the Catholics, who had started a run on the banks—so the story went—in order to disrupt the economic system and thus prepare the way for Rome's seizure of power. A.P.A. speakers told crowds of unemployed that their jobs had gone to a flood of immigrants unloosed on America by papal agents. To prove their charges, the agitators invented and distributed very widely a document entitled, "Instructions to Catholics," supposedly from the Pope. From this, the credulous learned that Rome was preparing desperate measures to get jobs for Catholic immigrants: "In order to find employment for the many thousands of the faithful who are coming daily to swell the ranks of our catholic army, which will in due time possess this land, we must secure control of . . . every enterprise requiring labor . . . this will render it necessary to remove or crowd out the American heretics who are now employed." [37]

Since the depression embittered class conflict, the A.P.A. profited from social as well as economic frustrations. For lower-middle and working class people bewildered by the clash of organized capital and organized labor, the A.P.A. preached the same message carried by the smaller nativist societies of the eighties—but preached it more widely and explicitly. Industrial unrest was explained as simply another form of papal subversion. According to the A.P.A., the Catholics, sometimes in the person of T. V. Powderley, were fomenting strikes and labor problems as part of a larger plot to overthrow American institutions. Protestants were warned to avoid all unions dominated by papists, to discard the strike as a useless device, and to place no confidence in free silver. This advice made so strong an impression that Eugene Debs, the militant labor leader, and Ignatius Donnelly, the fiery Populist, called the A.P.A. an instrument designed by railroad magnates to disorganize labor unions. In fact, A.P.A.-ism did have a disruptive impact on unionism, and not only among railroad employees. In the coal fields of Pennsylvania and Illinois this internecine strife checked a United Mine Workers' organizing drive; in many cases it tore existing locals apart.[38] Yet, along with a covert anti-union bias, the A.P.A. also reverberated with vague alarms at plutocracy. Strictures on monopoly appeared in the pages of its publications, Traynor promised to wring justice from "soulless corporations and greedy syndicates," and one A.P.A. council (championing small business against monopolies) resolved that no one should be allowed to accumulate more than a million dollars.[39]

These attitudes, although important for understanding the A.P.A.'s appeal, formed no part of its official creed. Far from dealing directly with social and economic conflicts, Protestant nativism converted them into religious and nationalistic ones. The association deliberately excluded the major issues of the day when it drew up a formal program early in 1894. It proposed simply to defend "true Americanism" against the "subjects of an un-American ecclesiastical institution" by fighting for a free public school system, for immigration restriction, and for a slower, more rigid system of naturalization.[40]

A.P.A. spokesmen regarded the immigration question as second only to the religious one, but it was distinctly secondary. Although unofficially they made drastic demands at times, their lobbying for restriction was slight and ineffective.[41] This was largely because of the organization's curiously mixed membership. In its quest for power the A.P.A. welcomed support wherever anti-Catholic nationalism flourished. Such sentiment throve among foreign-born Protestants from Canada, Britain, and Scandinavia. Many of these newcomers found in their own Protestant traditions a source of identification with America; and they hated the Irish, to whom they felt culturally superior but who seemed proportionally more successful than they in capturing local political offices. Accordingly, the A.P.A., while claiming "America for the Americans," appealed to "all who will be true Americans," regardless of nationality, race, or place of birth.[42] So many Scandinavians joined that the A.P.A. organ in Minneapolis merged with a leading Scandinavian newspaper. British Canadians flocked in and even extended the association across the border into Canada. In many places, Orangemen, born in Britain or Canada, formed the nucleus.[43] Traynor himself was Canadian-born and held the vice-presidency of the Grand Orange Lodge along with the presidency of the A.P.A. Sometimes these naturalized groups favored immigration restriction, but not for their own nationality. An explicit and emphatic anti-foreigner campaign could swiftly alienate the northern European A.P.A.-ers.[44]

It was safer to stress the Catholic issue; the oath, which all members took, never to vote for a Catholic, indicates the A.P.A.'s governing preoccupation. By endorsing some candidates and condemning others as pro-Roman, "advisory boards" in each city and state manipulated the votes of the membership and of sympathizers. Since support went almost invariably to Republican candidates, Democrats denounced the organization roundly, while Republicans tended to temporize. In the spring of 1893 the A.P.A. showed substantial strength in midwestern municipal and school board elections, and that fall it contributed to William McKinley's phenomenally successful re-election as Ohio governor. The next year it took an active interest in elections in nearly half of the states. Both were Republican years; consequently, the A.P.A. was able to claim much more strength than it really had. But it did help to send a number of sympathizers to Congress. In a few states, notably Michigan, Kentucky, and Nebraska, the organization enjoyed the favor and confidence of the Republican high command.[45]

Much energy blew off in the form of propaganda, particularly through the lectures of ex-priests and nuns exposing the horrors of convent life. Very generally, A.P.A. members boycotted Catholic merchants and discriminated against Catholic labor. On the other hand, the amount of physical violence produced by the anti-Catholic hysteria of the nineties was not great. Rocks were sometimes thrown through priests' windows, and infuriated Catholics repeatedly attacked A.P.A. lecturers,[46] but no successful lynching occurred. There were three Protestant-Catholic riots, two of which involved the A.P.A. directly. One of these, a day-long battle that raged in and around the saloons of Montana's leading mining town on the Fourth of July, 1894, resulted in two deaths. The other was a general shooting fray at a polling place in Kansas City, Missouri, during the municipal election that year. An A.P.A. leader and several Catholics were killed.[47] In these and other instances the A.P.A. created some violence, partly because it had belligerent adversaries.

The supreme violence occurred inside men's heads. Anti-Catholicism reached a climax in ideology rather than action by absorbing and reflecting the decade's rampant jingoism. Since religious nativists had always regarded Catholics as disloyal adherents of a foreign potentate, the anti-Catholic tradition was easily susceptible to jingoist influence. Eyeing their Catholic neighbors, Protestant nationalists could enjoy a tingling sense of confronting the waiting soldiery of an enemy state. In the mid-nineties, without the provocation of actual international friction, the papacy took a place alongside Chile, Italy, and Great Britain as one of the powers against which an inflamed populace prepared to do battle.

Fears of a long-range papal scheme to overthrow American institutions had bothered a good many Protestants during the early nineteenth century, but only in 1893 did Americans gird themselves to meet an imminent Catholic uprising. Early that year Traynor's newspaper, the Detroit *Patriotic American,* gave wide circulation to a document that disclosed the impending popish plot. The document was a bogus encyclical addressed to American Catholics by Pope Leo XIII. It absolved them from any oaths of loyalty to the United States and instructed them "to exterminate all heretics" on a certain date in September. A Minneapolis agitator, Burton Ames Huntington, improved on the story in a book designed to show that seven hundred thousand papal soldiers—organized in all large American cities—were ready to spring into rebellion at a moment's notice. Rome's policy, he asserted, was to force "us Americans . . . to rebel against Rome's usurpations" and then to carry out a counterrevolution under the pretext of restoring law and order. He urged his readers to organize and arm themselves but not to start anything.[48] The whole book quivered with a militant nationalism much like that evoked by the diplomatic crises of the period.

Reprinted throughout the nativist press, in leaflets and in handbills, these tales struck panic far and wide. Catholic meetings were spied upon for evidence of military preparations. In Toledo the mayor, the police commissioner, and others bought Winchester rifles to repel an anticipated invasion, and many A.P.A. members were afraid to go to bed at night. The Catholic war scare had greatest impact, however, in midwestern rural areas where "flesh-and-blood" Catholics were virtually nonexistent and the enemy lay far away in the cities. Illinois farmers feared to leave home lest Romanists burn their barns and houses. A rural schoolteacher in Minnesota went about heavily armed for weeks to defend himself against the anticipated massacre. A large part of the population in some of the smaller towns of Ohio was terrorized by bloodcurdling reports of the preparations for war which the Catholics in Columbus were supposedly making.[49]

This phase passed in a few months. Indeed, the vitality drained out of the whole anti-Catholic movement well before the other currents of late nineteenth century nativism subsided. While other xenophobias were still growing, anti-Catholicism began to decline in the latter part of 1894. In part it was discredited by internal dissensions which were splitting the A.P.A. Like every secret

political organization in American history, the A.P.A. lent itself
to exploitation for private advantage. Office-seekers used it and
then ignored it; factions wrestled for control of it. After the election of 1894 failed to produce results commensurate with the leadership's hopes, the strife increased. Traynor led an unsuccessful
movement for establishing a third party, others insisted on endorsing McKinley, and the society virtually fell apart over this issue
in the spring of 1896.[50] Meanwhile tension between the old American and immigrant wings seems also to have caused numerous
defections. Many Scandinavians lost sympathy with the A.P.A.
as its anti-foreign tinge became increasingly emphatic; in Minnesota the order started downhill in the spring of 1894, while it was
still advancing elsewhere.[51]

In addition to these disruptive tendencies, the A.P.A. suffered
from the limitations of anti-Catholic nationalism. This idea no
longer provided an adequately comprehensive expression of nativist
ferment. Whatever respectability the tradition had once possessed
was largely gone. In an increasingly secular culture, enthusiastic
religion was passing out of middle-class life, and without it the
belief that popery lay behind the major national perils was hard
to sustain. Furthermore, by the late nineteenth century many
Catholics had become assimilated into "respectable" society, making editors and politicians reluctant to lose their support by expressing sentiments critical of their religion. No outstanding political leader adhered publicly to the anti-Catholic line which Hayes,
Grant, and others had followed in the early seventies. *Harper's
Weekly* retreated from its earlier ebullience into a cautious neutrality,[52] and only two or three articles sympathetic to the A.P.A.
appeared in the general magazines. Even many Protestant clergymen who were outspokenly anti-foreign avoided the anti-Catholic
theme.[53] The A.P.A.'s old-fashioned nativism had little attraction
for the higher strata of American society.

By the same token this tradition-bound nativism failed to profit
from new and rising xenophobias. It lacked a race consciousness
that might have appealed to the South—the A.P.A. welcomed
Negro support[54]—and among particular nationalities it had eyes
only for the menace of the Irish. Although the A.P.A. feared
aliens in general, it never appreciated the shift that was under way
in the sources of immigration. A product of the Middle West, the

association arose and flourished most vigorously in a section which had as yet no great number of southern and eastern Europeans. The A.P.A. spent its declining strength belaboring the Irish stand-ard-bearers of Catholicism while other nationalities were moving into the orbit of American nativism.

Nationalism and the New Immigrants

Unlike the older Catholic population, the southern and eastern Europeans who had begun to arrive in considerable numbers during the 1880's lived in the American imagination only in the form of a few vague, ethnic stereotypes. They occupied, in other words, no distinctive place, either separately or collectively, in the traditions of American nationalism. In the 1890's, for the first time, they became a significant factor in the growth of nativism. An initial distrust, compounded largely out of their culture and ap-pearance, swelled into a pressing sense of menace, into hatred, and into violence. This process went forward essentially along two lines: first and most commonly, the general anti-foreign feelings touched off by the internal and international shocks of the late nineteenth century were discharged with special force against these new targets so that each of the southeastern European groups appeared as a particularly insidious representative of the whole foreign menace; secondly and more slowly, a campaign got under way against the new immigration as a unique entity, constituting in its difference from other foreign groups the essence of the na-tion's peril. The first type of attack was midwife to the second. The new immigrants had the very bad luck to arrive in America en masse at a time when nativism was already running at full tilt, and when neither anarchist nor Jesuit afforded a wholly satisfac-tory victim for it.

The hostilities which southeastern Europeans faced depended partly on their increasing prominence on the American scene. During the early nineties, peasants and Jews poured out of south-ern and eastern Europe in ever larger numbers, fleeing from pov-erty and inhumanity to a new promised land. Cutthroat competi-tion among the transatlantic steamship companies eased their flight; steerage rates on first-class boats dropped to $10 or even less. The depression sharply reduced all immigration, but the new current never fell below one hundred thousand persons per year—a level it had first reached in 1887.[55] More exclusively than most older immigrant groups, the new ones swarmed into the slums, the factories, and the mines. Either urbanites or industrial workers, and usually both, they played a role in American life that lent itself to nativist interpretation. In the crowded places where they made their homes, they lived as a class apart, the least assimilated and most impoverished of the immigrants. Hence, they symbolized vividly the social and economic ills with which nativists identified the immigrants generally. Fears of developing class cleavage could easily center on them; and with less perversion of logic than anti-Catholicism required, the problems of depression and unrest could be associated with them. Above all, each of the southern and eastern European nationalities seemed to Americans in some way a disturber of the peace, thereby focalizing the fear of foreign-bred discontent.

On the other hand, the new immigrants, although vulnerable as symbols of a general foreign problem, did not yet stand out readily as a collective entity. Until 1896 the old influx from northern and western Europe surpassed the southern and eastern European current. All in all, at least 80 per cent of the European-born population of the United States in the mid-nineties still derived from those accustomed sources—Germany, Great Britain, Scandinavia, France, Switzerland, and the Low Countries. Furthermore, concentration of settlement limited the impact of the new groups. While a few coastal cities and industrial complexes felt their arrival sharply, large parts of the country hardly knew them at all. Two-thirds of the first-generation Italians, for example, settled in the mid-Atlantic and New England states.[56] Most of America was just beginning to learn of their presence, largely at secondhand. Consequently most of the hatred of Italians, Slavs, and Jews consisted of general anti-foreign attitudes refracted through specific national stereotypes.

The Slavic coal miners of Pennsylvania illustrate very well how the new immigration inherited a wider, pre-existing animus. They acquired the immigrant's standard reputation for disorder in an unusually simple, direct form. The American mind contained, apparently, no distinctive "Slavic" stereotype, comparable to Italian and Jewish stereotypes, which might have individualized the hostile response.[57] Consequently Slavic and Magyar laborers impressed public opinion at large simply as foreigners par excellence: uncivilized, unruly, and dangerous.

The impression fed upon the Slavic coal miners' sporadic but increasing involvement in labor unrest. Ironically, while other workingmen continued to despise them as cheap and docile competitors, the general public fixed its eyes on their lapses from docility. Already the Slavs had incurred the indignation of employers for participating in the coke strike of 1886; during the greater industrial conflicts of the nineties, they encountered the hostility of the whole middle-class community. By 1891, when Henry Clay Frick precipitated a strike of fourteen thousand coke workers by posting a new wage scale, Slavic and Magyar nationalities well outnumbered the older immigrants and native Americans in the bituminous fields.[58] Although British and Americans led the strike, it was generally interpreted as an uprising of "Huns," who, in the words of the New York *Tribune*, were "the most dangerous of labor-unionists and strikers. They fill up with liquor and cannot be reasoned with." The company brought in nonunion workers, a step which resulted in riots and vandalism on the part of the strikers. In this tense situation, a crowd of "Huns," returning from a mass meeting, passed a frightened detachment of state militia guarding a company store. Someone fired a shot, the strikers fled, and the militia fired two volleys after them. Ten dead and fifty wounded immigrants littered the road. According to the *Tribune*, the militia's action was "upheld by businessmen and all law-abiding people in the entire region." [59]

Frick finally succeeded in breaking the strike, though he was to face a similar walkout three years later. This time an immigrant mob killed Frick's chief engineer, causing the Pittsburgh *Times* to report that the whole region was "trembling on the brink of an insurrection. Never before were the dangerous foreigners so thoroughly aroused." A sheriff's posse, equally aroused, pursued the escaping strikers, shooting several and arresting 138 for murder. No sooner was this strike defeated than a general work stoppage throughout the bituminous coal fields ensued, bringing its quota of violence and police brutalities.[60]

The bloodiest episode occurred in 1897. While the United Mine Workers Union was leading the new immigrants to victory in the bituminous fields, an attempt to launch a strike in the anthracite country provoked disaster. About 150 Polish and Hungarian strikers, entirely unarmed, set out from Hazleton, Pennsylvania, toward a nearby town, intent on urging the men there to join the walkout. The sheriff, persuaded by the coal owners that an organized march was illegal, gathered a posse of 102 deputies to intercept it. As the strikers came in sight, the sheriff ordered them to return. Someone struck him, frightening him into commanding the deputies to fire. They poured volley after volley into the surprised and terrorized crowd as it stampeded in flight. They killed twenty-one immigrants and wounded forty more. The sheriff, a former mine foreman, explained that the crowd consisted of "infuriated foreigners . . . like wild beasts." Other mine foremen agreed that if the strikers had been American-born no blood would have flowed.[61]

In the case of the Italians, a rather similar fear of "infuriated foreigners" took a different twist. Anti-foreign sentiment filtered through a specific ethnic stereotype when Italians were involved; for in American eyes they bore the mark of Cain. They suggested the stiletto, the Mafia, the deed of impassioned violence. "The disposition to assassinate in revenge for a fancied wrong," declared the Baltimore *News*, "is a marked trait in the character of this impulsive and inexorable race." Every time a simple Italian laborer resorted to his knife, the newspapers stressed the fact of his nationality; the most trivial fracas in Mulberry Street caused a headline on "Italian Vendetta."[62] The stereotype conditioned every major outburst of anti-Italian sentiment in the 1890's. The distinctive nativism which swarthy *paesani* experienced took the guise of social discipline applied to alleged acts of homicide.

Time and again, lynching parties struck at Italians charged with murder. In 1891 a wild rumor that drunken Italian laborers had cut the throats of a whole American family in West Virginia set off further rumors of a pitched battle between a sheriff's posse and the assassins. In 1895, when the southern Colorado coal fields were gripped by violent labor strife, a group of miners and other residents systematically massacred six Italian workers implicated in the death of an American saloonkeeper. A year later a mob dragged three Italians from jail in a small Louisiana town and hanged them.[63] The biggest incident convulsed New Orleans—and then the whole country—at the beginning of the decade. The city combined southern folkways with all of the social problems of the urban North, and as the most southerly of American ports, it was the haven of a large migration from Sicily. In 1891 the superintendent of police was murdered under conditions which pointed to the local Sicilian population. Wholesale arrests followed in an atmosphere of hysteria. The mayor issued a public appeal: "We must teach these people a lesson that they will not forget for all time." The city council appointed a citizens' committee to suggest ways of preventing the influx of European criminals. But when some of the accused were tried, the jury (which may have been suborned) stunned the city by refusing to convict. While officials stood idly by, a mob proceeded "to remedy the failure of justice" by lynching eleven Italian suspects. With apparent unanimity local newspapers and business leaders blessed the action.[64]

At that point jingoism intruded upon what had begun as a local, internal episode, transforming it into a nation-wide commotion and a diplomatic crisis. Italy sought redress for the victims' families and punishment of the mob that murdered them. Secretary of State James G. Blaine treated the plea cavalierly, whereupon Italy abruptly recalled her minister in Washington. Internal hatred and external conflict now interacted directly, producing an explosion of feeling against Italy and enormously magnifying the fear of Italian-Americans. A belief that the Italian fleet might suddenly descend on the United States gained fairly wide credence, and patriots flexed their muscles in preparation. Italians within the country now appeared as a potential fifth column; obviously these people could not be depended upon in times of national danger. There were reports of Italian immigrants riddling an American flag with bullets; a rumor circulated that several uniformed corps of Italians were drilling in New York.[65] In Wheeling, West Virginia, miners went on strike because their employer refused to discharge two Italians; the strikers vowed they would not work with men "allied to a nation that was trying to bring about a war with the United States." A patriotic society demanded war if Italy continued shipping criminals to the United States. The *Review of Reviews* saw two lessons in the affair: that America must have a navy to protect itself from "wanton insult," and an immigration policy to keep out "the refuse of the murder-breeds of Southern Europe." [66]

Clearly, as the *Review* pointed out, a revival of Americanism was emerging from the New Orleans incident. Not just Italian immigration but the whole immigration question was dramatized as nothing had dramatized it since the Haymarket Affair. The press, the pulpit, and the magazines rang with demands for stringent restriction. The influential *Nation* concluded that a secure modern state rested on community of language and proposed therefore to limit immigration to English-speaking applicants. This severe idea met considerable favor.[67]

The third major group in the new immigration, the Jews, was also buffeted by the nativism and jingoism of the nineties. They had, of course, their own unique status, fixed by the ancient Shylock stereotype; they stood for chicane rather than crime or revolution. (The American public had heard little as yet about the radical labor movements stirring in the New York ghetto.) [68] But the Jews' supposedly unscrupulous greed now seemed as potentially subversive as the doings of bloodthirsty Italians, "furious Huns," or Irish papists. Hatred, rooted in much the same conditions, lashed them all in rather similar ways.

The Jews felt, too, the violence endemic in that period. Beginning in the late eighties, the first serious anti-Semitic demonstrations in American history occurred in parts of the lower South where Jewish supply merchants were common. In several parishes of Louisiana debt-ridden farmers stormed into town, wrecked Jewish stores, and threatened to kill any Jews who remained in the area. During the worst year, 1893, night-riders burned dozens of farmhouses belonging to Jewish landlords in southern Mississippi, and open threats drove a substantial number of Jewish businessmen from Louisiana.[69] Persecution in northern cities generally took the form of personal taunts and assaults. Russo-Polish Jews had been stoned occasionally in the early eighties, and in the next decade this petty kind of Jew-baiting became much more common.[70] One serious incident broke out in a New Jersey mill town in 1891. Five hundred tending boys employed in the local glass works went on a rampage when the management hired fourteen young Russian Jews. Three days of riotous demonstrations caused most of the Jewish residents to flee from the area.[71] In one sense the Jews came off a little better than the other minorities; apparently no lives were lost in any of these episodes.

A substantial ideological onslaught accompanied the physical assaults, however. In response to the tensions of the 1890's, the Shylock stereotype—which tended to obscure distinctions between the relatively well-to-do German Jews and the newcomers from eastern Europe—assumed a new potency. To some nativists, the Jews were capable of dominating or ruining American business. Tradition connected Jews with gold, which was becoming one of the major touchstones of internal strife. After 1890 the government's determination to maintain the gold standard excited enormous discontent and defined the great political issue of the period. Since greedy, destructive forces seemed somehow at work in the government and economy, suspicion dawned that a Jewish bid for supremacy was wreaking the havoc America could not control. Agrarian radicals, absorbed in a passionate crusade for free silver, sometimes yielded to this conjecture, but the idea was not theirs alone. The patrician Henry Adams concluded that the United States lay at the mercy of the Jews, and a New York workingman vowed: "The Russian Jews and the other Jews will completely control the finances and Government of this country in ten years, or they will all be dead. . . . The hatred with which they are regarded . . . ought to be a warning to them. The people of this country . . . won't be starved and driven to the wall by Jews who are guilty of all the crimes, tricks and wiles that have hitherto been unknown and unthought of by civilized humanity." [72]

Here too jingoism played a part. It was not enough for jingo-inflamed nativists to see the Jews solely as an internal threat. They were a people without a national state or center of power: an *international* people. Since gold was becoming, in fact, a more and more firmly established international standard, millions of Americans associated their country's troubles with an international medium of exchange and felt themselves in the toils of a world-wide money-power. Did the Jews perhaps have an international loyalty above all governments, a quenchless resolve to rule the world themselves? For at least a few nativists, the new tendency to see America's adversaries operating on a world stage inflated the

Jewish peril from one of national subversion to one of world domination. An occasional eastern conservative detected a clandestine Jewish league controlling the money markets of the world, or blamed the depression on Jewish bankers who were said to be shipping America's gold to Europe.[73] Western agrarians not infrequently slipped into similar allusions. Minnesota's Ignatius Donnelly wrote a utopian novel, *Caesar's Column*, prophesying a totally degraded society ruled by a Jewish world oligarchy. The greatest of the silverites, William Jennings Bryan, bluntly accused President Cleveland of putting the country in the hands of the English Rothschilds.[74]

In nineteenth century America, even so, the menace of world Jewry was undoubtedly less important than related fears of Italians and Catholics. Certainly the vision of an Italian fifth column precipitated more immediate consequences, and the expectation of a papal uprising created greater hysteria. The chief significance of the "International Jew" lay far in the future. Denationalized and universal, the symbol curiously mingled jingoism with isolationism. It was less a summons to fight than a command to withdraw, and its full impact would not come until American nationalism reverted from a strategy of belligerent intervention to one of belligerent isolation.

For understanding late nineteenth century nativism, it is not the latent possibilities of the new anti-Semitism which need emphasis, but rather the common qualities in the assaults on the various new immigrant nationalities. No longer scorned simply for "mere habits of life," each of the major groups from southern and eastern Europe stood forth as a challenge to the nation, either endangering American institutions by unruly behavior or threatening through avarice to possess them. In lashing out at each of these ethnic groups, a distraught society secured a whole set of new adversaries.

On the other hand, the discovery that the miscellaneous Slavs, Jews, and Italians constituted a collective type, a "new immigration," dawned more gradually. The concept of a new immigration would seem to have been largely the work of cultivated minds rather than a simple derivative of popular instincts. Certainly mass opinion in the nineties pictured the Italian, the Slav, and the Jew chiefly within the context of a general foreign peril. The fact of a rising influx of southern Europeans with unusually low living standards had been mentioned as early as 1884 in the discussion of the contract labor bill but did not receive much notice. Occasionally in the late eighties and with increasing frequency after 1890, a few keen observers in the East pointed to the proportional decline of northwestern European entrants. After 1890, as the comfortable belief faded that this was a mere, temporary eddy in the migratory stream, a handful of nativist intellectuals confronted the problem of defining the general threat which the whole movement from southern and eastern Europe raised to the nation's destiny.

Neither of the major traditions of nativist thought quite fitted the problem. The anti-radical theme, with its fears of imported discontent, applied to Europeans as a whole, and surely the new immigrants presented a more docile appearance than did Irish labor leaders or the German anarchists who hanged for the Haymarket Affair. Anti-Catholic nationalism, aside from failing to account for the new Jewish immigration, reeked of religious fanaticism which literate and cultured people now disavowed. On the eve of the A.P.A.'s rise to national prominence, a typical nativist intellectual rejoiced that the present movement against immigration would be free from attacks on Catholics.[75] There was, however, a third nativist tradition—weaker than the other two but more adaptable to the purpose at hand. The old idea that America belongs peculiarly to the Anglo-Saxon race would define the special danger of the new immigration if one assumed that northern Europeans were at least first cousins to the Anglo-Saxons.

Eastern patrician intellectuals had been the keepers of the Anglo-Saxon tradition since the Civil War, and in the climate of the nineties it was not difficult for some of them to convert a doctrine that defined their own sense of nationality into censure of an immigrant throng that displayed few common traits except the indubitable fact that it was not Anglo-Saxon. Hardly had the new immigration begun to attract attention when race-conscious intellectuals discovered its hereditary taint. In 1890 the Brahmin president of the American Economic Association alerted his fellow scholars to the new tide of "races of . . . the very lowest stage of degradation." About the same time Henry Cabot Lodge noticed the shift away from northwestern Europe and began to bristle at its racial consequences.[76]

When Lodge raised the banner of race against the new immigration, it acquired its most dangerous adversary. As Massachusetts' scholar-in-politics, he dominated both the intellectual and legislative phases of nativism. To this dual role, Lodge's own interests and values imperiously summoned him; he embodied in remarkable degree some of the major forces underlying late nineteenth century xenophobia. From his precise Vandyke beard to his clipped Boston accent, Lodge was the model of a patrician. He was steeped in English culture—English to the last fiber of his thought, said Henry Adams—in pride of ancestry, and in nostalgia for New England's past. During the 1870's he had plunged into a study of the Anglo-Saxons; a thesis on early Anglo-Saxon law brought him the first Ph.D. that Harvard conferred in political science.[77] Secondly, connected with Lodge's race consciousness was a morbid sensitivity to the danger of extensive social change. He had a lively repugnance for both the rising plutocracy and the restive mob, and he felt acutely the general nativist response to class conflict. By 1888, as a fledgling Congressman, he was pointing to the diminishing supply of free land in the West and the growth of unrest in the East as reasons for restricting immigration. Finally, while attacking immigration in domestic affairs, Lodge was adopting a belligerent stance in foreign affairs.[78] His campaign against the new immigration during the 1890's interlaced with a jingoist crusade for expansion. Lodge the jingo hated England as much as Lodge the Anglo-Saxon loved the English; accordingly, his diplomatic belligerence took the form of an assertion of American power, his pleas for restriction a defense of the English race. But these and other inconsistencies in the life of the cold, cultivated little Senator were merely logical. They were resolved at another level—in the emotions of nationalism which shaped and guided his career.

Although the Anglo-Saxon tradition in the mid-nineties still swayed few outside of an eastern elite, through Lodge and others around him that elite occupied a position of strategic influence. Both the ideological instrument and the political leadership necessary to bring into a single focus the chaotic resentments against the new immigrant were therefore at hand.

Immigration Restriction

For all of the hysterias and hatreds of the decade, federal policy was hard to change. From the founding of the republic, nativists had never succeeded in permanently undoing the nation's tolerant, *laissez faire* policy toward European immigrants. Only once had that policy been seriously endangered—when the Federalists in 1798 passed the famous Alien Acts. One of these extended the residence requirement for citizenship from five to fourteen years; a second authorized the President to expel foreigners by executive decree; a third gave him still broader power over enemy aliens in case of war. Although these measures had an intimidating effect for a brief period, they did not become fully operative. In 1802 the Jeffersonians repealed the new naturalization law and restored the old five-year requirement. The Alien Friends Act lapsed by its own terms in 1800.[79] The Alien Enemies Act lingered on the statute books unused and forgotten.

The nativist upsurge in the mid-nineteenth century left federal policy even less touched. Nor did the new excitements of the eighties and nineties really overturn the existing pattern. New and significant legislative trends started, but the decisive action for which nativists pressed just barely escaped their grasp. Immigration was one of the cornerstones of the whole social structure, and a cosmopolitan ideal of nationality was woven deeply into America's Christian and democratic heritage. The stone could not be dislodged or the ideal renounced with ease.[80]

The raising of naturalization requirements had customarily formed the chief legislative objective of nativists. At bottom, they sought to limit the political power of the foreign-born, the ballot being the main practical prerogative of citizenship. Demands for lengthening and tightening the system of naturalization—an outgrowth of every nativist movement after 1789—burst forth again in the 1880's and 1890's. Some wanted to double the waiting period; some would raise it to twenty-one years. The cry came from all sorts of sources: from anti-Catholics bent on political power for themselves, from businessmen looking for a nativistic alternative to immigration restriction, from municipal reformers anxious to purge corruption from civic life.[81] Indeed, there were good grounds for stricter naturalization, with agents of both parties herding immigrants before pliant judges, paying for their naturalization papers, and then escorting them to the polls. But neither party would surrender the privilege; the system continued unchanged. And while immigrants voted in eastern cities by fraud, in the early eighties they did so legally in approximately eighteen western and southern states and territories. The fact that voting qualifications were set by the individual states had permitted many of them to offer the ballot to new settlers upon a simple declaration of intention to become a citizen. A trend back to the historic limitation of suffrage to citizens began in the late eighties, but at the end of the century eleven jurisdictions still granted aliens the right to vote.[82]

At the national level the principal nativist effort was shifting from the question of naturalization to that of immigration restriction. The springs of modern American nativism lay in the social and economic problems of an urban-industrial society. Few nativists could regard a limitation of the foreign vote as much of a remedy for those problems. The loss of the ballot would not prevent anarchists from fomenting a revolution, or stay the rift between classes, or counteract depressions, or stop the new immigrants from polluting Anglo-Saxon blood, or keep Italian criminals and Jewish bankers from subversive activity. To cope with these dangers, the nativist was certain that the United States would have to reduce and refine the stream of immigration. Restriction became his overriding aim.

From the outset the Republican party provided the main vehicle for restrictionist sentiment. It never monopolized or committed itself wholly to the movement, but it supplied the principal leaders, most of the energy, and most of the votes. Throughout the North and West the party tended to attract those who thought of themselves as "the better sort." It seemed the guardian of respectability, morality, and standing. In those regions the party appealed to most of the people alarmed at the growth of class antagonisms: middle-class reformers, Brahmin intelligentsia, the more substantial workingmen (to whom it offered restriction as a supplement to tariff protection), and the great bulk of white-collar folk conscious of status and tradition.[83] Furthermore, in the East, where the immigration question was most pressing, the Democratic party since its inception had allied itself with the foreign-born. This alliance, cemented by the Irish, disqualified it as an instrument of nativism.

In the 1880's, restrictionists got no farther than the laws of 1882 and 1885, both designed to meet specific, local situations. Although nativist clamor produced a number of bills and a widely publicized Congressional investigation,[84] no action occurred until 1890, when anti-foreign sentiment was becoming more widespread. Then William E. Chandler, a veteran Republican stalwart from New Hampshire, took charge of the Senate's first standing committee on immigration and, together with a House committee, launched a determined drive for stiffer controls.

The first objective was to establish thoroughgoing and effective federal regulation. Neither of the measures enacted in the previous decade was functioning well. The immigration law of 1882 left a conflicting division of authority between federal officials and the unpaid charity agents to whom the seaboard states delegated the actual work of inspecting immigrants. The contract labor law of 1885 did not touch the large number of immigrants who made no contracts abroad and paid their own passage on the strength of promises or advertisements of jobs circulated by steamship companies or other interests.[85] In order not to jeopardize legislation correcting these conditions, the immigration committees temporarily put aside plans for reducing the absolute number of immigrants and concentrated instead on regulation and "selection."

The outcome was the law of 1891, which laid a permanent administrative foundation for national control of immigration. First of all, the statute placed immigration wholly under federal authority. The year before the federal government, aggravated by the lax ways of New York's Board of Emigration Commissioners, had terminated its contract with the latter, had assumed sole jurisdiction over immigration at the port of New York, and had begun to build on U. S.-owned Ellis Island the depot which will be remembered as long as the story of the immigrants survives.[86] The new law confirmed this situation and made it general.

Secondly, the act prescribed practical means of enforcing existing regulations. It compelled steamship companies to carry back to Europe all passengers rejected by the United States inspectors. This had the effect of making the private ticket agents in Europe America's most effective immigration inspectors, since the companies held their agents responsible for the return passage. Equally important, the act contained the first effective provision for deporting aliens already in the United States. Aliens who entered illegally might be expelled within one year. So could any alien who became a public charge during that time "from causes existing prior to his landing." Third, the act added further excluded categories to those of 1882 and 1885. Polygamists and "persons suffering from a loathsome or dangerous contagious disease" were declared inadmissible; and the contract labor law was broadened to exclude immigrants encouraged by employers' advertisements. Such solicitations also became illegal in themselves.[87]

This act remained the framework of America's immigration policy for many years; but though tighter and more extensive, the regulations left the nativists far from satisfied. Chandler's Senate committee quickly turned some of its attention to schemes for restriction. In the fall of 1892 events seemed suddenly to play into its hands. Cholera had crept out of Asia into eastern Europe two years earlier; now it rode into New York harbor on an immigrant ship of the Hamburg-American line. In the general excitement that followed, President Harrison proclaimed a special quarantine, ordering the detention for twenty days of any ship carrying immigrants to the United States. This had the effect of bringing immigration almost to a standstill for a time.[88] It also gave the restrictionists an opening. With infection knocking at the gates and the President's action a stopgap measure, perhaps they could stampede Congress into suspending all immigration for one year and then use that time to put across a permanent system of restriction. The rank and file of legislators, however, would not be stampeded. Instead of acting on the suspension bill which Chandler's committee reported, Congress reformed America's crude public health laws. As a substitute for compulsory suspension, a provision of the new Quarantine Act gave the President permission to halt immigration if he deemed the regular procedures inadequate.[89] Neither Harrison nor his successors invoked that power.

In those early years before the depression galvanized nativism into a nation-wide crusade, the most popular scheme for permanently restricting immigration involved the requirement of a certificate from an American consul overseas attesting to the good character of each emigrant from his area. This idea, proposed as early as 1837, gained new popularity in the late 1880's.[90] After 1890 its most persistent champion was William A. Stone, a Republican Congressman from Pennsylvania. At the behest of the Junior Order United American Mechanics and other nativist societies in Pennsylvania, Stone worked hard for a measure combining consular inspection with exclusion of anarchists and a stiff head tax of $20 on all immigrants. When this failed, he cut out the latter two provisions and offered consular inspection by itself. The watered-down bill finally passed the House of Representatives in 1894, but the Democrats who controlled the Senate substituted an entirely innocuous measure, and a deadlock between the two houses ensued.[91]

Meanwhile a restrictive plan more radical than the consular-certificate idea was slowly coming forward. The progressive economist Edward W. Bemis, one of the first intellectuals to perceive a shift in the sources of immigration, proposed in a series of lectures in 1887 that the United States should exclude all male adults unable to read and write their own language. This, he contended, would help American wage-earners by reducing by 50 per cent the influx of nationalities with a low standard of living—the Italians, Poles, and Hungarians. The proposal made no headway until Henry Cabot Lodge took it up early in 1891. For him and for most subsequent advocates it was chiefly a means of discriminating against "alien races" rather than of elevating American workingmen. The literacy restrictionists realized that consular inspection would not discriminate between nationalities and that a large head tax would establish a blatantly undemocratic property qualification. The literacy test, on the other hand, provided a highly "respectable" cultural determinant which would also minister to Anglo-Saxon sensibilities. "No one," said Senator Chandler in 1892, "has suggested a race distinction. We are confronted with the fact, however, that the poorest immigrants do come from certain races."[92]

Now with Chandler's help, Lodge pressed for the literacy test at every opportunity; and the increasing antipathy toward the new immigration strengthened his hand. He was still far from victory when two events in 1894 brought a host of new adherents. In that disaster-ridden year Congress felt the full consequences of the depression. The fall elections swept the Democrats from control of the Senate and installed Republican majorities in both houses. The Republicans would now have the power to carry a thoroughgoing restrictive measure. At about the same time the Immigration Restriction League appeared in Boston and commenced a remarkable, nation-wide campaign to guide public opinion toward the literacy test.

The league was born at a meeting of five young blue bloods in the law office of Charles Warren, later a noted constitutional historian. Although the founders hoped for a time to build the league into a mass movement, its active members never exceeded a handful. Probably no more than twelve ever came to a meeting. The founders were practical-minded intellectuals from well-to-do, long-established families, steeped in Boston ways and Boston ideas. They had all attended Harvard College in the late 1880's and had then gone on to graduate work in the Lawrence Scientific School or the Harvard Law School.[93] They were determined to mount a counteroffensive against the strange invaders who seemed so grave a threat to their class, their region, their country, and their race.

From beginning to end, two men dominated the league. The more aggressive of them, Prescott F. Hall, had just opened a legal practice. He had a variety of interests, but for the rest of his life nothing ever mattered as much to him as the league. He was a gaunt, sunken-eyed figure, the product of an intensely over-protected childhood in an old Boston family, and throughout life he struggled continually with insomnia and ill health. But his mind was sharp and arrogant and proud. At Harvard he developed a passion for Wagnerian music and German philosophy and a life-long interest in medicine and biology.[94] His classmate Robert De-Courcy Ward was his right-hand man; in nineteen years Ward missed only a single league meeting except when absent from Boston. Twenty-seven years old at the league's inception, Ward was Hall's senior by one year and was about to enter a lifelong career first as instructor and then as professor of climatology at Harvard. Cooperating with them were several Boston philanthropists, including Joseph Lee, president of the Massachusetts Civic League, Samuel B. Capen, president of the Boston School Committee and of the Municipal League of Boston, and Robert T. Paine, Jr., one of the vice-presidents of the last. John Fiske was persuaded to accept the purely honorary presidency of the Immigration Restriction League, and various other illustrious names graced its letter-head.[95]

The league devoted itself single-mindedly to agitation for the literacy test. It sent speakers to address local Boston groups, it distributed propaganda leaflets throughout the country, and it engaged in direct legislative lobbying in Washington. In all this it tried to maintain a dignified and factual tone. Its first publication referred elliptically to the great danger of a change in America's race lines, but its arguments centered chiefly around data designed to prove that southern and eastern Europe—in sharp contrast to northwestern Europe—was dumping on the United States an alarming number of illiterates, paupers, criminals, and madmen who endangered the "American character" and "American citizenship." Since public opinion was ripe for these views, the league's publicity got a wide hearing. After a year's time, the league reported that over five hundred daily newspapers were receiving its literature and that the great bulk of them were reprinting part of it, sometimes in the form of editorials. The league also made a strenuous effort to sell the literacy test to organized labor, but with mixed effect.[96]

By the time the new Republican Congress assembled in December 1895, the league had working relations with its nativist leaders. Lodge, now a Senator, introduced and took charge of a literacy bill drawn up by the league. Congressman McCall of Massachusetts submitted the same bill to the House of Representatives. It was stringent, providing for the exclusion of both men and women over fourteen years of age if they could not read and write some language. Lodge led off for the measure with a violent harangue on the dangers threatening America's racial foundations, and in the House, McCall also urged the literacy test as a clear line of distinction between the Anglo-Saxons and the southern Europeans.[97] All of the nativist ferment of the past ten years was now coming to a head in an atmosphere of unrelieved depression, intense jingoism, and great political tension. During the spring of 1896 a sudden revival of Italian immigration added a final impetus to the restriction movement. All immigration had slacked off in the early years of the depression. Now a new wave of Italian migrants nearly swamped the facilities at Ellis Island.[98]

One factor still gave the politicians pause. Would the literacy test win or lose votes for the party that carried it? Public opinion seemed overwhelmingly favorable to some form of restriction, but what of the immigrants? As yet southern and eastern Europeans counted for little in American politics, but the older immigrant groups counted for much, and their attitude was by no means certain. Party managers pointed out the danger of taking up the question on the eve of a national election. In the House, however, they failed to suppress the issue. In two days of fierce debate, the bill passed by 195 to 26.[99] Lodge had less success forcing a vote in the Senate. The best he could do was to secure an agreement which left the bill as unfinished business to be called up when Congress reconvened after the elections.[100]

As soon as the new session opened in December, the Republican Senate caucus pressed for action on the immigration bill. With the help of most of the Democratic Senators, the literacy test won by a topheavy margin. Supremely confident, the jubilant restrictionists then secured a conference committee which "harmonized" the House and Senate versions by writing a more drastic measure than either house alone had adopted.[101]

But the conferees had gravely miscalculated. The crest of nativism had passed. It started ebbing the moment that William Jennings Bryan lost the election of 1896. In the midst of immense relief at the triumph of McKinley and of the status quo, alert conservatives noted an astonishing fact. Foreign-born voters in half a dozen midwestern states had much to do with the Republican victory. Without their overwhelming support, McKinley might well have lost. In the light of immigrant conservatism, anti-radical nativism began to seem less relevant.[102] Furthermore, a vociferous immigrant opposition to the literacy test was crystallizing. German newspapers, which were keenly conscious of their political influence, were especially outspoken against the bill; moreover, the federal immigration commissioner reported that the entire foreign-language press condemned it. By February 1897, when the final conference report came before the Senate, this opposition was taking effect. The report went through by a bare majority.[103]

Now it seemed clear that the Lodge forces in the Senate lacked the votes to override a Presidential veto if Grover Cleveland chose to disapprove the bill. And disapprove he did. Partly he objected to a House amendment of the original league bill prohibiting Canadian residents from crossing the border to work in the United States, a clause certain to stir up ill will in Canada. But his main contentions ran against the literacy test itself. A man with a strong sense of personal integrity and a steady faith in the ways of the fathers, Cleveland denounced the bill for upsetting tradition and hinted that the criterion of illiteracy was hypocritical. Don't make illiteracy a pretext for exclusion, he said in effect, if what you fear is something else.[104] The House of Representatives speedily overrode the veto; the Senate took no action.

With assurance unshaken, the Immigration Restriction League and its allies looked forward to confronting a more sympathetic President with similar legislation in the following year. How could they know that an era in the history of nativism was coming to an end? How could they know that sixteen years would pass before another Congress submitted to another President the proposal which Edward Bemis had devised?

Chapter Five

The Return of Confidence

For the poorer classes America is still the land of opportunity, and their hearts cannot be alienated. . . . The ideals,
the opportunities . . . of our democracy change the immigrants into a new order of men.
—Charles B. Spahr, 1900

The campaign banners of 1896 hailed mild-mannered William
McKinley as the advance agent of prosperity, and for once an election slogan proved wonderfully prophetic. Hardly had he taken
office when the economic skies began to clear. After a four-year-
long prostration, the business cycle started upward again. Soon
new discoveries of gold and better ways to refine it restored authority and flexibility to the accustomed medium of exchange.
Agrarian radicalism collapsed; farmers returned to raising more
corn and less hell. Industry too basked in the spreading glow of
harmony. Strikes continued, but the bitter industrial warfare of
preceding years did not. Instead, doctrines of cooperation between
capital and labor diffused through the ranks of each; after 1900
the country was treated to the strange spectacle of great tycoons
and the principal union leaders counseling with one another at the
pleasant luncheons of the National Civic Federation. All in all, as
the nineteenth century came to a close, American civilization
seemed to gain its second wind.

An early indication that the social and economic basis of nativism was crumbling came in the winter of 1897-98. Lodge reintroduced the Immigration Restriction League's literacy bill. McKinley
had given the cause his blessing, and the league took special pains
to remind every Congressman that the American Federation of

THE RETURN OF CONFIDENCE 107

Labor was now on record for the bill. The Senate passed it largely on party lines; only one Republican opposed it, few Democrats favored it.[1] But the House was less submissive to party discipline. For one thing, the immigrants were now lobbying against the measure as vigorously as the nativists lobbied for it. Early in 1898 several nationalities combined to organize the Immigration Protective League, a temporary counterpoise to the Restriction League. Also, officers of 150 German societies issued a combined protest against any restrictive legislation as a revival of Know-Nothingism and warned that it would hasten the already alarming decline in German immigration and German-American culture.[2] These threatening statements troubled many a western Republican from immigrant districts.

A deterrent at least as important as the foreign vote, however, was a new complacency born of reviving prosperity. Confidence first crept back in the sections where nativism was most recently and least well established—the West and South. Some of the old boom and booster psychology returned to the more sparsely settled areas of the country. Buoyed by unfolding opportunities, optimists now ridiculed the fear that the United States was overcrowded. In California agriculture expanded so swiftly that farmers short of hired hands even demanded relaxation of the Chinese exclusion law. As for the literacy bill, the House of Representatives kept postponing consideration of it.[3]

Conquest and Harmony

Hard on the heels of this new confidence in the health of American society came a new confidence in America's position in the world. The jingoism of the early and mid-nineties culminated in an exhilarating little war with Spain. The victory, won swiftly and in a holiday spirit, required few strains or sacrifices. The brief struggle raised no fears of disloyalty among the foreign-born, for Spanish immigration to the United States was always negligible. So nationalism, without abating a whit, grew heady and exultant. Anxieties over global dangers and rivalries diminished when the first test of modern American power gave the nation a fresh sense of vitality. Concern over internal dissension was engulfed in a joyous consciousness of national unity.

There were those, like the National Education Association, who outspokenly rejoiced that the war was bringing a new solidarity to the American people. "More than one American," the French ambassador in Washington observed, "hopes that the war will definitely create a Nation out of the mass of heterogeneous populations." [4] Others, in a flush of pride and satisfaction, simply forgot that the immigrants had seemed a problem. After the Spanish-American War began, it became impossible to get consideration for the literacy bill in the House of Representatives; the issue was rudely brushed aside. The Immigration Restriction League, its ardor exhausted and its hopes deflated, lapsed into a state of suspended animation. In 1899 the formerly nativistic *Nation* reported complacently, "There is now general satisfaction with the defeat of the bill establishing the educational test for immigration." [5] Other magazines that had teemed with attacks on immigration earlier in the decade now fell completely silent on the matter. Anti-Catholicism broke down even more completely than other forms of nativism during the war with Catholic Spain. The shattered remnants of the American Protective Association shrank entirely out of sight, and a perilous schism rent the hardy Junior Order United American Mechanics. [6]

The adventures of 1898 in the Caribbean and the Philippines led on into imperialism. In acquiring far-flung dependencies on the pattern of the great European powers of the day the United States, significantly, met no real opposition from other empires; it felt no obstruction of the mission it proclaimed for itself. The summons to take up the white man's burden, preached by a few before 1898, was accepted in a genial, lighthearted mood. What a dazzling field for American achievement opened now among "backward" island peoples! What proof was here of America's ability to tread the world stage! Thus the acquisition of an empire fortified the confidence renewed by prosperity, by relief from class conflict, and by a psychologically invigorating war.

In curious ways the colonial experiment even helped to restore the ideology of assimilation by reviving the old quasi-cosmopolitan theory of nationality. At first glance the intellectual impact of imperialism may seem altogether hostile to cosmopolitan values. Did not imperialists pride themselves on their superiority over "lesser breeds beyond the law"? Did they not, like the expansionists of the 1840's, give an unprecedented vogue to race-thinking by preaching an Anglo-Saxon destiny for world dominion? It is true that the events of 1898 popularized the Anglo-Saxon tradition as nothing had done before,[7] and in the long run, whatever magnified the racial strain in American thought would prove damaging to an assimilationist outlook. But for the moment Anglo-Saxon imperialism actually worked the other way. It was the disgruntled opponents of a "large policy" who argued that colonial possessions would bring unassimilable races within the national structure and thereby shatter the country's homogeneity. Exuberant empire-builders spurned so defensive an outlook. Brushing aside nativistic fears of racial pollution from subject peoples or from the new immigration, triumphant imperialists recaptured the optimistic kind of Anglo-Saxonism which had flourished in the mid-nineteenth century. Race-thinking, in celebrating the fulfillment of an appointed task, assumed the air of promise and achievement that surrounded the new status it justified. The imperialists' belief that the mighty impulse of the Anglo-Saxon race—now at the meridian of its strength—had driven America forth to conquer and redeem, expressed an exaltation transcending any fear of threat or dilution. It had no need of an adversary.[8] Nor could this creed permit serious doubts of America's ability to incorporate and dominate inferior races. If destiny called the Anglo-Saxon to regenerate men overseas, how could he fail to educate and discipline immigrant races at home? The newcomers, therefore, tended to figure among the lesser breeds whom the Anglo-Saxon was dedicated to uplift.[9]

No one illustrated better how national confidence tempered race-thinking than Edward A. Ross. One of the most race-conscious of American social scientists, Ross drew invidious contrasts between the Teutonic and other races in his first important book, published in 1901, and thereafter throughout his life.[10] In the early twentieth century, however, pride in America's powers of assimilation kept Ross's contempt for European immigrants from developing into alarm. While characterizing the new immigrants as "beaten members of beaten breeds . . . that . . . lack the ancestral foundations of American character," he exulted in America's capacity to transform them. He marveled at the "change a few years of our electrifying ozone works in the dull, fat-witted immigrant." As late as 1908 Ross offered an extensive analysis of America's success in assimilation, concluding that "the vortical suction of our civilization is stronger now than ever before." [11]

The relaxed, assimilationist mood of the new century also brought the melting-pot concept of a mixed, evolving race back into prominence. "Our confidence in the American race of the future," wrote the *Outlook*, "is due to the commingling on this continent of the blood and the characteristics of many peoples quite as much as to the unhampering environment of a new land." A scientist added: "Just as cross-fertilization is beneficial to plant life, the intermingling of peoples in this country must produce the most beautiful, most intellectual, and most powerful race of the world . . . the American, even to-day, presents the highest type of beauty which ever adorned the earth." And a popular journalist concluded: "It might even be said that the man of purest American blood is he who has the most cosmopolitan lineage." [12]

This remarkable collapse of nativism during the last years of the nineteenth and first years of the twentieth century ran exactly counter to the currents of immigration. The return of confidence coincided with a surge of immigration caused by a tremendous torrent from southern and eastern Europe. While migration from northern Europe remained at a low ebb, in 1899 the new immigration began a fantastic nine-year climb. In 1900 it reached three hundred thousand for the first time. In 1903 it passed six hundred thousand. In 1907 it stood at an all-time high of close to a million.[13] Now, there was no ignoring the vast Jewish population of New York City, the grimy Slavic settlements that clustered in industrial areas of the East and Midwest, or the troops of Italian laborers hewing and toiling from coast to coast. A sharp eye could also detect stranger faces appearing in the immigrant crowd—Greeks, Syrians, Armenians.

Older Americans lost none of their personal repugnance for men so alien. Discrimination and withdrawal undoubtedly increased, forcing the strangers to live and work apart; there were even objections to riding on the same streetcars with "lousy dagoes." [14] What did decline was fear—fear that immigration endangered the nation. The loss of a sense of national menace in the face of increasing cultural diversity indicates how much the ebb and flow of nativism has depended on larger changes in the course and character of American nationalism. When new conditions quieted both internal and international tensions, nationalism regained such buoyancy and radiance that little room was left for anti-foreign fears.

Of course, the complacent mood of the age of confidence never entirely returned. Clocks did not turn back. The crisis of the eighties and the strains of the nineties left a heritage of policies and ideas that were submerged but not dissolved. In the twentieth century those policies and ideas could reappear more easily and swiftly because their foundation rested in the nineteenth.

In 1901 the assassination of President McKinley illustrated both the enduring sensitivity of the nativist heritage and its weakness in the springtime of the new century. The man who killed McKinley unleashed a short-lived wave of xenophobia. Leon Czolgosz was an anarchist of American birth but obviously foreign extraction, and his act instantly brought back alarm over immigrant radicalism. Mobs attacked anarchists in Pittsburgh and elsewhere. In New York the office of a Yiddish anarchist newspaper was wrecked.[15] Excited nationalists determined, in the words of Senator Chauncey M. Depew, to "stop the reservoirs of European anarchy pouring into our country." Still, the nativist response was gentle and temperate compared with the terrified reaction to the Haymarket Affair fifteen years before. Many more commentators drew a distinction between anarchists and the mass of immigrants in 1901 than in 1886.[16]

Despite its relative mildness, the revival of anti-radical nativism enabled immigration restrictionists to pick up where they had left off and to build on nineteenth century precedents. A bill to exclude and deport alien anarchists—something which all of the unrest of the late nineteenth century had failed to bring about—materialized as soon as Congress convened. The idea was then incorporated in a general bill, recommended by the United States Industrial Commission, which also codified and, in certain minor respects, tightened other immigration regulations. Most important, it extended from one to three years the time within which an alien might be deported for becoming a public charge and made him deportable regardless of whether the cause of dependency arose before or after arrival in the United States. The sponsors deliberately kept the literacy test out of the bill, fearing its defeat if any general limitation on immigration were included.[17]

Nevertheless, a hard core of militant restrictionists had survived the debacle of nativism. Organized labor, having learned to distinguish between old and new immigrations, still looked forward to curtailing competition from the latter. Nor had the Immigration Restriction League abandoned hope for the literacy test. Determined to exploit the anarchist scare, the league came to life in the fall of 1901 after three years of inactivity. It raised enough money from wealthy old Boston families to hire a lobbyist in Washington and with the help of Senator Lodge launched an aggressive campaign.[18] First the league spread word that the literacy test would keep out the ignorant foreign masses susceptible to anarchistic blandishments. Then it stirred up the Junior Order United American Mechanics and scores of national trade unions to deluge Congress with petitions.[19] The American Federation of Labor for the first time cooperated actively in bringing pressure to bear on Congress. President Roosevelt gave the cause his blessing in his annual message to Congress. A good many businessmen, disturbed at the menace of imported anarchy, reverted to nativism, and the National Board of Trade came out in favor of the literacy test.[20]

With this backing and perhaps also with the aid of uneasiness created by the great anthracite strike of 1902, the Immigration Restriction League succeeded in attaching its literacy test as an amendment to the general immigration bill in the House of Representatives.[21] For all of Lodge's efforts in its behalf, however, the literacy test got nowhere in the Senate. "There was no more show of passing that bill with that amendment on it in the Senate," said a disgusted Congressional supporter, "than there would be of passing a temperance proposition in the German wards of Cincinnati." Railroad and steamship interests fought it, westerners and southerners declared that it would hamper their development, and even the more nativistic East showed little interest in it.[22] To save the rest of the bill, its Senate managers reluctantly agreed to drop the educational clause. Then the Senate version speedily became law.[23]

Although it contained no generally restrictive provision, the immigration law of 1903 represented an important nativistic achievement. By forbidding the admission and authorizing the deportation of foreign proponents of anarchism, the law penalized newcomers for their opinions for the first time since 1798. United States officials began exercising their new power at once. John Turner, a mild-mannered English anarchist who made his second trip to the United States in 1903, was arrested by a bevy of secret service men and deported before he had a chance to speak in public.[24] Here was no miscarriage of justice as in the Haymarket Affair, but rather the small beginnings of a permanent and portentous federal policy.

Significant consequences of the new barrier to foreigners with disagreeable ideas still lay far in the future; by the end of the year the furor over anarchists had dissipated. The whole brief flurry of anti-immigrant feeling subsided just as swiftly. Confidence prevailed so widely in 1904 that even Lodge conceded the absence of a demand for an immigration plank in the Republican platform and agreed to its omission; it did not reappear until 1912. In 1904 also the outstanding sociologist William I. Thomas announced that race prejudice was easily dispelled and would in fact become insignificant as advances in communication brought human groups in closer contact with one another. H. G. Wells, on a visit from England a little later, gathered the impression that all Americans above forty and most of the rest were enthusiastic advocates of unrestricted immigration.[25]

As in the last years of the nineteenth century, economic well-being supported much of the continuing tolerance of foreigners in the 1900's. Indeed, the enormous growth of the American economy produced a positive demand for more immigrant labor in the mid-years of the new decade—a demand unparalleled since the post-Civil War period. Some of the calls came from the West; as late as 1910 a new Colorado Board of Immigration was enticing Italian farmers to the state.[26] By far the greatest efforts to attract immigrants were made in the South. Big cotton farmers were enjoying an extraordinary wave of prosperity. Cotton mills shot up in the Piedmont country so rapidly that they outproduced first New England and then all the rest of the country. Southern railroads were still expanding. All of these interests faced an unusual labor shortage, for southerners were deserting the section faster than outsiders arrived.[27] Negroes particularly were quitting the farms for the cities, and the cities for the North. Some advocates of European immigration hoped that it would not only solve the southern labor problem but also accelerate the Negro exodus.[28]

Supported by powerful urban newspapers in the region, southern businessmen, landlords, and large farmers started this fresh campaign for immigrants in 1903. They sent agents to Europe, distributed literature, conferred with federal immigration officials, and held a series of resounding conventions.[29] From 1903 to 1907 seven southern states organized or reactivated immigration bureaus. South Carolina paid the passage of a shipload of Belgian cloth workers, who were greeted at Charleston by a cheering crowd, a free lunch, and a flow of official oratory. Little of this enthusiasm extended to southern Europeans, but they too had a surprising number of apologists.[30]

Northern business interests did not need to organize and agitate and maneuver for immigrants. Europeans flocked gladly and in ever larger numbers into the bustling cities above the Potomac. There the corporations had only to learn how to use the immigrants most profitably and guard against a revival of the restriction movement. While apostles of the New South struggled with pathetically little success to attract foreigners, their northern associates undertook a parallel program of exploitation and defense. This meant a decisive shift away from the anti-foreign and restrictionist tendencies dominant in American business in the 1880's and 1890's. The conversion of the great northern industrialists to an unqualified support of immigration was more significant than all the promotional clamor in the South.

At first, the unskilled peasants of southern and eastern Europe had entered only restricted segments of American industry. They got a start as construction workers or in the simple, back-breaking tasks of the extractive industries. In the early twentieth century the new immigrants also spread rapidly into the factories. Tremendous technological advances mechanized many industries so extensively that inexperienced foreigners could tend semi-automatic machines without understanding them. Steel, rubber, textile, and other plants no longer required a skilled worker to run each individual machine. Instead, the skilled, Americanized employees became superintendents of unskilled foreign gangs. Employers acquired a larger appreciation of the value of southern and eastern European immigrants, and by 1909 the latter comprised a third or more of the entire labor force of the principal industries of the country.[31]

In the course of relying increasingly on the new immigrants, industrialists perfected a system for mastering them. Employers of large immigrant forces learned to "balance nationalities," in other words to take advantage of the diversity and tensions among the many peoples of southern and eastern Europe. By judiciously mixing many nationalities, the employer could keep them divided and incapable of concerted action in their own behalf.[32] To be sure, the United Mine Workers had already gathered in great numbers of eastern European coal workers, but for the most part unskilled immigrant labor remained tractable and unorganized. Industrialists could now feel confident of controlling their cheap but sometimes restive labor supply. They ceased to fear the foreign radicalism and unrest that had disturbed them in the eighties and nineties and again briefly in 1901 and 1902. The National Board of Trade signaled the shift in business attitudes by opposing the literacy test in 1904—an exact reversal of its position a year before. Thereafter the board became a firm advocate of more, rather than less, immigration.[33]

About the same time the business press burst forth in praise of the enriching foreign tide. The *Commercial and Financial Chronicle* shifted to the defense of immigration because of the need for unskilled labor; the *Journal of Commerce*, the *Wall Street Journal*, and the New York *Commercial Bulletin* took the same position.[34] Powerful eastern newspapers subject to a business ideology cast off an earlier nativist outlook. The New York *Times*, the Philadelphia *Public Ledger*, and even that pillar of New England orthodoxy, the Boston *Transcript*, renounced their former xenophobia and rejoiced over the immigrants. America, they chorused, is still a growing place full of opportunity for an expanding population.[35]

The currents of nativism slowly gathered force again in the latter part of the 1900's, but instead of drifting with them, business interests organized a stubborn resistance. The National Board of Trade was ill equipped for aggressive pressure-building. The National Civic Federation, which developed a friendly interest in immigration in 1905, proved still less competent. Since it rested on a partnership between labor and capital, the federation could not go far in championing immigration without alienating its trade union membership. A Civic Federation-sponsored national conference on the subject had to content itself with a few limited, noncontroversial recommendations.[36] Big business at last found a vehement champion of lax immigration policies in 1907, when the National Association of Manufacturers entered the lists. The N.A.M. established a committee on immigration, complained of labor shortages in many industries, announced that new blood strengthened any race of people, and looked forward to relaxation of the mild immigration controls then in effect.[37] Henceforth, James Emery, the N.A.M.'s astute lobbyist, haunted the committee rooms whenever Congress showed signs of tampering with immigration. The return of confidence in the early twentieth century thus roused an economic opposition to nativism that was as determined as it was selfish.

Progressive Democracy

As the first decade of the twentieth century advanced, more and more of its adventurous optimism flowed into reform. Progressivism gradually replaced imperialism as the central interest in the public mind. The crusading fervor dedicated at the turn of the century to uplifting the little brown brother beyond the seas turned into a domestic struggle against the trusts, the bosses, and the "interests." Powerful in its sense of righteousness, its middle-class base, and its vision of democracy, the progressive movement wrought the first great conscious change in American institutions since the Civil War.

In full and overflowing measure, the progressives shared the confidence of their generation. Untroubled by the bitter class conflicts of the late nineteenth century, they escaped for the most part the forebodings of impending catastrophe that weighed upon the middle-class reformers who preceded them. Secure in the knowledge of their own respectability and certain that history was on their side, the progressives felt little urge to seek foreign sources of America's problems. William Allen White remarked that discontent had shaved its whiskers, washed its shirt, and put on a derby.[38] His comment described a movement that had little need of nativism.

Many progressives, to be sure, were clearly troubled by the increasing magnitude of immigration. Some of them espoused the cause of organized labor and shared its feeling that the newcomers threatened the unions and the living standards they were fighting for.[39] A larger number, especially progressives from rural and small-town backgrounds, deeply distrusted the big city. In that center of moral pestilence, alien settlement now concentrated more exclusively than ever before. The almost complete identification of the immigrant with his urban environment prevented a sympathetic response toward either on the part of many reformers. Furthermore, a strain of elitism made some progressive intellectuals contemptuous of malingerers on the highway of progress. The sociologist, Edward A. Ross, one of the most nativistic of progressives, defined democracy as government by talent, not by the "narrow, short-sighted, muddle-headed . . . average man." His Wisconsin colleague, John R. Commons, opened an influential book on immigration by taking issue with the equalitarian assumptions of the Declaration of Independence.[40]

Divided though it was on ethnic issues, progressive sentiment on balance probably weighed against nativism in the halcyon years before 1910. Buoyed by their own self-assurance, progressives were often attracted to the equalitarian idealism that Ross and Commons thought unrealistic. Compared with previous middle-class reformers, progressives drew from the hopeful atmosphere of the early twentieth century a larger confidence in the capacity of ordinary people to set things aright if given the means to do so. Believing ardently in the people, they sometimes included the immigrants in that category. They located evil primarily in the economic environment, and when they did so consistently they could respond to the immigrant as an innocent victim of bad conditions. The *Arena*, a liberal journal which had quaked at the foreign peril in earlier years, now accused nativists of blaming immigrants for the failures of America's own economic institutions. And when Mr. Dooley, the comic sage of Progressive America, heard that foreigners don't assimilate, he replied that America's digestion had gone wrong from too much rich food: " . . . if we'd lave off thryin' to digest Rockyfellar an' thry a simple diet like Schwartzmeister, we wudden't feel th' effects iv our vittels," declared Mr. Dooley.[41]

No part of the progressive movement sloughed off its former xenophobia more thoroughly than did the campaign against municipal corruption. Unlike previous civic reformers, progressives uncovered connections between urban bosses and the business interests they protected. The foreign-born voter ceased to bear the brunt of the blame for misgovernment. Lincoln Steffens' pioneering exposé, *The Shame of the Cities*, held American business responsible and dismissed talk about the foreign vote as hypocritical. Frederic C. Howe made the same shocked discovery after starting in Cleveland politics with an exactly opposite impression. Throughout the 1900's, the National Municipal League paid virtually no attention to the immigrant until its president, Charles J. Bonaparte, happily informed the members that "the admirable assimilative processes of our orderly freedom are turning out Americans with as much facility as Dickens' sausage factory, which was capable of turning paving-stones into sausages." [42]

An economic interpretation of political problems could not dispel all concern at how the immigrants cast their votes, but legislation could end the more flagrant scandals. The Naturalization Act of 1906 finally terminated the wholesale distribution of citizenship papers on the eve of elections. Under easygoing Jeffersonian legislation that had lasted more than a century, as many as five thousand separate state courts were administering naturalization with no central supervision whatever. Corruption had flourished for decades. In addition to the thousands of immigrants naturalized for voting purposes on the eve of elections, many others secured bogus American citizenship papers in order to return to their native lands exempt from a subject's duties. Partly in response to State Department protests, the reform measure in 1906 restricted naturalization to certain courts, laid down a standardized procedure for them to follow, and established a federal Division of Naturalization to supervise the whole process.[43] The law ignored entirely the old nativist demand for lengthening the residence requirement for citizenship. It aimed not at disfranchising the immigrant but at ending the conditions under which his vote was sold. It succeeded brilliantly and in doing so completed the separation between nativism and municipal reform.

Yet confidence was far from devotion. The progressives of the early twentieth century were unafraid, but in general they were also indifferent and aloof. Like the rest of their generation, they felt little enmity toward the immigrants but little identification with them either. A social and ideological gulf yawned between the well-established groups afire with visions of change and the uprooted folk who had already experienced more change than they could comprehend. The progressives seldom understood the strangers as fellow men with special problems of adjustment. They could be tolerant enough; they could often accept the old ideal of America's cosmopolitan nationality. But they could not believe that the newcomers might be significantly influencing American culture; at least they could not think so and retain their equanimity. Most native-born progressives in the early years of the century viewed the immigrant as a passive entity, malleable and still to be molded under the influences of American society. He was, in Charles Bonaparte's metaphor, sausage-meat. In beings so passive and remote the ordinary progressive took no great interest.[44]

The logic of democracy, however, pointed beyond this negative tolerance. It pointed to a respect for the integrity and importance of all people, toward a cooperative concern with the problems of every group. Most progressives, while convinced of the solvent power of democracy, applied it largely to political and economic inequalities. That it might reform relationships among men of varying creeds or colors or cultures did not impress them. On the other hand, some progressives glimpsed an ampler democratic vision. In addition to nativists like Ross and a larger group that was indifferent to ethnic issues, the progressive movement produced a small number of democratic humanists. In the cities a few early twentieth century liberals came into close enough contact with the immigrants to see them whole, to learn that poverty and isolation afflicted them in special ways, and to realize that democracy involved a social dimension which was unfulfilled as long as America simply took its foreign peoples for granted.

The beginnings lay in the social settlements. These had appeared in the slums of New York, Chicago, and other cities in the 1890's in response to the same rift between classes that aroused the nativists. Whereas the nativists struggled for social unity through hatred, the young men and women who moved into settlement houses hoped to bridge the class gulf through love. They went beyond traditional humanitarianism in two respects: in wanting to work with the people of the slums as well as for them, and in wanting to learn from them as well as teach them.[45] Since the poorest sections of the cities were the foreign quarters, most of the people with whom settlement dwellers worked were immigrants. The democratic, experimental philosophy behind the settlements contrasted sharply with the nativistic tendencies of most late nineteenth century humanitarians and reformers. Of all old-stock

Americans, settlement workers gained the fullest understanding, compassion, and respect for the new immigration.

Under the impact of the progressive movement, the settlements' attitude toward the foreign-born gradually spread to the ranks of professional social workers. Until the end of the nineteenth century, social work had been largely synonymous with charity, and for the most part its practitioners had loudly bewailed the immigrant flood that was swamping their resources. But now a philosophy of alleviation was giving way to one of prevention and social action. Welfare agencies, like municipal reformers and progressives generally, were discovering economic roots to the problems they faced. Instead of attributing poverty to moral weakness or to "hereditary pauperism," social workers turned toward the environment and toward its reconstruction.[46] Some of the leading settlements were becoming veritable nurseries of reform, and as social workers fell into line they too saw the immigrants not as an oppressive burden but as an oppressed minority. In 1904 the organ of the New York Charity Organization Society shifted from hostility to unqualified sympathy for the foreign-born, and the National Conference of Charities made the same transition more gradually during the decade. After 1910 very few social workers who had intimate contact with foreign groups favored a further restriction of immigration.[47]

Although the professional servants of society rallied behind a generous admission policy, their primary concern was with the treatment which the immigrants received after arrival. What needed reforming was the neglect and exploitation of the newcomers. They deserved educational opportunities to reduce their special handicaps and their special isolation; they should have protection from both Americans and their own fellow countrymen who took advantage of them. Combating indifference as much as nativism, social workers in the latter part of the progressive period planted the seeds of a public welfare program directed specifically at immigrant needs. This program flowered, however, under other influences and deserves a fuller discussion in a later context.[48]

Along with a positive interest in the immigrants' welfare came a sense of their positive value to America—not just as hewers of wood and drawers of water, but as enriching additions to the whole culture. The traditional theory of America's cosmopolitan nationality emphasized the triumph of unity over diversity. Although the country was supposed somehow to gain from the blending process, no one had pointed proudly to the immigrants' concrete contributions to the final amalgam. The few progressive groups who actually worked with foreigners moved a step beyond the usual conception of assimilation.

Here again the settlements pioneered, because they respected foreign customs and approached the foreigners' problems in an empirical way. Experience soon taught a sensitive settlement founder like Jane Addams that the prevailing American contempt for the immigrant's past snarled his adjustment to the new environment. She saw particularly that a ruthless American chauvinism often infected the children of the immigrants, turning them against their parents and exposing them to the worst in their new surroundings. Experimentally, Jane Addams discovered that the settlements could check family disorganization by extending an appreciative welcome to Old World heritages. Several settlements began in the nineties to develop programs for conserving and celebrating the holidays, customs, folksongs, and languages of the nationalities in the neighborhood. In encouraging the newcomers to preserve the "best" in their own traditions, settlement leaders argued that each immigrant group had a tangible contribution to make to the building of American culture. Miss Addams and others came to believe that a more genuinely cosmopolitan society might emerge out of the mingling of old and new.[49]

Originally a means of enhancing the foreigners' self-respect, the doctrine of "immigrant gifts" soon turned into a defense of the foreign-born from nativist attack and a justification for reform efforts in their behalf. The settlement people disseminated the doctrine widely after 1900, urging the general public as well as other social workers to appreciate the cultural contributions the strangers might make to American life.[50] Allied reform elements absorbed the idea. The community center movement, which began about 1910 as an extension of the settlement ideal of unifying the jangling groups in urban areas, quickly appropriated the belief that America would gain by giving the immigrants greater opportunity to express their own inherent values. The chairman of the California State Commission of Immigration and Housing adopted a similar point of view, and New York's Governor Charles Evans Hughes was one of the early political leaders to praise the foreigners' contribution to American life.[51]

A measure of these broader sympathies was passed along from the secular advocates of social welfare to the exponents of the Social Gospel, now the commanding force in American Protestantism. In the nineteenth century Josiah Strong and other Protestant reformers had regarded the foreign-born as a national menace, and the Protestant churches generally had shown too plain a hostility toward immigrants to take much thought for their religious or material welfare.[52] Now the major denominations, moving more serenely on the currents of reform, developed a general interest in the strangers as fellow men—and as potential Protestants. The tasks of assimilating and evangelizing immigrants became linked to the whole religious attack on social problems. Although many churchmen could not entirely shed their fear and distrust, at least some Social-Gospelers adopted the "contributions" theory of assimilation. Directors of immigrant educational programs established by religious bodies warned their followers to emphasize America's indebtedness to its many peoples. The Home Mission Council, a broad federation of Protestant groups, sponsored a special week in which the churches were to undertake immigrant welfare projects and indoctrinate their congregations with respect for the newcomers' contributions.[53]

Thus the widening human sympathies of the progressive era called forth a new version of the cosmopolitan ideal of American nationality—a version emphasizing cultural accretion rather than racial blending. Undoubtedly the concept of immigrant gifts lent a certain status and dignity to the foreigner qua foreigner. Yet none of the progressives carried the idea very far; it represented a modification of the melting-pot tradition rather than a break from it.

One could talk in generalities about immigrant gifts far more easily than define them. No one even tried to discriminate what was "best" in the immigrants' past and worth preserving, from what might be bad or worthless. When examples of specific gifts came to mind, they turned out invariably to be things to which Americans attached slight importance: folk dances, music, exotic dishes, handicrafts, perhaps certain literary fragments. The contributions that charmed sympathetic progressives had no bearing on American institutions or ideals. A pageant prepared for Fourth of July celebrations expressed the gifts idea neatly. In this solemn drama immigrant groups in native costumes performed their national folk dances in an "offertory spirit" before a white-robed figure of America.[54] It was all very genteel and uplifting, and very far removed from the rough, sweaty, painful adjustments that converted Europeans into Americans.

The Immigrants Fight Back

Of all the groups who, through confidence or conviction, helped to turn back the tide of nativism, none was as resolute as the immigrants themselves. Already they had taken an active part in defeating the literacy test in 1897 and 1898, at the outset of the new era. In the twentieth century the immigrants stood out more and more among the forces mobilized against the returning currents of anti-foreign sentiment. In time, the general public assurance nourished by internal well-being and external conquest deteriorated, and large numbers of progressives renounced their jaunty optimism. Eventually, even the business support of immigration lost much of its vitality. But for the immigrants it was a matter of self-defense. Every symptom of reviving nativism aroused a fiercer, more militant immigrant opposition. Through individual appeals to public opinion, through organizations, and through political pressure, the immigrants fought back.

The burden of defense fell chiefly on the new immigrants. In contrast to the general anti-foreignism prevalent in the late nineteenth century, the attack now centered overwhelmingly on the peoples of southern and eastern Europe. The ties of common interest which elicited a united immigrant protest against restriction in 1897 were loose at best, and in the process of assimilation increasing numbers of old immigrants and their descendants were adopting the nativist distinction between themselves and the newer nationalities.

The rupture was not absolute, for some elements of the old immigration remained active in the resistance to nativism. The German-American Alliance, representing more than a million and a half members, signed an agreement with the Ancient Order of Hibernians in 1907 to oppose all immigration restriction. The Irish leaders who dominated the Catholic Church and in some sections bossed the Democratic party championed the interests of their southern and eastern European followers.[55] But the main effort had to come from the Slavic nationalities, the Magyars, the Italians, and the Jews. Of these, the Jews played by far the most significant role. Alone among all of the new nationalities, the Jews had an intelligentsia capable of reaching the American public and wealthy leaders well established in American life. They had also a keen sensitivity to slights and injuries and a tradition of fighting for their rights. They could supply much of the leadership and driving force for the immigrants' cause.

The foreign-born spokesmen who joined battle with the nativists in the early twentieth century thought and wrote in the most conventional terms. Although they sometimes paid lip service to the new theory of immigrant gifts, on the whole they praised America rather than the immigrant. They were keepers of the hallowed doctrines of cosmopolitan Americanism. Time and again they reiterated the mission of the United States to succor and shelter the oppressed. The course of recent history might have weakened the force of this idea, but Irish and Jewish leaders knew what it meant and gave it continuing life.[56] Just as insistently, they echoed the traditional view of assimilation. Themselves products of the assimilative process, they were sure that America could continue to build a homogeneous nationality from a mixture of all comers. They wanted so much to demonstrate the nation's powers of absorption that they tended to treat the immigrant as a being whom America cleansed, transformed, and uplifted.

Two renditions of this idea, one in a play, the other in an autobiography, said most compellingly what a legion of immigrant writers expressed in various ways. Israel Zangwill, an English author, never settled in the United States himself but directed an emigration society which helped thousands of Russian Jews to do so. Out of his enthusiasm for America he wrote *The Melting-Pot*, a rhapsodic melodrama which began a tremendously popular run in 1908. The play permanently attached a vivid symbol to the old assimilationist ideal of American nationality. America, so the moral went, was God's fiery crucible, consuming the dross of Europe and fusing all of its warring peoples into "the coming superman." [57] Four years later, Mary Antin carried the melting-pot idea to its logical extreme. Like the characters in Zangwill's play, this lyrical immigrant girl had fled from Czarist Russia. Her ecstatic autobiography, *The Promised Land*, was a sustained hymn to America for obliterating the immigrant's past and giving him an entirely new life. "I have been made over," she wrote happily. "I am absolutely other than the person whose story I have to tell." [58]

Even the most original immigrant intellectual, a great social scientist, analyzed assimilation as if it were a one-way process by which America completely transformed its new peoples. Franz Boas, who became the leading anthropologist of the day, brought a lifelong devotion to historic American ideals with him when he arrived from Germany as a youth. Both a Jew and a democrat, he took a keen interest in puncturing the claims of race-thinkers. Theories about the superiority of mixed races he dismissed as hardly more scientific than those about the greatness of pure ones. True to the assumptions of progressivism, his own thinking recurred constantly to the concrete facts of physical and social environments. As applied to European immigration, this environmentalist approach led him to a startling anthropological vindication of the melting-pot idea.

In 1911 Boas published, as part of a huge federal investigation of immigration, a study designed to prove that the American environment was recasting the most persistent hereditary traits of immigrants. Since the shape of the head was then regarded as one of the most stable indices of race, Boas measured the head forms of second-generation immigrants and found a considerable change from the parent stock. If long-headed types grew shorter and round-headed types grew longer, Boas concluded that all of the immigrants' bodily and mental characteristics must be powerfully affected by American conditions. His report aroused immediate interest and was widely taken as proof of the rapid assimilation of all strains to a common "American type" with a uniform "American face." [59]

For men presumed to be so passive and pliable, the immigrants were showing themselves wonderfully active. Along with the ideological thrusts of the Boases and the Zangwills, a second prong of the immigrant defense effort formed in politics. In the right to vote—the keystone of the American political structure—the foreign-born had a weapon against nativism hardly less significant than the assimilationist tradition. The new immigrants were just beginning to enter politics in defense of their own interests in the early years of the twentieth century. Their appearance as a sizeable political force spelled new difficulties for the nativist campaign to restrict immigration.

As America's ethnic composition shifted, the Democratic party through its urban machines retained the allegiance of a substantial number of foreign voters. Irish politicians continued to function for the Democrats as brokers of the foreign vote. But what made that vote a dangerous impediment to nativism was a successful bid by the Republican party for a share of it. The Republicans dominated national politics in the first decade of the twentieth century. Furthermore, the G.O.P. had served as the principal channel of restrictionist agitation. Now the attraction of southern and eastern European voting blocs to the Republican column ended the party's effectiveness as a nativist instrument. The shift of big business to an anti-restrictionist point of view undoubtedly helped to break the Republican-nativist alliance, but before business opposition to nativism had fully crystallized the Republicans were already feeling the pressure of their new supporters.

The coming of the new immigration gave the Republicans an opportunity to undermine Democratic strength in urban areas by mobilizing Italian, Slavic, and Jewish voters. About the turn of the century, contacts developed in various ways. Organizations like the Hungarian Republican Club of New York appeared, and began to receive minor federal patronage.[60] In the Pennsylvania coal districts a wily Polish editor named Louis Hammerling entered into arrangements with Senators Mark Hanna and Boies Penrose, receiving a subsidy which he used to influence foreign-language newspapers in favor of Republican candidates. Hammerling was a master of fraud and intrigue. He served so well in the campaigns of 1904 and 1908 that some of his wealthy Republican friends then helped him set up an advertising agency, the American Association of Foreign Language Newspapers, which placed national advertising in the pages of the immigrant press for the first time. Through lucrative contracts which were his to give or withhold, Hammerling acquired a power of life and death over struggling foreign-language newspapers. And with him, politics and business were inextricably entwined.[61]

On the other hand, many Russian Jews in New York City proved responsive to reform campaigns and to diplomatic heckling of Czarist Russia. James Bronson Reynolds, head worker of a social settlement on the Lower East Side, won considerable Jewish support for the Citizens' Union, which fought Tammany in 1897. Reynolds became a close adviser of Theodore Roosevelt both on social problems and on immigration, directed the Society of the Friends of Russian Freedom, made official reports on the Jewish plight in eastern Europe, and continued to campaign for the Republican party in New York City. By 1903 Roosevelt was trying hard to conciliate Jewish and other critics of the administration of the federal immigration laws.[62]

Meanwhile a third force was intensifying competition for immigrant votes. Both inside and outside of party politics William Randolph Hearst exerted no little influence in behalf of the foreign-born, for he gave them raucous support and received in return their devoted loyalty. Raised in the stormy politics of Denis Kearney's San Francisco, Hearst learned early that a newspaper with bold type, simple ideas, and passionate appeals for social justice could command the pennies and the votes of the immigrant working class. He became the knight-errant of the tenements, denouncing religious prejudices while arousing class and national prejudices, posing as the great American champion of the maltreated Jews in Russia, and noisily publicizing the personal thanks of the Pope for relief funds that the Hearst papers collected when Mount Vesuvius erupted. He succeeded so well that at least one observer characterized the "yellow press" as the immigrants' Bible. For years, therefore, the growing chain of Hearst newspapers fulminated against further restrictive legislation and also against strict enforcement of existing laws.[63]

Hearst's campaign for the governorship of New York on the Democratic ticket in 1906 alarmed Republican progressives seriously. Just when they seemed to be making real headway in immigrant precincts, Hearst threatened to outbid them. On the eve of the election, as reports poured into the White House that Hearst was about to sweep New York City's Lower East Side, Roosevelt acted. He appointed Oscar Straus as Secretary of Commerce and Labor, thereby elevating a Jew to the Cabinet for the

first time and giving him control over the department which supervised immigration.[64]

The first major test of the influence which the new nationalities
and their strangely assorted allies could exert over Congress came
in the same year. For reasons that will appear later, a resurgence
of nativism made immigration restriction once more an issue. The
restrictionists seemed rejuvenated enough to secure a strong measure embodying the literacy test. Several foreign groups raised a
hue and cry against it, the Jewish protest being by far the most
vigorous. Nissim Behar, a Jewish welfare worker, organized the
National Liberal Immigration League for the sole purpose of defeating restriction bills. Edward Lauterbach, Jewish philanthropist
active in Republican politics, became its president, and a list of
prominent old-stock members gave the organization an air of altruism. Behar launched a whirlwind campaign of political pressure,
but he had hardly begun when Lodge maneuvered the literacy test
through the Senate.[65]

By the time the bill reached the House, immigrant opposition
was taking hold. Straus persuaded the leading Catholic prelate,
Cardinal Gibbons, to write a letter to Theodore Roosevelt opposing the literacy test. Among Republican Congressmen, Straus
spread a warning that passage of the literacy test would mean the
loss of their party's growing support in the foreign districts of the
cities. Leaders of Jewish philanthropic societies gathered in Washington to fight the bill, while the National Liberal Immigration
League organized mass meetings in the large cities and pelted Congressmen with resolutions.[66] President Roosevelt, although at heart
in favor of the measure, dared not intervene openly in its behalf.

Still, the bill would have gone through if the leading "organization" Republican, Speaker Joe Cannon, had not stood like a rock
against it. Part of Cannon's determined opposition undoubtedly
stemmed from his hostility to organized labor (now clamoring for
action) and from his pro-business sympathies. But also he and the
party managers around him clearly saw that enactment of the
literacy test would jeopardize the party's strength among naturalized voters.[67] As the representative of a mining district that was
drawing heavily on foreign labor, Cannon understood wherein industrial interests and ethnic loyalties coincided. While the progressives stayed largely on the sidelines, the expanding confidence

of American business and the defensive strength of the immigrants achieved expression through the crusty old conservative from Illinois.

Since some wavering Congressmen were exposed to pressure from the trade unions and other restrictionist groups, the first step toward defeating the literacy test in the House of Representatives was to prevent a record vote on it. This was accomplished by Cannon's henchmen on the Rules Committee, who reported a special rule precluding the possibility of a separate yea-and-nay vote on the literacy proviso. Then, as debate started, Cannon called a substitute to the Speaker's chair and took personal command on the floor. Still it seemed that the literacy test would pass. A motion to strike it from the bill failed by thirteen votes on a simple division. Tellers were called for a recount. Cannon took a stand in the well of the House, buttonholing Congressmen as they crowded down to the tellers. One after another, twenty opponents of the motion yielded to the fierce old man and switched or withheld their votes. Once the literacy test was dropped, it was an easy matter to drive the emasculated bill to passage.[68]

Now it remained only to subdue the Senate, whose representatives on the conference committee clung to the restrictionist provision as stubbornly as Cannon's appointees rejected it. A conference deadlock lasted for eight months, until the anti-Japanese agitation in California stirred the President to intervene. To appease the rancorous authorities of San Francisco, Roosevelt promised to secure immediate passage of the immigration bill with a new amendment prohibiting Japanese entry into the United States from Hawaii. Still, Cannon would not move. Only if the Senate drops the literacy test will the House agree to this bill, he told the President's emissary. Swallowing his own convictions, Roosevelt turned to the Senate and urged Lodge to abandon European restriction in the interest of Japanese restriction. To this plea the Senate conferees gave way, and the bill became law in the only form that the ruler of the House would accept.[69]

As finally enacted, the immigration act of 1907 was a triumph for the opponents of European restriction in all respects but one. Each arriving immigrant was required to pay a head tax of $4—twice the entrance fee then in force. On the other hand, the act enlarged the discretionary authority of the Secretary of Commerce and Labor to admit borderline cases; it established in the Bureau of Immigration a division of information, designed by anti-restrictionists to promote the distribution of immigrants by finding jobs for them outside the big cities; and it set up a commission charged with making an exhaustive investigation of the impact of immigration on the nation. The last idea crept into the law as a substitute for the literacy test. It had the merit of sounding constructive, and above all it would afford a breathing spell, postponing another nativist assault until the opposition to restriction was better organized.[70]

The anti-restrictionists had had a narrow squeeze, and they knew that the issue was far from settled. Perhaps they sensed that the ruthless power of the Speaker might not again avail them, though they could not foresee that it would be broken before the immigration question came to a head again. Yet they could count on building more durable barriers to legislative action. Big business was just beginning to take an active part in resisting restriction. The masses of naturalized Americans from southern and eastern Europe had shown only a fraction of their potential voting strength, and every ship was bringing more recruits. The victors of 1907 resorted to the delaying action of a lengthy investigation in the belief that time was on their side.

In a limited sense it was. Every year the new immigrants and their allies put up a more energetic defense. From a larger point of view, however, they had made too little and too sluggish use of a crucial interlude. The complacent optimism of the early twentieth century could not, in the nature of things, last for very long; the social and economic problems of the industrial age were certainly far from solved. Henceforth, confidence in the future of American society would have to rest increasingly on the use of organized intelligence to preserve and fulfill what fortune initially provided. With the extension of centralized direction over the national life, immigration would surely come under purposeful control. Yet the friends of the immigrant had simply adopted on the issue of restriction a frozen posture of defending the status quo. The progressive spirit reacted to ethnic problems too ambiguously to be of much help. So the opportunity to think out an immigration policy that might be both realistic and democratic was lost.

Chapter Six

Toward Racism:
The History of an Idea

> It need not puzzle us that Malay and Papuan, Celt and Roman, Saxon and Tartar should mix. . . . The best nations are those most widely related. . . .
> —Ralph Waldo Emerson, 1856

> "You cannot dodge the Mendelian law, my boy. Like begets like, but in a union of opposites we get throwbacks. . . . You're not going to run the risk of mongrelizing the species, are you?"
> —Peter B. Kyne, 1923

Hardly any aspect of American xenophobia over its course from the eighteenth to the twentieth century is more striking than the monotony of its ideological refrain. Year after year, decade after decade, the same charges and complaints have sounded in endless reiteration. Variously combined, formulated, and documented, adapted to different and changing adversaries, rising and falling in intensity and acceptance, nearly all of the key ideas persisted without basic modification.

But in one major respect the pattern of nativist thought changed fundamentally. Gradually and progressively it veered toward racism. Absent from the strictures of the eighteenth century nationalist, notions of racial superiority and exclusiveness appeared in the mid-nineteenth, but they were to undergo a long process of revision and expansion before emerging in the early twentieth century as the most important nativist ideology. Several genera-

131

tions of intellectuals took part in transforming the vague and somewhat benign racial concepts of romantic nationalism into doctrines that were precise, malicious, and plausibly applicable to European immigration. The task was far from simple; at every point the race-thinkers confronted the liberal and cosmopolitan barriers of Christianity and American democracy. Ironically and significantly, it was not until the beginning of the present century, when public opinion recovered much of its accustomed confidence, that racial nativism reached intellectual maturity.

Of course racial nativism forms only a segment, though a critical and illuminating segment, of the larger evolution of race consciousness in modern times. The greater part of the complex phenomenon which is now fashionably called "race prejudice" lies beyond the scope of this book; its history is tangled and still largely unwritten. What concerns us is the intersection of racial attitudes with nationalistic ones—in other words, the extension to European nationalities of that sense of absolute difference which already divided white Americans from people of other colors. When sentiments analogous to those already discharged against Negroes, Indians, and Orientals spilled over into anti-European channels, a force of tremendous intensity entered the stream of American nativism.

The whole story of modern racial ferment, nativist and otherwise, has two levels, one involving popular emotions, the other concerning more or less systematic ideas. Most of the emotions flow from a reservoir of habitual suspicion and distrust accumulated over the span of American history toward human groups stamped by obvious differences of color. The ideas, on the other hand, depend on the speculations of intellectuals on the nature of races. The distinction is partly artificial, for the spirit of white supremacy—or what may be labeled race-feeling—has interlocked with race-thinking at many points. Indeed, their convergence has given the problem of race its modern significance. But at least the distinction has the merit of reminding us that race-feelings and explicit concepts about races have not always accompanied one another. The Anglo-Saxon idea in its early form did not entail the biological taboos of race-feeling. Nor did the pattern of white supremacy, in all likelihood, depend at the outset on formal race-thinking. Traditional religious beliefs, often hardly articulated at all, served the pragmatic purposes of the English colonists who enslaved Negroes and who scourged Indians as Satanic agents "having little of Humanitie but shape." [1] However, the evolution of white supremacy into a comprehensive philosophy of life, grounding human values in the innate constitution of nature, required a major theoretical effort. It was the task of the race-thinkers to organize specific antipathies toward dark-hued peoples into a generalized, ideological structure.

To the development of racial nativism, the thinkers have made a special contribution. Sharp physical differences between native Americans and European immigrants were not readily apparent; to a large extent they had to be manufactured. A rather elaborate, well-entrenched set of racial ideas was essential before the newcomers from Europe could seem a fundamentally different order of men. Accordingly, a number of race-conscious intellectuals blazed the way for ordinary nativists, and it will be useful to tell their story before turning in later chapters to the popular emotions their ideas helped to orient.

From Romanticism to Naturalism

Two general types of race-thinking, derived from very different origins, circulated throughout the nineteenth century. One came from political and literary sources and assumed, under the impact of the romantic movement, a nationalistic form. Its characteristic manifestation in England and America was the Anglo-Saxon tradition. Largely exempt through most of the century from the passions of either the nativist or the white supremacist, this politico-literary concept of race lacked a clearly defined physiological basis. Its vague identification of culture with ancestry served mainly to emphasize the antiquity, the uniqueness, and the permanence of a nationality. It suggested the inner vitality of one's own culture, rather than the menace of another race. Whereas some of the early racial nationalists attributed America's greatness (and above all its capacity for self-government) to its Anglo-Saxon derivation, others thought America was creating a new mixed race; and, such was the temper of the age, many accepted both ideas at the same time. But whether exclusive or cosmopolitan in tendency, these romantics almost always discussed race as an ill-defined blessing; hardly ever as a sharply etched problem. During the age of confidence, as Anglo-Saxonism spread among an eastern social elite well removed from the fierce race conflicts of other regions, it retained a complacent, self-congratulatory air.

Meanwhile a second kind of race-thinking was developing from the inquiries of naturalists. Stimulated by the discovery of new worlds overseas, men with a scientific bent began in the seventeenth and eighteenth centuries to study human types systematically in order to catalogue and explain them. While Anglo-Saxonists consulted history and literature to identify national races, the naturalists concentrated on the great "primary" groupings of *Homo sapiens* and used physiological characteristics such as skin color, stature, head shape, and so on, to distinguish them one from the other. Quite commonly this school associated physical with cultural differences and displayed, in doing so, a feeling of white superiority over the colored races. On the whole, however, the leading scientific thinkers did not regard race differences as permanent, pure, and unalterable. A minority insisted that races were immutable, separately created species; but the influence of this polygenist argument suffered from its obvious violation of the Christian doctrine of the unity of mankind. For the most part, early anthropologists stressed the molding force of environmental conditions in differentiating the human family.[2]

In the course of the nineteenth and early twentieth centuries, the separation between the two streams of race-thinking gradually and partially broke down. Racial science increasingly intermingled with racial nationalism. Under the pressure of a growing national consciousness, a number of European naturalists began to subdivide the European white man into biological types, often using linguistic similarity as evidence of hereditary connection. For their part, the nationalists slowly absorbed biological assumptions about the nature of race, until every national trait seemed wholly dependent on hereditary transmission. This interchange forms the intellectual background for the conversion of the vague Anglo-Saxon tradition into a sharp-cutting nativist weapon and, ultimately, into a completely racist philosophy.

Behind the fusion—and confusion—of natural history with national history, of "scientific" with social ideas, lay a massive trend in the intellectual history of the late nineteenth and twentieth centuries. Hopes and fears alike received scientific credentials; and men looked on the human universe in increasingly naturalistic terms. In religion, literature, philosophy, and social theory ancient dualisms dissolved. Human affairs and values were seen more and more as products of vast, impersonal processes operating throughout nature. The Darwinian theory represented a decisive step in this direction; in the eyes of many, it subsumed mankind wholly under the grim physical laws of the animal kingdom.

While the whole naturalistic trend encouraged race-thinking and lent a sharper flesh-and-blood significance to it, Darwinism added a special edge. By picturing all species as both the products and the victims of a desperate, competitive struggle for survival, Darwinism suggested a warning: the daily peril of destruction confronts every species. Thus the evolutionary theory, when fully adopted by race-thinkers, not only impelled them to anchor their national claims to a biological basis; it also provoked anxiety by denying assurance that the basis would endure. Although most Anglo-Saxonists still identified their race with an indwelling spiritual principle, now they had also to envision the bearers of that principle as combatants in the great biological battle raging throughout nature.

On the other hand, it is not true that Darwinian (and Spencerian) ideas led directly to an outburst of racial nativism or to an overriding hereditarian determinism. The whole scientific revolution of the nineteenth century merely prepared the way and opened the possibility for those developments. Actually, the evolutionary hypothesis left major obstacles to a rigidly racial creed.

First of all, the general climate of opinion in the early Darwinian era inhibited the pessimistic implications of the new naturalism. What stood out in the first instance, as the great social lesson of the theory of natural selection, was not the ravages of the struggle for survival but rather the idea of "the survival of the fittest." To a generation of intellectuals steeped in confidence, the laws of evolution seemed to guarantee that the "fittest" races would most certainly triumph over inferior competitors. And in their eagerness to convert social values into biological facts, Darwinian optimists unblinkingly read "the fittest" to mean "the best." They felt confirmed in their supremacy over the immigrants, who in turn seemed the winnowed best of Europe. Darwinism, therefore, easily ministered to Anglo-Saxon pride, but in the age of confidence it could hardly arouse Anglo-Saxon anxiety.

Secondly, Darwinism gave the race-thinkers little concrete help in an essential prerequisite of racism—belief in the preponderance of heredity over environment. Certainly the biological vogue of the late nineteenth century stimulated speculation along these lines, but the evolutionary theory by no means disqualified a fundamentally environmentalist outlook. Darwin's species struggled and evolved within particular natural settings; they survived through adaptation to those settings. This aspect of the theory ultimately impressed itself so forcefully on American social scientists that toward the end of the century one of them acclaimed the doctrine of evolution for actually discouraging racial as opposed to environmental interpretations.[3] And while liberal environmentalists drew comfort from the new scientific gospel, it left the race-thinkers with no definite knowledge of how hereditary forces function or persist. Darwinism explained only the survival, not the appearance, of biological variations from pre-existing types. The origins of and relationships among races remained obscure.

Obviously both of these difficulties would have to be overcome if the Anglo-Saxon nationalism of the 1870's was to evolve into a fully effective instrument for race-feelings. Even to begin the transition the race-thinkers would have to cast loose from Darwinian optimism, discarding the happy thought that the fittest, in the sense of the best, always win out. That done, they would still lack a strict racial determinism. To divorce race entirely from environment and to put biological purity at the center of social policy, American nationalists would need further cues from the developing natural sciences.

Patricians on the Defensive

Americans were slow to take that second and more drastic step. Although sweeping theories and pretentious sciences or pseudo-sciences of race developed in continental Europe in the late nineteenth century, American intellectuals of that period knew practically nothing of them. Nor did American scientists make any contributions to race-thinking similar to those of Broca, Ammon, or Lapouge. In the United States psychologists dealt with individuals rather than groups, sociologists with institutions rather than peoples. Anthropologists immersed themselves in narrowly empirical studies of primitive folk, chiefly the Indians.[4] The movement toward racism was an up-hill fight in democratic America.

But a number of Anglo-Saxon nationalists in the eighties and nineties did begin to break away from evolutionary optimism. At first, instead of trying to qualify or rebut the principle of the survival of the fittest, the race-thinkers simply turned from complacent contemplation of America's Anglo-Saxon past to an anxious look at its future. This swing to a defensive outlook marks the initial phase of racial nativism. It required no fresh intellectual stimulus; it was precipitated by the general crisis in American society.

The same internal crisis that reactivated the older nativist traditions crystallized the new one. Until unrest and class cleavage upset the reign of confidence in the 1880's, the assimilationist concept of a mixed nationality had tempered and offset pride in Anglo-Saxon superiority. But when the Anglo-Saxon enthusiasts felt their society and their own status deeply threatened, they put aside their boasts about the assimilative powers of their race. They read the signs of the times as symptoms of its peril. Contrary to an impression widespread among historians, the new racial xenophobia did not originate as a way of discriminating between old and new immigrations. It arose from disturbances, within American society, which preceded awareness of a general ethnic change in the incoming stream. At the outset, Anglo-Saxon nativism vaguely indicted the whole foreign influx. Only later did the attack narrow specifically to the new immigration.

The current social scene presented a troubling contrast to the image of America that Anglo-Saxon intellectuals cherished. The tradition of racial nationalism had always proclaimed orderly self-government as the chief glory of the Anglo-Saxons—an inherited capacity so unique that the future of human freedom surely rested in their hands. But now the disorders of the mid-eighties cast doubt on the survival of a free society. The more anxious of the Anglo-Saxon apostles knew that the fault must lie with all the other races swarming to America. Did they not, one and all, lack the Anglo-Saxon's self-control, almost by definition? So, behind the popular image of unruly foreigners, a few caught sight of unruly races; and Anglo-Saxon nativism emerged as a corollary to anti-radical nativism—as a way of explaining why incendiary immigrants threatened the stability of the republic.

The explanation came out clear-cut in the convulsion that followed the Haymarket Affair. A writer in a business magazine stated the racial lesson of the riot in the baldest terms: anarchy is "a blood disease" from which the English have never suffered. "I am no race worshipper," he insisted, "but . . . if the master race of this continent is subordinated to or overrun with the communistic and revolutionary races, it will be in grave danger of social disaster." [5] During the same fateful summer a leading Congregational theologian equated race and unrest in words so sharp that he withheld them from publication for a year and a half. The Reverend Theodore T. Munger, an exponent of evolutionary theology, had long admired the Anglo-Saxons, the most highly developed, the most individualistic, and indeed the most Christian of races. As he surveyed the strife of 1886, he saw "anarchism, lawlessness . . . labor strikes, and a general violation of personal rights such as the Anglo-Saxon race has not witnessed since Magna Charta. . . . This horrible tyranny is wholly of foreign origin." Fundamentally, however, the problem was not just foreign. It was "physiological": how to restrict immigration "so that the physical stock shall not degenerate, and how to keep the strong, fine strain ascendant." [6]

Compared to the common and simple attack on radical *foreigners,* the attack on radical *races* was at first a minor theme. Indeed, it did not immediately displace the older kind of race-thinking. During the eighties many Anglo-Saxonists still clung to the traditional pride and confidence in America's powers of assimilation. Josiah Strong, for example, was still celebrating the absorptive capacities of the Anglo-Saxons after he had begun to attack the immigrants as socially disruptive. And in 1890 James K. Hosmer's glowing constitutional history of the Anglo-Saxon race still conceded that racial mingling invigorated it, although Hosmer was equally certain that immigration was diluting the Anglo-Saxons' blood and subverting their social order. [7]

During the 1890's, as the social crisis deepened, racial nativism became more defined and widespread. If one may judge, however, from Congressional debates, newspapers, and the more popular periodicals, Anglo-Saxonism still played a relatively small part in public opinion. The rising flood of popular xenophobia drew much more upon conventional anti-foreign ideas.

On the whole, the Anglo-Saxon tradition in its new nativistic form still found its support within the patrician circles where it had persisted throughout the age of confidence. Now, as then, the race-thinkers were men who rejoiced in their colonial ancestry, who looked to England for standards of deportment and taste, who held the great academic posts or belonged to the best clubs or adorned the higher Protestant clergy. Some, like Frank Parsons or Albert Shaw, were active reformers, especially in the municipal field. But, in general, racial nativists worshipped tradition in a deeply conservative spirit, and in the tumult of the nineties it seemed to them that everything fixed and sacred was threatened with dissolution. Among them were Episcopalian Bishop A. Cleveland Coxe, who added the final "e" to his family name in order to re-establish its antique spelling; [8] Woodrow Wilson, then a historian with aristocratic sympathies, a disciple of Burke and Bagehot who believed heartily in evolution because it moved so slowly; John W. Burgess, who brought from German seminars a love for "the race-proud Teutons" rather than the Anglo-Saxons and whose political science proved that racial amalgamation endangered private enterprise; and of course Henry Cabot Lodge, who mourned for the days when society venerated the old families, their traditions, and their ancestors. No one expressed the state of mind in this group better than the Presbyterian clergyman in New York who thought nature's great principle of inequality endangered by a "specious humanity," liberty-loving Anglo-Saxons beset by socialistic foreigners, and the intelligent people in the clutches of the unintelligent. [9]

A substantial number of these patrician nativists belonged to the cultivated intelligentsia of New England, the region where the Anglo-Saxon idea was most firmly entrenched. There the proportion of foreign-born in the total population was rising more sharply than in any other part of the country. There too the declining vitality of the native culture contributed to a defensive attitude. Brahmin intellectuals such as Lodge, Henry Adams, and Barrett Wendell knew that the historic culture of New England had entered its "Indian Summer," and the knowledge gave them added cause to see their race and region beleaguered by the alien.[10] In other places also a pessimistic spirit was creeping into intellectual life as the century waned. What the German writer Max Nordau was calling "vague qualms of a Dusk of the Nations" darkened various minds receptive to social anxieties or to the grimmer implications of Darwinian naturalism. But New Englanders particularly succumbed to the melancholy, *fin de siècle* mood and gave it a racial form. Thus at Harvard, Barrett Wendell, whose English accent matched his Anglophile interpretation of American literature, was settling into the conviction that his own kind had had its day, that other races had wrenched the country from its grasp for once and all.[11]

Many if not most of these men in the early nineties remained oblivious of the new immigration, assuming that the immigrants as a whole lacked the Anglo-Saxon's ancestral qualities. However, the avant-garde of racial nationalists was discovering during those years the shift in the immigrant stream. The discovery was important, because it lent a new sharpness and relevance to race-thinking. By making the simple (and in fact traditional) assumption that northern European nationalities shared much of the Anglo-Saxon's inherited traits, a racial nativist could now understand why immigration had just now become a problem. Also, the cultural remoteness of southern and eastern European "races" suggested to him that the foreign danger involved much more than an inherited incapacity for self-government: the new immigration was racially impervious to the whole of American civilization! Thus Anglo-Saxon nativism, in coming to focus on specific ethnic types, passed beyond its first, subordinate role as a corollary to anti-radical nativism. It found its own *raison d'être*, and in doing so served to divide the new immigrants from their predecessors in an absolute and fundamental way. Racial nativism became at once more plausible, a more significant factor in the history of immigration restriction, and a more precisely formulated ideology.

Three prominent intellectuals of the day illustrate this evolution in the Anglo-Saxon idea. Each of them embarked on anti-foreign agitation in the loose terms provoked by the internal events of the eighties, and each of them ended by fixing on the new immigration as constitutionally incapable of assimilation.

Nathaniel S. Shaler, the Kentucky-born geologist who presided over the Lawrence Scientific School at Harvard, was in some ways a reluctant and unlikely nativist. One of the most benign of individuals, Shaler felt a real sympathy for disadvantaged groups; and his professional training impressed upon him the large influence of the physical environment in creating human differences. But his early southern background had given Shaler an indelible race consciousness. He easily shared the belief of his Brahmin colleagues that American democracy rested on an English racial heritage. At first he stated the racial argument against immigration in class terms, contending that the immigrants threatened social stability because, as peasants, they lacked the Americans' inborn instinct for freedom. In 1894, however, he shifted to a more specific and sweeping attack on the new immigration. Instead of indicting the immigrants as a whole, he now drew a sharp racial contrast between northwestern and southeastern Europeans, maintaining that the new "non-Aryan" peoples were wholly different from earlier immigrants and innately impossible to Americanize.[12]

Henry Cabot Lodge arrived by a similar route at the same conclusion but carried it much further. What was perhaps his earliest public attack on immigration reflected simply a nationalist reaction to the crisis within American society. At that time, in 1888, he actually repudiated the injection of racial considerations into political issues. His own Anglo-Saxonism still conformed to the traditional eulogistic pattern.[13] Events, however, soon turned his attention to invidious racial comparisons.* In 1891 Lodge published a statistical analysis, which cost him much time and effort, concerning "the distribution of ability" in the American population. By classifying the entries in a biographical encyclopedia, he tried to show "the enormous predominance" of an English racial strain over every other in contributing to the development of the United States. Although the figures in this study suggested the inferiority of every non-English group in America, thereafter Lodge concentrated his fire on the new immigration, arguing that

---

* In 1890, for largely partisan reasons, Lodge brought to a head a Republican drive to enact a Force Bill designed to insure Negro suffrage in the South. The attempt failed; in fact, it brought down upon Lodge the condemnation of "the best people" of Massachusetts. The next year, instead of opposing racial barriers, Lodge proceeded to champion them by opening his campaign in Congress against the new immigration. See James A. Barnes, *John G. Carlisle, Financial Statesman* (New York, 1931), 188.

it presented a supreme danger transcending political or economic considerations: it threatened "a great and perilous change in the very fabric of our race." [14]

To support this view, Lodge went far beyond his American contemporaries in the direction of a racial philosophy of history. During a summer in France in 1895, he happened upon a new book by Gustave Le Bon, *The Psychology of Peoples*. Le Bon was a poetic social psychologist, an enemy of democracy, and a man who lived in dread of an imminent socialist revolution. His book treated nationalities as races and races as the substrata of history. Only through crossbreeding, according to Le Bon, could a race die or miss its destiny. He saw little hope for continental Europe but thought that the English, alone among European races, had kept their purity and stability. Lodge took these ideas back to the United States and repeated them practically verbatim on the floor of the Senate in 1896 in leading the fight for the literacy test. Without restriction of the new immigration, he warned, America's fixed, inherited national character would be lost in the only way possible—by being "bred out." [15]

Lodge was exceptional both in his direct contact with European race-thinking and in the degree to which he embraced an ideal of racial purity. It was not so easy for others to ignore the influence of environment or to understand how a supposedly backward, inferior type could overwhelm the puissant Anglo-Saxons.

A third member of the Yankee upper crust moved more cautiously into racial nativism but exerted in the long run a more telling intellectual influence. Francis A. Walker, president of the Massachusetts Institute of Technology and one of the outstanding economists of his day, was virtually the only American who made an original contribution to nativist thought in the late nineteenth century. Unlike Lodge, Shaler or the rest, Walker faced up to the key Darwinian issue of the survival of the fittest.

When he awoke to the menace of the foreign-born during the great labor upheaval of the mid-eighties, it was not race but rather the European's characteristic "insolence and savagery" that gave Walker visions of "great cities threatened with darkness, riot, and pillage." He continued to think of labor unrest as the most important aspect of the foreign peril and, in fact, never indulged in comprehensive racial theorizing. But as early as 1890 he trembled at a new influx of totally unassimilable races, representing "the very lowest stage of degradation." That these were laggards in the struggle for existence Walker had no doubt. Lest anyone should still defend the old Darwinian notion of migration as a selective process bringing America the most energetic and enterprising of Europeans, Walker neatly turned the tables, declaring that natural selection was now working in reverse. Due to the cheapness and ease of steamship transportation, the fittest now stay at home; the unfit migrate. The new immigrants, he declared in phrases that rang down through the restriction debates of the next three decades, "are beaten men from beaten races; representing the worst failures in the struggle for existence. . . . They have none of the ideas and aptitudes which . . . belong to those who are descended from the tribes that met under the oak trees of old Germany to make laws and choose chieftains." [16]

But still there was the hard question: How and why can such unfit groups endanger the survival of America's strong native stock? Walker held the clue long before it occurred to him to ask the question. As superintendent of the United States census of 1870, he had noticed that the rate of population growth in America was declining. At the time and for many years afterward he interpreted the decline very sensibly as a result of urbanization and industrialization. Then, when the events of the eighties and early nineties turned his attention to the racial significance of immigration, the old problem of population growth appeared in a new light. Might not the dwindling birth rate be a prudential response by the old American stock to a Darwinian struggle with immigrants capable of underbidding and outbreeding them? With an ingenious show of statistics, Walker argued in 1891 that the reproductive decline was occurring largely among the native population and that immigration rather than domestic conditions was responsible for it. In order to compete with cheap foreign labor, he said, Americans preferred to reduce the size of their families rather than lower their standard of living. Thus the foreign-born were actually replacing the native stock, not reinforcing it; in the very act of maintaining social and economic superiority, native Americans were undergoing biological defeat. In view of the new influx from southern and eastern Europe, Walker was sure that this long process of replacement would now enter an increasingly ominous stage.[17]

From a racial point of view, the argument had the disadvantage of resting on social and economic determinants and therefore failing to make any real distinction between immigrant types. Nevertheless, it did effectively counter Darwinian optimism while defining the foreign danger in plainly biological terms. Like Lodge's bluster about crossbreeding, Walker's birth-rate hypothesis suggested that unobstructed natural selection might insure the survival of the worst people rather than the best. The recasting of the Anglo-Saxon tradition into the mold of a gloomy, scientific naturalism was under way.

Optimistic Crosscurrents

Before this naturalistic trend made further headway, in fact before nativists paid much attention to Walker's theory, events temporarily twisted race-thinking in a very different direction. The fears and forebodings that were pushing Anglo-Saxonism toward sharper, more dogmatic formulations suddenly lifted at the end of the century; a new era bright with hope and flushed with well-being relieved the need to define enemies and explain failures. At a time when every xenophobia subsided, racial nationalism softened, relaxed, and resumed once more its historic air of triumphant confidence. Yet, oddly, it flourished as never before.

Actually, two currents of racial nationalism had developed among American intellectuals during the 1890's. One was defensive, pointed at the foreigner within; the other was aggressive, calling for expansion overseas. Both issued, in large measure, from the same internal frustrations; both reflected the same groundswell of national feeling. But one warned the Anglo-Saxon of a danger of submergence, while the other assured him of a conquering destiny. By 1898 the danger and doom were all but forgotten, and the conquest was made. An easy and successful adventure in imperialism gave racial nationalism both an unprecedented vogue and a cheerful tone. In a torrent of popular jubilation over the Anglo-Saxon's invincibility, the need to understand his predicament scientifically dissolved in a romantic glow.[18]

Imperialists happily intent on absorbing Filipinos and Puerto

Ricans felt little doubt of the Anglo-Saxons' powers of assimilation. Instead of Lodge's dread of racial mixture and his insistence on the fixity of the Anglo-Saxon folk, the country now heard once more the earlier theory of John Fiske: that Anglo-Saxons possess a unique capacity to merge with other peoples while retaining their own dominant traits. Franklin H. Giddings, the first professor of sociology at Columbia University, dressed up in scientific language the old notion that immigration was recapitulating in the United States the same blend of European strains from which the English had originally emerged. His proof that the United States was still English moved the editor of the *Ladies' Home Journal* to congratulate the home of the oppressed for its success in assimilation.[19] Others admitted that America's racial composition was changing but insisted that its Anglo-Saxon (or Teutonic) ideals were imposed on all comers. Albert Shaw, once one of the leading racial nativists, explained his shift away from a restrictionist position by asserting that America's power to assimilate had increased. Another imperialist felt so strong a sense of national homogeneity that he gave a new definition to the term Anglo-Saxon. All who stand together under the stars and stripes and fight for what it represents, he declared, have a right to that proud designation.[20]

Of course, there was another, less uplifting side to this frame of mind. The prime object of the imperialist ideology, after all, was to justify imposing colonial status on backward peoples. Every Anglo-Saxonist knew that the United States was taking up "the white man's burden" in extending American control over the dark-skinned natives of the Philippines, Hawaii, and Puerto Rico. Under these circumstances the Anglo-Saxon idea easily associated itself with emotions of white supremacy. In other words, while welcoming the immigrant population into the Anglo-Saxon fold, imperialists were also linking their ideal of nationality to a consciousness of color. Although a romantic idealism temporarily blurred the ideological sharpness of racial nationalism, at a deeper and more permanent level the Anglo-Saxon would henceforth symbolize the white man par excellence.

The imperialist excitement itself lasted only a short while, leaving the Anglo-Saxon tradition freighted with race-feelings and exposed again to a defensive, nativistic reaction. Overseas adventures lost their savor as soon as they engendered difficult moral problems and serious international entanglements. As early as 1901 the bloodshed necessary to impose United States rule on the "new-caught, sullen peoples" of the Philippines was deflating enthusiasm for expansion. And by 1905, when Japan emerged as a new world power menacing American interests in the Far East, American opinion was nervously repudiating the conquering, global destiny of a few years before.[21] Confronted by the "Yellow Peril," the Anglo-Saxon abandoned his rampant stance and resumed a somewhat defensive posture.

There were various indications in the early years of the twentieth century that race-thinking was entering a fretful, post-imperialist phase. One very direct reflection of the change of mood came in a book published in 1905 by a United States Army surgeon on his return from a tour of duty in the Philippines. In *The Effects of Tropical Light on White Men*, Major Charles E. Woodruff passed a depressing verdict on the racial results of imperialism. The blond, blue-eyed race, he argued, is born to command and to conquer; but in expanding southward from its foggy, overcast homelands in northern Europe it always succumbs to intense sunlight, which only the brunette races can withstand. And as Woodruff glanced apprehensively at the complexion of the immigrants pouring into the United States at the time, he added a significant afterthought. Perhaps the blond Teutons cannot expect to survive even under the climatic conditions prevailing throughout most of the United States.[22] Woodruff displayed all of the color feelings aroused by imperialism and none of its buoyant idealism. Much the same can be said of the gloomy tracts that California's leading race-thinker, Homer Lea, wrote in the next few years on the decline of American militancy and the spread of the Yellow Peril.[23]

Among other racial nationalists the reaction from imperial euphoria brought back the vague fears of the nineties about the Anglo-Saxons' stamina. They spoke of the old stock becoming decadent and being elbowed aside, of the Anglo-Saxon race as doomed, of the native Americans suffering from all manner of moral, physical, and psychic deterioration, due in large measure to immigration. Since nativism was at a low ebb in the early years of the century, the complaints usually sounded a mournful note rather than a belligerent or defiant one. Professor George E. Woodberry, one of the old-guard literary critics, even tried to find some comfort in the dismal spectacle. Lecturing on "race power" in literature in 1903, he suggested that the dissolution of the English race would fulfill a historic, sacrificial principle by which each great race succumbs in order to bequeath its heritage to a broader humanity.[24]

A less spiritually satisfying but more scientific explanation of the Anglo-Saxon's flagging energies could be found in Francis A. Walker's theory that immigration discouraged reproduction among the older stock. The theory was more and more widely discussed, with hardly anyone equipped statistically to challenge it.[25] Instead of critical scrutiny, Walker's sober argument now got a popular currency as it was inflated into the more grandiose concept of "race suicide." This happened in a curiously roundabout fashion. In 1901 Edward A. Ross used Walker's ideas in an address before the American Academy of Political and Social Science to explain how unchecked Asiatic immigration might lead to the extinction of the American people. When a higher race quietly eliminates itself rather than endure the competition of a lower one, said Ross, it is committing suicide. At the time, Ross was too confident of America's powers of assimilation to write about European immigration in these terms.[26] Before "race suicide" did become directly pertinent to the problem which Walker himself had had in mind, Theodore Roosevelt simplified it into an argument against birth control. For all of his booming optimism, Roosevelt could not entirely repress lurking doubts over the future. His nativist tendencies being in check, he discharged his anxieties through vague, thundering appeals to mothers to arrest the suicide of "the race" by having more children.[27]

The President's campaign for fecundity popularized the notion of race suicide. During the period from 1905 through 1909 the general magazines published over thirty-five articles dealing directly with the topic. Once it became a minor national phobia, the original, nativistic implications of the idea speedily reasserted themselves. In reply to a Rooseveltian tirade, *Harper's Weekly* remarked caustically in 1905 that exhortation would have little effect on the native birth rate as long as unlimited European immigration continued to reduce it. Soon books were being written to warn that race suicide would "toll the passing of this great Anglo-Teuton people" and the surrender of the nation "to the Latin and the Hun." [28] In the end, the whole discussion probably caused more race-thinking than reproduction. At least it brought to a wider audience the racial pessimism previously confined to a limited group of upper-class intellectuals.

It would be wrong to suppose, however, that any despairing note sounded very loudly or struck very deeply during the first decade of the twentieth century. Pessimistic anxieties crept about the fringes of American thought; at the heart of it was a supreme confidence. As the ebullience of imperialism ebbed away, much of the slack in American spirits was taken up by another enthusiasm. Progressivism inherited and sustained a good deal of the verve and exuberance which imperialism had generated. Many of the empire-builders of 1900 became apostles of social reform in the following years,[29] their crusading élan shifting from expansion abroad to improvement at home. As long as progressivism kept that psychological tone, as long as it radiated a sense of promise and victory, it limited the impact of imperialism's other heritage of race-thinking.

Furthermore, the premises of progressive thought, as well as its optimistic spirit, blunted the force of Anglo-Saxon nativism. By renewing faith in democracy, progressivism tended to challenge belief in racial inequalities. By concentrating on environmental reconstruction, it implicitly disputed all racial determinisms. At a time when politicians, public, and intelligentsia, alike, quickened with a vision of intelligence recasting environment, the Anglo-Saxon tradition faced powerful opposing currents. If nativistic intellectuals were to capitalize on the race consciousness left in the wake of imperialism, they would have to breast the mainstream of progressive thought.

Thus the race-thinkers of the early twentieth century belonged in considerable degree to the same social minority that had sustained the Anglo-Saxon tradition during the late nineteenth. Conservative patricians were less likely than most Americans to share the prevailing optimism and environmentalism. To men like Lodge and the founders of the Immigration Restriction League, like Major Woodruff and Professor Woodberry, the crusading spirit of progressivism brought little solace. Surely reform was not restoring the more stable social order of the past, and those who above all valued family and tradition often relapsed into a gloomy view of their racial future once the appeal of imperialism faded.

A number of patrician intellectuals, it is true, were caught up in the wave of social reform and surrendered some of their ethnic worries in the process. Theodore Roosevelt, for example, who had applauded Lodge's racial tirade in 1896 and rushed off to France an order for Le Bon's books, by 1904 was calling into question the whole tendency to use racial criteria in judging nationalities.[30] But others of Roosevelt's background felt increasingly their own social displacement in a democratic age and hugged ever more tightly —in Henry James' words—"the honor that sits astride of the consecrated English tradition." [31]

In short, when imperialism subsided, the Anglo-Saxon tradition moved again in the nativist direction it had taken during the early and mid-nineties. Yet the subsequent compulsions of empire-building and progressive reform decisively affected its course—one in a positive, the other in a negative, way. Imperialism left a heritage of race-feelings that enriched the emotional appeal of Anglo-Saxon nativism; progressivism challenged its intellectual basis. The democratic, environmentalist outlook adopted by most of the leading social scientists and historians of the Progressive era weakened the intellectual respectability of the confused, ill-defined concepts of race prevalent in the nineteenth century. To vindicate its intellectual pretensions and rationalize its emotional tone, the Anglo-Saxon tradition more than ever needed restatement in the form of a scientific law. And this was exactly what happened.

Enter the Natural Scientists

In the 1890's nativist intellectuals had barely begun to think of European races as a biological threat or to associate national survival with racial purity. Even Walker's birth-rate theory offered no logical reason to suppose that the country would suffer from the replacement of old stock by new. Perhaps the most serious intellectual handicap of American race-thinkers before the twentieth century was the lack of a general scientific principle from which to argue the prepotency of heredity in human affairs. But at the turn of the century, when social science and history came increasingly under the sway of environmental assumptions, biologists advanced dramatic claims for heredity and even helped to translate them into a political and social creed.[32]

The new science of heredity came out of Europe about 1900 and formed the first substantial contribution of European thought to American nativism after the time of Darwin. The study of inheritance suddenly leaped into prominence and assumed a meaningful pattern from the discovery of the long-unnoticed work of Gregor Mendel and its convergence with August Weismann's theory of germinal continuity. Together, these hypotheses demonstrated the transmission from generation to generation of characteristics that obeyed their own fixed laws without regard to the external life of the organism.

Amid the excitement caused in English scientific circles by these continental discoveries, Sir Francis Galton launched the eugenics movement. Galton, who was England's leading Darwinian scientist, had long been producing statistical studies on the inheritance of all sorts of human abilities and deficiencies. But it was only in the favorable climate of the early twentieth century that he started active propaganda for uplifting humanity by breeding from the best and restricting the offspring of the worst. To Galton, eugenics was both a science and a kind of secular religion. It certified that the betterment of society depends largely on improvement of the "inborn qualities" of "the human breed," and Galton preached this message with evangelical fervor.[33] Thus he provided biologists and physicians, excited over the new genetic theories, with a way of converting their scientific interests into a program of social salvation—a program based wholly on manipulation of the supposedly omnipotent forces of heredity.

In the latter part of the 1900's the eugenics movement got under way in the United States, where it struck several responsive chords. Its emphasis on unalterable human inequalities confirmed the patricians' sense of superiority; its warnings over the multiplication of the unfit and the sterility of the best people synchronized with the discussion of race suicide. Yet the eugenicists' dedication to a positive program of "race improvement" through education and state action gave the movement an air of reform, enabling it to flourish in the ambience of progressivism while still ministering to conservative sensibilities. By 1910, therefore, eugenicists were catching the public ear. From then through 1914, according to one tabulation, the general magazines carried more articles on eugenics than on the three questions of slums, tenements, and living standards, combined.[34]

The leading eugenicist in America was Charles B. Davenport, a zoologist of tremendous ambition and drive who established the country's first research center in genetics at Cold Spring Harbor, Long Island. Davenport's father, a descendant of one of the Puritan founders of New England, was a genealogist who traced his ancestry back to 1086, and Davenport himself often mourned "that the best of that grand old New England stock is dying out through failure to reproduce." His early experiments at Cold Spring Harbor were devoted to testing the Mendelian principles in animal breeding; by 1907 he was beginning to apply them to the study of human heredity. In 1910 he persuaded Mrs. E. H. Harriman to finance a Eugenics Record Office adjacent to his laboratory with the aim of compiling an index of the American population and advising individuals and local societies on eugenical problems. Over a course of years she poured more than half a million dollars into the agency, while Davenport—already one of America's leading biologists— gave the rest of his life to studying the inheritance of human traits and spreading the gospel of eugenics.[35] An indefatigable organizer, Davenport was also one of the leaders of the American Breeders' Association, where the eugenics agitation first centered. Established in 1903 by practical plant and animal breeders who wanted to keep in touch with the new theoretical advances, the association enlarged its field in 1907 to embrace eugenics.[36]

The racial and nativistic implications of eugenics soon became apparent. From the eugenicists' point of view, the immigration question was at heart a biological one, and to them admitting "degenerate breeding stock" seemed one of the worst sins the nation could commit against itself. It was axiomatic to these naïve Mendelians that environment could never modify an immigrant's germ plasm and that only a rigid selection of the best immigrant stock could improve rather than pollute endless generations to come. Since their hereditarian convictions made virtually every symptom of social disorganization look like an inherited trait, the recent immigration could not fail to alarm them.[37] Under the influence of eugenic thinking, the burgeoning mental hygiene movement picked up the cry. Disturbed at the number of hereditary mental defectives supposedly pouring into the country, the psychiatrists

who organized the National Committee for Mental Hygiene succeeded in adding to the immigration bill of 1914 an odd provision
excluding cases of "constitutional psychopathic inferiority." [38] By
that time many critics of immigration were echoing the pleas in
scientific periodicals for a "rational" policy "based upon a noble
culture of racial purity." [39]

None were quicker or more influential in relating eugenics to
racial nativism than the haughty Bostonians who ran the Immigration Restriction League. Prescott F. Hall had always had a hypo-
chondriac's fascination with medicine and biology, and his associate, Robert DeCourcy Ward, was a professional scientist. They
had shied away from racial arguments in the nineties, but in the
less favorable atmosphere of the new century their propaganda
very much needed a fresh impulse. As early as 1906 the league
leaders pointed to the new genetic principles in emphasizing the opportunity that immigration regulation offered to control America's future racial development.[40] Two years later they learned of
the eugenics sentiment developing in the American Breeders' Association. They descended upon it, and soon they were dominating
its immigration activities. The association organized a permanent
committee on immigration, of which Hall became chairman and
Ward secretary. Ward proceeded to read papers on immigration
legislation before meetings of eugenicists, and for a time the two
considered changing the name of their own organization to the
"Eugenic Immigration League." [41] Meanwhile they seized every
occasion to publicize the dogma that science decrees restrictions on
the new immigration for the conservation of the "American
race." [42]

Obviously the eugenics movement had crucial importance for
race-thinking at a time when racial presuppositions were seriously
threatened in the intellectual world. But basically the importance
of eugenics was transitional and preparatory. It vindicated the
hereditarian assumptions of the Anglo-Saxon tradition; it protected
and indeed encouraged loose talk about race in reputable circles;
and in putting race-thinking on scientific rather than romantic
premises it went well beyond the vague Darwinian analogies of
the nineteenth century. On the other hand, eugenics failed utterly
to supply a racial typology. In their scientific capacity, the eugenicists—like their master Galton—studied individual traits and reached

conclusions on individual differences. When they generalized the defects of individual immigrants into those of whole ethnic groups, their science deserted them and their phrases became darkly equivocal. Indeed, the more logical and consistent eugenicists maintained that America could improve its "race" by selecting immigrants on the ground of their individual family histories regardless of their national origins.[43]

In the end the race-thinkers had to look to anthropology to round out a naturalistic nativism. Anthropology alone could classify the peoples of Europe into hereditary types that would distinguish the new immigration from older Americans; it alone might arrange these races in a hierarchy of merit and thereby prove the irremediable inferiority of the newcomers; and anthropology would have to collaborate with genetics to show wherein a mixture of races physically weakens the stronger.

American anthropology remained cautiously circumspect on these points. The influence of the foreign-born progressive, Franz Boas, was already great; in 1911 he published the classic indictment of race-thinking, *The Mind of Primitive Man*. In the absence of interest on the part of American anthropologists, a perfected racism depended on amateur handling of imported ideas. In a climate of opinion conditioned by the vogues of race suicide and eugenics, however, it is not surprising that scientifically minded nativists found the categories and concepts they needed without assistance from American anthropologists.

Again the inspiration came from Europe. There, chiefly in France and Germany, during the latter half of the nineteenth century anthropologists furnished the scientific credentials and speculative thinkers the general ideas out of which a philosophy of race took shape. The first of the thoroughgoing racists, Count J. A. de Gobineau, reached a limited audience of proslavery thinkers in America on the eve of the Civil War and then was forgotten. His successors were even less effective. Once in a while an immigrant writer tried to translate some of this literature into terms that might appeal to an American public, but the stuff simply was not read.[44] Not until the beginning of the twentieth century did the invidious anthropological theories which had been accumulating in Europe for over thirty years reach a significant American audience. And when they did, they were delivered in a characteristically American package.

William Z. Ripley was a brilliant young economist who had the kind of mind that refuses to stay put. In the mid-nineties, before he was thirty years old, Ripley was teaching economics at the Massachusetts Institute of Technology, while simultaneously developing a unique course of lectures at Columbia University on the role of geography in human affairs. In its conception this course reflected Ripley's conviction of the basic importance of environmental conditions in molding the life of man; but he quickly came up against the problem of race. The question led him to the controversies among continental scholars on the anthropological traits of European peoples, and he chose the locale of Europe as a crucial test of the interplay of race and environment. In *The Races of Europe*, a big, scholarly volume appearing in 1899, he anatomized the populations of the continent, pointing temperately but persistently to ways in which physiological traits seemed to reflect geographical and social conditions.

This was cold comfort to nativists, but the book had another significance apart from the author's well-hedged thesis. Ripley organized into an impressive synthesis a tripartite classification of white men which European ethnologists had recently developed. For the first time, American readers learned that Europe was not a land of "Aryans" or Goths subdivided into vaguely national races such as the Anglo-Saxon, but rather the seat of three races discernible by physical measurements: a northern race of tall, blond longheads which Ripley called Teutonic; a central race of stocky roundheads which he called Alpine; and a southern race of slender, dark longheads which he called Mediterranean.[45] Here was a powerful weapon for nativists bent on distinguishing absolutely between old and new immigrations, but to make it serviceable Ripley's data would have to be untangled from his environmentalist assumptions.

It is ironical that Ripley himself did some of the untangling. For all of his scholarly caution he could not entirely suppress an attachment to the Teutonic race that reflected very mildly the rampant Teutonism of many of the authorities on which he relied. In the early twentieth century the new genetic hypotheses and a growing alarm over the new immigration turned his attention from environmental to inherited influences. He began to talk about race suicide and to wonder about the hereditary consequences of the mixture of European races occurring in America.

Before abandoning anthropology completely to concentrate in economics, Ripley delivered in 1908 a widely publicized address in which he suggested an answer to the old problem of how the crossing of superior and inferior races can drag down the former. His roving eye had come upon the experiments that some of the Mendelian geneticists were making on plant and animal hybrids. Hugo De Vries and others were demonstrating how hybridization sometimes caused a reassertion of latent characters inherited from a remote ancestor. The concept of reversion was an old one, discussed by Darwin himself, but the rise of genetics brought it into new prominence. Ripley fastened on the idea and raised the question whether the racial intermixture under way in America might produce a reversion to a primitive type.[46] In contrast to the theory of race suicide, this doctrine—torn from the context of genetics and applied to the typology of European races—provided a thoroughly biological explanation of the foreign peril. Presumably race suicide might be arrested by legislation and by education raising the immigrant's standard of living; but reversion seemed remorseless. All of the pieces from which a sweeping statement of racial nativism might be constructed were now on hand.

The man who put the pieces together was Madison Grant, intellectually the most important nativist in recent American history. All of the trends in race-thinking converged upon him. A Park Avenue bachelor, he was the most lordly of patricians. His family had adorned the social life of Manhattan since colonial times, and he was both an expert genealogist and a charter member of the Society of Colonial Wars. Always he resisted doggedly any intrusion of the hoi polloi. On his deathbed he was still battling to keep the public from bringing cameras into the zoo over which he had long presided.[47]

In addition to a razor-sharp set of patrician values, Grant also had an extensive acquaintance with the natural sciences and a thoroughly naturalistic temper of mind. Beginning as a wealthy sportsman and hunter, he was the founder and later the chairman of the New York Zoological Society, where he associated intimately with leading biologists and eugenicists. In the early years of the twentieth century he published a series of monographs on North American animals—the moose, the caribou, the Rocky Mountain goat. He picked up a smattering of Mendelian concepts and, unlike his eugenicist friends, read a good deal of physical anthropology too. Ripley's work furnished his main facts about European man, but he also went behind Ripley to many of the more extreme European ethnologists. Thus Grant was well supplied with scientific information yet free from a scientist's scruple in interpreting it.

By 1910 Grant's racial concepts were clearly formed and thoroughly articulated with a passionate hatred of the new immigration.[48] He showed little concern over relations between whites and Negroes or Orientals. His deadliest animus focused on the Jews, whom he saw all about him in New York. More broadly, what upset him was the general mixture of European races under way in America; for this process was irretrievably destroying racial purity, the foundation of every national and cultural value.

Grant's philippic appeared finally in 1916. It bore the somber title, *The Passing of the Great Race*, summing up the aristocratic pessimism that had troubled nativist intellectuals since the 1890's. Everywhere Grant saw the ruling race of the western world on the wane yet heedless of its fate because of a "fatuous belief" in the power of environment to alter heredity. In the United States he observed the deterioration going on along two parallel lines: race suicide and reversion. As a result of Mendelian laws, Grant pontificated, we know that different races do not really blend. The mixing of two races "gives us a race reverting to the more ancient, generalized and lower type." Thus "the cross between any of the three European races and a Jew is a Jew." [49] In short, a crude interpretation of Mendelian genetics provided the rationale for championing racial purity.

After arguing the issue of race versus physical environment, Grant assumed a racial determination of culture. Much of the book rested on this assumption, for the volume consisted essentially of a loose-knit sketch of the racial history of Europe. The Alpines have always been a race of peasants. The Mediterraneans have at least shown artistic and intellectual proclivities. But the blond conquerors of the North constitute "the white man par excellence." Following the French scientist Joseph Deniker, Grant designated this great race Nordic. To it belongs the political and military genius of the world, the daring and pride that make explorers, fighters, rulers, organizers, and aristocrats. In the early days, the American population was purely Nordic, but now the swarms of Alpine, Mediterranean, and Jewish hybrids threaten to extinguish the old stock unless it reasserts its class and racial pride by shutting them out.

So the book turned ultimately into a defense of both class and racial consciousness, the former being dependent on the latter. The argument broadened from nativism to an appeal for aristocracy as a necessary correlative in maintaining racial purity. Democracy, Grant maintained, violates the scientific facts of heredity; and he was obviously proud to attribute feudalism to the Nordics. Furthermore, Grant assaulted Christianity for its humanitarian bias in favor of the weak and its consequent tendency to break down racial pride. Even national consciousness ranked second to race consciousness in Grant's scale of values.

This boldness and sweep gave *The Passing of the Great Race* particular significance. Its reception and its impact on public opinion belong to a later stage in the history of American nativism, but its appearance before America's entry into the First World War indicates that the old Anglo-Saxon tradition had finally emerged in at least one mind as a systematic, comprehensive world view. Race-thinking was basically at odds with the values of democracy and Christianity, but earlier nativists had always tried either to ignore the conflict or to mediate between racial pride and the humanistic assumptions of America's major traditions. Grant, relying on what he thought was scientific truth, made race the supreme value and repudiated all others inconsistent with it.

This, at last, was racism.[50]

Chapter Seven

The Loss of Confidence

Heredity will tell the story of our greatest woes. It is like inoculating a whole nation of people with leprosy, that can be eradicated from the blood only by a racial lapse, through decades of time, to rejuvenating savagery.
—Charles Major, 1910

In the decade from 1905 to 1915, while patrician nativists were building a systematic ideology, popular nativism was struggling to recover the vitality it had had in the mid-nineties. From 1906, when the literacy test reappeared in Congress, to the beginning of American involvement in the First World War, the jaunty self-assurance with which America as a whole had greeted the twentieth century was slowly deteriorating. Xenophobia was steadily on the rise. Although we may take 1905 or 1906 as its starting point, resurgent nativism did not announce itself with the explosive force of a second Haymarket riot. Nor did it, in all probability, regain even at the end of the period the hysterical intensity of the 1890's. Yet the prewar revival of nativism has major significance. It prepared the way for the greater passions of the war years, and it also set in motion trends that reached fulfillment once the war was over.

This most obscure of all periods in the history of American nativism eludes any simple or easy analysis. It started during relatively happy, abundant years, when most people felt sure that reform was liquidating the problems of the nineteenth century. Furthermore, anti-foreign feelings steadily gathered strength at a time when the dominant force of progressivism was also surging upward in potency and enthusiasm. To understand the growing vigor of nativist movements in the late years of the Progressive era one must take account of many things: of changes in the pattern of immigration; of ideas, inherited from earlier periods, that had little to do with a progressive spirit; and of certain alterations that occurred in that spirit itself.

The Ethnocentric Background

All through the Progressive era, through its years of confidence and through its returning doubts, the human tide rolled in from crowded Europe. From a low point in 1897 the current ascended to its zenith in 1907 and then fluctuated at a level above 650,000 per year until the outbreak of the World War. At no time in the nineteenth century had such numbers crossed the Atlantic. On the other hand, the proportion of native- to foreign-born in the total population did not substantially vary, and the cityward movement of the native population more than kept pace with the increasing urbanization of the immigrants. Percentagewise, the immigrants were barely holding their own.

What was changing significantly was their destination and their composition. Like the major domestic migrations, the transatlantic current was moving more than ever toward the cities; despite the efforts of private agencies and of the federal Division of Information, established in 1907, Europeans no longer in any number found homes in the small towns or the countryside of America. Also, the new immigration from southern and eastern Europe now thoroughly overshadowed the dwindling stream from Germany, Scandinavia, the Low Countries, and the British Isles. In the period from the Spanish-American to the World War the new immigration was nearly three and a half times the size of the old.[1] Few nativists, except the anti-Catholic crusaders who could never forget the Irish, now failed to attribute great importance to the shift in nationalities. Around this distinction between old and new—not around the general anti-foreignism that had prevailed in the 1890's—the return of nativism clearly centered.

The collapse of widespread hatred at the turn of the century by no means dispensed the new immigrants from the distaste which older Americans had always felt for their culture and appearance. Since only a small segment of progressive opinion sought positive values in the foreigners' way of life, a traditional ethnocentric aversion spread with the growing numbers of the newcomers and their increasing prominence on the American scene.

Among the score or more of nationalities now funneling through Ellis Island, only Italians and Jews were commonly distinguishable in American eyes from the nameless masses who accompanied them, and Italians and Jews continued to suffer the most resentment. The Italian still bore as vividly as ever the stigma of impassioned crime. During the ebb of nativism in the early years of the century, headlines in metropolitan newspapers trumpeted the tale of Italian blood lust incessantly: "Caro Stabs Piro . . . Cantania Murdered . . . Ear-Biting Crime . . . Rinaldo Kills Malvino . . . Gascani Assaulted . . . Vendetta Near Oak Street. . . ."[2] Doubtless the reports inspired less terror than they had a decade earlier, partly because the public was learning that the violence was almost entirely intramural. Italian lawlessness ignited no further jingoist explosions and precipitated fewer lynchings. Nevertheless, it was universally believed that serious offenses were rapidly increasing—as they probably were. Lax American law enforcement was attracting to the United States a considerable number of Sicily's bandits; here, through blackmail and murder, they levied tribute on their intimidated countrymen more successfully than they had at home. By 1909, when a combined drive of American authorities and Italian community leaders began to reduce these activities, the image of a mysterious Black Hand Society, extending from Italy into every large American city, was fixed in the public imagination.[3]

Although the Jews were certainly not exempt from the new immigrants' general reputation for criminality,[4] on the whole the anti-Semitic stereotype pointed to private misbehavior rather than public misdemeanor. With the return of confidence, the nationalistic fears of the 1890's, that the Jews were wrecking the American economy and conspiring to rule the world, had vanished; no one now accused the Jews of subversive activity. Nor were they so liable to physical attacks, except in the foreign quarters.[5] But what did persist, and indeed advance, was the older Shylock tradition, the notion of the Jews as an immoral, unmannerly people, given to greed and vulgarity. The general American materialism and social climbing that followed the Civil War had thrown this image into relief and had set in motion a corresponding pattern of social discrimination. Throughout the late nineteenth century, beneath the stormy surface of harsher sentiments, this tendency to judge Jews as acquisitive barbarians and to recoil from association with them affected ever larger segments of American society. In the Progressive era social anti-Semitism was still spreading.

Part of the explanation for the sharpening of discrimination at a time of relative tranquillity lay in the swift upward thrust of the new Jewish immigrants. Like the German Jews who preceded them and whose social ascent had occasioned the earliest prohibitions, the refugees from Czarist persecution had a dynamism rare among foreign groups. They quit the slums in conspicuous numbers, produced an affluent class of real estate speculators and clothing manufacturers, and alone among recent immigrants sent a good many of their children to college.[6] As they rose, native Americans threw new obstacles across their path. Already shut out of clubs, most summer resorts, and many private schools, Jews found it increasingly difficult in the early twentieth century to enter college fraternities and faculties. Restrictive covenants became common in urban residential areas.[7] More important, job opportunities were beginning to contract. Sons and daughters of eastern European Jews were edging into the white-collar world and finding office managers unwilling to employ them.[8]

Because of their exceptional mobility, the Jews met the most economic discrimination, but at the same time other new groups ran athwart middle-class proscriptions. Italian applicants for clerical jobs often felt obliged to call themselves French or Spanish or Turkish,[9] just as some Jews denied their national origin. As if to demonstrate that the pattern of discrimination did not apply exclusively to any single nationality, state legislatures enacted prohibitions on the entry of all aliens into certain specialized occupations. In the nineteenth century, discriminatory legislation had aimed largely to exclude the immigrant from the relatively unskilled occupations he first sought out. But at the turn of the century states began to outlaw the unnaturalized foreigner from various white-collar jobs. Some revised their codes to require American citizenship of all attorneys. New York in 1909 adopted the same stipulation for private detectives. Michigan prohibited the issuance of a barber's license to any alien. About 1909 a successful legislative campaign to deny nondeclarant aliens acceptance as certified public accountants got under way. Three eastern states went entirely beyond the vocational field to regulate avocations. New York in 1908 required aliens to pay $20 for a hunting license, as against $1 for citizens. A little later Pennsylvania flatly prohibited aliens from hunting and so from possessing shotguns, rifles, or dogs of any kind. In two counties of Massachusetts it became a crime for an alien to pick wild berries or flowers except on his own property.[10]

Yet none of this unfriendliness necessarily signified a rebirth of the nativist spirit. Conceivably the coldness, the repugnance, and the exclusions could have resulted simply from the growth of the new immigrant population. Nativism cut deeper than economic jealousy or social disapproval. It touched the springs of fear and hatred; it breathed a sense of crisis. Above all, it expressed a militantly defensive nationalism: an aroused conviction that an intrusive element menaced the unity, and therefore the integrity and survival, of the nation itself. The coming of the new immigration had contributed to late nineteenth century xenophobia, and its presence played a more crucial role in the twentieth century, but at both times the intensity of the hostility reflected larger factors in the American situation.

For clues to the distinctive sources of the new nativism one must turn to its earliest significant symptom: the fresh and surprisingly vigorous effort to enact a literacy test in 1906. This fourth failure to secure what had been defeated in 1897, in 1898, and again more dismally in 1902, revealed the emerging influence of the newer immigrants in American politics; but the narrow margin and desperate measures by which Uncle Joe Cannon and his immigrant allies prevented passage of the literacy test also signaled a recrudescence of nativist power. Here several of the tangled threads of modern American xenophobia first intersected, some old, others just coming into view. The incident furnishes a starting point for unraveling them.

Early on the Congressional scene appeared pressure groups which had labored for similar legislation in previous years: the veterans of immigration controversies. The patrician intellectuals of the Northeast, while busy modernizing their ideology, had not changed their legislative tactics. The Immigration Restriction League, still supported by old New England families, was carrying on in 1905 and 1906 as it had since the 1890's. Sensing a shift in public opinion, the league hired a new Washington lobbyist and prepared another campaign. Henry Cabot Lodge again cooperated with the league in the Senate, although with unwonted circumspection. Seemingly the multiplication of immigrant votes in Massachusetts (and perhaps the pressure of business opinion) lent a certain prudence to Lodge's activities. He never again exercised the initiative and leadership on restriction which he had taken during the nineties. In his impetuous son-in-law, Congressman Augustus Gardner, the league had a more aggressive spokesman in the House of Representatives. It was Gardner who forced the immigration bill out of the standpat Rules Committee and who struggled vainly against Speaker Cannon's stratagems.[11]

Organized labor too returned to the fray and returned with unprecedented vitality. The unions had played a rather limited role in nineteenth century movements for general restrictions on immigration. Even in the feeble, literacy test campaign of 1902 the American Federation of Labor had not acted with conspicuous vigor or resolution. By 1906, however, conditions had changed, and labor's heart was in restriction. In the years from 1897 to 1904, a period of relative harmony between capital and labor, the A.F.L. grew enormously, in no small measure by recruiting native American artisans. Because of this expansion and also because most A.F.L. unions ignored the masses of unskilled workers, the proportion of native-born in the organization was evidently increasing; it was losing touch with its own immigrant roots.[12] The decline of immigrant influence in the federation might alone account for the organization's heartier acceptance of restriction, but after 1904 another factor gave a positive impetus to the idea. A massive attack by organized business threw organized labor on the defensive. The unions stopped growing, blocked by boycotts, open-shop campaigns, and in some measure by employers' handling of cheap immigrant labor (notably through the practice of "balancing nationalities"). This display of corporate power whetted resentment against men who seemed more than ever pliant tools of the corporations. Fearful, angry, and discouraged, the A.F.L. for the first time turned to immigration restriction with determination. The literacy test became one of its cardinal legislative objectives, as it warned recalcitrant Congressmen of retaliation at the next election.[13]

The strange alliance of patricians with union labor, an alliance which linked A.F.L. President Samuel Gompers and Henry Cabot Lodge in the only common endeavor of their two careers, would not of itself have made much headway against the powerful forces arrayed in opposition. The gathering resistance to restriction by big business and by the new immigration was creating a coalition at least as strong as the Lodge-Gompers axis, and because both alignments cut across party divisions, neither the Republican nor the Democratic party could serve as a nativist vehicle. The traditionally restrictionist groups needed substantial outside support for any show of strength, and this meant a shift in at least some sectors of public opinion. The shift was occurring in 1905 and 1906, chiefly in two regions of the country.

The veteran restrictionists felt the new wind that was rising in one section. In fact, they set their sails to catch it. Gompers later recalled: "When the Japanese school issue originating in San Francisco focused attention on the Japanese phases of the immigration question . . . there developed an opportunity of getting action on immigration." Lodge had the same perception. "This intense feeling on the Pacific Slope," he wrote to Theodore Roosevelt in the summer of 1905, "may help us to get some good general legislation . . . on the anti-Japanese-Chinese agitation supported by the labor people we might win." [14]

Neither Gompers nor Lodge realized that another section was taking their cause just as much or more to heart. The South as well as the Far West was stirring with nativist ferment. In fact, two southerners seized the initiative in Congress. An Alabaman, Oscar W. Underwood, was the first to raise the immigration question when the legislators convened in December 1905. Breaking irrelevantly into another debate, Underwood instructed the House on the pure whiteness of the old immigration in contrast to the mixture of Asiatic and African blood coursing in the veins of southern Europeans. When the Senate took up the issue a few months later, the literacy test was not introduced by the more cautious Lodge but rather by Senator F. M. Simmons of North Carolina. Simmons appealed fervently for the preservation of Anglo-Saxon civilization against immigrants who "are nothing more than the degenerate progeny of the Asiatic hoards [*sic*] which, long centuries ago, overran the shores of the Mediterranean . . . the spawn of the Phoenician curse. . . ." [15]

Grass Roots of Anglo-Saxon Nativism

With these words, a new phase in the history of American nativism inauspiciously began. Although beaten in the legislative fight of 1906-07, the southern and western opponents of immigration, together with the eastern restrictionists, pressed steadily forward in succeeding years. And just as steadily the importance of the West and South in the nativist coalition grew, until the preponderant strength of the movement came from those outlying regions, where the main object of attack, the new immigration, was least numerous.

Throughout that whole vast area one prevailing quality and character stamped the anti-foreign drive from the outset. It was racial; it rang with the shibboleths of the Anglo-Saxon tradition. Yet the southern and western nativists knew little or nothing about the racial science that was beginning to affect literate northern circles. For some time the crude bombast of cotton Senators and California statesmen owed hardly anything to the pretentious doctrines of race suicide, eugenics, and racist anthropology. South and West were sectional spearheads of a popular kind of racial nativism that arose parallel with but was not dependent upon the new racial ideology.

The taproot of the reaction was gnarled and massive, imbedded deeply in the common folkways of the two areas. The South and the Pacific Coast alike thought of themselves as a "white man's country." They had long struggled—in different degrees and in different ways—to maintain white supremacy, often without the aid of a systematic ideology. From Seattle to Savannah primitive race-feelings, wrought deeply in the American character, flourished as nowhere else in the United States. Projected on the new immigration, these ancient feelings gave southern and western nativism its peculiar energy.

On the West Coast, as Lodge and Gompers appreciated, the Japanese question precipitated the racial anxieties which infected attitudes toward Mediterranean and eastern European peoples.

Anti-Japanese sentiment, gathering strength slowly after 1900 as immigration from Nippon increased, burst forth in a raging flood in 1905. Alive with hysteria, the California legislature unanimously called for Japanese exclusion, boycotts of Japanese businesses began, and the San Francisco School Board ordered the segregation of Asiatic pupils. The fires of anti-Oriental hatred cast at least a pale reflection on European outsiders. California newspaper editorials excoriating the Japanese had a way of broadening into appeals to preserve America for Americans. The Asiatic Exclusion League, an organization formed in 1905 which soon claimed over one hundred thousand members, resolved that *all aliens* should be disarmed in order to prevent insurrection. Other anti-Japanese agitators on the West Coast trembled at the dangerously inferior blood pouring across the Atlantic from southern Europe as well as across the Pacific. Far Western Congressmen repeatedly tried to attach anti-Japanese provisions to general immigration measures, and in doing so they became one of the foremost blocs in the whole restrictionist movement. Occasionally a representative of the West Coast might regret that the literacy test was not more directly a test of blood and race, but by 1912 not a single member of Congress from the eight westernmost states voted against the literacy proviso.[16]

The threat of the "Yellow Peril" to white America touched a responsive chord in the South, the only other section of the country which sympathized quickly and widely with California's war against the Japanese.[17] Southerners also sensed the general, nativist significance of the Japanese issue, as the comments of Underwood and Simmons on the semi-Asiatic ancestry of southeastern Europe suggested. Fundamentally, however, the South's hostility to the new immigration reflected its own long-standing "ethnophobia"; the Japanese were settling in a section of the country so remote from the South that their presence could not concern it vitally. At bottom it was the Negro issue that stirred southern anxieties about European and Asiatic immigrants alike. For decades the South, above all other regions, had cherished race-feelings in order to keep the white man irrevocably superior to the black. Now, Dixie spokesmen warned time and again that one race problem was bad enough without further endangering white supremacy through immigration. In 1912 southern Senators voted 16 to 1 for the literacy test; southern Representatives 68 to 5.[18] And in both houses they supplied the driving force behind the measure.

The extension of southern and western race-feelings to include European immigrants seems, therefore, a simple and "natural" development as long as one does not ask why it occurred when it did. Both sections had nourished a pride of race for a very long time; yet only in the twentieth century did these regional patterns of white supremacy breed a related attack on the European newcomers. If residents of the Pacific Coast discovered a Japanese menace only after 1900, they had fought another Oriental people, the Chinese, ever since the 1850's. It is significant that the anti-Chinese movement in the Far West in the late nineteenth century had not contributed directly to other anti-foreign phobias. Although the basic Chinese exclusion law was enacted in 1882, the year of the first general immigration law, the Congress that passed the two measures sensed no connection between them. At no time in the nineteenth century did immigration restrictionists argue that Chinese exclusion set a logical precedent for their own proposals. The two issues seemed so different that foreign-born whites felt no embarrassment in leading the anti-Chinese crusade, while San Francisco's most bitterly anti-European nativists held entirely aloof from the war on the Oriental.[19]

The nativist eruption in the South presents a still more difficult puzzle, for the Negro—unlike the Japanese on the West Coast—had always been there, and his presence never ceased to trouble the southern mind. Yet southern views on immigration underwent an astonishing revolution in the early twentieth century. Like the West, the South had shared in the nation-wide nativism of the mid-nineties, but what panic it felt then took a largely anti-radical and jingoist form. Southern spokesmen in the late nineteenth century seldom attacked immigrants in terms of race, and some invoked the unity of "the great Caucasian race" in resisting immigration restriction. Moreover, economic interests kept every kind of nativism so well in check that in January 1898, southern Senators voted 15 to 3 against the literacy test, supplying more than half the opposition to it.[20] A decade later the South was becoming the nativist section par excellence, its spokesmen soon to be prominent in every anti-foreign movement.

Undoubtedly one reason for the blossoming of these long encysted race-feelings lay in the character of the Europeans who were now arriving. The predominance of new over old immigration—a trend which was clearly appreciated in the early 1890's only in the Northeast—was now becoming apparent to Americans in every part of the country. Everywhere the thought of European immigration now suggested strange images of Mediterranean, Slavic, and Jewish types, rather than the familiar German, Irishman, or Scandinavian. The new groups did, on the whole, have an exotic look about them for ethnological as well as cultural reasons, and in sections with a highly developed race consciousness their whiteness was easily open to question. "The color of thousands of them," warned Congressman Thomas Abercrombie of Alabama, "differs materially from that of the Anglo-Saxon." [21]

Along with a general realization that the whole stream of immigration was changing, southerners and westerners were beginning to see a substantial number of the newcomers with their own eyes. In the early twentieth century a good many southern and eastern Europeans worked their way westward to the Pacific Coast. By 1907 they formed, together with the Mexicans and Asiatics, the great majority of the general construction workers and railway section hands. They provided a very large part of the common labor in mills and fisheries, while the Italians and Portuguese aroused sharp jealousy by duplicating the success of the Japanese in intensive truck farming. During the decade the total number of new immigrants in the Far West more than tripled.[22] At the same time a relatively less important but not insignificant stream was seeping into the South. Outside of New Orleans and a few adjacent parishes, the South had known hardly any new immigrants until the very end of the nineteenth century. Then they became somewhat more common: Italian farmhands and railroad workers, eastern European shopkeepers and miners, scattered widely enough to be noticeable. While the South's small population of northern European birth declined between 1900 and 1910, the number of southern and eastern Europeans more than doubled.[23] Both the southward and westward movements were only trickles compared to the great tide pouring into the North; the whole area beyond the Rockies and below the Mason and Dixon Line had only half as many new immigrants as did New York City. But sections deeply sensitive to complexion and cast of features readily detected a swarthy face.

In the South, the newcomer's "in-betweenness" seemed a double threat. He might endanger not only the purity of the white race but also its solidarity. In other words, the foreigners, partly because of their low cultural and social status, more largely because they had no background of southern traditions and values, might relax the pattern of white supremacy. Particularly the Italians, who sometimes worked beside the blacks on large plantations, seemed to lack a properly inflexible spirit. In the little town of Tallulah, Louisiana, for example, the coming of five Sicilian storekeepers disturbed the native whites because the Italians dealt mainly with the Negroes and associated with them nearly on terms of equality. They violated the white man's code. In a few years a quarrel over a goat resulted in the lynching of all five. In another locality the whites tried to keep the color line sharp and clear by barring Italian children from the white schools.[24] Meanwhile the Negroes too distrusted the "Third Force" entering the southern racial world, for the newcomers did their work and sometimes came as their competitors. Booker T. Washington echoed the sentiments of white nativists by warning that southern European immigration might create "a racial problem in the South more difficult and more dangerous than that which is caused by the presence of the Negro."[25]

To explain the nativistic thrust of southern and western race-feelings solely in terms of a change in immigrant types is, however, to tell only half of the story. If we conclude that the penetration of the new immigration into the South and West automatically activated the color phobias of those areas, we do little justice to the distinctive essence of all nativisms. In every guise, the nativist stood always as a nationalist in a defensive posture. He chose a *foreign* adversary, and defined him, in terms of a conception of the nation's most precious and precarious attributes. Along with the social impact of the new immigration, the South and the Far West in the early twentieth century were also tingling with the ideological stimulus of a new nationalism. Perhaps the kind of nationalism that flourished in the wake of the Spanish-American War did as much as anything else to enable the guardians of white supremacy to discharge their feelings on the new foreign groups.

Ordinarily, the almost instinctive pride and arrogance with which white men met black and yellow and red men in North America bore little relation to a nationalist spirit. The pattern of white supremacy crystallized long before the birth of American nationalism, and in the nineteenth century the latter, despite its gradual assimilation of race-ideas, remained largely detached from primitive race-feelings. The exaltation of white supremacy in the antebellum South had actually served to weaken national loyalty; and California's anti-Chinese hysteria had presented itself largely as a defense of "white civilization," not as an explicitly nationalist movement.[26] At the turn of the century, however, the Anglo-Saxon idea of American nationality was so widely popularized that the racial egoisms of South and West could easily permeate a nationalism ideologically adapted to receive them. The expansion of the Anglo-Saxon tradition at the turn of the century, while preparing the way toward racism among northern intellectuals, also opened a wider field for the popular hatreds at the grass roots of the South and West.

Every section of the country shared in the jubilant Anglo-Saxonism touched off by the victories of 1898. The South, though somewhat less enthusiastic about a colonial policy than other parts of the United States, found the ideological by-products of the new departure deeply satisfying. The imperialist theory of the superiority of the Anglo-Saxons seemed to southerners to vindicate their own regional pattern. White supremacy was becoming, in Professor C. Vann Woodward's phrase, the American Way. It was perhaps not entirely coincidental that the period of overseas expansion coincided with a general tightening of race lines within the South through disfranchisement and sterner segregation laws.[27] Moreover, the Spanish-American War itself set the South firmly in the midstream of American nationalism. As long as the bitter heritage of disunion dominated southern thought—and much sectional hatred persisted through the 1870's and 1880's—nearly all of the animus against outsiders centered on the northern Yankee. The War of 1898 completed a stage in sectional reconciliation by turning the martial ardor of the Confederate tradition into a patriotic crusade, by linking all parts of the country in a common purpose, and by giving the South an opportunity to demonstrate a passionate national loyalty.[28] Relatively secure now in its own acceptance in the Union, the South could join wholeheartedly in other crusades for national homogeneity, especially when racial sentiment synchronized with nationalism. Southerners (like New Englanders) had been proud of their Anglo-Saxon ancestry since ante-bellum days; in the twentieth century they found it easy to boast that this inheritance, buttressed by the code of white supremacy, made the South the real bastion of true Americanism. The testimony of Congressman Martin Dies, Sr., of Texas, before a House committee is a fair illustration of how the southern assault on the new immigration blended race-feelings with the ideas of Anglo-Saxon nationalism.

> MR. DIES. As the little turtle, when the egg hatches on the sea shore instinctively makes for the water, so these beaten races of earth instinctively turn to the head of the government as the great father . . . I would quarantine this Nation against people of any government in Europe incapable of self-government for any reason, as I would against the bubonic plague. . . . I will admit the old immigration of the English, Irish, Germans, Scandinavians, and Swedes, the light-haired, blue-eyed Anglo-Saxons, or Celts—I mean the nations I have enumerated—
>
> THE CHAIRMAN. Pure Caucasians?
>
> MR. DIES. Yes; they were great in their own country and great in our country.[29]

Apparently a somewhat similar process took place on the Pacific Coast, local race-feelings blending with nationalism, though usually in a milder and less explicit way. In both sections imperialism created a congenial atmosphere for nationalizing the spirit of white supremacy. Moreover, there were special incentives in the Far West for the offensive spirit of imperialism to lapse into a defensive nativism. Due to its geographical location, this region undoubtedly felt more keenly than other parts of the country the frustrations and difficulties to which the expansionist policy of 1898 soon led. In the flush of confidence at the turn of the century many westerners looked forward to vistas of enterprise and adventure in the Orient. But instead of substantial benefits the "large policy" bore bitter fruit of international rivalry and insecurity. Japan's stunning victories over the ponderous Russian war machine in 1904-05 placed her in a position to threaten America's new stakes in the Far East. As a result the West Coast felt a double sense of crisis: added to an internal fear of Japanese blood was an external fear of Japanese power. One exacerbated the other. From 1905 on, war scares recurrently agitated the Pacific states, and California nativists commonly looked upon Japanese immigration as a quasi-military invasion of soldiers and spies.[30] Consequently western race-feelings gained a nationalistic dimension not only from the philosophy of imperialism but also from the international discord that expansion engendered.

Homer Lea, the leading theoretician of the Yellow Peril, summed up the nationalist aspects of western nativism in their most naked and pretentious form. Lea, a frail, wizened Californian who worshiped power and spent most of his life playing at war, argued that nations flourish only through expansion and conquest. He believed implicitly in the mission of the Anglo-Saxon to rule the world, but in Japan he feared that America had met a race-enemy which was its match in militancy. In 1909 his most influential book, *The Valor of Ignorance*, worked out in startling detail a prediction of Japanese military occupation of the West Coast. The widening stream of European immigration, Lea warned, is augmenting the Japanese danger by sapping America's racial strength and unity.[31]

It remained, however, for a novelist to translate this creed into a frontal assault on the new immigration and to disseminate it far and wide. Jack London, the West Coast's most popular writer, came gradually to a fully nativistic position via an ingrained sense of white supremacy and an extensive education in imperialistic race-thinking. As a roustabout on the San Francisco waterfront he learned the white man's arrogance in boyhood. By 1900 he was reveling in the Anglo-Saxons' destiny to seize the earth for themselves. As a correspondent in the Russo-Japanese War he felt less assurance, turning from racial braggadocio to warnings about the Yellow Peril.[32] Finally, around 1913, London wrote in rapid succession two novels which showed "the dark-pigmented things, the half-castes, the mongrel-bloods" of southern and eastern Europe swamping the blond, master race in America. In both books the protagonists saw visions of their ancestors roving westward in beaked ships and winged helmets. In one, the heroine's name was Saxon.[33]

Both Lea and London echoed the biological pessimism—the appeal to iron laws of heredity, the morbid speculations on racial defeat—which eastern nativist intellectuals were adding to the Anglo-Saxon tradition in the early twentieth century. Both wrote for a nation-wide audience, and both indicate that by 1910 the sophisticated theories of the patrician East were beginning to intermingle with the popular nativisms of the West and South. By no means was the exchange all in one direction. If new doctrines spread gradually beyond an eastern elite, the mass sentiments of the West and South found an increasingly sympathetic response in the rest of the country. No part of the United States was immune to the spirit of white supremacy; in all sections native-born and northern European laborers called themselves "white men" to distinguish themselves from the southern Europeans whom they worked beside.[34] And everywhere Anglo-Saxon nationalism, bereft of the exhilarating prospect of continued overseas expansion, was reverting to the defensive.

To this nation-wide trend the primitive race-feelings emanating from the South and Far West gave a constant spur. The East and Midwest, although inclined to depreciate anti-Japanese hysteria, could not entirely escape the influence of the Yellow Peril agitation and its broad racial implications. After 1908, for example, the national Socialist party abandoned a cosmopolitan immigration policy under the racist urgings of one of its western leaders.[35] Anti-Negro feeling radiated northward more easily than anti-Oriental feeling spread eastward. In northern attitudes toward Negroes a derogatory trend, evident since Reconstruction, sharpened during the 1900's under the pressure of an increasing Negro influx; and a series of race riots bloodied the streets of the Midwest.[36] All this affected the image of the new immigration. As early as 1905 the *Outlook* asked if immigration might "so add to the serious race problems we already have that it will endanger the success of America's task." In every section, the Negro, the Oriental, and the southern European appeared more and more in a common light.[37]

The best single index to the nation-wide growth of Anglo-Saxon nativism was the hardiest, most vigorous of the nativist fraternal orders, the Junior Order United American Mechanics. Its career mirrored the history of popular xenophobia. Largely anti-Catholic during its formative years before the Civil War, the

Junior Order's emphasis shifted to anti-radicalism in the 1880's and 1890's. At the turn of the century the order declined in size and energy; then another successful period set in. Membership rose from 147,000 in 1904 to 224,000 in 1914. Significantly, much of the growth seems to have come from expansion into the South and West.[38] The order took a very active part in the restrictionist campaign of 1906 and continued to agitate throughout the period. While anti-Catholicism persisted as a distinctly subsidiary part of the order's program, its former concentration on foreign radicals yielded to a primary fear of foreign races. Indeed, the organization echoed almost every theme in the racial polyphony. Its national chairman worried lest southern European immigrants should intermarry with Negroes, as in Latin America. The order's California council affiliated with the Asiatic Exclusion League and announced that southern Europeans were semi-Mongolian. The national chaplain told a House committee quite simply that he wanted "the kind to come from which we came . . . I glory in my kinship. My father, on one side, was a German, my father upon the other was an Englishman. . . . That is the kind we want and can absorb. . . . They belonged to that independent race . . . who . . . came with the idea already imbedded in their hearts and minds of the beauties of self-government." [39]

Yet one should not overemphasize the strength of this nationwide trend. Although racial nativism tugged at men everywhere in the United States, during the prewar years it never established a really firm grip on public opinion outside of the South and the West Coast. Those were its strongholds; the aroused and pervasive race-feeling of those areas touched the East and Midwest only to a limited degree. A spirit of confidence, sustained by the triumphant march of progressive reform, remained widespread throughout the era, and in the Northeast the regnant values of progressivism tended to inhibit racial anxieties. As long as northeastern progressives took to heart their optimistic faith in environmental reform, they held the Anglo-Saxon tradition in check. But this was not true of the South or of the Far West. There, without anguish and with no apparent sense of inconsistency, reform-thinking accommodated itself to race-thinking; progressivism was for white men only. No prominent easterner exhibited such wildly contradictory attitudes as Jack London, a radical champion of social justice for exploited and submerged classes who was forever glorifying the ruthlessness of supermen and master races.[40]

Meanwhile the southern brand of progressivism actually reinforced the racial reaction. Concerted opposition to immigration crystallized in the South about 1905, in the form of a counterattack against the large landlords and business interests then engaged in a promotional campaign for European manpower. To many the power of organized wealth seemed to be undoing the South's long struggle to maintain race purity.[41] Much of the leadership in fighting the immigration promoters came from the fast-growing Farmers' Union, the largest farmer organization in the South, which leveled a fierce propaganda barrage at the state immigration bureaus and at the whole influx from southeastern Europe and Asia.[42] In South Carolina, Cole Blease, idol of the cotton mill operatives, seized upon the issue in 1908. The next year the state abolished its immigration bureau and prohibited its officials from encouraging immigration in any way. Several other states reduced the activities of their agencies, and by 1910 the promotional drive was moribund, the victim of a progressivism charged with racial nativism.[43]

Anti-Radical and Anti-Catholic Revivals

During the early twentieth century anti-radicalism and anti-Catholicism languished everywhere in the United States. Except for a flurry at the time of McKinley's assassination, the anti-radical tradition was dormant through the whole decade of the 1900's.[44] Anti-Catholicism fared worse yet; even within the Junior Order United American Mechanics it faded into the background. Undoubtedly the progressive mood, along with all of the other factors which renewed national confidence, helped to check these xenophobias. A people with great expectations of building a better society could perhaps afford a certain nonchalance toward radical critics of the present one; and a crusade clearly fixed on close-at-hand symbols of economic privilege pointed away from shadowy religious targets.

At least such was the case when the progressive impulse was fresh and young. In the last years of the prewar era, when reforms seemed more abundant and reformers more ebullient than ever, the specters of foreign revolution and of popish despotism once more grew visible on the American scene. They reappeared more slowly than Anglo-Saxon nativism, and neither of these older anti-foreign traditions won the general vogue race-thinking now enjoyed. But the seemingly unpropitious circumstances under which anti-radicalism and anti-Catholicism came to life make their renewal a subject of moment. Unlike racial nativism, which had started up from factors largely independent of the prevailing progressive faith, the anti-radical and anti-Catholic revivals after 1910 were direct outgrowths of the ongoing currents of social protest. In the end, the ferment of reform revived anxieties which it had initially helped to repress.

The great underlying change running through the Progressive period was one of tempo. Year by year the innovating spirit whirled faster and faster, overrunning old objectives, generating new schemes for reform, raising men's level of expectation ever higher, broadening into a force that stirred every nook and cranny of American life. By 1910 the excited talk of reformers about "social democracy," breaking the "money trust," shackling the judiciary, and emancipating the "new woman" suggested that a reconstruction of some of the country's major institutions, from the banking system to the home, lay in the offing.

As progressivism moved from first successes toward grander visions, it showed signs of accumulating stress. On the right, conservative opposition tightened. The Republican party was dividing by 1910, and President Taft, once regarded as a loyal standard-bearer by reformers, now assailed them for exciting a class spirit. Within the broad movement of liberal opinion intellectuals were discovering divergent trends and weighing distinctions between the older American freedom and a planned society. On the left, an astonishing number of people were growing impatient with all the progressive promises. Longings too vast for any kind of moderate leadership to fulfill played into the hands of a new type of southern demagogue, like Cole Blease, or in other areas strengthened the Socialist party. In 1910 the Socialists elected their first mayors and congressmen; two years later the party polled the highest percentage of a Presidential vote it would ever receive. Meanwhile the most militant radicalism crackled in the West, where lumberjacks and harvest hands joined the Industrial Workers of the World and brandished the strike as a revolutionary weapon.

Here were conditions faintly reminiscent of those in the 1880's. Symptoms of a head-on clash between capital and labor, a sense of increasing class conflict, dissatisfactions blurring immediate objectives and conjuring up vaguer issues: all these tugged again at the bonds of social unity. To be sure, the profound anxieties of the earlier period were muted by the continuing vitality of the progressive impulse. But some who found the pace of change too rapid, and others for whom it was too slow, drifted uneasily toward the psychology of the late nineteenth century, with its fears for the survival of the social order, with its compensatory nationalisms.

It was among men who deeply distrusted the whole current of innovation that anti-radical nativism reawakened after 1910. A generation earlier the dread of an approaching social catastrophe had touched a wider range of opinion, liberal as well as conservative. In the progressive era, when even the Socialist party was winning a certain respectability, few except the most orthodox took to heart the peril of revolution. Among them, however, labor militancy again inspired dismay: in place of the half-forgotten anarchists the Industrial Workers of the World came into view. What if the Wobblies were an essentially indigenous group? They swept a good many immigrant workers into their rough-and-tumble ranks, and they were "un-American" enough to preach class war.

In the Pacific Northwest a chunky hard-faced newspaper editor vaulted into national politics by mobilizing nativistic opposition to the I.W.W. Albert Johnson published a small daily at Gray's Harbor, the lumbering center of southwestern Washington. Early in 1912, when local businessmen put him forward as a standpat Republican candidate for Congress, he was known largely as a booster, a jolly after-dinner speaker at commercial clubs, and a foe of conservation. Then an I.W.W.-led strike of the lumber mills paralyzed the local economy. Johnson made a state-wide reputation by leading an armed citizens' movement which broke the strike, ran the leaders out of town, secured the recall of the mayor, and tried to punish the foreign laborers who obeyed the strike call by announcing that preference in re-employment would be given to native Americans. The peppery editor turned his own Congressional campaign into a holy war against radicalism and for immigration restriction, raging at the I.W.W. as a flag-hating foreign conspiracy out to wreck the country.[45] He defeated the incumbent, who ran as a Progressive, and carried his crusade to Congress, where he soon alienated other restrictionists by the embarrassing violence of his proposals.[46]

The same year the I.W.W. burst into the East, where it organized the new immigrant workers in textile mills. Cruelly exploited by employers and rejected by the A.F.L., the unskilled immigrants turned temporarily to the "One Big Union" where all workers were on an equal footing. A bitter but victorious I.W.W. strike at Lawrence, Massachusetts, involving twenty-two thousand workers of sixteen nationalities, signaled the new foreign threat. This thunder on the left awakened conservative alarm in the East. Convinced that all radical experiments endangered "the solidarity of the Nation," organs such as the New York *Evening Sun* were equally sure that "the first considerable development of an actually revolutionary spirit comes today, and comes . . . among the un-American immigrants from Southern Europe." In the next few years anti-radical nativism formed a minor but persistent undercurrent in middle-class thinking.[47]

While the prevailing, progressive spirit confined anti-radicalism to right-wing groups, anti-Catholicism reappeared in an entirely different quarter. About the same time that foreign revolutionists were beginning to excite conservative nativists, a dread of foreign Romanists came to life on the nativist left. Both fears emerged out of the increasing restlessness of the day: one as a reaction against it, the other as a perverse expression of it.

The new religious xenophobia contained all of the traditional ideological ingredients: ex-priests lecturing on the moral iniquities of confessional and convent; warnings about Catholic political conspiracies; widespread rumors that the faithful were drilling nightly in church basements in preparation for an armed uprising.[48] More remarkable were the progressive sympathies and aspirations that often shone through the hatred. To be sure, Protestant nativism had long had a certain liberal flavor, in contrast to the conservative bias implicit in anti-radical nativism. Since the Enlightenment, Americans had tended to look upon the Pope as a reactionary despot, hostile to liberty and progress alike. One could always point to the Inquisition or the Syllabus of Errors, and more than once native reformers balked by the opposition of Irish immigrants had moved easily into an anti-Catholic crusade.[49]

The new religious xenophobia in the years after 1910, while building on the historic identification of popery with tyranny, went significantly further. It frequently displayed a subdued but unmistakably progressive response to social problems; its principal spokesmen hinted that the Pope stood in the way of all social improvement; and there is reason to suspect that much of the energy behind the movement came from a displacement or distortion of anti-monopolistic sentiment. Whereas, in the days of the American Protective Association, anti-Catholic agitators betrayed a horror of revolt as well as reaction, their counterparts in the 1910's railed largely at reaction. The former approach suggested dissatisfactions not yet disciplined by the hard immediacies of reform. The latter suggested an overflow of discontents which reform *had* canalized. It is hard to explain the rebirth of anti-Catholic ferment except as an outlet for expectations which progressivism raised and then failed to fulfill.

A frustrated southern radical, a man of the people who had battled for economic democracy since 1890, started the new crusade against Rome. Tom Watson led the hosts of Populism in the nineties and spurred Georgia progressives in the mid-1900's. His feverish campaigns brought little permanent benefit to the farmers he loved, and by 1910 his prestige was clearly waning, though he still commanded a devoted following through his personal organ, *Watson's Magazine*. Without abandoning entirely his old agitation against corporate privilege, Watson shifted to a primary attack on the Catholic peril. A trivial but much publicized incident apparently precipitated his change of course. The Pope cancelled a scheduled interview with the former vice-president of the United States, Charles W. Fairbanks, because Fairbanks had first visited a group of Methodist missionaries in Italy. A defense of the Pope's conduct in the Hearst press sent Watson into a rage. He decided to expose the Catholic plot against democracy, America and the home.[50] Soon the issue became a consuming passion with Watson, the immigrants entering indirectly as the agents of Rome.

"There is a foreign foe at our gates," he thundered, "and that foe is confidently expecting the spies within to unlock the portals. Those domestic traitors are the voracious Trusts, the Roman Catholic priesthood . . . the Knights of Columbus. . . ." His propaganda followed the traditional anti-Catholic line so closely that it relied on tracts written eighty years before, but there were progressive undertones as well.[51]

Another wayward reformer established a much more successful nativist publication the year after Watson's conversion. In Aurora, Missouri, a small town in the Ozark highlands with a declining population, Wilbur Franklin Phelps founded in 1911 a national "patriotic" weekly called *The Menace*. Phelps, a country editor who had worked up from the printer's trade and who always prided himself on his progressive outlook, was already publishing the local Aurora newspaper. Soon *The Menace* completely overshadowed it. In a year circulation rose to 120,000, in two years to over five hundred thousand, in three years to a million. Along with the paper grew a large publishing plant which employed 135 people, did a rousing mail-order business printing anti-Catholic books, and arranged engagements for anti-Catholic lecturers.[52]

Nothing interested *The Menace* very much except a Roman one. It alleged, for example, that the Vatican was now ordering subversive Italian immigrants to the United States instead of Irish, having learned that the Irish became Americanized too quickly. The paper's most notorious sally was against the Knights of Columbus, who, according to an oath *The Menace* helped to publicize, pledged their fourth degree members to a war of extermination and mutilation against all heretics.[53] At the same time the paper wore a progressive air. It said that the Catholic Church was trying to obstruct all progressive legislation and was combining with big business to break the labor unions; it showed a vague, guarded sympathy with the Socialists; and it warned all reformers that no progressive development of democracy could succeed unless everyone united to preserve America's free institutions against the common foe.[54]

Phelps' paper shared with *Watson's Magazine* a second characteristic that defines the sources of the new religious nativism. Both were published in country towns with a population of four thousand or less. So also were a number of other nativistic sheets that sprang up in their wake. From 1912 through 1914 a score of less successful imitators appeared, often in such unlikely communities as Mankato, Minnesota, Anderson, Indiana, Magnolia, Arkansas, or Moravian Falls, North Carolina. Nearly every important urban newspaper denounced the spirit these rustic journalists represented. Anti-Catholic nationalism found some city support, notably among Protestant railroad employees who had taken a prominent part in the A.P.A. and who still felt threatened by their Irish fellow workers. Nevertheless, the broad base—as the New York *Times* pointed out—now lay in rural areas.[55]

This inverted the structure of former anti-Catholic movements and marked a historic transition in the character of Protestant nativism. During the nineteenth century the tradition drew its main strength from the larger towns and cities where Catholics were actually settling.[56] Even in the 1890's, when the excitement invaded the midwestern countryside in a grotesquely jingoistic form, anti-Catholic xenophobia remained primarily an urban movement. But in the twentieth century it re-emerged most actively in rural America, where adherents of the hated faith were relatively few.

This shift tied in with a trend already under way in the late nineteenth century: the extrusion of religious nativism from the citadels of middle-class culture. Among educated urban groups, nationalism, like almost everything else, was gradually secularized. Penetrating down the social scale, the secular outlook softened religious frictions, turned aggressive impulses to other adversaries, and forced each successive wave of anti-Catholic hysteria farther from the centers of cultivated society. What had issued from Boston, New York, and Philadelphia in the 1840's radiated from the smaller cities of the Middle West in the 1880's and finally found its most valiant champions among the hicks and hillbillies.

They, at least, had never abandoned the old-time religion. In fact they were beginning in the years after 1910 to pass over to the offensive against the diluted doctrines and moral laxity of their urban brethren. The rise of a militant rural fundamentalism coincided with the upsurge of rural nativism. Perhaps the two came partly from a common need, aggressive fundamentalism ministering to the same unfulfilled urges that sent rural Protestants crusading against popery. At any rate the reassertion of the straight Gospel truth undoubtedly quickened the rural war on Rome. In large parts of the South, Catholics were so uncommon that nativists found popular sentiment harder to rouse than in the Midwest, but in both areas the movement was definitely taking hold. In both, barnstorming evangelists lent an apocalyptic fury to the assault; and the devout could often be seen going to church with the Bible in one hand and *The Menace* in the other.[57]

At the same time this anti-Catholic propaganda often lacked genuine religious feeling.[58] A political and social emphasis connected much of it so directly with an unsatisfied progressivism that one wonders if a tendency to lose faith in the pattern of reform did not affect rural groups in some special way. The progressive movement did not belong to rural America, as the agrarian crusades of the late nineteenth century had. Farmers joined it readily enough and hoped for much from it, but city folk controlled it, and city folk could best appreciate the substantial victories it achieved. Big business was a long way off from many country people. Sometimes it was hard for them to tell whether the trusts or some grander power was really thwarting them.[59]

The significance of both anti-Catholic and anti-radical nativism in the late Progressive period lies in their origins, not in their achievements. Neither reached far enough to have an important impact at the time. The No-Popery tradition, though strong in propaganda outlets, suffered particularly from inadequate organization. As always, Protestant nativists needed the striking power of political secret societies. Several such groups cropped up: the Guardians of Liberty in 1911, and some time later the Covenanters (who covenanted to have no dealings with Catholics) and the Knights of Luther.[60] None, however, made much impression, perhaps partly because of ineffective leadership. The most important body, the Guardians of Liberty, was formed by several retired army and navy officers and up-state New York civic leaders of respectable antecedents. The former United States Chief of Staff, General Nelson A. Miles, became the Chief Guardian. The Guardians aimed primarily at defeating any political candidate "who owns superior temporal allegiance to any power above his obligation to . . . the United States." Initially their principles also included opposition to corporate monopolies. But the Guardians insisted on agitating in a genteel way, and at least until 1914 they remained a negligible influence.[61]

1914: Summit of Prewar Nativism

By this time, corrosion of the confidence in unity and homogeneity that America had regained at the turn of the century was well advanced. All of the anti-foreign and anti-Catholic traditions, though they remained largely separate from one another, were gaining momentum, and each was firmly grounded on international or internal problems which a generation of progressives had failed to solve. In 1914 nativism displayed symptoms of hysteria and violence that had been rare or nonexistent since the 1890's. The war then beginning in Europe played no part in these anxieties; they reflected domestic conditions. As if to complete the pattern of peacetime xenophobia, the economy slid from a recession in 1913 into a depression the next year. Not a major depression, perhaps, but a strain on prices and employment sufficient to embitter existing animosities.

Most obviously the depression preyed on the nativistic susceptibilities of workingmen, who now coveted the inferior jobs the immigrants held. "I see employment furnished to foreigners every day at good pay where Americans are not wanted," wrote a down-and-out descendant of colonial stock. "I have reached the limit, I have been out of work until I can stand it no longer." [62] In Arizona the State Federation of Labor, supported by the miners, secured as an initiative measure a law requiring all employers of more than five workers to recruit at least 80 per cent of their labor force from American citizens. As a general and drastic restriction on the employment of foreigners in private industry, the law was unprecedented, and the United States Supreme Court soon declared it in violation of the Fourteenth Amendment. On the other hand, the Supreme Court was adjusting itself to milder discriminatory statutes. In the 1890's it had invoked the Fourteenth Amendment against laws excluding aliens from employment on public works. But now the Supreme Court upheld a New York statute of that nature when the Bricklayers' Union demanded its enforcement against unnaturalized Italians engaged in building the New York subways. In effect the Justices endorsed the discharge of the Italians, in conformity with the law, on the ground that the state in selecting its employees should have the same freedom that private employers enjoy—the freedom to discriminate against any group.[63]

While private and public discrimination against immigrant work-men increased, the anti-Catholic movement also pushed ahead dur-ing the hard times of 1914 and early 1915. The circulation of *The Menace* grew by leaps and bounds, reaching a high point of 1,507,923 in April 1915. In addition to the stimulus of economic tensions, the paper benefited considerably from Catholic efforts to suppress it by securing its exclusion from the mails.[64] Meanwhile anti-Catholic proposals were coming under discussion in several state legislatures. Arkansas and Missouri, for example, considered an official inspection of sectarian hospitals and convents; Texas meditated public supervision of parochial schools.[65]

Furthermore, for the first time since 1894, religious xenophobia became a substantial factor in the 1914 elections in some areas, notably in the New York gubernatorial campaign. In that state William Sulzer, a flashy, insincere progressive who had been re-moved as Democratic Governor the year before on proof of cor-ruption, was seeking popular vindication. The Democratic candi-date was Martin Glynn, a Catholic supported by the Tammany forces that had engineered Sulzer's impeachment. After Sulzer failed narrowly in an attempt to seize control of the collapsing Progressive party, he organized his own, the American party, claimed that the Tammany bosses had framed him, and exploited all of the anti-Catholic commonplaces as openly as he dared. The Guardians of Liberty, now a formidable force in up-state areas, turned their back on the tarnished ex-Governor and endorsed the Republican candidate as the surest way to defeat Glynn. Despite this division in the anti-Catholic vote, Sulzer showed remarkable strength in several up-state counties. Some staunchly Republican rural districts capitulated to him almost en masse.[66]

Elsewhere the year of depression brought back another phe-nomenon of the nineties. Flashes of lawless fury seared relations between old and new Americans. In the mining country of south-ern Illinois, long a dark and bloody ground which was now ac-quiring a very large foreign population, a street brawl resulted in the death of one Italian and two native Americans. The only sur-vivor, an Italian, was promptly lynched under circumstances which suggested collusion on the part of the local mayor. A few months later, in another mining town, a mob wrenched an Italian from jail and hanged him; he had been arrested on the faintest suspicion of complicity in an attempt to assassinate a mine superintendent.[67] The most dramatic incident occurred in Georgia, where economic resentment, frustrated progressivism, and race consciousness combined to produce a classic case of lynch law. The victim this time was not a poor Italian worker but a well-to-do Jewish employer.

Leo Frank, the son of a wealthy New York merchant, managed an Atlanta pencil factory which employed female labor at low wages. When one of the factory girls, Mary Phagan, was found murdered on the premises, unsubstantiated rumors of sexual perversion helped to fix suspicion on Frank. Most aroused were the working classes, who saw in Frank a symbol of the northern capitalist exploiting southern womanhood. Although he was convicted in frantic haste, the carpenter, the blacksmith, the millhand, and the motorman kept saying, "He will never hang. He's rich and Mary Phagan has no friends." According to later reports, overt anti-Semitic sentiment played little part at this initial stage.[68]

All through 1914, evidence of the flimsiness of the case against Frank accumulated. Wealthy northern Jews financed a determined legal battle for a new trial. Leading Georgia newspapers and prominent Atlanta clergymen supported the appeal for justice. This shift in cultivated opinion, together with mounting "outside interference," only inflamed the masses.[69] Hatred of organized wealth reaching into Georgia from outside became a hatred of Jewish wealth. From one end of the state to the other the story went: "The Jews have said that no Jew has ever been hanged and that none ever will be." Tom Watson threw himself into the fray, with enormous effect. The hostility to corporate privilege which he was already shunting toward the Pope had found a closer, more popular target in Leo Frank, and by the end of the year, Watson's tirades against the attempt of "Big Money" to invade and subvert the Georgia courts were growing increasingly anti-Semitic.[70]

Finally all the fears of the populace seemed confirmed; the victim was almost literally snatched from the scaffold when the Governor at the last minute commuted his sentence to life imprisonment. Most of the urban press in Georgia praised or defended the Governor's action; the bulk of the population plunged into hysteria. Boycotts of Jewish merchants began; throughout the state nightly mass meetings howled for retribution; at the murdered girl's grave the Knights of Mary Phagan pledged themselves never to rest until the crime was avenged; and Tom Watson now saw the hand of a world-wide "Invisible Power." [71]

The dénouement was practically inevitable. A band of citizens from Mary Phagan's home town took Leo Frank from the state prison, carried him 175 miles across the state, and butchered him almost in their own back yards. This ended the affair but not its consequences. In the last stages of the Frank Case, anti-Semitism regained the fiercely nationalistic twist it had acquired briefly in the nineties; and it assumed also an explicitly racial tone. About the time of the lynching Tom Watson marked this ideological advance:

> It is a peculiar and portentious [*sic*] thing, that one race of men
> —*and one, only*,—should be able to convulse the world, by a
> system of newspaper *agitation and suppression*, when a member
> of that race is convicted of a capital crime against another race.
> . . . From all over the world, the Children of Israel are flocking
> to this country, and plans are on foot to move them from Europe
> *en masse* . . . to empty upon our shores the very scum and
> dregs of the *Parasite Race*.[72]

Something bigger than a local episode was in the air, something nourished by all the forces of racial nationalism, distorted progressivism, and economic decline. Before the Frank Case attracted nation-wide attention, a leaflet circulated in the streets of San Francisco. "Mr. White American," it warned, "if you have any race pride or patriotism, you will organize for the protection of your race." [73] San Franciscans had read words like that directed against the Orientals for a long time. But this leaflet was against the Negroes—and the Jews.

The Failure of Restriction

Like every other manifestation of nativism, the immigration restriction movement gathered strength year by year through the late Progressive period. Its points of special intensity rested where they had in 1905-1907: the South, the Far West, the native-born working class, and the patrician intellectuals. It also received general support in public opinion, and whenever restriction came to a vote in Congress it rolled up overwhelming majorities. The most remarkable aspect of the movement was its repeated failure; it accomplished nothing. Each Congress confronted a flurry of immigration bills. Not one of them of any consequence became law for a decade after the essentially anti-restrictionist measure of 1907. There are few better examples of the toughness and conservatism of American institutions than this steady persistence of a traditional immigration policy in the face of widespread demands for change.

In this case, as in many others, the status quo survived blow after blow for two related reasons. Despite the militancy of certain groups, the immigration issue was not yet deeply felt throughout the country as a whole. Restriction sentiment, though general, was not generally intense; a substantial part of the American population seemed to regard the question as one of secondary importance. And in the absence of an imperious, nation-wide clamor, strategically situated minorities could prevent either of the major political parties from committing itself resolutely on the issue. The minorities that blocked restriction had the additional advantage of appealing to traditional American ideals.

Big business constituted one of those minorities; through the National Association of Manufacturers, the American Iron and Steel Institute, and leading chambers of commerce it spoke out against disturbing the country's open gates.[74] Far more active and vocal, however, were the immigrants. The southern and eastern European opposition to restriction, partially demonstrated in 1906, swelled into a mighty, insistent chorus in the next few years. The federal immigration investigation authorized in the 1907 law gave the immigrant leaders the breathing spell they hoped for, and by the time another Congressional showdown arrived, the chaotic masses of the slums and tenements formed a pressure group of formidable size.

No single organization played a dominating role, though the National Liberal Immigration League tried to direct strategy. From its New York offices, it developed a network of connections with big city representatives in Congress. It was able, for example, to reward Congressman James M. Curley by sending volunteer workers from various cities to Boston to help in an election. Also the league laid down a barrage of propaganda designed to appeal to conservative American opinion, opposing restriction on the ground of manpower needs while favoring stricter deportation and naturalization regulations. It clearly sought rapport with like-minded business groups and received some of its financial support from the Susquehanna Coal Company, the Hamburg-Amerika Line, and the Compagnie Générale Transatlantique.[75]

A very important factor in inciting and sustaining the immigrants' interest in the anti-restriction campaign was the foreign-language press, which teemed with lurid accounts of injustices under present legislation and the danger of worse. Although little of this journalistic ferment went beyond its immediate audience, the immigrant press had one strong voice in high councils in the American Association of Foreign Language Newspapers. This agency of Louis Hammerling's, mingling business with politics, kept its member papers loyal to the Republican party in return for corporate advertising; and at least it tried to keep the Republican leaders loyal to the immigrants. It served other interests better than the foreigner's, but it gave immigrant editors a voice in party councils, reminding the administration of the support it received from 508 newspapers with a vital stake in a generous immigration policy.[76]

The principal vehicles of immigrant pressure were the national societies—numberless organizations of every size and description ranging from the great German-American Alliance to a tiny Lithuanian club on the South Side of Chicago. Delegates from a score of Polish benevolent societies, from Italian federations, and from Jewish associations trooped before Congressional committees, sometimes stumbling over their English, sometimes speaking with the commanding eloquence of Louis Marshall, head of the American Jewish Committee. In the large cities the societies combined to organize mass meetings; everywhere they circulated petitions.[77] In addition, some immigrant opinion also reached a larger public through the great immigrant church, for Roman Catholic leaders at various times expressed an unofficial opposition to restriction.[78]

While the immigrants mobilized their forces and the United States Immigration Commission ground through its vast investigation, the nativists fumed impatiently. At first they used the legislative lull to try to secure more drastic administration of existing statutes. The Immigration Restriction League directed its fire at

Oscar Straus, Roosevelt's Secretary of Commerce and Labor, who frequently exercised his authority to overrule harsh decisions which the Commissioner of Immigration, a former labor leader, made in the cases of individual immigrants. But with Roosevelt's support, Straus continued to administer the law with humanity. His successor in the Taft administration, Secretary Charles Nagel, was another second-generation immigrant who followed a similar course.[79] Meanwhile, the A.F.L. was sniping futilely at the Bureau of Immigration because of its new Division of Information, established under the law of 1907. The division functioned in a very small way as an employment agency for newly arrived immigrants; the A.F.L. charged it with strikebreaking. Finally the restrictionists tried to cut off the appropriation for the Immigration Commission in order to force out its report more quickly; and again they failed.[80]

At last, in 1911, the commission issued its report in forty-two volumes. Its recommendations were largely technical, but it took a moderately restrictionist position. The commission endorsed the old device of a literacy test; it favored on economic grounds a reduction in the supply of unskilled immigrant labor; and it cast its mountainous social and economic data in the form of an invidious contrast between the northwestern and southeastern Europeans in the United States at that time. Instantly, the struggle reopened in Congress, with anti-restrictionists still pursing Fabian tactics. For a year they kept the commission's recommendations bottled up in committees. Restrictionists finally got a general bill out of the Senate committee in 1912 and attached the literacy test to it on the floor. In the House, however, the Democratic leadership proved as recalcitrant as Speaker Cannon had been in 1906. A presidential election was imminent; this was no time to antagonize the foreign vote. Southern Democrats raged at their party for cowering before foreign flags, but the Rules Committee refused to release an immigration bill before November.[81]

Never have the political parties made greater efforts to curry favor among the immigrants than in the election of 1912. Each party, the Republican, the Democratic, and the Progressive, established adjunct organizations to work among the foreign-born during the campaign. Taft scarcely campaigned at all, but at least he tried to hold the immigrants. In the last days of the campaign he spoke in honeyed words about their influence on America, and the chairman of the Republican National Committee promised that Taft would veto the literacy test if re-elected. Hammerling faithfully supplied pro-Taft editorials to the foreign-language papers under his domination. He admitted disbursing more than $100,000 of Republican campaign funds and was said in some cases to have paid editors not to print advertisements for other candidates.[82]

On the Democratic side Woodrow Wilson labored throughout the campaign under the embarrassing handicap of having to repudiate over and over again the contemptuous phrases he had written about southern and eastern European immigrants in his *History of the American People* a decade before. Flaunted by his enemies, those sentences evoked indignant protests from immigrant societies. Wilson countered by lavishing admiration on the Poles, the Italians, and others. In a letter to an Italian-American which the Democratic National Committee distributed by the hundreds of thousands, Wilson declared: "America has always been proud to open her gates to everyone who loved liberty and sought opportunity, and she will never seek another course under the guidance of the Democratic Party."[83]

Theodore Roosevelt's new Progressive party adopted the most positive approach, due to the influence of social workers. Calling itself "the Party of Social Justice," the Progressive party welcomed social workers and incorporated bodily into its platform a sweeping program for social security worked out by a committee of the National Conference of Charities. The program included pledges to protect the immigrant from exploitation and to promote his assimilation and education. Frances Kellor, who was already pioneering in exactly this area, became a national committeewoman of the Progressive party and probably did more than anyone else to direct Roosevelt's growing reformist zeal toward the special plight of the urban immigrant.[84] The Junior Order United American Mechanics denounced the Progressive party for those promises to the foreign-born, but Roosevelt captured the imagination and the loyalty of a large proportion of southern and eastern European voters. In three out of the four New York City districts that gave Roosevelt a plurality, Slavs and Russian Jews constituted the great majority of the electorate.[85]

After this interparty demonstration of affection for the immigrants, Congress returned to the business at hand. Both houses hastily completed action on a general immigration bill recodifying all previous legislation and limiting admission to those able to read some language, the immediate family of a qualified immigrant being excepted. The measure came before President Taft in the closing weeks of his term of office. Taft was genuinely divided in his own mind on the issue. Since he had a business sense of the immigrants' economic contribution and considerable confidence in America's powers of assimilation, he was inclined to veto; but until the last minute no one knew what he would do.[86] In the end Taft vetoed and submitted to Congress the unfavorable recommendations of his Secretary of Commerce and Labor, Charles Nagel, as his reasons for doing so. Nagel was a prominent corporation lawyer with deep roots in the German community of St. Louis. To him illiteracy meant a lack of opportunity, not of ability; America needed the labor and could supply the literacy.[87] The Senate overrode the veto, but the House failed to do so by a margin of five votes. The voting followed the characteristic line-up that had emerged out of twentieth century nativism: the South and Far West almost unanimous for restriction, the urban areas of the North strongly against it, and considerable opposition lingering in the old immigrant districts of the Midwest.[88]

Woodrow Wilson, the new President, brought to Washington a bold program of economic reform that filled the rest of the year. The restrictionists had to wait for the next session of Congress. Early in 1914 their turn came. Southern Democrats now headed the immigration committees of both houses, and concern over rising unemployment was adding to all of the other nativist pressures. In the House of Representatives, the bill which Taft vetoed was revived, strengthened by broader provisions for the exclusion and deportation of revolutionists, embellished with the eugenic category of "psychopathic constitutional inferiority," and rushed to passage.[89] The Senate was prepared to follow suit when it began to wonder about Wilson. No one really knew his attitude on the question, but Jewish leaders were calling at the White House, and Wilson's Catholic secretary, Joe Tumulty, was said to exercise a baneful influence over him.[90] "Cotton Ed" Smith, chairman of the Senate Committee, confronted the President before proceeding further and discovered a reluctant opponent. Wilson tried to deflect Smith from restriction to a plan for distributing immigrants to rural areas—something that a rural nativist could only regard with horror.

To another southern Senator, Wilson later justified his own position on the literacy test in unusually frank terms: "I find myself in a very embarrassing situation about that bill. . . . I myself personally made the most explicit statements at the time of the Presidential election about this subject to groups of our fellow-citizens of foreign extraction whom I wished to treat with perfect frankness and for whom I had entire respect. In view of what I said to them I do not see how it will be possible for me to give my assent to this bill. I know you will appreciate the scruple upon which I act." [91]

Wilson in those days dominated his party to an unusual degree; Smith hesitated to defy him. Nevertheless, the Senate Immigration Committee decided after a month of doubt to press for action. Wilson's whole manner on the issue was constrained. Perhaps he might adopt a hands-off policy in the end. The matter dragged on through the spring and early summer. By then the Democratic leaders in the Senate were cocking their eyes toward another election. Despite a threat of a southern filibuster, they refused to allow time for debate until December.[92] So the literacy test waited again until the immigrants had cast their votes. Then the Senate passed the bill easily, and it went to the White House in January 1915.

Wilson proved inflexible. Apart from motives of political expediency, he had undoubtedly sloughed off his earlier fears of the immigrant as he responded to progressivism, and he was especially struck by the failure of the bill to exempt from the literacy test refugees from political persecution. (Congress had resisted strong pressure for such an exemption exerted in the interest of Russian Jews by the American Jewish Committee and the Friends of Russian Freedom.) [93] This failure gave Wilson an opportunity to stand on the high ground of traditional American idealism. His veto message rested four-square on an eighteenth century doctrine which immigrant spokesmen had kept alive: the idea of America's cosmopolitan mission to provide a home for the oppressed. The proposed legislation, Wilson declared, "seeks to all but close entirely the gates of asylum which have always been open to those who could find nowhere else the right and opportunity of constitutional agitation for what they conceived to be the natural and inalienable rights of men. . . ." [94]

For the third time in American history the literacy test received a Presidential veto, and for the third time its supporters tried to override executive disapproval. But Wilson apparently did more than disapprove. According to current reports, he brought the administration's patronage powers to bear to pick off Congressmen sympathetic to the literacy test. On February 4, 1915, the House of Representatives failed by four votes to pass the bill over the President's veto.[95] The dikes of interest and tradition still stood against the flowing nativist tide.

On the same day Imperial Germany announced a policy of unrestricted submarine warfare in all the waters surrounding the British Isles.

Chapter Eight

War and Revolution

We are 100 per cent American in the State of Wyoming, and we are going to remain 100 per cent American.
—Governor Frank Houx, 1918

The deadly convulsion in Western civilization that began in 1914 did not significantly impinge on American intellectual history until the following year. At first Europe seemed a long way off. Americans felt safely sheltered from the upheaval not only by a broad expanse of ocean but also by their own virtually unanimous determination to stay at peace. An overwhelming majority of native Americans sympathized with Britain through ties of geography and history, and the militarism evident in Germany affronted the prevailing pacifist mood itself; but few leaders of American opinion supposed that any latent preference for one side or the other would really compromise a neutral stance.

For all of its devotion to peace, the United States was psychologically prepared to react to an international challenge with nationalistic fervor. The Progressive era had built up a crusading spirit, a sense of dedication to high ideals. It had drawn powerfully on a modernized evangelical impulse, investing a secular crusade with religious significance, making the struggle against bosses and monopolists a way of battling for the Lord. By 1915 the reform leaders had nearly exhausted their capacity for constructive domestic achievement. Wilson's program was very largely on the statute books, and the Congressional elections of 1914—fought wholly on domestic issues—had set back reformers generally. On the other hand, the moral energy of the age, its appetite for splendid tri-

194

umphs over the forces of evil, was far from appeased. While progressivism was losing coherence as a practical program, its messianic zeal remained unquenched. This yearning idealism took a new lease on life when the specter of German militarism arose. Freed from the lagging drive for internal reform, the progressive spirit expanded into a global crusade.[1] This exalted sense of righteousness beat upon America throughout the war years, giving an almost religious significance to the struggle for victory abroad and unity at home.

In another way too there was continuity between a waning progressivism and the developing war spirit. We have already observed a slackening of confidence, an accumulation of tensions, as the progressive movement reached its crest in the immediate prewar years. Men were groping again for national unity, alarmed at unhealed or widening rifts of class, of race, of ideology. Perhaps a vigorous assertion of American rights functioned in some measure to submerge the drift and clash of purpose in domestic affairs. Undoubtedly the growing nativism of 1910 to 1914 formed a backlog of sentiment for and a bridge of transition into the greater nationalism of the war period.

Hyphens and Preparedness

If these and other impulses from an earlier day deeply colored the American response to the international crisis, the fact still remains that a new era was at hand; for the issues of 1915 inaugurated a tremendous alteration both in the course of American history and in the character of American nativism. While modern wars have generally imparted a fresh vigor to the tide of nationalism, they have often calmed the waves of nativism borne along within that tide. Certainly the wars that America fought in the nineteenth century had (whatever their other effects) diverted nationalism temporarily from nativist channels. The struggle with Germany, however, called forth the most strenuous nationalism *and* the most pervasive nativism that the United States had ever known.

The World War caused the first big international conflict between America and a country which had been sending to it a large and cohesive immigrant population. Despite the volume of new immigration, Germans still comprised the largest single nationality among the foreign-born. They numbered more than 2.3 millions,[2] and behind the first-generation immigrants stood countless others with attachments to the culture from which their fathers and forefathers came. What had occurred in a limited and partial form during the Italian war scare of 1891 and the friction with Japan after 1905 now erupted on a colossal scale and with classic purity. The Germans fell subject, not to any of the specific nativist traditions, but rather to the plain and simple accusation in which every type of xenophobia culminated: the charge of disloyalty, the gravest sin in the morality of nationalism.

The fury that broke upon the German-Americans in 1915 represented the most spectacular reversal of judgment in the history of American nativism. During the post-Civil War age of confidence the initial distaste for German customs had rapidly worn away. Public opinion had come to accept the Germans as one of the most assimilable and reputable of immigrant groups. Repeatedly, older Americans praised them as law-abiding, speedily assimilated, and strongly patriotic. In 1903 a Boston sociologist pronounced the Germans the best ethnic type in the city. In 1908 a group of professional people, in rating the traits of various immigrant nationalities, ranked the Germans above the English and in some respects judged them superior to the native whites.[3] These opinions rested on substantial foundations of social and economic prestige. By and large the Germans had risen out of the working class. They were businessmen, farmers, clerks, and in a few cases highly skilled workmen. Among workers in the major industries, a German was more likely to own his own home than was a native white.[4]

The friendliness they were used to meeting contributed to the Germans' undoing. Adversity had not disciplined the German-American leaders to meekness or restraint. Accustomed to acceptance and respect, they pressed for what they wanted confidently, even belligerently. Were they not, through the mighty German-American Alliance, the best organized foreign-language group in the country? Thus, when the European holocaust called forth their strong sympathies for the Fatherland, they rallied loudly and openly to influence American foreign policy. In the winter of 1914-15, as munitions shipments flowed out in ever larger quantities to the Allies, German-Americans launched a massive campaign for an embargo on the export of war supplies.[5] An embargo would have offset Britain's natural advantage over Germany in securing supplies from the United States. Although the German-Americans described their proposal as the only genuinely neutral course, Americans interpreted the agitation as an attempt to undermine the nation's cherished neutrality in the interest of a foreign power. They responded to the embargo movement with the first passionate outburst of anti-German hysteria. On January 30, 1915, just a few days before the German government declared submarine warfare on Great Britain, representatives of every large German-American organization met in Washington in a show of strength that sent a shiver through public opinion. The New York *Times* editorialized: "Never since the foundation of the Republic has any body of men assembled here who were more completely subservient to foreign influence and a foreign power and none ever proclaimed the un-American spirit more openly." [6]

The recoil from organized German-Americanism had hardly begun when policies of the German government made matters far worse. Within the week following the embargo conference, the first instances of sabotage executed by agents operating from the German embassy in Washington came to light. Bungling attempts to smuggle bombs onto American ships or to wreck American factories occurred fairly regularly during the following months. Each cast a darker shadow across the whole German community in the United States. At the same time the Reich embarked on a submarine campaign which soon spilled American blood. Through popular thinking there spread an image of the German-American community riddled with treason and conspiring under orders from Berlin. As early as February wild rumors told of German-American intentions to invade Canada. By August there was common talk that German-Americans were rejoicing over the death of American citizens on torpedoed ships; and whispers told of a mysterious multiplication of German street bands spreading propaganda by playing "The Watch on the Rhine." Before long public opinion transformed the German-American Alliance into a vast engine of the German government.[7]

The more a web of international conflict entangled the Americans, the fiercer grew their insistence on national solidarity and the more certain their feeling that the country was dangerously divided. Instead of unifying America, the issues of foreign policy and internal security in 1915 and 1916 created a sense of deeper disunities. Since the agitation against German-Americans arose from this free-floating nationalistic anxiety, not from dislike of specifically German cultural traits, it tended to assume a vague, generalized form. From the very beginning, the phraseology of the attack was directed less at Germans as such than at an entirely disembodied category: the "hyphenated American," i.e., the immigrant of divided loyalty. The *Literary Digest* asserted in October 1915 that the hyphenate issue was the most vital one of the day.[8]

The two most distinguished men in public life lent their influence to the anti-hyphenate campaign. Theodore Roosevelt bestrode the movement; Woodrow Wilson surrendered to it; and together they illustrated the change that the progressive impulse was undergoing. Roosevelt stood out as the standard-bearer and personification of "unhyphenated Americanism." Through all the turns of his protean career the Rough Rider had followed the fixed star of militant nationalism. Though he emphasized various functions and ends of state power at different times, he was always happiest when invoking its authority and glory. Long before, as a jingo and an ardent immigration restrictionist in the 1890's, Roosevelt had upbraided immigrants who failed to break loose from every Old World tie. Then, during the years of reform, the democratic and humanitarian strains in his character (encouraged by political expediency) brought him into sympathy with those who wanted to use the state in behalf of hyphenated minorities; in 1912 he championed a "New Nationalism" that would bind the foreign-born closer to the rest of America by a broad federal welfare program. But with the scent of battle in his nostrils in 1915, he swung back to his earlier view of the hyphen as a menace rather than a challenge.

Now he denounced every kind of divided loyalty as "moral treason." He insisted on one maxim for all Americans, regardless of birth or ancestry, "and that is the simple and loyal motto, AMERICA FOR AMERICANS." Roosevelt regularly cautioned the public that his attacks concerned only the "German-Americans who call themselves such" or the "professional German-Americans," not "the Americans of German origin," and he believed that his fairness toward unhyphenated people who happened to have German names or lineages justified the harshness of his assault on "those who spiritually remain foreigners in whole or in part." [9] Doubtless his audiences felt that the distinction clothed their hatreds with righteousness too.

By the time of the election of 1916, Wilson had also picked up the loyalty issue and was assailing the hyphenates. Unlike Roosevelt, Wilson did not mention any national group by name, and he always asserted that the disloyal people formed but a small minority of the foreign-born population. Nevertheless, he and his party exploited the hyphenate theme much more effectively than did the Republicans, who hoped to profit from the Germans' animosity toward the President. While the Republican candidate Charles Evans Hughes tried uneasily to temper the anti-German speeches that Roosevelt was making in his behalf, Wilson executed one of the master strokes of the campaign by defiantly repudiating the "hyphenate vote" in a stinging letter to an Irish agitator.[10]

The whole excitement over undivided loyalty developed hand in hand with another nationalist movement stemming from the European war. Preparedness, the term that described the campaign for national defense in 1915 and 1916, constituted an appeal for strength analogous to the anti-hyphenate demand for unity. The two causes, each full of alarm at the weakness of the republic, naturally supplemented one another. The preparedness movement tended, in fact, to aggravate anti-German nativism, partly because its emotional tone suggested vague dangers of foreign aggression, partly perhaps because it was easier to play up an internal menace than to show how European armed forces could threaten the United States. Psychologically the hyphen could serve as surrogate for enemy fleets or armies.

Certainly it was not accidental that the first Congressional advocates of preparedness were Augustus P. Gardner and Henry Cabot Lodge, the most fervent immigration restrictionists in politics in the Northeast, nor was it happenstance that the principal preparedness societies, the National Security League and the American Defense Society, evolved into leading instruments of wartime nativism.[11] Similarly, Theodore Roosevelt's thunderous campaign for military preparedness paralleled his trumpeting against the hyphenates, while President Wilson said little about hyphens until he gave up his opposition to armaments. Until the fall of 1915, Wilson resisted pressure for substantial increases in the country's armed forces. Then, in coming out for preparedness, he expressed a temperate alarm at voices speaking with "alien sympathies." In December, when the President began to appeal vigorously for defense appropriations, he struck out harshly at those immigrants "who have poured the poison of disloyalty into the very arteries of our national life . . . America never witnessed anything like this before. . . . Such creatures of passion, disloyalty, and anarchy must be crushed out." [12]

Unlike the attack on hyphens, the crusade to arm America had to overcome bitter opposition from native groups, but this friction at an hour of seeming national peril only heightened the military enthusiasts' fear of disunity. The tremendous preparedness parade on New York's Fifth Avenue in 1916 moved beneath a great electric sign that summarized the essential principle growing out of the whole international crisis: "Absolute and Unqualified Loyalty to Our Country." [13] The monolithic adjectives of that flashing sign summoned Americans toward a concept of national unity surpassing any they had known.

Greatly as the temper of American nationalism changed during those years of painful neutrality, the alterations were far from complete. The inflation of loyalty was just beginning, and the anti-German, anti-hyphenate movement—for all of its sound and fury—was still a matter of talk; it did not yet involve concrete proscriptions and reprisals. The period from the beginning of 1915 until America's entry into the war stands as a transitional one, in which a good deal of anti-foreign sentiment continued to function within the older, prewar patterns.

Although preoccupation with the German issue tended to push all other nativisms more or less into the background, the new situation affected the older traditions in different degrees. Anti-Catholicism sustained the greatest setback. In one of those sudden collapses that have marked its history the anti-Catholic movement shrank like a pricked balloon in 1915. The circulation of *The Menace* reached a high point of 1,507,923 in April and thereafter fell steadily and swiftly. It lost a million subscribers in little over a year and soon was reduced to futility. Meanwhile most of its journalistic competitors either ceased publication or changed policy. The

Guardians of Liberty disappeared from sight. A Knights of Columbus Commission on Religious Prejudices, established in 1914, disbanded in 1917 in a joyful mood.[14] The decline must have resulted partly from the economic upswing of 1915—from the prosperous returns on a flood of Allied purchases. But undoubtedly the breakup of Protestant xenophobia also reflected a shift of attention from the Pope to the more substantial and exciting menace of the Kaiser. Instead of invigorating anti-Catholicism, anti-Germanism stole its thunder. The two movements, so similar in their imagery of disloyal fifth columns acting under orders of a foreign "despot," had competitive appeals; for the papacy could not very readily be equated with Prussianized Germany.

Racial nationalism during those transitional years proved more resistant to the shift in public interest, though it too lost ground at a time of conflict between the American people and their Teutonic racial cousins. Many of the patrician intelligentsia of the East remained faithful to the Anglo-Saxon tradition, which at least ministered to their strong pro-British sympathies. Among them, the scientific race-thinkers pursued their inquiries uninterruptedly. Eugenicists followed with intense interest the studies that Aleš Hrdlička, an eminent anthropologist, began in 1914 to determine, by cranial measurements, if a race of Old Americans really existed. Madison Grant's book appeared in 1916 with only a casual reference to the war as another deplorable example of an old suicidal blood rage among the Nordics. It is noteworthy, however, that the book received rather little notice at the time.[15]

Meanwhile other racial nativists were tempering their ideas to the exigencies of the new international crisis, the chief problem being to eliminate any Germanic flavor from the Anglo-Saxon tradition. Some of the most ardent Anglophiles, assuming that the Anglo-Saxons alone constituted the truly American element, viewed the hyphenate vote as a threat to Anglo-American racial ties and thus to the source of American liberty.[16] This new distinction between hyphenated Teutons and unhyphenated Anglo-Saxons meant, of course, ignoring the latter's supposedly Teutonic origins. The Anglo-Saxonists, in effect, had to secede from the larger Teutonic race—a maneuver which they executed with dispatch. The psychologist G. Stanley Hall, for example, trained in German universities and long an apostle of Teutonism, now decided that "there was something fundamentally wrong with the Teutonic soul," and thereafter lavished his admiration on Anglo-Saxons alone.[17] After 1915 little more was heard in the United States about the origins of liberty in the forests of Germany.

The third proscriptive tradition, anti-radical nativism, had not reached by 1914 an intensity at all comparable to that of the other two. Apparently it had only minor importance during the next two years. Nonetheless, a radical spirit interfered in general with the solidarity that nationalists were increasingly demanding, and left-wing groups formed an important part of the opposition to preparedness. That fear of foreign radicals was far from dead was plainly evident in the immigration law passed in February 1917. This omnibus measure contained very broad anti-radical provisions evolved before the outbreak of the European war under urging from Albert Johnson and other foes of the I.W.W. The anarchist clause of 1903 was expanded in two ways: first, to exclude from the United States not only individual advocates of violent revolution but also those who advocated sabotage or belonged to revolutionary organizations; second, to deport any alien who at any time after entry was found preaching such doctrines. Thus organizational membership ("guilt by association") became a test of exclusion, and, in contrast to the original three-year time limit on deportation, an alien revolutionist might be sent back to his homeland even for beliefs acquired after long residence in America.[18]

The whole law provides the best illustration of how older xenophobias persisted into the neutrality period, interacting with the new anxiety over hyphenated loyalties. The 1917 statute was essentially the immigration restriction bill that Wilson had blocked in February 1915; the subsequent German crisis supplied the impetus for reviving and enacting a measure grounded in prewar problems. By the time the law was finally passed, it served no immediately restrictive purpose; the European war had already reduced emigration far more drastically than any legislator could hope to do. Proponents of a literacy test, however, warned that once the war ended a real deluge would begin.[19] Also they made much of the hyphenate issue. In their arguments all of the customary complaints against southern and eastern European immigration mingled somewhat incongruously with the fresh excitement over divided loyalties. Some observers noted that the nationalities which the literacy test was designed to penalize were showing, in contrast to the shocking behavior of German-Americans, "almost incomprehensible" restraint. Nonetheless, the German example suggested that one could never tell when a foreigner might betray the country to an enemy. To the Chicago *Tribune* the problems created by the war in Europe demonstrated the need for a more "intense and inspiring nationality" and made immigration restriction a phase of national defense.[20]

Before the measure became law, the old lure of the immigrant vote in a national election once more forced a delay. The Democrats, who posed in 1916 as the party of pure Americanism, warily took foreign influence into account at the very time their platform was denouncing it. Democratic publicists might accuse the Republican Presidential nominee of truckling to the foreign vote, but a Democratic Senatorial caucus meanwhile agreed not to take up the immigration bill until after the election. A group of southern Democrats revolted against the caucus decision but were brought to heel.[21]

As soon as Wilson was safely re-elected, the Senate passed the bill with only seven negative votes. Wilson, still keeping faith with the immigrants, vetoed it for a second time. Most big city newspapers endorsed the President's action, as did the United States Chamber of Commerce; but anti-hyphenism gave the restrictionists the extra margin they needed to override the veto. In the final tally the bill met virtually no opposition outside of industrial centers.[22] After a quarter of a century of agitation and more than a score of favorable votes in Congress on literacy bills, a provision excluding from the United States adult immigrants unable to read a simple passage in some language was enacted on February 5, 1917. There were two important exceptions. An admissible alien might bring in members of his immediate family despite their illiteracy, and in the interest of Russian Jews the same exemption applied to all aliens who could prove they were fleeing from religious persecution. Significantly, refugees from political persecution received no such exemption.

The law was a comprehensive one, based originally on recommendations of the United States Immigration Commission, which had been revived and expanded in each Congress since 1911. It codified existing legislation, added to the excluded classes "persons of constitutional psychopathic inferiority," "vagrants," and chronic alcoholics, and raised the head tax from $4 to $8. Along with the new prohibitions on alien radicals, the statute also established an Asiatic "barred zone" which served to exclude Hindu and East Indian labor. For reasons of diplomacy the Wilson administration managed to ward off a similar ban on Japanese, thus retaining the Gentlemen's Agreement which Roosevelt made with Japan in 1907.[23]

With this act, the question of immigration restriction rested for a time. The leaders of the Immigration Restriction League, at a quiet victory dinner in Boston's Union Club, began at once to plan additional barriers,[24] but America's entry into the World War was imminent, and Congress would take no further interest in the question until after the war. Already most nativistic anxieties centered on the lingering alien rather than the entering immigrant. Once war came, the immigrant qua immigrant disappeared from view, while fear of the alien absorbed the whole of American nativism and grew a hundredfold.

100 Per Cent Americanism

When President Wilson delivered his somber war message to Congress in April 1917, almost every member of the excited audience before him was waving or wearing an American flag.[25] The sight was impressive—and symbolic. The declaration of war ushered in a new ideology, rooted in the transitional years of 1915 and 1916 but now grown full scale. Though first visible through the preparedness and hyphenate movements, the change was not confined to any specific aspect of American nationalism. It amounted to nothing less than an alteration in the whole texture of nationalist thought. This pervasive shift came on the wings of a freshly minted phrase. By converting the negative term "unhyphenated Americanism" into a positive and prescriptive one, writers and orators of the war years created the expression "100 per cent Americanism." Like most simple phrases, this one implied far more than it said. Without rising to the dignity of a systematic doctrine, 100 per cent Americanism expressed, or connoted, a cluster of assumptions.[26] To understand its components and its dynamics is to reach the essence of wartime nativism and the spirit of much that followed in the postwar years.

Above all, 100 per centers belligerently demanded universal conformity organized through total national loyalty. Nothing in this demand was wholly new; certainly not loyalty, certainly not conformity. Partly because of the great social diversity within the country and the relatively limited force of government and custom, America had long since developed a remarkable degree of conformity through the sway of public opinion. European observers since de Tocqueville had repeatedly commented on how effectively Americans regulated one another through the pressure of collective judgment. Never before the First World War, however, had the urge for conformity blended so neatly with the spirit of nationalism. As a result, 100 per centers regarded the maintenance of the existing social pattern as dependent on the individual's sense of complete identification with the nation—a sense of identification so all-embracing as to permeate and stabilize the rest of his thinking and behavior.[27]

But passive assent to the national purpose was not enough; it must be grasped and carried forward with evangelical fervor. In addition to equating loyalty with conformity, patrioteers stressed the inculcation of a spirit of duty. Steady, uniform subordination of other interests to one national endeavor imposed a heavy psychic strain on a loose-knit, individualistic society; to practice conformity ardently all citizens must have a high sense of obligations and responsibilities laid upon them by the nation. Patriotism therefore was interpreted as service; the public was scolded for having thought too much in the past about its rights and privileges. About the time of America's entry into the war, the press inaugurated a country-wide contest for the best statement of a national creed which would emphasize the citizen's duties. The result, "The American's Creed," became a part of classroom ritual, an ever repeated reminder that love of country is to be understood in terms of duty. Meanwhile Theodore Roosevelt was thundering: "we must sternly insist that all our people practice the patriotism of service . . . for patriotism means service to the Nation. . . . We cannot render such service if our loyalty is in even the smallest degree divided."[28]

Millions of civilians displayed the same evangelical temper in

flocking to serve the war effort through countless voluntary organizations, drives, and pledge-signings—activities that often acquired a semi-obligatory status. The essential duty, however, consisted in right-thinking, i.e., the enthusiastic cultivation of obedience
and conformity. A newspaper editor who headed the Iowa Council of Defense spelled out three specific imperatives for every citizen: to join a patriotic society, to preach the impropriety of con-
sidering terms of peace, and "to find out what his neighbor
thinks." [29]

Thus the primary sanction on which 100 per centers depended
to enforce a crusading conformity was exhortation. Verbal appeals seemed so potent, and the calculated manipulation of opinion
was practiced to a degree so unprecedented that men began to
talk of "propaganda" as a kind of modern magic. [30] But techniques
of persuasion, no matter how high-pressured, seemed only partly
adequate to discipline the well-disposed, and entirely inadequate to
punish the disaffected. As their tempers rose, 100 per centers fell
back increasingly on the punitive and coercive powers of government to execute their mandates. The war was enlarging the scope
of governmental action in all sorts of ways, building on precedents
which reformers had supplied for protecting the community by
extending the functions of the state. Without often realizing they
were doing so, 100 per centers took part in the general statist
trend. For all their faith in pep talks, they also brandished a club.

An explanation for this whole temper of mind is not hard to
find: it was caused by the unexpected exigencies of modern war
impinging on traditional American habits and ideas. The struggle
with Germany suddenly imposed enormous tasks upon a loose-
knit, peaceful society, calling for an immense output of manpower
and material. The war seemed so encompassing, so arduous, that
the slightest division of purpose or lack of enthusiasm appeared an
intolerable handicap to it. Only a single-minded, even simple-
minded, dedication to a presumably single national objective could,
it was believed, prevent other interests or loyalties from competing
or conflicting with the luminous will of the nation. To achieve
this kind of unity, wartime nationalism drew heavily on the crusading impulse that had flowed both through imperialism and
through progressivism. The same intense belief in the power of
ideals to accomplish social objectives, the same reliance on exhor-

tation, the same moral energy, were now at work in the summons to national service. In this sense 100 per cent Americanism was the final fruit of a generation of political moralizing, though now the missionary spirit was turning toward the strengthening of existing institutions rather than the creation of new ones.

One must distinguish, therefore, between this American response to total war and the totalitarian nationalisms that have developed in other parts of the modern world. One hundred per cent Americanism involved no conscious repudiation of other social values such as individual freedom, but rather a refusal to recognize any legitimate conflict between such values and conformity; no hostility to the existing social order, but rather a zeal to maintain it; no desire to build an omnipotent state, but rather an appeal to state power only as a court of last resort when public opinion seemed incapable of enforcing conformity.

Though this new nationalism outlawed many kinds of deviation, it had already discovered its primary target in the formative years of 1915 and 1916. On the hapless German minority 100 per cent Americanism broke with great force as soon as the United States entered the war. Ironically, the German-Americans now suffered far more than they had during the neutrality period for a resistance which they no longer offered to the nation's purpose. Sabotage ceased with the flight of official German agents to Mexico when war was declared. Before long the German-language newspapers, at least in their public professions, embraced a blatant patriotism.[31] The 100 per centers, however, saw evidence of conspiracies everywhere. In the month before the United States entered the war, tales poured into the War and Justice Departments, often from highly responsible people, about secret organizations which were planning an earthquake of explosions under the direction of the German General Staff once hostilities commenced. Army commanders, especially in the Middle West, braced themselves to suppress insurrections that never materialized.

The fear of organized plots survived every disappointment and triumphed over every symptom of tranquillity. German-American Red Cross volunteers were widely believed to be putting ground glass in bandages and in food sent out to soldiers. Others were supposed to be selling court plaster containing tetanus bacilli, spreading influenza germs, or poisoning wells.[32] The Hoboken

Council of Six wanted the city placed under martial law to suppress a "Whispering Propaganda Organization" led by German-Americans. The President's secretary, Joseph Tumulty—a target of anti-Catholicism in the early years of the Wilson administration—felt called on to issue a formal newspaper statement denying that he had been shot as a German spy. The closing of many normal channels of communication and criticism stimulated the circulation of all sorts of rumors, so that the air was full of stories of transports sunk, Red Cross sweaters on sale in department stores, and governmental plans to confiscate all savings. Both press and government intensified the anti-German hysteria by branding such reports as inventions of German agents. Thus the Food Administration warned the public that a rumored shortage of salt, matches, and laundry blue was "the result of the latest efforts of pro-German propagandists." [33]

With the minions of the Kaiser moving in such mysterious ways, 100 per centers felt sure that the nation would never be safe until every vestige of German culture had been stamped out. German societies dared not hold public meetings or outings even in cosmopolitan New York. Many patriots clamored for suppression of all German-language newspapers, and in numerous areas local officials banned their sale.[34] A special act of Congress repealed the charter of the German-American Alliance. A campaign to eliminate German from the public school curricula made considerable headway on the theory that the study of the language served to inculcate un-American ideas. A poll of 1,200 public school systems in March 1918 showed that about one out of seven had already dropped German. The proportion was much higher in the South (almost 40 per cent), and wherever classes remained open, enrollment was dwindling rapidly. Before the war ended, some whole states—Delaware, Iowa, Montana, and others—banned the teaching of German. Meanwhile German opera was boycotted, sauerkraut became "liberty cabbage," and many towns, firms, and individuals with German names changed them. All of these repressive drives received much encouragement from the American Defense Society, a propaganda organization of wealthy conservatives and militarists.[35] Born in 1915 to agitate for preparedness, it lived on to become an embodiment of the 100 per cent philosophy.

Inevitably the zeal to expunge disloyalty and to "swat the Hun" roused a spirit of violence. Theodore Roosevelt advised shooting or hanging any German who showed himself disloyal,[36] and eminent clerical spokesmen demanded the death penalty for German propagandists. Plainer citizens meted out their own brand of informal justice. Mobs occasionally destroyed a German's books or musical instruments. Sometimes a German was forced to kiss the American flag. Passion mounted in the spring of 1918 as American troops went into action against the great German offensives unleashed on the Western Front. Supposedly seditious utterances by Germans and others provoked frequent public floggings or tar-and-feathering parties. Some of the worst vigilante groups in the Midwest and in California called themselves the Knights of Liberty. The climax came in April when a mob of miners lynched a German alien on the bloody ground of southern Illinois, where Negroes and Italians had met a similar fate in days of peace.[37]

In large measure these acts of repression and reprisal by private groups and local communities reflected the 100 per center's conviction that the federal government was timid and even criminally negligent in dealing with traitors. Popular indignation was rising against a nerveless government hampered by inadequate authority or paralyzed by respect for law. Were not thousands of disloyal utterances going unpunished? Were not German spies constantly being caught and then released without trial? Was not the government's anti-German propaganda, asked the American Defense Society, so pacific as to give aid and comfort to the enemy? Many 100 per centers believed that the weakness of federal action compelled them to take the law into their own hands.[38] This pressure from below for a more potent and coercive national state pressed hard on the Wilson administration. The government never went nearly as far as super-patriots wanted, but to some extent it was infected by 100 per-centism, and to some extent it was driven to appease it.

At the outset federal policy showed an uneasy but notable restraint. Unsatisfied with existing conspiracy statutes, Congress passed the Espionage Act in June 1917, which penalized individuals for false statements designed to obstruct the war effort or to aid the enemy. Although somewhat ambiguous, the measure appeared on its face to outlaw only those statements which constituted dangerous acts; not all deviant opinions.[39] To deal with the acts and statements of enemy aliens the government had a far more summary weapon at its disposal. During the first great anti-foreign scare of 1798, the Alien Enemies Act had given the President arbitrary control over unnaturalized subjects of a hostile power during wartime; he could arrest, restrain, regulate, and deport them by fiat. Alone among the Alien and Sedition Acts, this one remained in force, and Wilson invoked it as soon as war was declared. However, only a small fraction of the half million German aliens in the United States was molested under this authority. Sixty-three deemed most dangerous were seized at once; about 1,200 were arrested in the course of the year. By contrast, Britain interned all German aliens (some forty-five thousand); and Portugal, which was almost as secure from invasion as the United States, expelled them en masse from the country.[40]

The initial restraints upon American policy were progressively whittled away. Federal judges proceeded to flout a strict construction of the Espionage Act and to mete out long prison sentences to individuals who said that war violated the teachings of Christ or enriched profiteers. Attorney General Thomas W. Gregory tried to prevent indiscriminate prosecutions, but his own ability to distinguish between dangerous and innocuous utterances became somewhat blurred. Like many others in responsible positions, he was torn between passion and principle. Although he set himself against the demand of the Assistant Attorney General, Charles Warren, for imposing martial law on the country, Gregory felt keenly the prevalent criticism of federal laxity. Spurred by public opinion, he asked Congress to enlarge the Espionage Act slightly. It responded in May 1918 with more than he had bargained for—the draconic Sedition Act. Any opinion deemed disloyal, any contemptuous reference to the American flag, form of government, or Constitution, became subject to a twenty-year sentence.[41]

Meanwhile the Justice Department was hustling greater numbers of German aliens into internment camps under the President's summary powers. The total of enemy aliens arrested on Presidential warrants rose from 1,200 at the beginning of 1918 to 6,300 ten months later. Regulations governing the conduct of German aliens who remained at large were tightened, requiring them to register and forbidding them to move without official permission. Also the Justice Department in 1918 found a way of stripping "disloyal" naturalized Germans of their citizenship, and Gregory prepared a drive for denaturalization proceedings.[42]

Super-nationalist tendencies also came to bear on the federal government through secret societies of volunteer spy-hunters. One of the most satisfying ways by which a 100 per center disqualified from military service could answer the urge for duty and conformity was to take part in a society engaged in ferreting out disloyalty. A number of such societies appeared around the time of America's entry into the war, including (according to one report) the Anti-Yellow Dog League, composed of boys over ten who searched for disloyalists and claimed a thousand branches throughout the country.

The Justice Department, daunted by the puny size of its own staff of three hundred investigators, gave a kind of unofficial blessing to several of the secret bodies.[43] One of them, the American Protective League, secured a unique status as a semiofficial auxiliary to the Justice Department and grew to phenomenal size. Established by a Chicago advertising executive, A. M. Briggs, in March 1917, with the Justice Department's approval, in a few months the league mushroomed into an organization of more than 1,200 separate units functioning in nearly every locality in the United States. Its members were largely business and professional men, who financed it through their own contributions supplemented by subsidies from large corporations. According to the league's claim, it attracted a total of 250,000 members, each equipped with an impressive badge and imbued with 100 per cent fervor. To middle-aged soldiers of the home front, the league supplied the gratifications of participating in a secret, oath-bound society, the respectability of operating more or less within the law, and above all the opportunity to clothe themselves in the authority of the national state. By joining, any "red-blooded patriot" could become a policeman.

As their primary task, A.P.L. "operatives" pried into men's opinions. They carried out investigative assignments referred to them by the Bureau of Investigation and later by the War Department's Military Intelligence Division, and flooded public officials everywhere with unsolicited, melodramatic information. Reports on "seditious and disloyal utterances" comprised their main stock in trade, these often consisting of gossip, hearsay, and misinformation offered from malevolent motives. Sometimes the silent were browbeaten into public confessions of thorough loyalty; sometimes those who might have spoken critically were silenced by advance warnings. The authorized history of the A.P.L. records such feats as the following: "Prowers County, Colorado, investigated fifty cases of mouth-to-mouth propaganda, a notable case in its annals being that of a German Lutheran minister who refused to answer the question as to which side he wished to win the war. . . . He asked for time. The next day he declared very promptly that he wanted the United States to win. He was instructed to prove this by preaching and praying it in private as well as in public, which he agreed to do." [44]

The league performed other chores as well, sometimes with a muscular vigor that disturbed its official sponsors. It checked up on people who failed to buy Liberty bonds, looked for draft evaders, spotted violators of food and gasoline regulations, and took a suspicious interest in citizens living in luxury without visible means of support. Attorney General Gregory tried to restrict the league to investigative work, but the desire of its members to police their communities could not always be held in check. In New York they took part in a mass roundup of draft evaders. In Cleveland they broke up meetings of a Socialist local. In Milwaukee they threatened members of the Machinists Union with immediate induction into the Army, and German aliens who tried to change jobs with internment. In at least two cities league members served as strikebreakers to prevent walkouts of policemen and firemen who wanted higher pay.[45] "It is safe to say," Gregory reported to Congress with truthful pride, "that never in its history has this country been so thoroughly policed. . . ." [46]

A Common Cause

Although wartime nationalism bore down most severely and painfully on the German element, obviously a conformist ethic that applied so broadly to the whole American population could easily jeopardize other immigrant groups as well. Conceivably, 100 per cent Americanism could have unleashed a general xenophobia against all aliens. To what extent did this in fact occur?

Certainly the war created a more widespread concern than

Americans had ever before felt over the immigrants' attachment to their adopted country. Decades of xenophobia in all parts of the country had failed to touch a substantial part of the native public in any primary or significant way. Now that national solidarity was at such a premium, many Americans had a sense of discovering a momentous issue hitherto only dimly grasped.

Statistics alone were disturbing enough. An estimate by the Bureau of the Census in 1917 showed that the American population included about 4,662,000 people born within the boundaries of the Central Powers, half of them Germans and the other half a queer conglomeration of nationalities from Austria-Hungary, Turkey, and Bulgaria. Altogether, about one-third of America's foreign-born derived from enemy territory. An overwhelming majority of those who had come from the countries allied with Germany had not yet acquired American citizenship;[47] and when the United States declared war on Austria-Hungary in December 1917, its subjects became enemy aliens. Furthermore, their significance for the American war machine was crucial. The Slavic and Magyar nationalities originating in the Dual Monarchy now dominated the eastern coal fields, formed perhaps two-thirds of the labor force in the iron and steel industries and an equal proportion in the slaughterhouses, and worked in most of the munitions factories.[48]

The Slovaks, Slovenes, Magyars, Bohemians, and all the rest of the great mass from eastern Europe were not Teutonic, to be sure, nor did American opinion ever view them in quite that light. To the United States the enemy was Germany. The other Central Powers seemed (when one thought about them at all) not so much the allies of the Kaiser as his pawns. Nevertheless the thought that the adversary had at least a technical claim on the sympathies of millions in the industrial heart of America was deeply disquieting.

What was worse than the size and the strategic position of the alien population was its apartness. The impulse for unity crashed against the plain, frightening fact that the new immigrants lived in a social universe so remote from that of the Americans on the other side of the tracks that they knew practically nothing of one another. The average citizen's acquaintance with the immigrants scarcely went beyond some unpleasant concepts about their character and the conditions under which they lived. Of their inmost loyalties he knew nothing but suspected much when the war began. In a magazine article entitled "Invaded America," Samuel Hopkins Adams described the millions born on enemy soil in a manner characteristically vague and characteristically ominous: "Reckon each as a pound of dynamite—surely a modest comparison. . . . Not all these enemy aliens are hostile. Not all dynamite explodes." [49]

The general apprehension about alien influence highlighted an anomalous condition surviving in seven western states. Operating on constitutions written in the frontier era, Indiana, South Dakota, Nebraska, Kansas, Missouri, Arkansas, and Texas still permitted aliens to vote on the mere declaration of intention to become citizens. Since the 1880's a number of other states had eliminated this right, but during the same period the nativists' preoccupation with the issue of immigration restriction had left the question of alien suffrage largely unattended. In 1917 the realization that aliens, many of them legally enemies, might control elections in certain districts, caused a determined movement for limiting suffrage to citizens only. Three states amended their constitutions in 1918, and the rest followed suit in the immediate postwar years. [50]

Meanwhile compulsory military service bore more heavily on citizens than on aliens and thus added to the resentments and anxieties inherent in the war situation. The Selective Service Act of May 1917 exempted enemy aliens and all other aliens who had not declared their intention to become citizens; on the other hand, quotas were apportioned on the basis of total population. Consequently, as the draft began to cut deeply into the country's manpower, it took a disproportionate number of citizens from communities with a large alien population. Along with indignation that young aliens should be enjoying the fruits of war prosperity while citizens filled up the military quotas, there was concern lest the induction of too many native-born workers in mill towns and other industrial areas should disturb "American control" of plants by causing the elevation of aliens to supervisory posts. In 1918 a new system of apportioning quotas was instituted and ended most of the dissatisfaction. [51] There remained the problem of a relatively small number of declarant aliens from neutral countries who sought exemption from military service on the basis of treaties the United States had with their homelands. In an act of July 1918, Congress yielded to the claim of treaty obligations but stipulated that to secure exemption, such aliens must withdraw their first papers and in doing so would be forever barred from citizenship.[52]

All in all, a foreigner was well advised to conduct himself with unusual circumspection in an atmosphere so highly charged. There was, for example, the case of a foreign-looking man, unable to speak English, who ripped a Liberty Loan poster from a Cleveland trolley car. The other occupants of the car mobbed him, and only a timely arrest saved him from what might have become a lynching. He proved to be an illiterate Pole infuriated by the poster's illustration: the glaring visage of the Kaiser.[53]

Yet, despite the indiscriminate anti-foreign suspicions omnipresent in the war mood, incidents of this kind were unusual. Toward the German, American opinion showed little restraint; toward the rest of the immigrant population it showed a great deal. The average non-German alien passed through 1917 and 1918 unscathed by hatred, and often touched by sympathy. The logic of 100 per cent Americanism was against him, but the war also created powerful forces which held that logic in check. Latent hostilities toward hyphenated nationalities became overt only in the case of the Germans. An incident in Texas, where a corrupt governor in the course of a general assault on the state university tried to oust all aliens from the faculty, stands alone in the annals of the war.[54] This was the paradox of American nationalism during the First World War. On the one hand it created an unappeasable and unprecedented demand for unity and conformity. On the other, it saved the foreigner from the persecutory or exclusionist consequences of this demand as long as he was non-German and showed an outward compliance with the national purpose. To a remarkable degree the psychic climate of war gave the average alien not only protection but also a sense of participation and belonging.

In this respect the First World War resembled previous American wars. Like the Civil War and the Spanish-American War, the struggle with Germany drained many internal antagonisms out of American society, turning them instead onto the common enemy. The people were seeking national unity through fraternity *and* through hatred, developing modes of sympathy as well as repression. Foreign groups usually excluded from community affairs were invited to take part in Red Cross projects, Liberty Loan drives, and a host of similar activities. In the oneness of the war effort, nationalities, churches, and classes found a common ground. A sociologist studying a Vermont industrial city in the mid-1930's met many residents who still looked back nostalgically to the social homogeneity of 1917, when some of the traditional ethnic and religious barriers had broken down.[55] This spirit of community flourished side by side with 100 per cent Americanism, each providing an approach to unity. Perhaps they complemented one another, but to a considerable extent the achievement of fellowship tempered the force of fear and compulsion.

The most powerful of all of the symbols of loyalty was military service. The complaints about "alien slackers" that grew out of the inequities of the draft act made little impression beside the immigrant soldier's bright reputation for patriotism and valor. The prestige which the foreign-born had won fifty-five years before at Fredericksburg, Antietam, and Shiloh was won again on the battlefields of France. Despite the nondeclarant and enemy aliens' right of exemption from the draft (an exemption which great numbers of them waived), the foreign-born constituted about 18 per cent of the United States Army. This was somewhat more than their share of the total population.[56] Not only immigrant leaders but all who wished to stress the cohesiveness of a fighting America exalted the foreigners' service record. Popular military commentators evinced a sense of relief at the immigrant response to the test of war. The government's official propaganda agency, the Committee on Public Information, made much of the decorations which individual immigrants received. A Victory Liberty Loan poster by the famous illustrator, Howard Chandler Christy, painted perhaps the most vivid image. It showed an Honor Roll full of outlandish foreign names and above the caption, "Americans All!"[57]

A deliberate effort was made to emphasize the loyal cooperation of the immigrants on the home front also. At the instigation of the C.P.I., communities throughout the country organized great pageants on the Fourth of July, 1918, with every available nationality conspicuous in its native costumes and in its demonstrations of patriotism. Even the German-Americans were not entirely excluded from the ceremonial joining of hands. They too had American war heroes to whom orators could point, and in the parade at Sandusky, Ohio, a group of them marched with a banner inscribed "100% Americans of German birth and descent." [58] Little wonder that a leading Protestant periodical, the *Missionary Review*, exclaimed indulgently, "These handicapped races are showing such loyalty, such devotion to our country, that we are realizing our former undemocratic, unchristian attitude toward them." [59]

This tendency to play up the common ties of interest and purpose among old and new Americans was strengthened by the very real hatred most Austro-Hungarian immigrants displayed toward their official fatherland. The bulk of immigrants from the Dual Monarchy were subject nationalities who saw an Allied victory as an opportunity for their own people to secure independent statehood. The foreign districts of American cities bubbled with agitation and propaganda for such independence movements—a kind of hyphenate activity which served to demonstrate the attachment to American war aims of many technically enemy aliens. If the Magyars, who dominated half of Austria-Hungary, failed to share this enthusiasm for disrupting their homeland, they apparently kept their resentments to themselves. [60] The general impression that Austro-Hungarian aliens had little sympathy with their home government reinforced the implicit distinction Americans drew between Germany and her allies. The federal government treated unnaturalized immigrants from the other Central Powers very differently from unnaturalized Germans. After the belated declaration of war with the Dual Monarchy, Wilson refrained from applying to its subjects in the United States any of the enemy alien regulations which hampered all German aliens. The press, according to the *Literary Digest*, tended to applaud Wilson's action in parting "the goats of German nationality from the sheep who owed allegiance to the Hapsburg Kaiser. . . ." [61]

The Nativist Traditions in Wartime

To a considerable extent, the spirit of a common cause also laid its inhibitions on the older patterns of nativism. Many hatreds functional to peacetime tensions were expensive luxuries during war, and any type of xenophobia not directly relevant to the conflict between the United States and Germany had little chance to prosper. Accordingly, the tendency, already manifest in the preparedness period, to subordinate other nativist ideas to the new international challenge was steadily pursued.

Two of the historic traditions of American nativism ran counter to the common purpose. Anti-Catholicism was generally discouraged and remained at low ebb; speculation that the papacy sympathized with Germany was denounced as "Hun propaganda" designed to divide America.[62] Nor did racial nativism make headway while the United States was aligned with Italy and Japan against the masters of northern Europe. Very few racial attacks on foreign groups appeared in the general books and magazines. The leading race-thinkers strove primarily to bring their theories into harmony with the spirit of the hour. Madison Grant brought out a hastily revised edition of The Passing of the Great Race in 1918, eliminating references to early American settlers as Teutonic and declaring that most present-day inhabitants of Germany are Alpines rather than Nordics. A physician, William S. Sadler, wrote a whole book to prove the latter point, arguing that 90 per cent of the German Nordics had been killed off in the wars of the previous three hundred years. This indicated, according to a lurid report in the Hearst press on the views of Professor Henry Fairfield Osborn, that the modern German population was actually descended from Asiatic barbarians.[63] There is no evidence, however, that these readjustments gave racial nationalism any wartime vogue.

On the other hand, the third of America's anti-foreign traditions fitted very usefully into the mood and circumstances of the war years. Whereas anti-Catholicism and racism could only strain existing bonds of unity, anti-radicalism served to counteract an existing disunity. All religions and races joined willingly in the war effort; many radicals did not. Consequently a nationalist attack on radicals gathered great strength during 1917 and 1918. It supplemented and interacted with the reigning anti-German hysteria, forming a subordinate but important outlet for 100 per cent Americanism.

When war came, the conditions which had discouraged fears of revolutionists during the Progressive period were reversed. Then, the strong current of enthusiasm for social change had confined anti-radical hysteria to a conservative minority; and since a great part of America was then responding to varying degrees of reform, the line between progressive and revolutionary opinion dimmed.

The war, however, had precisely the opposite effect. It put a premium on stability rather than dissent, and it created a sharp distinction between liberals and radicals. Liberals, like most groups in wartime America, restricted or suspended their own struggle, in the interest of harmony. Radicals alone remained unregenerate enough to oppose the war itself in a relatively outspoken and organized way.

While nationality groups such as the Germans and Magyars publicly avowed their support of the war, left-wing spokesmen denounced it as a capitalistic blood-bath. Just about all of the meager anti-war propaganda in the United States came from the I.W.W., from tiny anarchist groups, and from the dwindling Socialist party, at least until they were bludgeoned into silence. Horrified at what seemed outrageous disloyalty, 100 per centers poured upon members of these groups, regardless of nativity, a hatred second only to their abomination of the hyphenated German. A provision in the Espionage Act banning disloyal literature from the mails was used largely against left-wing publications, and an important motive behind the sweeping Sedition Act was a desire to clamp down on radical sentiment more completely.[64]

The attack on radicalism was thoroughly interwoven with the anti-German hysteria. The equation between the two was partly an outgrowth of the whole anti-radical tradition, with its assumption that militant discontent is a foreign importation, and partly a reflection of the new inclination to see the hand of the Kaiser in any divisive symptom. Any radical critic of the war was customarily designated a "pro-German agitator." [65] Then too the frustrating scarcity of disloyal acts among German groups undoubtedly encouraged the belief that the crafty Hun was actually working through left-wing organizations.

Although Socialists were occasionally horsewhipped, frequently arrested, and generally silenced, anti-radicalism now as in the late Progressive era found its chief target in the I.W.W. To the Wobbly organizers a class loyalty transcended any national loyalties. In the early summer of 1917, when the organization reached a peak membership of about one hundred thousand, it had no compunction about stopping work in the copper mines and launching a series of strikes among the exploited, migratory workers in the northwestern lumber camps. This action raised the most overt challenge that was to occur during the war to the new spirit of patriotic conformity. Convinced that German influence lay behind it all, the middle-class public responded with extraordinary violence. Sheriffs' posses and armed citizens' committees expelled more than 1,300 miners thought to be Wobblies from points in Arizona. One large group was met at the California border by a similar armed committee which threatened to shoot both the guards and their prisoners if they set foot in California. New Mexico vigilantes stopped a similar deportation from Arizona, with the result that federal authorities had to take charge of the captives. In Butte, Montana, a half-breed Indian active in the I.W.W. was lynched. Throughout the western states vigilante groups were springing up, and men were talking about further "neck-tie parties." [66]

Western state legislatures began to pass "criminal syndicalism" laws, severely penalizing membership in any organization advocating violence. On the other hand, state authorities felt helpless to halt the violence of their own enraged citizenry. A group of western governors appealed for federal action against the I.W.W. to forestall further mob action against it. Attorney General Gregory, who shared the suspicion that Germany was financing the I.W.W., probably needed little encouraging. In July 1917, he ordered the internment of all German aliens found to be I.W.W. members. But still the popular clamor for more drastic steps continued. On September 5, therefore, Gregory began a thoroughgoing campaign of repression. His agents descended on every I.W.W. hall in the United States. Further raids and confiscations of literature followed, resulting in all in the arrest of more than three hundred I.W.W. leaders, who were tried chiefly for violating the Espionage Act. Another group, consisting of non-German aliens identified with the I.W.W., was seized through the collaboration of the Immigration Bureau and the American Protective League and held for deportation under the new immigration law. [67]

In deportation the nation grasped its absolute weapon against the foreign-born radical. During the World War, deportation assumed a wholly new significance. In the nineteenth and early twentieth centuries it had had a purely instrumental function. It was a way of enforcing the existing laws regulating immigration—a way of sending back recently admitted aliens who should have been stopped at the port of entry because of specific excludable qualities. Deportation, therefore, never received wide public attention until the war period. Then nationalists glimpsed broader potentialities in what had been purely an administrative instrument; they began to envisage it as a major public policy in its own right. They saw it as a means of purifying American society. Through deportation and the threat of it, the nation might rid itself of divided loyalties. In this broad sense deportation now became a subject of considerable comment. "We are going," said the chairman of the Iowa Council of Defense, "to love every foreigner who really becomes an American, and all others we are going to ship back home." The ex-president of the Native Sons of the Golden West added that every foreigner "must live for the United States, and grow an American soul inside of him, or get out of the country." [68] In short, the popular concept of deportation expanded to fit the ideals of 100 per cent Americanism.

The immigration law of 1917 furnished an initial opportunity to experiment along these lines. By permitting the Department of Labor to deport aliens implicated in certain kinds of radicalism regardless of how long they had lived in the United States before the offense occurred, the statute freed the weapon of deportation from the simple and limited function of enforcing the immigration code. However, after beginning to arrest aliens active in the I.W.W. in the winter of 1917-18, the government discovered that for purposes of deportation the law was less commodious than it had appeared on first glance. Although immigrants could be excluded, alien residents of long standing could not be expelled merely for membership in a subversive organization. Deportation in such cases depended on proof that the man had personally advocated subversive doctrines. In order to carry out the campaign against foreign Wobblies, therefore, the Justice and Labor Departments in 1918 asked Congress to authorize the deportation of any alien simply on grounds of belonging to an organization which advocated revolt or sabotage. Congress passed the bill in October with no opposition, and with little comprehension of the momentous step it was taking.[69]

Even with this broader dispensation, only the beginnings of an anti-radical purge were possible while the war lasted. By disrupting normal diplomatic relations and maritime connections, the war prevented the government from effecting more than a few individual deportations. In almost all cases the Secretary of Labor, who had official jurisdiction in the matter, postponed action until the end of hostilities.[70] Furthermore, anti-radicalism remained a subsidiary manifestation of the 100 per cent spirit as long as the German menace was unquelled. It was one thing to call the radicals German agents but quite another to equate radicalism with the whole foreign population. Thus the war laid both the legislative and ideological foundations for a nationalistic, anti-radical crusade but curbed its channels of expression.

Big Red Scare

On Armistice Day a close observer might have guessed that the anti-radical tradition would make trouble for the immigrants in the months ahead. It is unlikely that he could have predicted the full fury of the Big Red Scare. Who could have foreseen that the emotions stirred up by the war would persist so violently into the postwar era? Yet the survival of 100 per cent Americanism under peacetime conditions is one of the great keys to the storm of xenophobia that followed in the wake of battle. An unappeased demand for the kind of conformity which only an extremely belligerent nationalism might provide flowed on for years, making World War I a major turning point in American nativism.

It is hard to explain the tug of wartime passions on the postwar mind except in terms at least partly psychological. The clamor for absolute loyalty, continuing relentlessly into peacetime, spoke, perhaps, an unwillingness to surrender the psychic gratifications the war had offered. Along with death and sacrifice the war had brought the warmth of a common purpose into millions of lives; it had touched them far more heroically than ever before with the moral idealism of the early twentieth century; it had given them catharsis for a host of aggressive impulses. These were experiences to cherish deeply, and men who had discovered them in the heat of national conflict had little difficulty supposing that the war had not ended, that the adversary had merely assumed another guise and still presented a deadly challenge to loyalty and a summons to hatred. Although other wars, too, had left violent emotional aftermaths, the martial spirit of 1918 could adapt itself to changing issues and fasten itself on changing enemies with unusual flexibility:

the new creed of total loyalty outlawed so many kinds of dissent. Projected into the postwar world, the 100 per cent ideology gave war hatreds a wide and various field.

With the collapse of the German onslaught in November 1918, therefore, Germanophobes rallied swiftly and easily to repulse the foreign revolutionist. The latter—already stamped as an ally or agent of the Hun—merely moved from a subordinate to a central position on the enemy front. So interlocked and continuous were the anti-German and anti-radical excitements that no date marks the end of one or the beginning of the other. In the summer of 1918, after the new Bolshevik government of Russia had made an abject peace with Germany, stories circulated in the United States to the effect that the Kaiser actually controlled the Soviet régime. The Committee on Public Information confirmed this illusion by releasing a sensational report from one of its officials, Edgar Sisson, which sought to prove that the Bolshevik leaders were German agents. After the armistice the equation between Germanism and Bolshevism enabled a Senate committee investigating pro-German propaganda in the United States to shift smoothly to an inquiry into Bolshevik propaganda.[71] All through 1919 much hatred and suspicion of German influence lingered, erupting time and again in the charge that Teutonic machinations lay behind every symptom of unrest. In early 1920 New York state's famous Redhunter, Clayton R. Lusk, was still proclaiming that paid agents of the German Junkers had started the radical movement in America as part of their plan of world conquest.[72]

The undercurrent of 100 per cent Americanism running through both waves of xenophobia appeared still more clearly on the organizational level. When the war ended, the American Protective League had no intention of dissolving. It looked forward to a happy career ferreting out new disloyalties, sharpened its surveillance of radical meetings, and tried to work out with the United States Naturalization Service an arrangement for investigating every applicant for citizenship. Attorney General Gregory soon decided, however, that public opinion might not tolerate a secret system of citizen espionage under peacetime conditions. He and the national directors of the league had to apply considerable pressure to persuade the organization to disband. At that, some local divisions continued under other names, such as the Loyal American League of Cleveland, which kept trying to help public officials in suppressing disloyalty and disorder.[73]

A new organization, operating with no pretense of secrecy or of official status, stepped into the league's shoes as the guardian of national orthodoxy. This was the American Legion. Being a veterans' organization, the legion perpetuated more directly than any other group the corporate values of the war experience, the solidarity, the fellowship, the special identification with the nation. It took form in France in the early weeks of 1919, launched by a group of Army officers who were concerned about the morale of restless, homesick troops. They were alarmed too at signs of radical ferment on all sides, and from the beginning leaders of the legion thought of it as an agency for defending America from revolution. A constitution was drawn up pledging the organization "To foster and perpetuate a one-hundred-percent Americanism." Of this it soon became a veritable incarnation. It kept alive the whole cluster of war hatreds (against Germans, "alien slackers," and Wobblies), pressed for stronger military defenses and a stronger sense of duty to the nation, sowed patriotic propaganda broadcast, and in the sweep of its attack on radical dissent proved a pillar of the economic status quo. Although the national leaders tried to chart a respectable course, during 1919 and 1920 representatives of local posts attacked left-wing meeting places and newspapers, helped to break strikes, and otherwise flexed their muscles.[74]

While a coercive zeal to maintain absolute loyalty endured after the armistice, the gentler, more spontaneous aspects of wartime national unity disappeared. With the end of hostilities, individuals and groups who had pulled together soon pulled apart. This postwar loss in actual homogeneity had as much to do with bringing on the Big Red Scare as did the continuing pressure of 100 per cent Americanism. The sense of community, which had confined wartime nativism within fairly narrow channels and which had given status to all who took part in the great common cause, was swept away after the armistice. Thus the 100 per cent impulse survived, but the principal barrier which had held it in check disappeared. In place of the very high degree of harmony prevailing in 1917 and 1918, the country shook in 1919 under a wave of class conflict unparalleled since the turbulent nineties.

After shackling their own freedom of action for two years in the interest of national unity, both capital and labor kicked loose like young colts. Businessmen, resentful at the swift growth of unions under government benediction during the war, set themselves to crush any sign of labor militancy. Workers, on the other hand, determined to keep abreast of the booming cost of living. Beyond that, they were fired by visions of social reconstruction, by bright hopes of a brave new world rising in the morning of peace and victory. The highly respectable railroad brotherhoods came out for government ownership of the railroads; the United Mine Workers proposed nationalizing the coal mines, organizing a labor party, and establishing a program of compulsory health insurance. At the same time strikes flared more widely than ever before in American history.

To the left of most of the labor movement, a similar dynamism surged in radical groups, which, rebounding from wartime restrictions, were magnetized by forces radiating from the new Russia. About fifty radical newspapers began publication in the year after the armistice, many of them anticipating an imminent social cataclysm. Out of the Socialist party, which was shaken apart by the ferment, arose at least two communist parties, both small but bubbling with insurrectionary élan. A number of little anarchist groups became active. Nor was all the excitement verbal. On December 30, 1918, bombs exploded on the doorsteps of two Philadelphia judges and a police superintendent, and similar attempts on the lives of public officials occurred sporadically over the next few months.[75]

Although American labor and the American left were, generally, in upheaval, foreign-born workers and radicals played a very prominent part. In addition to the anarchists, the great majority of American communists had a recent immigrant background. The bulk of Russian peasants in the United States seemed sympathetic to the Bolshevik régime.[76] Also some of the biggest strikes occurred in basic industries manned largely from the new immigration. The first blaze of labor unrest after the war broke out in the textile industry, beginning with thirty-five thousand New York garment workers in January and spreading throughout New England and the mid-Atlantic states. The great majority of the strikers were recent immigrants, and in some places such as Lawrence, Massachusetts, the English-speaking employees remained at work while the foreigners went out. In the autumn, at the height of the Red

Scare, the great steel strike drew together 376,000 workers, largely from the unorganized masses of southern and eastern Europe, despite the companies' best efforts to exploit nationality cleavages.

As part of a fierce counteroffensive, employers inflamed the historic identification of class conflict with immigrant radicalism. In advertisements and interviews they confirmed impressions that the strikes represented alien outbreaks intended to inaugurate an actual revolution.[77] It is little wonder that the immigrants got rough treatment. Out of fear, some factories discharged all their Russian employees, and many others adopted a policy of refusing to hire them. One company advised its workers to give discontented foreigners "a good swat on the jaw." In Lawrence, mounted police with flailing clubs charged orderly meetings.

In Gary, Indiana, a vigilante of the "Loyal Legion" gave this report on how it maintained "law and order" during the early days of the steel strike:

> A bunch of these foreigners, six or eight times the number of our posse, met us this side of the tracks, and we went into them. I told the men with me not to trouble too long with a man. Our method of work was to grab a man's right arm with the operator's own left hand, then bring down the blackjack across the hand bones or wrist of the man thus caught. One rap was enough, and after one of those people had got that we could go on to the next man, as he could not make any more trouble. We have a nice hospital in Gary. There were thirty-five people in there the next day with broken wrists and hands.[78]

Other 1919 strikes principally involved native-born workers, but it was inevitable that every step in the breakdown of class unity should lead a public conditioned by the belligerent qualities of the new nationalism, and by the long anti-radical tradition, deeper into nativism. As early as February a general strike of sixty thousand old-line union men in Seattle turned the country's fears of a foreign insurrection into sheer panic. That foreign agitators had provoked the "uprising" was axiomatic; that it marked the actual beginning of a communist revolution was hardly less so. Even Woodrow Wilson's staunchly liberal aide, Joe Tumulty, thought the Seattle strike was "the first appearance of the soviet in this country."[79] Thus the wartime tendency to distinguish between pro-German radicals on the one hand and the rank and file of loyal foreigners on the other gave way to an impression that radicalism permeated the foreign-born population, that it flourished among immigrants generally and appealed to hardly anyone else. One journalist admitted that a few of the Bolsheviks might be native-born but dismissed these as tame and innocuous. "The foreign element, on the other hand, is absolutely destructive. . . ." [80] Never before had anti-radical nativism stirred the public mind so profoundly. During 1919 and the early months of 1920 no other kind of xenophobia even approached it in terms of vogue and impact.

On all levels of government, authorities moved to crush the Reds. Local police made many raids and arrests on their own initiative. It was not uncommon, for example, for Russian workers of suspicious appearance to be seized, held overnight, and then released. A wave of repressive legislation swept through state legislatures. Fourteen of them in 1919 enacted criminal syndicalism laws, following or expanding upon the example which five states had set during the war. Under these laws a vigorous program of prosecutions for organizational membership or for opinion ensued; in a three-month period the state of Washington convicted eighty-six individuals of membership in the I.W.W., which was now regarded as an American appendage of the Bolsheviks. [81]

The federal government, however, had no similar powers to cast anyone into prison simply for his beliefs or associations. The Espionage and Sedition Acts had enabled federal officials to outdo the states in this respect while America was fighting Germany, but the authority conferred by these statutes lapsed with the end of hostilities. The United States government possessed only one legal instrument for stamping on the propaganda activities which the postwar radicals conducted. It could deport the foreigners who supposedly were causing all the trouble; or, rather, it could deport those who had not acquired citizenship. This limitation on federal power tended to accentuate the anti-foreign emphasis in the Red Scare, for the whole weight of the distinctively national attack on radicalism fell upon the immigrants. [82]

In 1919 the clamor of 100 per centers for applying deportation as a purgative rose to an hysterical howl. "Nothing will save the life of this free Republic if these foreign leeches are not cut and cast out," said Mrs. George Thacher Guernsey, president-general of the Daughters of the American Revolution. Patriotic, veteran, and fraternal organizations demanded more vigorous federal action and sterner legislation. The Farmers National Congress recommended to the United States Justice Department: "burn a brand in the hide of those fellows when you deport them so that if they ever dare return the trade mark will tell its tale and expose them." When the question arose as to where deportees could be sent, one Senator suggested that the North Pole would be a good place. "I do not care where they go, so they get out of here," he said. At the annual picnic of the North Dakota Association of Southern California a speaker advised: "These murderous wild beasts of our otherwise blessed republic should be given a bottle of water and a pint of meal and shoved out into the ocean on a raft, when the wind is blowing seaward." [83] Again, as during the war, a supernationalist public opinion urged the federal government along the path of coercion.

Although deportation was acquiring new significance as a technique of suppression and purification, administratively it was divorced from the domestic law enforcement agencies of the nation —a situation which from the outset hampered execution of a mass expulsion of alien radicals. The historic connection of deportation with the regulation of immigration placed jurisdiction in the hands of the Secretary of Labor, within whose department the Bureau of Immigration functioned. As a repressive agency the Department of Labor proved a weak and uncertain reed. On the one hand, the Commissioner of Immigration, Anthony Caminetti, had (despite his Italian parentage) the instincts of a 100 per center; it was he who had directed the roundup of alien Wobblies during the war and who had initiated action for the new deportation law of 1918.* The Secretary of Labor, on the other hand, was a Scottish-born labor leader named William B. Wilson with a liberal record and a distrust of the doctrine of guilt by association. A rubicund, good-natured man, Secretary Wilson paid far more attention to labor problems than to immigration, and his views on deportation were not always clear or consistent. But before anyone could

---

* Caminetti, a Californian, was the first Italian-American to be elected to Congress. His appointment as Commissioner of Immigration in 1913 had taken control of the bureau out of the hands of labor leaders and was undoubtedly an earnest of President Wilson's desire to placate the immigrants!

actually be sent out of the country, the Secretary had to sign a warrant ordering the step. Also, in cases arising under the 1918 law which authorized deportation on grounds of organizational membership, he had to certify the organization as subversive. Wilson did not regard mere I.W.W. membership as a crime against the nation, and he consistently refused to certify the I.W.W.[84]

Consequently a full-fledged deportation campaign was slow to develop. In February 1919, the Immigration Bureau rushed to Ellis Island thirty-nine of the alien Wobblies it had seized the year before, hoping to expel them immediately. The press hailed the move with wild rejoicing as the first federal blow against radicalism—a grand clean-up of "bewhiskered, ranting, howling, mentally warped, law-defying aliens." [85] The Secretary's attitude, however, compelled the immigration authorities to furnish evidence that each candidate for deportation had personally advocated revolution or sabotage. This was a difficult task and, together with other legal complications, forced the bureau to release all but a handful. Throughout the spring and summer the pursuit of individual aliens suspected of radical views continued, but only a trickle of deportations resulted.[86]

Meanwhile public opinion was growing daily more impatient for action. So was the Justice Department, with its strong and established predilection for 100 per cent policies. A new Attorney General, A. Mitchell Palmer, took over from Gregory in March 1919. Palmer's bulldog jaw belied his simple, placid face. Once the implacable opponent of the political bosses and liquor interests in Pennsylvania, he approached the war against Germany with the same crusading belligerence. As Alien Property Custodian during the war, he showed his mettle in scourging the Hun and won national prominence. He was an ambitious man as well: his eye rested lovingly on the White House.[87] The failure of Palmer's agents to find the perpetrators of several bombing episodes in April must have exasperated him considerably, and when another infernal machine battered the front of his own home in June, Palmer was ready to go with the current. He appealed to Congress for a special appropriation, telling the frightened legislators that he knew exactly when the Reds were planning "to rise up and destroy the Government at one fell swoop." [88] The appropriation became available during the summer, and with it Palmer created a new division of the Bureau of Investigation for the war against radicalism. In anticipation of a peacetime sedition law, the division proceeded to assemble data on all revolutionary activities; for more immediate action it offered its services to the Department of Labor. The latter agreed to the participation of Justice agents in carrying out a program of deportation, and inasmuch as Secretary Wilson's scruples about guilt by association did not extend to a radical organization of Russian immigrants, the Union of Russian Workers, this was chosen as the first target.

On November 7, 1919, the second anniversary of the Bolshevik régime in Russia, Palmer's men descended on Russian meeting places in eleven cities and seized hundreds of members of the organization. Screening for once was swift. Little more than a month later 249 aliens, most of them netted in the November raids, were on a specially chartered transport en route to Finland. From there they traveled overland to Russia through snows and military lines. Some had to leave behind in America their wives and children, at once destitute and ostracized.[89]

Palmer, by this dramatic move and by a simultaneous injunction crushing a national coal strike, filled a power vacuum. Woodrow Wilson lay helplessly ill, a broken and exhausted President, and the Attorney General emerged as the strong man of Washington. For a moment he seemed almost to be converting 100 per cent Americanism into a system of government.[90] Certainly, with fewer powers than his wartime predecessor, he applied more singlemindedly the principle of securing conformity by calling in the police.

Basking in the popularity of his anti-Russian raid, Palmer now prepared a mightier blow. On January 2 the Department of Justice, aided by local police forces in thirty-three cities, carried out a vast roundup of alien members of the two communist parties. Officers burst into homes, meeting places, and pool rooms, as often as not seizing everyone in sight. The victims were loaded into trucks, or sometimes marched through the streets handcuffed and chained to one another, and massed by the hundreds at concentration points, usually police stations. There officials tried to separate out the alien members of radical organizations, releasing the rest or turning them over to the local police. Many remained in federal custody for a few hours only; some lay in crowded cells for several weeks without a preliminary hearing. For several days in Detroit eight hundred men were held incommunicado in a windowless corridor, sleeping on the bare stone floor, subsisting on food which their families brought in, and limited to the use of a single drinking fountain and a single toilet.[91] Altogether, about three thousand aliens were held for deportation, almost all of them eastern Europeans.

The brazenness of these proceedings (executed through the closest cooperation between the Justice Department and the Bureau of Immigration) is all the more striking in view of the fact that the Secretary of Labor had not yet formally declared membership in either the Communist party or the Communist Labor party a deportable offense. Indeed, Secretary Wilson was largely incapacitated by illness during the winter of 1919-20. He yielded grudgingly to pressure from Caminetti and Palmer in authorizing warrants of arrest for the January raids. Once they occurred, he accepted the accomplished fact and decided that membership in the Communist party fell under the ban of the deportation law of 1918. The Assistant Secretary of Labor, Louis F. Post, was made of sterner stuff, however. In March, while final deportation action was still pending, Post temporarily became Acting Secretary of Labor and set himself athwart Palmer's path.

Post, a seventy-one-year-old liberal with sad eyes and a scholarly Vandyke beard, had been a crotchety reformer ever since he read Tom Paine as a child. He was a leading single-taxer, a Swedenborgian, and a defender of academic freedom. With the ardor of another Voltaire he undertook a meticulous review of each of the cases at hand. Wherever evidence of party membership seemed faulty or wherever the government lacked proof that the man knew what he was doing when he joined the party, Post canceled the deportation order and freed the immigrant. When Secretary Wilson returned to office, he upheld Post's policy, and by July 2,202 prospective deportees had been set loose. Post endorsed the deportation of 556 others, and in time most of these went their exiled way,[92] but the drive to purge the alien radical had suffered a mortal setback. Palmer fumed at Post for coddling and encouraging Bolsheviks, and a group of 100 per cent American Congressmen tried to impeach him for disloyalty. The public hysteria, however, was breaking. Before a Congressional committee, Post turned on his critics with a savagely brilliant defense. Instead of unanimously excoriating him, many newspapers commended the pugnacious old liberal for simply doing his duty.[93]

Actually the Big Red Scare was nearly over, Post's personal intervention coinciding with much larger changes. First of all, the seething labor unrest of 1919, which formed the social basis of the anti-radical spirit, faded early in 1920. The great steel strike collapsed in January amid the wreckage of labor's postwar dreams, and the unions passed to the defensive. The return of industrial peace dissipated the fear of imminent revolution. Especially among industrialists, many of whom had joined in the cry of alarm, the easing of class tensions produced a deep reaction. Now that the immigrant seemed docile again, his bosses recalled his economic value. In purely business terms, a rampant anti-radical nativism could cut off industry's best source of manpower. A number of business leaders began actively defending the foreign-born from the charge of radicalism. The Inter-Racial Council, which was a mouthpiece for some of America's biggest tycoons—men like Cleveland H. Dodge, E. G. Grace, Thomas W. Lamont, and Daniel Willard—came out flatly in April 1920 against the common association of immigrants with unrest, demanded a reform of deportation proceedings, and urged the public to take a friendly attitude toward ethnic minorities. Its chairman, T. Coleman du Pont, asserted that native Americans created most of the industrial disturbances and that the immigrant's critics were suffering from "sheer Red hysteria, nothing more." The head of the National Founders Association took the same view. The American Constitutional Association, an organization of a thousand West Virginia business leaders formed in 1920 to defend the interests of the coal operators and to promote the open shop, said, "Bolshevism was conceived in America by Americans." [94]

Just at the moment when industrial strife was abating, the Redhunters were overreaching themselves. In their zeal to repress radicalism they were ranging farther and farther from the orbit of nativism. As long as anti-radicalism kept its link with nationalism and struck chiefly at groups on the fringes of American life, it awakened no significant protest. But by the early months of 1920 the repressive spirit was beginning to threaten the heart of American political processes. Throughout the fall Palmer had been pushing hard for a peacetime sedition law which would enable him to punish citizens as well as aliens for their opinions and associations. In January such a bill passed the Senate. A number of conservative groups such as the American Newspaper Publishers Association instantly turned their fire on so general an abridgement of freedom. At the same time the New York legislature evicted five of its duly elected members simply because they were Socialists. This unconstitutional abrogation of the decision of an electorate seemed to many a danger to American political institutions and thus a very different matter from the simple hounding of foreigners. The Bar Association of the City of New York, led by Charles Evans Hughes, sparked a reverberating protest.[95]

The Attorney General's best efforts to keep the Red Scare alive came to nought. In April he announced that a gigantic bomb plot and general strike would erupt on May Day. Nothing exploded except the jeers of Palmer's now vociferous critics. Twelve of the leading jurists in the United States issued a statement declaring that the Justice Department's illegal practices had stirred up more revolutionary sentiment than any group of radical propagandists could have created. A subcommittee of the Republican National Committee advised against further repressive measures. Congress did enact one more anti-radical law in June, forbidding aliens under pain of deportation to possess revolutionary literature; but a general sedition law ceased to be a political possibility. Although Palmer veered toward a more cautious course, his political prospects rapidly waned. In 1924 the *Saturday Evening Post* could look back with amusement at the nation's former concern over radicals, dismissing it as "nothing but the last symptom of war fever." [96]

By then anti-radical nativism had indeed shrunk to minor significance. Nevertheless the *Post* was dead wrong in assuming that the United States had recovered from the distempers of 1915 to 1919. The specific fevers of war and revolution passed; but a hardy virus was still at work. As social conditions changed—different in 1919 than in 1918, and altered again in 1920—they modified the expression of nationalism but preserved its inner spirit. Nothing occurred in 1920 to destroy the ongoing force of 100 per cent Americanism. In spy-hunting and in Red-hunting it assumed only the first of its evolving forms.

Chapter Nine

Crusade for Americanization

"Maybe if we'd season th' immygrants a little or cook thim thurly, they'd go down betther," I says. . . . "But what wud ye do with th' offscourin' iv Europe?" says he. "I'd scour thim some more," says I.

—Mr. Dooley

Nation building is to be in the future a deliberate formative process, not an accidental . . . arrangement.

—Frances Kellor

Until the twentieth century, native Americans had not supposed that national homogeneity depended, necessarily or desirably, on special pressures to assimilate the immigrants. Surely assimilation would follow readily enough from the general institutions and atmosphere of American society, unless of course an especially vicious immigration appeared on the scene; and in that case America could restrict its entry or its influence. Thus virtually the whole American response to foreign minorities was contained in two general attitudes: on the one hand, rejection and withdrawal; on the other, a confident faith in the natural, easy melting of many peoples into one. When fearful of disruptive influences, the Americans sought to brake the incoming current or to inhibit its political power; otherwise they trusted in the ordinary processes of a free society.

In contrast, some of the multinational states of Europe had adopted a third approach to unity. In Russia and in Hungary, for example, dominant nationalities tried to force or stimulate absorption of entrenched minorities. Drives to impose a unitary national

234

culture by repressing minority languages, churches, and names created storms and stresses from which the United States long and happily escaped. Part of the difference was due to the more fluid character of America's ethnic groups. In Europe most minorities were fixed in place and rooted in the soil of an ancient culture they were determined to preserve. But immigration brought the United States uprooted peoples who wanted to share in large degree in the new national life; cohesion developed without coercion. Equally important, nineteenth century Americans did not really demand a high level of national solidarity. Their country had achieved its own loose kind of homogeneity in the very course of accepting a variety of peoples and institutions. And since the American concept of freedom sanctioned a various and flexible ethnic pattern, a large measure of diversity was taken for granted.

Yet America did not forever avoid a version of the European experience. When neither a preventive nativism nor the natural health of a free society seemed sufficient to cope with disunity, a conscious drive to hasten the assimilative process, to heat and stir the melting pot, emerged. From its tiny beginnings at the end of the nineteenth century to its height in the First World War, the movement for Americanization was another indication of the growing urgency of the nationalist impulse. Americanization brought new methods for dealing with the immigrants; it significantly altered the traditions of both nativism and confidence. At the same time, the movement embraced the underlying spirit of both traditions. Within the crusade for Americanization the struggle between nativistic and democratic instincts persisted.

Prewar Origins

The institution, above all others, on which nineteenth century Americans relied to further such ethnic unity as they required was the common school. "Education," declared a New York high school principal with characteristically American faith in that commodity, "will solve every problem of our national life, even that of assimilating our foreign element." [1] The education to which he referred, however, consisted of the standard regimen applied to all children alike. The schools made almost no effort to single out the immigrants for special attention. Although a few eastern cities in the latter part of the century opened special night school classes in English, and sometimes civics, for foreigners, such programs functioned on a very modest scale.[2] As an organized, articulate movement, Americanization did not receive its primary impetus from educators. The impulse came from two civic-minded groups who had little in common with one another except a felt need for closer social unity. From different points of view both groups reacted to the stresses of urban, industrial conditions, which were forcing America's peoples into increasing interdependence.[3]

The social settlements faced the problem from a humane perspective. There a whole generation of humanitarians discovered how deep was the cultural gulf dividing the people of the slums from the rest of society. Beginning in the 1890's, the settlements undertook the first practical efforts toward social integration of the new immigrant nationalities with the older America. Yet places like Hull House and the University Settlement aimed at Americanization only in the loosest sense of the term. They laid no special emphasis on English or civics classes. They tried to bind together and complete a neighborhood, not to make a nation. On the whole they did more to sustain the immigrant's respect for his old culture than to urge him forward into the new one. One of the great lessons the settlements discovered was that the normal, assimilative influences in America often worked too harshly. Immigrant families were divided; the children developed a brassy, swaggering Americanism in their yearning for acceptance. The settlements, therefore, sought to temper as well as improve the ordinary course of assimilation by providing a receptive environment for Old World heritages. Preaching the doctrine of immigrant gifts, Jane Addams and her fellow workers concentrated less on changing the newcomers than on offering them a home.[4]

A second, and closer, approach to Americanization came from another side of the 1890's: not from its hopes of reform but from its nationalist anxieties. Since the whole Americanization movement reflected a demand for a more tightly knit nation, it was characteristic that the campaign got its essential start from the new patriotic hereditary societies.

Led by the Daughters of the American Revolution, several of these societies embarked on programs of patriotic education designed to indoctrinate the adult foreigner with loyalty to America. In 1898 the Buffalo chapter of the D.A.R. prepared lectures on American history and government to be delivered in foreign languages to men who would soon be voting. Other chapters joined in the work of teaching the "spirit of true Americanism," some directing their attention to immigrant children.[5] The Society of Colonial Dames in 1904 launched a somewhat more extensive program, including scholarships to train experts for such patriotic educational work, the sponsorship of lectures and civics classes, and the preparation of appropriate literature. The Sons of the American Revolution, stirred into action by the assassination of President McKinley, soon outdid the ladies' groups. By 1907 the S.A.R. was devoting half of its income to the job of making aliens into good citizens. Its main achievement was a pamphlet purveying to immigrants advice and information about America. A million copies were printed in fifteen languages and distributed by employers, night schools, and other organizations, and even by the United States Department of Commerce and Labor, which endorsed the project and bore part of the printing expenses.[6]

Throughout their Americanizing efforts the patriotic societies preached a loyalty that consisted essentially of willing submissiveness. Above all, in the words of the D.A.R., they "taught obedience to law, which is the groundwork of true citizenship." [7] The main object of such self-constituted champions of America was to combat the danger of immigrant radicalism or discontent; their chief motive, fear. The settlements, on the other hand, had acted in response to a human need, rather than a political or economic threat; their gentler kind of assimilation arose from sympathy, not from dread. One program drew support from nativistic groups and emotions, the other from the tolerant, cosmopolitan traditions of American democracy.

These were the two sides of the Americanization movement. The impulse of fear and the impulse of love ran throughout its whole course, clashing in principle though in practice sometimes strangely blended. One current tended to soften the movement, orienting it toward the welfare of the immigrant; the other steeled it to an imperious demand for conformity. Out of fear, the Americanization movement fostered a militant nationalism, and by this means it eventually made its widest, most fervent appeal to the native-born public. But Americanization worked most successfully

upon the immigrants through love. It was part of the paradox of
the movement that the side which evoked the most ardent American response produced the slightest positive results.

During the confident years at the beginning of the century,
when ethnic fears did not cut deeply, the kind of Americanizing
which some of the patriotic societies attempted elicited only a
moderate interest; the general public attitude remained indifferent.
On the other hand, the atmosphere of Progressive America encouraged the settlement approach toward immigrants. Although
Americanization never became a major issue in the Progressive era,
it made most headway by enlisting the support of urban progressives who had an awakened social conscience and a cosmopolitan
view of democratic tasks. Under the promptings of sympathy,
Americanization broadened into a drive to combat neglect and
exploitation; it merged into the pattern of reform. Significantly,
the first appearance of the issue in national politics was in the 1912
platform of the Progressive party. For the first time a political
party denounced "the fatal policy of indifference and neglect
which has left our enormous immigrant population to become the
prey of chance and cupidity," and proposed federal action "to promote their assimilation, education and advancement." [8]

Social workers were responsible for the Progressive plank, and
social workers played a key role in fostering ethnic integration,
though they did not characteristically call it Americanization.
Lillian Wald, for example, defined the task as one of "fusing these
people who come to us from the Old World civilization into . . .
a real brotherhood among men." [9] A similar spirit increasingly
permeated the Protestant Social Gospel. For liberal Protestants the
cause had a special attraction as an essential preliminary to evan-
gelization. They chided the churches for maintaining an attitude
of snobbish aloofness toward the alien and called for an expanded
and democratized home-missions campaign.[10] Perhaps the most successful of the efforts under religious sponsorship came from the
Young Men's Christian Association which during those years was
turning from missionary work to a program of social service. Under the direction of Peter Roberts, a trained sociologist, the "Y"
began in 1907 to organize evening classes in English and civics for
foreigners. Roberts developed his own system for teaching prac-

tical English conversation to foreign-born adults, and by 1914 his volunteer instructors had some thirty thousand students.[11]

To Roberts, as to many of the humanitarian Americanizers, the immigrant seemed a blessing if redeemed and uplifted but a danger if left alone. A call to preserve American ideals was fairly commonly interwoven into pleas for service to mankind.[12] In fact, the individual who emerged in the last years of the Progressive era as the presiding genius of the still amorphous movement for Americanization combined to a unique degree the reformer's passion for social improvement with the nationalist's insistence on a single loyalty. Frances A. Kellor, half reformer, half nationalist, represented both sides of the Americanization movement. She gave it as much central direction as it was ever to receive, and through it she made her main contribution to American history.

A crisp, authoritative young lady with an instinct for order and organization, Frances Kellor took a law degree at Cornell before turning to sociology and social work at the University of Chicago and the New York Summer School of Philanthropy. At the turn of the century she plunged into the teeming tenements of New York as a fellow of the College Settlement. In 1904 she wrote *Out of Work*, a muckraking investigation of employment agencies exposing especially their victimization of women and immigrants. Employed thereafter by the Inter-Municipal Research Committee, Miss Kellor kept prying into the facts of urban social problems, drafting remedial legislation, and lobbying for its passage. More and more, the outcast state of the immigrant outraged her sense of justice.

By 1906 she had won the ear of Theodore Roosevelt, who was learning to value her advice on immigration laws.[13] For her part, Miss Kellor's devotion to Roosevelt's leadership grew with the years; in 1912 she became head of the Progressive party's research and publicity department. Also, her ideas increasingly reflected a Rooseveltian "New Nationalism." Always an apostle of industrial efficiency, she abhorred the chaos and waste of *laissez faire*. Through social research and national planning she hoped to organize and emancipate America's human resources, to rationalize opportunity, and to build a more unified nation. In one breath she preached social welfare and national discipline.[14]

Frances Kellor's direct involvement in Americanization began in

1908 when Governor Charles Evans Hughes, prompted by Lillian Wald, appointed the New York Commission on Immigration to inquire into the condition of aliens in the state. As secretary of the commission, Miss Kellor spent months visiting slums and vermin-infested labor camps, studying immigrant education and taking testimony on the exploitation of foreigners by employers and by their own fellow countrymen. The result was the first thorough, official state investigation of alien living conditions. It led to the establishment of a permanent state Bureau of Industries and Immigration under the direction of Miss Kellor. This agency supervised the newcomers' reception and distribution by hearing their complaints, preventing fraud, disseminating advice, and conducting continuing investigations. In time, the bureau's studies engendered further protective legislation regulating immigrant lodging houses, bankers, and steamship agents.[15]

Miss Kellor's work as a public servant (she was said to be the first woman to head a state bureau) by no means exhausted her restless determination to force justice and order upon American ethnic relations. Like any American with a cause, she needed an organization. It happened that one was at hand. In 1908 a group of public-spirited New England businessmen had launched in Boston the North American Civic League for Immigrants. Its founders, though not unmoved by sympathy, were chiefly concerned with protecting the status quo from the menace of ignorant, incendiary foreigners without resorting to immigration restriction. The league, therefore, combined aid with propaganda; it hired agents who advised new arrivals about jobs, housing, and transportation, and it sponsored widely publicized patriotic lectures in foreign languages in the evening schools. Miss Kellor, supported by a group of wealthy New Yorkers, organized a New York branch of the North American Civic League in December 1909.

But the branch and its parent soon parted ways. The New Yorkers developed a much broader, more imaginative program under Miss Kellor's direction. They employed all sorts of ingenious devices to stimulate education for immigrants and, most important, exerted constant pressure on the mid-Atlantic states for protective legislation.[16] While the New York effort followed a liberal direction, emphasizing state-supported social welfare, the parent league became increasingly reactionary. After the Lawrence textile strike of 1912, the Boston group, subsidized by New England industrialists, concentrated on sending agents into foreign communities to act as industrial spies and leaders of anti-strike movements. Early in 1914, therefore, the New Yorkers broke away completely to form the Committee for Immigrants in America, with Frances Kellor as vice-chairman and guiding spirit.[17]

Meanwhile the kind of governmental action which New York state had pioneered, and which the Kellor group did much to encourage elsewhere, was spreading. Pennsylvania, New Jersey, Massachusetts, Rhode Island, and California undertook investigations into immigrant life on the model of the original New York inquiry, and some of those states followed through with permanent agencies. The most vigorous action came from California, whose Commission on Immigration and Housing was directed by Simon Lubin. The commission began work by exposing the dreadful living conditions underlying the Wheatland hop fields riot of 1913; in time its recommendations led to public regulation of labor camps, a unique program of home teachers in foreign districts, and the most complete tenement and lodging house laws in the country.[18] At the same time the larger American cities were expanding their evening school classes in English for immigrants; by 1915 Chicago had 13 per cent of its total non-English-speaking population enrolled in school.[19] In all these ways the progressive conscience was reaching new dimensions.

Nevertheless, these uncoordinated local, state, and voluntary efforts left Frances Kellor unsatisfied. The New Nationalist within her clamored for centralized, federal action; Americanization was floundering "without a *national* goal or consciousness." Her new Committee for Immigrants in America set itself up, therefore, as a central clearinghouse to aid, advise, and unify all public and private agencies interested in the problem throughout the country. It sought both "a national policy . . . to make of all these people one nation" and a federal bureau to lead the way. At the moment the best Miss Kellor could get from the federal government was the enthusiastic interest of the Bureau of Education, which had little power and scant appropriations. Nothing daunted, the Committee for Immigrants persuaded its own well-to-do backers—people like Frank Trumbull, the railroad president, Felix Warburg, the banker, and Mrs. E. H. Harriman—to put up the money for establishing a Division of Immigrant Education within the Bureau of Education. The committee then provided this new unit with a staff of workers who proceeded to publicize the need for educational Americanization. Throughout its five-year life, the Division of Immigrant Education remained the subsidized creature of Miss Kellor's private pressure group.[20]

100 Per Cent Americanized

Molded by the social conscience and the growing national aspirations of the Progressive era the Americanization movement took definite form. It developed a broad program and a vigorous leadership. In a small way it was undoubtedly beginning to have some effect on the immigrants. What it lacked chiefly was followers. It failed signally to awaken a mass response in the American people. Then the war transformed it. In a few months Americanization blossomed into a great popular crusade. And as it swelled on the waves of wartime sentiment, the character of the movement subtly but profoundly changed.

"With startling suddenness," wrote one authority in 1916, "the effects flowing out of the war have brought to public attention aspects of immigration that heretofore have been regarded with unruffled complacency. It has consciously become all of a sudden of the very greatest importance to us as a nation that the immigrants whom we have welcomed into our society . . . should be an integral part of that society and not foreign to it. We have found that our forces for assimilating this foreign element have not been working. . . . We have suddenly been made to realize that . . . many of these . . . are not strangers to the hand that stabs in the dark or the lips that betray with a kiss." [21] Spurred by fear of the hyphen, the drive for national solidarity, the deepest force underlying Americanization, now reached far beyond its earlier demands.

Americanization pushed dramatically into the public eye in the spring and summer of 1915. The United States Bureau of Naturalization, set up in 1906 to supervise and standardize the admission of aliens to citizenship, had already begun before the European war to consider ways to encourage civic education for aspiring citizens and to make naturalization ceremonies more impressive.

As a publicity device the bureau persuaded the city fathers of Philadelphia to hold a great public reception for thousands of newly naturalized citizens on May 10, 1915. President Wilson came to the city of brotherly love for the occasion and delivered an important neutrality speech containing one of his noblest affirmations of the cosmopolitan sources of American nationality.

The event caused so much interest that the Committee for Immigrants in America eagerly seized upon the idea. It established an auxiliary, the National Americanization Day Committee, which organized similar receptions throughout the country on the Fourth of July, designating that holiday "Americanization Day." In a whirlwind campaign, Frances Kellor and her associates enlisted the cooperation of mayors, school authorities, churches, and civic groups, prepared data for speakers, and distributed suggested programs, buttons, and posters. When the Fourth arrived, 107 cities celebrated it as Americanization Day, and the country resounded with the committee's slogan, "Many Peoples, But One Nation." [22]

The tone was still liberal, and the emphasis still rested on social welfare; but the impulse behind the new interest in Americanization was fear of divided loyalties. The popular support which the movement had never had as a reform, now, with the waning of progressivism, poured out of an apprehensive nationalism. In this climate of opinion the leadership of the movement underwent a similar reorientation. The National Americanization Day Committee dropped the "Day" out of its title, largely absorbed the functions of the Committee for Immigrants in America, and continued the latter's role as the brain trust of Americanization. Still led by Frances Kellor, the group never entirely abandoned a humanitarian sympathy for the alien, but after the summer of 1915 it shifted its emphasis to a program of stimulating naturalization, breaking the immigrant's ties with the Old World, and teaching him an American culture. The earlier social objectives faded into the background. Loyalty was contrasted with "dual citizenship." The slogan "Many Peoples, But One Nation" gave way to a new one, "America First." Also, the National Americanization Committee deliberately tried to link its own objectives to the more powerful preparedness movement by interpreting Americanization as the civilian side of national defense. Miss Kellor appeared before the National Security League to warn of the internal peril from foreign influences. In the same year, 1916, her most breathless book, *Straight America*, pleaded for military preparedness, industrial mobilization, universal service, and Americanization as coessential to a more vital nationalism.[23]

The Americanizers were now gaining fresh recruits daily. The General Federation of Women's Clubs put its maternal shoulder to the wheel; the D.A.R. girded itself for more strenuous efforts; fraternal organizations saw an opportunity for patriotic service; educators, under pressure both from the Bureau of Naturalization and the Bureau of Education, revised their teaching methods and expanded their classes.

Significant support came from business organizations. In addition to patriotic motives and the desire to forestall unrest, many businessmen had good economic reasons to encourage Americanization. Just when a flood of Allied purchase orders turned the depression of 1914 into a rousing boom, the war cut off industry's supply of new manpower. For the first time since the Civil War the American economy was hurtling into flush times with no fresh stream of immigrant labor on which to draw. Confronted with the novel problem of labor conservation, many an employer saw in Americanization a means of increasing the efficiency, cooperation, and output of his present workers.

The Detroit Board of Commerce showed the way in 1915 with a massive civic campaign to get non-English-speaking foreigners into the night schools. Henry Ford, who was just then launching a spectacular experiment in welfare capitalism, set up his own Ford English School and compelled his foreign employees to attend it before and after work two days a week. Both the National Association of Manufacturers and the United States Chamber of Commerce then commended Americanization to their members. The chamber, which was led by some of the same people who were active in the National Americanization Committee, entered jointly with the latter into a general campaign for business support. (The ubiquitous Frances Kellor emerged as assistant to the chairman of the Immigration Committee of the Chamber of Commerce.) As a result, a good many businessmen inaugurated factory classes, distributed civics lessons in pay envelopes, and even subsidized public evening schools. A substantial segment of employers regarded these operations as quixotic, but those who did participate in them commonly thought that Americanization paid dividends in productivity and morale.[24]

America's entry into the war keyed up the whole agitation which had been developing over the preceding two years to a more intense and frantic pitch. Since victory itself might depend on the loyalty of the vast foreign population, a note of urgency and a plea for haste sharpened the entreaties for national solidarity. Furthermore, the crusade provided an outlet for civilian America's tremendous hunger to "do something" to help win the war. In a global encounter which touched off the most strenuous appeals for "service," Americanization took its place along with Liberty bond campaigns, food conservation, Red Cross work, the detection of disloyalty, and a dozen other voluntary drives as a way of enlisting on the home front. In some ways, Americanizing the alien was perhaps more satisfying than merely spying upon him because success seemed to depend on the same type of moral exhortation which sustained so much of the war effort. To a nation charged with evangelical impulses, Americanization was a mission of redemption; to a country of salesmen, it offered an adventure in high pressure salesmanship.

The movement had now grown too large and chaotic to conform to any central leadership. Although the National Americanization Committee kept issuing directives and recommendations and continued to exert much influence, enthusiasm overflowed the bounds of all authority or direction. Thousands of agencies were in some measure engaged: schools, churches, fraternal orders, patriotic societies, civic organizations, chambers of commerce, philanthropies, railroads, and industries, and—to a limited degree—trade unions. There was much duplication, overlapping, and pawing of the air. Many harassed their local school superintendents; others deluged the foreign-born with patriotic leaflets. Now that the preparedness movement was past, the National Security League and the American Defense Society developed a program of war propaganda which included public meetings in immigrant neighborhoods. Other groups dispatched speakers to instruct their fellow citizens on the duty "to go among our alien residents and to see that they understand the desirability of becoming citizens [and appreciate] the debt they owe to the country which is protecting them." [25] Among women's clubs there spread the practice of paying friendly, Americanizing visits to immigrant homes.

On one such occasion, according to a story current in Washington at the time, a group of Americanizing ladies was met by a Bohemian tenement dweller with the plea that they wait and come back next week. "What!" they protested. "You mean that you . . . want to put *off* your entrance into American life?"

"No, no!" the agitated Bohemian woman replied. "We're *perfectly* willing to be Americanized. Why, we never turn *any* of them away. But there's nobody home but me. The boys volunteered, my man's working on munitions, and all the rest are out selling Liberty bonds. I don't want you to get mad, but *can't* you come back next week?" [26]

The confusion was multiplied and exacerbated by competition between several federal agencies for primacy in the movement. The Bureau of Education, backed by continuing subsidies from the National Americanization Committee, worked very hard not only to foster immigrant education but also to mobilize all the forces interested in Americanization. The bureau, and its *alter ego*, the N.A.C., did manage in some degree to dominate the Americanization work which sprang up through the loose machinery of the Council of National Defense. The latter, acting on the recommendations of the N.A.C., urged the various state councils of defense to support the program of the Bureau of Education. In line with this objective, the state councils proceeded to create further machinery to "coordinate" the work of local, voluntary agencies; but little uniformity resulted. All this aroused the jealousy of the Bureau of Naturalization, which was pushing its own narrower program of citizenship classes in the public evening schools. The Bureau of Naturalization got the National Council of Defense to endorse its campaign too and then lobbied for legislative authority to absorb control over all federal aspects of Americanization.

At this point, in the spring of 1918, the Bureau of Education advanced suddenly into new terrain. The N.A.C. turned over its entire New York office and office force to the Bureau of Education. There Frances Kellor developed for the bureau a network of direct contacts with immigrant groups through foreign-language propaganda and through conferences with representatives of the several nationalities. Thus the bureau passed beyond the practice of coaching Americans in Americanization and began to work on the immigrants themselves.

But meanwhile the Committee on Public Information, the new federal agency for psychological warfare, was doing exactly the same thing quite independently. Through another social worker, Josephine Roche, the C.P.I. proved remarkably successful in directing advice and patriotic propaganda at more than a score of immigrant nationalities and giving them a sense of participation in the nation's cause.[27]

The organizational confusion in wartime Americanization was one mark of the feverish spirit which the movement now displayed; another was its prevailing ideology. The war carried much further the shift from sympathy to fear, from cosmopolitan democracy to jealous nationalism, which had displayed itself in the preparedness period. In large measure the Americanizers were swept up in the current of 100 per cent Americanism. Most of them gave themselves over to more or less the whole range of 100 per cent ideas: the insistence on a conformist loyalty intolerant of any values not functional to it; the demand for a high sense of duty toward the nation; the faith in a drumfire of exhortation and propaganda to accomplish desired social objectives; and the ultimate reliance on coercion and punishment. In short, by threat and rhetoric 100 per cent Americanizers opened a frontal assault on foreign influence in American life. They set about to stampede immigrants into citizenship, into adoption of the English language, and into an unquestioning reverence for existing American institutions. They bade them abandon entirely their Old World loyalties, customs, and memories. They used high-pressure, steamroller tactics. They cajoled and they commanded.

The drillmasters of Americanization made an appearance as early as the preparedness period. General Leonard Wood, one of the leading advocates of preparedness, suggested that universal military service would itself offer the best means of making unassimilated groups "understand that they are Americans."[28] There was some talk of applying economic compulsions to naturalization by giving job preferences to citizens, and Henry Ford's compulsory English School represented a pioneering attempt to apply the 100 per cent philosophy to education. The first thing that foreign-speaking employees learned in the Ford school was how to say,

"I am a good American." Later the students acted out a panto-
mime which admirably symbolized the spirit of the enterprise. In
this performance a great melting pot (labeled as such) occupied
the middle of the stage. A long column of immigrant students
descended into the pot from backstage, clad in outlandish garb and
flaunting signs proclaiming their fatherlands. Simultaneously from
either side of the pot another stream of men emerged, each pros-
perously dressed in identical suits of clothes and each carrying a
little American flag.[29]

With America's entry into the war, of course, 100 per cent
Americanization picked up momentum. Various official and semiofficial agencies foisted patriotic articles on foreign-language
newspapers. Schoolteachers in New York City made use of the
immigrants' children to circulate loyalty pledges for the signature
of their parents. The Cincinnati City Council closed down pool-
rooms operated by aliens, on the theory that such establishments
kept foreigners apart from American influences. The Governor of
Iowa issued a proclamation banning any language except English
in all schools, church services, conversations in public places or
over the telephone.[30] Congress struck its hardest blow in the Reve-
nue Act of 1918, which imposed on "non-resident" aliens an income tax rate twice as heavy as that for citizens and "resident"
aliens. The definition of a "non-resident" alien was never entirely
clear, but the act had the effect of driving thousands of foreign
workers to declare their intention to become citizens.

Meanwhile private individuals and groups often exerted sterner
pressures. Although few industrialists could afford to fire their
unnaturalized employees, many adopted and publicized a compromise policy of promoting only citizens or those in process of becoming citizens; scores of manufacturers in Chicago posted such an
announcement in their plants.[31] A more extreme threat was that of
deportation, the ultimate sanction of the 100 per center. What
better fate, indeed, did anyone who resisted assimilation deserve?
Accordingly a bill to deport all aliens who would not apply for
citizenship within three months was introduced in Congress in
1916, and during the war the idea of expulsion as an alternative
to assimilation was frequently discussed, though it could not yet
be implemented.[32]

Nothing better illustrated the drift of wartime Americanization than the views of Frances Kellor and her National Americanization Committee, still the chief claimants for leadership of the movement. Already pulled part way from its original course by the anxious militancy of the preparedness period, the committee in 1917 embraced much of the 100 per cent philosophy. So far had Miss Kellor and her wealthy associates swung from their early emphasis on reform that now they stressed the protection of the economic status quo. As a New Nationalist, Miss Kellor had always stood for rationalizing the business system instead of attacking it. Since her interest in efficiency and discipline never flagged, she slipped easily from the concepts of the welfare state to those of welfare capitalism once wartime apprehensions muted progressive aspirations.

Above all, the N.A.C. now urged the suppression of unrest and disloyalty, the elimination of conditions under which "anti-American" influences flourished, and the dissolution of minority cultures. To prevent strikes or other disaffection, the committee recommended a constant surveillance of aliens by means of a semiannual registration of the whole population. It established a Man-Power Engineering Service which advised employers how and where to use alien enemies in their plants and how to guard against sabotage. ("Let us insist frankly," the committee warned, "that a man born on another soil has to *prove* himself for America.") It demanded internment wherever proof of "anti-American sympathy" existed. ("There is no use temporizing.") And it proposed requiring all aliens to learn English and apply for citizenship within three years, or face deportation.[33] A note of sympathy remained, strangely blended with the sense of menace: the committee still criticized social discriminations and barbaric working conditions. But against an ounce of accommodation it balanced a pound of coercion.

Although 100 per cent Americanization constituted a major break from the old, easygoing confidence in assimilation, in comparison to similar movements in other countries it was mild indeed. Aside from the discriminatory tax law of 1918, the federal government and almost all of the state governments confined themselves to moral suasion in aiding Americanization; they did not, with the rarest exceptions, resort to force. All of the more extreme proposals of private zealots remained unrealized: deportation, a time limit on naturalization and adoption of the English language, suppression of the foreign-language press, mass internments, the denial of industrial employment to aliens. In part, this comparative restraint reflected the pressure of a democratic heritage; in part, however, it was due to the limits which the war itself imposed on 100 per cent Americanism. The need for immediate national unity was too pressing to permit a thorough indulgence in tactics which would surely breed wide resentment among aliens, thus intensifying their alienage. Too violent an assault on the immigrant would defeat the aim of speedily transforming him.

Nor were the inhibitions which the war laid upon wartime nationalism merely negative and expediential. Through military service and through countless voluntary community projects, the peoples of America drew together into a closer union than any they had known before. In dedication to a common cause, they found a good deal of the unity for which they sought. The cohesive sympathies of 1917 and 1918 certainly did not satiate the craving for conformity; but who can doubt that the fund of good will which most minorities enjoyed during those years softened the blows that fell upon them?

The International Nationalists

The forces that restrained the mailed fist of the 100 per center upheld the beckoning hand of the humanitarian; what checked one released the other. Although wartime fears diverted Americanization from predominantly liberal channels, the sunny side of the war spirit lent a certain encouragement to the liberal approach. The strategy born in the social settlements, though no longer the controlling strategy, got wide support from the fraternal idealism of a common cause. Americanization still pulled two ways.

Liberal Americanization did not pass from peace to war entirely unchanged. An early zeal for reforming the immigrant's environment had to give place, like all programs of social reconstruction, to the immediate exigencies of victory. Furthermore the democratic, cosmopolitan school shared a heightened national consciousness. By taking seriously the importance of *national* integration as well as *human* integration, the liberals entered more fully into a nationalist mood; they talked less about reform and more about America. Their Americanism, however, contained the same humane values that had been central to their reformism. They remained the keepers of the cosmopolitan traditions of American democracy.

In contrast to the high-pressure salesmen of Americanization, this group pleaded for appreciation of the immigrants' cultural heritages. The concept of "immigrant gifts," which the settlement founders had first preached to the immigrants themselves, served to define an ideal of nationality which could be set against 100 per cent theories. The latter, according to the liberal view, would deprive the nation of sources of strength and enrichment. One ideal called on America to enlarge its national character by accepting contributions, the other to protect that character by a quarantine on infections. One pictured the nation as great in the universal range of its ties and sympathies, the other as great in the purity of its separateness. One looked toward the future growth of a still unfinished nationality; the other looked back to the past perfection of a completed pattern.

During the war, as before, liberal Americanization drew its main support from social workers, from liberal clergymen, and from educators and intellectuals alert to the social implications of democracy. In terms as vague in their own way as those of the 100 per centers, a school superintendent appealed for a policy of Americanization which "welcomes the best of the culture, the arts, and the crafts of the Old World, that . . . we may be enriched with this spiritual inheritance"; Professor John Erskine deplored the tendency of Americans to impoverish their national character by too readily abandoning their various pasts; and John Dewey, a philosopher whose own sense of democracy had broadened through association with Jane Addams at Hull House, pleaded for "a unity created by drawing out and composing into a harmonious whole the best, the most characteristic, which each contributing race and people has to offer." [34]

These cosmopolitan views received a special stimulus from the idealistic internationalism that swept through the ranks of liberal intellectuals as the United States joined battle with Germany. Pacific and largely isolationist before the war, most of them embraced Woodrow Wilson's interpretation of American intervention as an altruistic dedication of the nation to the cause of mankind. Repudiating isolation as a myth in an interdependent world, they now insisted that America's universal ideals could be realized only through participation in the world community. Linking nationalism explicitly with internationalism, they argued that "the measure of national greatness is to be found in international service." [35] In a sense, the Wilsonian liberals applied the cosmopolitan attitudes they had shown toward the immigrants to the society of nations. Consequently they regarded liberal Americanization as the domestic equivalent of a federated world, and they believed the United States uniquely qualified to realize both goals. Some thought that the two endeavors depended upon each other.[36] Woodrow Wilson himself struck this note. He liked to argue that America's cosmopolitan nationality gave her a consciousness of touching elbows and hearts with all men everywhere and set for her a special vocation of world leadership. But Wilson's feeling for the immigrants was too abstract, too little a flesh-and-blood awareness of people in travail, to remain consistent. When immigrants seemed stubbornly unimpressed by America's mission to gird for war or to join the League of Nations, Wilson lashed out at them fiercely. "Hyphens are the knives that are being stuck into this document," he often charged in defending the Versailles Treaty.[37]

Insubstantial and prettily unreal as the cosmopolitan outlook often was, it did control the policies followed by some Americanizing agencies, thereby serving as an operative check on 100 per cent tendencies. The Delaware Service Citizens, for example, organized evening classes at which twenty-one nationalities sang their own songs and danced their native dances in native costumes. In Springfield, Illinois, a "Gifts of the Nations" class gave immigrants an opportunity to tell others about their homelands. The city of Cleveland, guided by Professor Raymond Moley of Western Reserve University, adopted one of the broadest of such programs, but when it tried to bring foreign and old-stock groups together in a common theater project, it found that good intentions and an appreciation of cultural gifts did not, alas, make people mingle.[38] Among federal agencies the liberal approach was most consistently applied by the Committee on Public Information. By emphasizing the Wilsonian war aim of national self-determination, the committee encouraged immigrant nationalities to associate the "best interests" of their homelands with the American cause; and on July

4, 1918, the C.P.I. organized throughout the United States gigantic demonstrations at which immigrants paraded their "gifts" and affirmed their loyalty.[39]

Whatever effectiveness these devices may have had during the war was soon lost when hostilities ended. The vitality of liberal Americanization depended very much on the high degree of actual national unity that existed during the war period. Once the centripetal pull of the war effort ceased, that sense of dedication to a common national purpose broke down. Among native-born liberals, Americanization, understood as a conscious fostering of nationalism, no longer seemed important after the war. Instead of identifying themselves with the nation, liberal intellectuals felt an increasing alienation from it as reaction followed victory. Instead of clinging to an idealistic, cosmopolitan nationalism, many of them in bitterness and disillusion repudiated all nationalisms, voluntary or coercive, international or parochial. Insofar as they still interested themselves in the immigrant's assimilation, they now thought of it on the whole as a social and economic problem which would pretty largely take care of itself under conditions of social and economic justice. The contributions theory formed the point of departure, for example, for an ambitious project of cooperative research into methods of Americanization which the Carnegie Corporation of New York initiated in the spring of 1918; but the volumes that finally came out of this inquiry in the early twenties said little or nothing about immigrant gifts. Instead, they analyzed the difficulties which immigrants faced in the United States in realistic, sociological terms. And in a book which presumed to speak for the postwar liberal mind, Frederic Howe, who had played an active part in Americanization in its early, progressive phase, now dismissed the problem of the alien as essentially a problem of reestablishing economic democracy.[40]

The decline of a spirit of national unity after the war weakened the sympathetic school of Americanization in another way too. The same sense of solidarity that had enlivened the interest of native liberals in patriotic causes had also helped to make the immigrants receptive to the movement as long as the war lasted. Liberal Americanizers, because they relied on voluntary incentives, very much needed evidence that the alien was well disposed and responsive to their appeal. During the war the immigrants reacted favorably or at least acquiescently to the advances of their mentors. They marched in parades, trooped to class, endured the patronizing attitude that sometimes accompanied liberal Americanization, and dared not protest against the lash of the 100 per centers. Once the crisis ended, however, a long-suppressed resentment burst loose. In recoiling from threats and pressures, the more articulate immigrant leaders often denounced anything that went by the name of Americanization. You threaten to outlaw our speech and memories, they said in effect, and at the same time coax us to deck ourselves out like exhibits in a circus and entertain you with our quaint dialects. An Italian editor summed it up bluntly. "Americanization," he wrote, "is an ugly word." [41]

The minority revolt against Americanization, a revolt accentuated by all of the other manifestations of 100 per cent Americanism, hurled large blocs of immigrants into compensatory chauvinisms of their own. Like the pan-African ferment among American Negroes, Zionism became a mighty force in American Jewish life, and among other European minorities nationalist organizations multiplied, each asserting its own defiant group consciousness. [42] Thus while old-stock liberals were turning anti-nationalist, immigrants were to an unprecedented degree trying to build their own separate nationalisms. Both began to look upon any effort at stimulating American national unity with distrust or even scorn. The cosmopolitan ideal of American nationality as a harmonious fusion of immigrant gifts lived on, to be sure, but not as a significant force. Stripped of most of its functional importance and partially discredited by a more realistic sociology, the gifts idea lingered in story and sentiment. It survived as a genteel tradition.

Meanwhile the decline of the cosmopolitan school of Americanization after the war left the 100 per centers very largely in possession of the field. Undaunted by the immigrants' increasing antagonism, they moved grimly into the breach.

Last Phase: Antidote to Bolshevism

In 1919 and 1920 the crusade for Americanization entered a final convulsive phase. Much creditable work continued to be done, with humanity and understanding, in teaching English to foreigners, especially through the development during and after the war of college courses which trained teachers specifically for such work.[43] But as a general movement Americanization now took on its most frightened and feverish aspect. Swept into the postwar era by an unspent longing for national unity, Americanization cast off some of the restraints imposed by wartime conditions and responded aggressively to the social schisms which opened as those restraints dissolved. The context within which the movement now functioned was the Big Red Scare. Americanization served, in fact, as the positive side of the 100 per cent program during the Red Scare, while anti-radical nativism formed the negative side. Through repression and deportation on the one hand and speedy total assimilation on the other, 100 per centers hoped to eradicate discontent and purify the nation.

The strategy of their campaign was little changed; it was simply more fully articulated. The war had taught them the power of propaganda and had suggested also the supplementary value of governmental coercion. They were prepared to indulge in the one fully and to employ the other with less hesitation. It seemed only fair and sensible to put every ounce of pressure possible behind Americanization in order to salvage the merely ignorant aliens and separate them from the vicious ones. The country could then, with a clear conscience, expel those who remained resistant.[44] The degree to which the patrioteers of 1919-1920 relied on Americanization as a weapon against unrest is indicated by the fact that New York state's Committee on Seditious Activities (the famous Lusk Committee that hounded liberals and radicals alike) devoted almost half of its 4,500-page report to Americanization. Similarly a United States Senate committee investigating the great steel strike of 1919 urgently prescribed Americanization as a means of preventing such conflicts in the future.[45]

In the vanguard now, sounding their alarms and rallying their hosts, were the patriotic societies. Two especially, both products of the war, clutched for leadership. The National Security League, the most powerful of the preparedness societies, had broadened its scope during the war to include Americanization in a general campaign of nationalistic agitation. In December 1918, it shifted gears, moving into a country-wide drive against Bolshevism; and Americanization leaped to the top of its agenda. "The battle to make the country safe is not won," it announced. "The enemy but wears a different guise." [46] The league, which was led by a group of excited corporation directors, was strictly a propaganda organization; it had great faith in the power of organized patriotism to uphold the economic status quo. Counting on deportation to take care of the "irreconcilable radicals," the league concentrated on preaching the 100 per cent ideal of patriotic docility to "the great mass, not yet hopeless, of aliens . . . neither speaking nor thinking American." Accordingly it formed a "Flying Squadron" of hundreds of speakers, who invaded the foreign quarters "to contradict the lies of agitators to ignorant aliens." It circularized employers to organize patriotic meetings in their factories; it set up a program to train teachers for Americanization work; and it vainly sought permission from the federal government to undertake the semiofficial role of investigating all applicants for citizenship. [47]

The American Legion, in its early years the supreme embodiment of the 100 per cent philosophy, leaned more toward the nativist side of the Red Scare and favored repressive tactics more than did the league. But the legion by no means neglected Americanization. At its first national convention in 1919 it established a National Americanism Commission with the particular task of stepping up the tempo of Americanization work in the schools and inciting them to a more vigorous inculcation of the legion's philosophy. Declaring that radicalism came mostly from the "non-American speaking population," the veterans also put pressure on Congress to require all aliens to learn "the American language." This done, the legion was sure that in the next generation foreign colonies would disappear and American ideals of government become secure. [48] Other patriotic societies, both old and new, took much the same view. In the Pacific Northwest the Constitutional Government League combined Americanization and anti-strike propaganda. In Chicago the United Americans enrolled 150 speakers, who kept track of radical meetings and sent a rival orator to the nearest corner whenever a meeting was held. The Daughters of the American Revolution issued in some fifteen languages a manual for immigrants, advising them to distinguish between liberty and license, learn the American way of living, revere the Constitution, save their earnings and pay their taxes, and refrain from dropping papers and rubbish in the streets. [49]

Industrialists too remained active in Americanization after the war, and though some of them gave way to hysteria, a substantial number avoided the extremities of the 100 per cent approach. They shared, to be sure, the anxious fear of Bolshevism, the reliance on patriotism to counteract it, and the association of loyalty with conformity. But as employers of immigrant labor, many of the big industrialists knew that it was to their own self-interest to deal gently with men already resentful at being pushed around; and as converts to "welfare capitalism" an increasing group of business leaders felt an obligation to cultivate the good will of their workers, both native and foreign. Consequently they shied away from tactics too overtly coercive, recommending a humane and kindly approach rather than an overzealous arrogance. "Imagine *yourself* adrift in a foreign-speaking land," declared the organ of the West Virginia coal operators; other manufacturers vaguely endorsed the golden rule.[50] On the whole those employers of foreign-born labor who took a serious interest in Americanization tried to practice it with a certain humanity; they tried to implement a set of 100 per cent assumptions, but diplomatically.

To no small extent their policy reflected the guidance of Frances Kellor, who gave up after the war her hopeless attempt to control and direct the whole Americanization movement and concentrated on working through business channels. Her associations with business leaders had increased during the war, as her contact with progressive reform had diminished. By the time the war ended and the specter of Bolshevism came to the fore, Miss Kellor was looking much more to business than to government for national unity and protection. Her National Americanization Committee's long-standing subsidization of the United States Bureau of Education ceased in March 1919. The connection would shortly have become illegal under a statute prohibiting the federal government from accepting financial aid from private organizations;[51] but Miss Kellor was already absorbed in another project. To replace the N.A.C. she was organizing a new society, of, by, and for American industry.

Its beginnings went back to a quiet dinner at Sherry's Restaurant in New York late in November 1918, at which Frances Kellor addressed fifty of the biggest employers of foreign-born labor in the United States. She warned them that Americanization had thus far had little success and that they would now face great unrest, with minority nationalisms sucking many foreign workers back to their homelands and Bolshevism spreading among those who remained. She proposed a somewhat oblique propaganda campaign by which industry might strengthen its grip on its labor force and "break up the nationalistic, racial groups by combining their members for America." With an initial subscription of $100,-000, Miss Kellor soon launched the Inter-Racial Council.[52] The inclusion of a number of "racial members" (conservative representatives of immigrant groups) gave the council the appearance of a cooperative enterprise and supplied it with minority contacts, but essentially it consisted of much the same group that had sponsored the National Americanization Committee. The millionaire T. Coleman du Pont became chairman, and the council soon enlisted the support of hundreds of industrial corporations.

In the interest of stabilizing industrial conditions, the Inter-Racial Council earnestly besought its followers to avoid strong-arm tactics of Americanization. It counseled "spontaneous Americanization, which, by indirect methods can be delicately but effectively stimulated." [53] The stimulated spontaneity amounted, however, to a veiled coercion. While furnishing its industrial members with pro-American films and advice on their labor problems, the council gave its main attention to dominating the foreign-language press. A unique opportunity arose in December 1918. The crafty Louis Hammerling, who had manipulated foreign-language papers for a decade, was discredited by a Senatorial exposé of services he had performed for liquor interests and for the German government. Some of the leading backers of the Inter-Racial Council seized the occasion to buy Hammerling's American Association of Foreign Language Newspapers and to install Frances Kellor as its new president. The association, which handled practically all of the national advertising in the immigrant press, then became the organ of the Inter-Racial Council. Miss Kellor eliminated the chicanery and political partisanship of Hammerling's régime, while continuing to use the association to control the policies of its member newspapers. The association's stranglehold on national advertising enabled it to flood immigrant editors' columns with patriotic articles, admonitions against emigration to Europe, and anti-radical propaganda.[54]

If the leading industrial Americanizers, tempering fanaticism with self-interest and fear with sympathy, avoided overt compulsions, it is also significant that the whole Americanization movement remained primarily a venture in persuasion. It continued to rely much more upon ideological pressure than upon the coercive power of government. Even for the most rabid 100 per centers, the force of law was ancillary to that of propaganda. After the wartime restraints on 100 per cent Americanism broke down, it still had to work within limits set by a hallowed distrust of state power and official regimentation. Indeed the general postwar reaction brought this distrust sharply in focus. Consequently, in 1919-1920, when the Red Scare gave a new urgency to Americanization, its legislative achievements were still modest. To be sure, a remarkable number of statutes were now enacted to add force to the crusade. But every effort to put new federal sanctions behind Americanization failed, and most of the laws passed by the states encouraged persuasion while stopping short of coercion.

A sustained campaign for broad federal support of Americanization began in 1918 and extended into 1920. The Bureau of Naturalization sponsored one bill, the Bureau of Education another and more extensive one. The latter measure provided for substantial federal aid to the states, on a dollar-matching basis, to finance the teaching of English to aliens and native illiterates. In behalf of this plan, Franklin K. Lane, Secretary of the Interior, organized national conferences and bombarded Congress with pleas for a common language as imperative to national self-protection. After the war there was much sentiment for making such a program of educational Americanization compulsory for all aliens, and in the form in which the bill finally came before the Senate in January 1920, it offered a federal grant only to those states which would require all adult aliens under forty-five to attend the course.[55] Congress, however, was in no mood to embark on new expenditures or to invest the federal government with new powers. The Bureau of Education had to withdraw from Americanization after its subsidy from the Kellor group ended, leaving the Bureau of Naturalization the sole federal agency still active. The latter continued, on a progressively reduced scale, its customary supervision of citizenship classes in the public schools.

Without federal aid, the states in 1919-1920 rushed in to press the crusade for Americanization. A deluge of legislation designed to counteract Bolshevism with nationalism poured out of state legislatures. As always, the principal effort centered on immigrant education. More than a score of states passed laws authorizing or strengthening night school classes in English for foreigners. Some gave local governments considerable financial support for such work; some also took over the propaganda activities which the state councils of defense had conducted among the foreign-born. At least two states, Idaho and Utah, yielded to the coercive spirit by requiring non-English-speaking aliens to attend Americanization classes.[56] Others went farther along the path of 100 percentism, accompanying their educational laws with certain legislative inhibitions on foreign influences. In 1919 fifteen states decreed that English must be the sole language of instruction in all primary schools, public and private. Several states followed the lead of New York in insisting that all public schoolteachers be citizens. Nebraska extended the same requirement to private schools and also stipulated that all meetings except religious or lodge meetings must be conducted in English.[57] Oregon, in the interest of Americanization, came close to outlawing the foreign-language press by requiring that all foreign-language publications display prominently a literal English translation of their entire contents. Two years later, in 1922, the same state passed what was perhaps the last and certainly one of the most severe of the Americanization laws, declaring that all children had to be educated in public rather than private elementary schools. Meanwhile, in 1920, California struck directly at alienage by ordering every adult male alien to register and pay a special annual poll tax of $10. Both the California poll tax and the Oregon school law were declared unconstitutional.[58]

With these statutes, the Americanization movement reached and passed its zenith. As a workaday endeavor to teach English and civics to foreigners in the public evening schools, the program had taken permanent root, and it endured. There, in the schools, it had its major institutional impact, and its most lasting effect was to give a powerful stimulus to all phases of adult education. (During the twenties a number of the agencies set up to supervise immigrant education became departments or divisions of adult education.)[59] But as a major expression of American nationalism, Americanization faded swiftly in the latter part of 1920 and in 1921.

Even before, signs of its approaching breakup were manifest. The defection of many of the liberal Americanizers once the war ended had already largely deprived the crusade of the spirit of sympathy so essential to its earlier successes. Then, in the fear-ridden atmosphere of the Red Scare, the movement lost in coherence as it gained in hysteria. To its most zealous proponents, Americanization began to seem a grander and more comprehensive thing than a simple effort to transform the immigrant. Like the 100 per cent Americanism behind it, the movement now appeared as an antidote for every kind of dissent and a panacea for all of the nation's ills. Men flushed with enthusiasm for the systematic inculcation of patriotism talked more and more in 1919-1920 about "the Americanization of America," rejoicing that the campaign was broadening into one that would "fortify the American Government through implanting and fostering a higher ideality in the individual citizen, whatever his birth." [60] This increasing diffuseness enabled all sorts of special interests to appropriate the idea for their own ends. Evangelical churches adopted the slogan, "Christianization and Americanization are one and the same thing"; the Americanization Fund of Los Angeles, established by ultraconservative businessmen, subsidized campaigns for the open shop and against the initiative law; an Athletes' Americanization League worked to provide free athletic equipment for every American youth on the theory that sports were "the logical antidote for unrest." [61] Abandoned as a reform and balked as a movement for speedy, wholesale assimilation, Americanization was losing contact with the immigrants.

Finally, in the course of 1920, two events—the onset of economic depression and the passing of the Red Scare—delivered the *coup de grâce*. The depression cut off much of the financial support. During the war and postwar boom, businessmen, by organizing factory classes, subsidizing propaganda campaigns, and contributing to the largest Americanization societies, had invested heavily in a movement that promised them a more efficient as well as a more American labor force. Now, however, as production levels slumped, as labor shortages eased and unemployment soared, Americanization no longer seemed worth the expense or effort. Factory classes folded up; even Henry Ford stopped stirring the melting pot. The rich income of the Inter-Racial Council dwindled, and after 1920 it disappeared from sight, bringing to a close Frances Kellor's long career as chaperone of the immigrants.[62] Yet funds were less basic to the vigor of the Americanization movement than were fears. Above all, the crusade came to an end because the collapse of the Big Red Scare dried up its emotional wellsprings. Once the specter of an imminent Bolshevik revolution dissolved, the crusade lost all urgency, lost, in fact, its whole immediate and pressing object.

This is not to say that foreigners no longer seemed a national menace after the early months of 1920. The sense of danger was still vivid; the 100 per center's thirst for conformity remained unslaked. But his conception of the foreign peril changed so profoundly that Americanization became wholly irrelevant to it. From fear of a radical danger, nationalists reverted in 1920 and thereafter to a racial bias. Radicalism, and the hyphenism that preceded it, had been ideological infections; presumably one might set up ideological defenses against them. But the racial danger was in the blood. Why try to educate men inherently incapable of receiving American ideals? Why try to change people who are biologically unchangeable? Why, the influential *Saturday Evening Post* now asked, try to make Americans out of those who will always be Americanski? [63] Why, indeed, put much faith in ideals at all? As early as February 1920, an extremely popular writer declared: "The whole theory of Americanization is one which J. J. Rousseau and T. Jefferson would call perfectly lovely if they were alive. It goes in well with a lot of these mentally subjective theories about altruism and democracy, which in my belief have pretty much brought America to ruin. . . ." [64]

The comment had perhaps a certain grain of truth. Americanization, even in its most coercive aspect, involved an appeal to the foreign-born. It rested, therefore, on a faith in the power of ideals and in the capacity of at least a good share of foreigners to respond to them. It was a venture in conversion and uplift. It drew, to be sure, on nativistic impulses and suspicions, but it served in a way to contain them. It turned part of the new fears of foreign influence which came out of the war into a positive program of emancipation rather than a wholly negative one of exclusion.

The dissolution of the movement left 100 per centers with a sense of failure and disillusion. Had they not tried their best to bring the great mass of newcomers into the fold? Did not the experiment prove the incorrigibly unassimilable nature of the material on which they had worked? America's task, 100 per centers now realized, was much simpler. Instead of struggling to transform the foreign-born, nationalists must concentrate on keeping them out. Thus, while the movement for the redemption of the alien ebbed in 1920, the old drive for the rejection of the immigrant passed all previous bounds.

Chapter Ten

The Tribal Twenties

> The old Americans are getting a little panicky, and no wonder. . . . America, Americans and Americanism are being crowded out of America. It is inevitable that there should be silly forms of protest and rebellion. But the Ku Klux Klan and the hundred percenters are fundamentally right from the standpoint of an American unity and destiny.
> —Ltr. to ed., *New Republic*, 1924

> . . . not nostrums but normalcy . . . not experiment but equipoise, not submergence in internationality but sustainment in triumphant nationality.
> —Warren G. Harding, 1920

During the night of August 5, 1920, and all through the following day hundreds of people laden with clothing and household goods filled the roads leading out of West Frankfort, a mining town in southern Illinois. Back in town their homes were burning. Mobs bent on driving every foreigner from the area surged through the streets. Foreigners of all descriptions were beaten on sight, although the Italian population was the chief objective. Time and again the crowds burst into the Italian district, dragged cowering residents from their homes, clubbed and stoned them, and set fire to their dwellings. The havoc went on for three days, although five hundred state troops were rushed to the scene.

The immediate background of the affair was trivial enough. Thousands of workers were idle and restless owing to a strike in the coal mines where the Italians and a large part of the native population were employed. A series of bank robberies, popularly attributed to a Black Hand Society, had lately occurred; this was followed by the kidnapping of two boys. The discovery of their bodies touched off the civic explosion.[1] The region, to be sure, had a bloody history. Violent anti-foreign incidents had occurred there during and before the war. But never on this scale.[2]

About the same time, an exuberance not wholly unrelated to the miners' frenzy sprang up elsewhere on the national scene in sundry ways. In California anti-Japanese hysteria, quiescent during the war, broke out again in the latter part of 1919 and rose to unprecedented heights during the election of 1920. A new law forbidding Japanese ownership of land passed by popular initiative; a fearful clamor against Japanese "picture brides" went up; and for the first time the agitation was beginning to have a real effect on eastern opinion.[3] In Georgia the 1920 primaries brought the old warrior, Tom Watson, back to the hustings to end his career with a successful campaign for a seat in the United States Senate. The issue was popery. Silenced by the federal government during the war because of his anti-war attitudes, Watson now heaped ridicule on the authors of the discredited Red Scare while crying up the peril of Catholic domination. Not to be outdone, the adjoining state of Alabama had recently set up a convent-inspecting commission to ensure that no Protestant maidens were held under durance vile.[4] Out of the Midwest in May 1920 came the opening blast of a propaganda campaign against Jews launched by Henry Ford, America's leading industrialist and a man idolized by millions. Almost simultaneously the most widely read magazine in the United States, the *Saturday Evening Post,* began to quote and urgently commend the doctrines of Madison Grant. At another intellectual level one of the country's foremost literary arbiters instigated a general critical assault on writers of alien blood and spirit for corrupting American literature.[5] And during that same summer, quite outside the public eye, an insignificant little society named the Ku Klux Klan was feeling a sudden flutter of life. The upheaval in West Frankfort was only the gaudiest of the portents signaling another great nativist wave that was boiling up in the wake of the Red Scare.

Blighted New World

In its basic patterns, the new ferment of 1920-1924 was far from new. The nativisms that came to the fore in 1920 essentially continued prewar trends. They consisted largely of hatreds—toward Catholics, Jews, and southeastern Europeans—that had gathered strength in the late Progressive era, reaching a minor crescendo in 1914. The war had simply suspended these animosities while American nationalism vented itself in other directions. Once the war and immediate postwar period passed, the two leading nativist traditions of the early twentieth century, Anglo-Saxonism and anti-Catholicism, reoccupied the field. Anti-radicalism, their historic partner, had grown hugely under the conditions which temporarily blocked the other two, but its collapse cleared the way for their revival.

As they passed into the 1920's, the Anglo-Saxon and anti-Catholic traditions retained the distinctive character that the prewar decade had stamped upon them. Racial nativism remained fixed on the new immigration (together with the Japanese), rooted in primitive race-feelings, and rationalized by a scientific determinism. It owed to the early twentieth century its prophet, Madison Grant, its southern and western political leadership, and its nation-wide appeal. Anti-Catholic nativism similarly exhibited the characteristics it had developed just before the war. Whereas racism knew no limits of section or class and preserved an air of respectability, anti-Romanism throve outside of the big cities and the cultivated classes. Reborn after 1910 in the small towns of the South and West, religious nativism resumed its prewar pattern of growth, feeding on the continuing surge of rural fundamentalism and the deepening frustration of progressive hopes. Despite the incongruities between religious and racial xenophobias, they had begun to intersect before the World War in the demagoguery of Tom Watson and, less melodramatically, in the program of the Junior Order United American Mechanics. After the war, the two traditions flowed together in the comprehensive nativism of the Ku Klux Klan, an organization which itself dated from 1915.

Yet the tempestuous climate of the early twenties is not to be accounted for simply as a resumption of storms after a temporary lull. The very fact that the lull did prove temporary, that old hatreds came to life after the war instead of being consumed by it, needs explanation. In some degree the causes lay in the objective circumstances of 1920. That year, as part of a general adjustment to peacetime conditions, two factors which time and again in American history had encouraged anti-foreign outbreaks vividly reappeared. One was economic depression, the other a fresh wave of immigration. During the latter months of the year the war and postwar boom collapsed. For a year and a half businessmen, farmers, and workers felt the pinch of hard times, with all the consequences of unemployment, credit stringencies, and tobogganing prices. Unfortunately for the immigrants, the economic downswing sychronized with a sudden revival of immigration. Virtually halted by the war, immigration had remained at low ebb through 1919 and into the early months of 1920. In the second half of 1919 so many aliens, flushed with wartime savings and embittered toward America, had returned home to Europe that immigration figures showed a net loss. But the tide turned decisively around the end of May 1920. By early September an average five thousand arrivals per day were pouring into Ellis Island. Before the year was out newspapers teemed with hostile comment on the relation between this torrential influx and the worsening unemployment problem. Some thought that immigration was undermining the whole economic system.[6]

A third well-known irritant to ethnic relations intruded into the postwar era, assuming somewhat more importance than it had hitherto displayed. Whereas the scale of immigration and the state of the economy had often contributed significantly to nativist movements, the association of foreigners with crime had not affected their reception to a comparable degree. Crime had helped to make anti-foreign stereotypes rather than anti-foreign hatreds. Prohibition, however, created a much more highly charged situation, for it precipitated a head-on collision between mounting lawlessness and a new drive for social conformity.

On the one hand, the Eighteenth Amendment attempted an unprecedented regimentation of morality by law. Although a tradition of reform originally sired the prohibition movement, its national triumph awaited the strenuous spirit of conformity which the war unleashed. Riding the wave of 100 per cent Americanism, the Drys identified their crusade to regulate behavior with preservation of the American way of life. On the other hand, constraint bred revolt. Prohibition aggravated the normal lawlessness of a postwar era by opening a vast illicit traffic in alcohol. The immigrants, whose own cultures imposed no alcoholic taboos, were

Wets by habit and conviction. The dazzling opportunities that prohibition created for organized gangsterism thrust immigrant children into a special notoriety, for city gangs had long recruited a
high proportion of their members in the disorganizing environment of foreign slum quarters. Thus the ban on alcohol hit the
immigrants two ways: it increased their conspicuousness as law-
breakers and brought down upon their heads the wrath of a 100
per cent American morality.

By the end of 1919 the press was commenting on a rising "crime
wave" and speculating on its alien origins,[7] but it remained for the
eruption at West Frankfort to demonstrate the intensity of the
hatred of foreign lawlessness. In the years ahead similar feelings
would find a powerful outlet through the hooded legions of the
Ku Klux Klan; in the Midwest the Klan delivered more real assaults on the bootleggers than on any other target. At the same
time, one state after another tackled the specter of the foreign
criminal with legislation to disarm all aliens. Wyoming took particular care to forbid the possession by aliens of "any dirk, pistol,
shot gun, rifle, or other fire arm, bowie knife, dagger, or any other
dangerous or deadly weapon." [8]

The resumption of immigration, the onset of depression, a wave
of crime—each of these formed part of a social pattern shaped by a
return to peace, and all three had precedents in the circumstances
of earlier peacetime eras in which nativism flourished. But if these
events help to account for the regeneration of historic xenophobias
in 1920, in themselves they can hardly explain the peculiar force
and magnitude that the reawakened hatreds now displayed. Indeed,
the alien lawbreaker owed his new significance as an anti-foreign
symbol more largely to a state of mind that had crystallized during the war than to the objective circumstances of the postwar
period. In many respects the level of hysteria in the early twenties
was a heritage of mind and spirit from the World War. Pre-1914
traditions supplied the massive roots of that hysteria; post-1919
conditions provided fertile soil for a new season of growth; but
100 per cent Americanism was the vital force that gave it abundant life.

On first thought one may wonder how the new nationalism survived so vigorously the transition from war to peace, when many
other wartime ideals were shipwrecked. It is important to realize

that during the years from 1915 to 1919, 100 per cent Americanism shared in the heady optimism that flourished during the war and collapsed soon after. If the guardians of an exclusive loyalty had nothing else in common with the cosmopolitan, democratic nationalists, at least they felt a common exaltation. Despite the obsessive fears that tortured the 100 per centers, they too looked forward to a brave new world once the nation had passed through its ordeal. To be sure, their assurance was a grimmer and narrower thing than that of their liberal opponents; real victory would require iron resolution and heroic measures. But a crusading idealism formed a fundamental part of the 100 per cent American outlook. The millennial expectations dominant in public opinion since 1898 had reached a culmination during the war period, deeply affecting almost the whole spectrum of American thought, and 100 per centers acquired much of their evangelical zeal from the general hope that the war's turmoil would usher in a purified, regenerate society. So Americanizers set about with a will to transform the immigrants; patriotic clergymen testified to the spiritually ennobling results of warfare; prohibitionists carried the point that outlawing alcohol would accomplish a general moral improvement and call for little enforcement at that; few seriously challenged President Wilson's vision of a new reign of peace founded on a league of nations.

Perhaps this utopian spirit could not long have survived unsullied under any circumstances. Certainly the harsh facts of the postwar world produced, during 1919 and 1920, a general disillusion. The quarreling at Versailles and the class strife that broke out at home and abroad began the process of deflation and embitterment. It went forward under the influence of partisan wrangling in Congress, economic depression, the manifest failure of Americanization, and the scandalous consequences of prohibition. The letdown seriously undermined democratic, cosmopolitan values, for many who held them abandoned a crusading stance, repudiating their ideals as delusive, nationalism as nasty, and society as unsalvageable. One hundred per cent Americanism, on the other hand, had a built-in shock-absorber which not only saved it from disintegrating but converted every disappointment into rebounding aggressiveness. Believing implicitly that the great source of evil lay outside of their own society, super-nationalists could not hold their own principles at fault when failure mocked them. The trouble must come instead from the tenacity and secret cunning of alien influences, together with a lack of sufficient solidarity on the part of true Americans in resisting them. The nation must gird anew against protean forces working in ever grander and more mysterious ways. Thus, instead of crippling the force of 100 per cent Americanism, the discouragements of 1919-1920 broadened the fears which it expressed and turned it against enemies vaguer and more elusive than either the German or the Bolshevik.

The persistence, then, of the fundamental premises of wartime nationalism was crucial to the nativist climate of the early twenties, but equally important was the loss of the spirit of confidence characteristic of the war years. In their own fashion, 100 per centers reflected the general psychological letdown. They ceased on the whole to look forward to a total defeat of the forces of darkness. The evil was too great, the world too deeply infected. Americans must concentrate their efforts on holding their present ground. In short, 100 per cent Americanism passed entirely to the defensive. Its aggressions took the form not of conquest but of a holding operation to save "the last best hope of earth." The result was an intense isolationism that worked hand in hand with nativism. By mid-1920 a general revulsion against European entanglements was crystallizing. In the debate over the Versailles Treaty an afterglow of Wilsonian ideals had lingered through 1919, and the League of Nations commanded immense support in public opinion (though with increasing qualifications) until the early months of 1920. By autumn not 10 per cent of the daily press, and hardly a single national magazine, still backed the league.[9] America now seemed vulnerable to European influences of every kind. Policies of diplomatic withdrawal, higher tariffs, and more stringent immigration restriction were all in order.

Flowering of Racism

Logically, a nationalism so committed to isolation, so distrustful of entanglements with Europe, should find expression in a general revulsion against all foreigners. Indeed, an indiscriminate anti-foreignism did extend far and wide in the early twenties. It echoed through the debate on the League of Nations; it swayed the policies of the American Legion and rumbled in the "konklaves" of the Ku Klux Klan; it unloosed a new torrent of state legislation excluding aliens from a great many occupations.[10] Nevertheless the most intense and significant anti-foreign feelings still focused on symbols of hatred more specific than the whole foreign population. One hundred per cent Americanism had greatest impact through interaction with older cultural traditions.

As the Red Scare subsided, the Anglo-Saxon tradition displayed more than ever the special magnetism it acquired in the prewar period. No other nativism spoke with equal authority or affected so much of American society. This was the flowering time of the semi-scientific racism that had burgeoned in the decade before the war. Although this ideology had the limitation (from a 100 per cent point of view) of not rejecting all Europeans, it was peculiarly well suited as a channel for the defensive nationalism of an age undergoing disillusion. In the nineteenth and early twentieth centuries racial nativism had developed in minds of a gloomy cast; it registered a failure of nerve on the part of an exhausted elite. Explicitly, racism denied the regnant optimism of the Progressive era; a pessimistic determinism imprisoned ideals within iron laws of heredity. Thus, when the utopian hopes of the war years dissolved, the harsh racial doctrines fitted a prevailing mood. Those doctrines not only explained the apparent imperviousness of the immigrant to Americanization. They also accounted for the failure of all efforts at universal uplift. And they showed that the United States could trust in no ideals save those that rested upon and served to protect the nation's racial foundations.

Intellectually the resurgent racism of the early twenties drew its central inspiration from Madison Grant's *The Passing of the Great Race*. The book had caused no considerable comment when first published in 1916, but now it enjoyed a substantial vogue. New editions appeared in 1921 and 1923, bringing total sales to about sixteen thousand copies.[11] Grant himself never became widely known in spite of sympathetic comments in the editorials of such influential publications as the New York *Times* and the *Saturday Evening Post*.[12] However, his emotionally charged formulation of a thoroughgoing racial philosophy stirred the imagination of many literate people. He inspired a bevy of popular writers and influenced a number of scholarly ones. More than anyone else he taught the American people to recognize within the white race a three-tiered hierarchy of Mediterraneans, Alpines, and Nordics, to identify themselves as Nordic, and to regard any mixture with the other two as a destructive process of "mongrelization."

Of all of the nativist ideologies, racism most directly contradicted the central democratic postulate of equal rights, and it is significant that Grant's ideas flourished at a time when the whole postwar reaction put democratic values at a discount. The Young Intellectuals were cheering H. L. Mencken's raucous denial of the possibility of a civilized life in a democracy; a chorus of lawyers and business spokesmen was proclaiming the United States a representative republic rather than a democracy;[13] the Harding administration was providing an uninspiring example of democracy in action. In this context race-thinkers tended generally to reflect the contemptuously anti-equalitarian outlook that had been one of the unusual qualities of Grant's book when it first appeared. For example, Prescott F. Hall, whose earlier racial diatribes had shown a certain caution and restraint, now characterized the "fatuous belief in universal suffrage" and "the lust for equality" as forms of paranoia.[14] Other nativist writers argued that science proves the "basic fact" of inequality or that democracy perpetuates mediocrity. Lothrop Stoddard, a lawyer in Brookline, Massachusetts, with a Ph.D. in history, wrote a whole book on the menace of the Under Man—the racially impoverished opponent of all elites.[15]

Stoddard was Grant's leading disciple. Unlike most of the new racist intellectuals, however, his main preoccupation concerned the rapid multiplication of the yellow and brown races and the danger —spectacularly stated in 1920 in *The Rising Tide of Color*—that they would soon overwhelm the whole white world. His disillusion with the outcome of the World War took the form of a belief that it was actually a civil war which had vitally impaired white solidarity. Consequently Stoddard was hardly a nationalist at all in any explicit sense. Nevertheless he agreed with Grant that the white man's salvation rested with the Nordics and that the immigration of inferior white races would mongrelize the Nordic into "a walking chaos, so consumed by his jarring heredities that he is quite worthless."[16] Grant, in fact, advised Stoddard during the writing of the book and contributed an introduction to it.

Other writers of the same school hewed to a Nordic nationalism.

Charles W. Gould's *America, A Family Matter* differed from *The Passing of the Great Race* only in adding some further data on the rise and fall of civilizations, culminating in the now threatened Nordic occupation of America. Clinton Stoddard Burr, in *America's Race Heritage*, rehashed Gould and Grant. His own contribution consisted of a statistical estimate of the numerical size of the various white races in the American population. His thesis, summarily stated, came down to this: "Americanism is actually the racial thought of the Nordic race, evolved after a thousand years of experience." Undoubtedly the most widely read of these effusions were the articles which Kenneth Roberts wrote for the *Saturday Evening Post* and which appeared in book form in 1922 under the title *Why Europe Leaves Home*. Two years before, the *Post's* editor, George Horace Lorimer, had sent Roberts to Europe to work up a series of articles on immigration. Roberts cast his findings into the framework of the Nordic theory, concluding that a continuing deluge of Alpine, Mediterranean, and Semitic immigrants would inevitably produce "a hybrid race of people as worthless and futile as the good-for-nothing mongrels of Central America and Southeastern Europe." [17]

Natural scientists eschewed such intemperate generalizations, but a number of them lent their authority to the racial philosophy in a polite and qualified way. Scientific race-thinking centered, of course, in the eugenics movement, which continued to agitate genteel and academic circles during the 1920's. With a few exceptions such as Edward A. Ross, Henry Pratt Fairchild, and Ernest F. Hooton, both social scientists and anthropologists remained hostile or indifferent to eugenics, but to a good many speculative biologists, physicians, and amateur scientists it still seemed the salvation of a world imperiled by the multiplication of the unfit.

From a nativistic point of view, postwar eugenics showed a significant advance over the early phase of the movement. American eugenicists were increasingly prone to interpret their data in terms of clear-cut racial differences as well as individually inherited differences. In other words, many of them were coming to accept the new racist categories as a framework for analyzing the inheritance of valuable and vicious traits. This trend was evident as early as 1918 in *Applied Eugenics*, the standard textbook on the subject. The authors relied on Madison Grant's interpretation of the biological danger which Nordic America faced from Mediterraneans and Alpines. And, to bring the racial cleavage to life, they appended to the narrative a flattering drawing of the "Old American" head—a high, well-developed head, the book gravely averred, denoting a very specialized type and an advanced evolution.[18]

Similar ideas reached a larger audience through the well-publicized sessions of the Second International Congress of Eugenics, which Henry Fairfield Osborn, prominent biologist and president of the American Museum of Natural History, brought to New York in 1921. Osborn was closely associated with Grant (who served as one of the Museum's trustees) and had supplied an introduction to *The Passing of the Great Race*. Osborn's welcoming address to the congress was the first of several warnings it heard on the subject of race-crossings.[19] In the next few years the Nordic theory and its implications for immigration restriction showed up in books by such well-known scholars as the Harvard geneticist Edward M. East and the Yale geographer Ellsworth Huntington. With breadth and sweep, Huntington's *The Character of Races* summarized the whole eugenic argument for a racial interpretation of history and for the control of man's biological development now that the conquest of the physical environment seemed nearly complete.[20]

Fundamentally, of course, the fusion of racism with eugenics meant that scientists who were not anthropologists were acquiescing in a disreputable anthropological theory. European anthropologists in the late nineteenth century had offered much evidence that the population of Europe might be classified into three general physical types; that these types carried with them hereditary cultural traits the scientists had never proved. Yet it was the cultural rather than the physical qualities of races that gave eugenicists and other nativists most concern. However much they might gloat over the external proportions of the "Old American" head, their main interest centered on what lay inside that head and how its contents differed from the moral, political, and intellectual characteristics of differently shaped crania. Grant's *The Passing of the Great Race* had simply assumed, on the basis of some scraps of historical data, a correlation between racial physique and racial culture. But loose historical assertions seemed hardly convincing to earnest eugenicists disciplined to the virtues of statistical analysis.

Their willingness to accept the Nordic theory depended to no small degree on a timely stimulus and a fresh group of allies which eugenics received in the postwar era from the field of psychology.

Although eugenicists had exercised their hereditarian bias before the war in counting the number of great men produced by various racial and national groups, they had had no way of comparing the supposedly inborn mental endowments of those groups as a whole. On the eve of the war, however, psychologists forged a wonderful new instrument for measuring some of the psychic differences between races. This was the intelligence test. Allegedly IQ scores did not reflect education. Were they not, therefore, independent of all environmental influences? So leading American psychologists contended. Just then, the war, by calling forth a mass army, fortuitously provided an opportunity for applying group tests on a large scale. Robert M. Yerkes, president of the American Psychological Association, and the corps of distinguished psychologists who aided him in the United States Army's new psychological testing program, gathered a mass of data on the intellectual ability of Negro, native white, and foreign-born soldiers. Published after the war, their studies showed what other investigators were simultaneously learning in testing school children: that northern Europeans scored almost as well as native whites, whereas soldiers born in Latin and Slavic countries averaged significantly lower.[21] Eugenicists seized avidly on these findings as a clinching proof of the racial philosophy and of the inferiority of the new immigration.

Although Yerkes and other psychologists deplored the extravagant statements in which nativistic popularizers of their work indulged, they themselves fell increasingly under the Nordic spell. In 1921 William McDougall, perhaps the most eminent social psychologist of his generation, advanced a racial interpretation of history based on the data of the intelligence tests. McDougall had long been an ardent eugenicist in England, but only after coming to the United States in 1920 did he emerge as a champion of Nordic superiority. Meanwhile, Yerkes and one of his Army colleagues, Professor Carl C. Brigham, were recasting into racial categories the evidence which they had assembled during the war on the intelligence of immigrant nationalities. Inspired by reading the books of Madison Grant and Charles W. Gould, the psychologists realized how neatly their own studies might serve to substantiate the conception of a hierarchy of European races in America. Thus Brigham's book, *A Study of American Intelligence*, triumphantly concluded: "The intellectual superiority of our Nordic group over the Alpine, Mediterranean and negro groups has been demonstrated." [22] With such authority to sustain them, it is little wonder that not only many eugenicists but also a broad segment of literate opinion in America accepted the tenets of racial nativism as proved truths of science.

For those who consulted the oracle of art as well as for those who bowed down to science, the same Nordic myths and prophecies were told. Literary critics paid little attention to eugenics itself, but a group of them had reasons of their own to preach a racial nativism. A whole school of literary traditionalists in the early twenties looked on American literature as a battleground where old-stock writers were defending the nation's spiritual heritage against onslaught from the spokesmen of alien races. Stuart Pratt Sherman first raised the standard of the nativist critics. Around it rallied Brander Matthews, Gertrude Atherton, and John Farrar, supported by the professors of English in many an American college. At the head and front of the enemy hosts stood H. L. Mencken, a belligerent champion of unorthodox and corrosive writers like Theodore Dreiser and James Branch Cabell, ridiculing with mischievous joy the pieties, the patriotisms, and virtually the whole culture of the United States. Proud of his own German background, Mencken gleefully accepted the definition of cultural values in racial terms. The Anglo-Saxons, he proclaimed, have lost the little capacity they may once have had for producing ideas; the country's intellectual life comes largely from men of foreign stock.[23] The enraged traditionalists felt that their own kind was indeed losing cultural leadership, and they struck back bluntly at the unassimilated aliens whose racial hatred for Anglo-Saxon ideals was mongrelizing language, literature, and society. Gertrude Atherton, a leading popular novelist, argued that in the process of "breeding out" the Nordic aristocracy, the Alpine race was spreading the poison of democracy throughout American culture.[24]

Public opinion echoed the perturbations of the nativist intelligentsia as never before. The general magazines teemed with race-thinking, phrased nearly always in terms of an attack on the new immigration. By no means all of the discussion displayed the sharp outlines of the Nordic theory. The more old-fashioned Anglo-Saxon concept sometimes served as well, while other writers spoke in behalf of "the American type" or "the old stock." [25] As scientific racism spread downward from patrician circles, it blended with the cruder Anglo-Saxon nativism that was pushing upward from the grass roots of the South and West. The two streams of racial nationalism reinforced one another: the national news magazine *Current Opinion* wrote about keeping America white with as much gusto as the Imperial Wizard of the Ku Klux Klan discussed the lessons of eugenics.[26] No one any longer, except possibly some immigrant spokesmen, claimed that America's genius derived from racial mixture. In the former muckraking weekly, *Collier's,* George Creel, who had shown much sympathy toward the immigrants during the war, now denounced them as "so much slag in the melting pot. Opposed at every point to the American or Nordic stock. . . ."[27]

At some point a fever in the public imagination becomes self-parodying, and criticism slips easily into ridicule. In the racial controversies of the early 1920s as reported by irreverent journalists, it is often hard to know what to take seriously. When Henry Fairfield Osborn argued learnedly that Christopher Columbus was actually a Nordic, did the proposition attract attention because it gave readers a good feeling about their country's origins or because it gave them a good laugh?[28] Was the New York *World* in 1924 making fun of racism by revealing that Dr. Alzamon Ira Lucas, a former Negro preacher, snake-oil salesman, and fortune-teller, was about to convene a Congress of Superior Caucasians at the Hotel Pennsylvania in the hope of awakening all Americans of Caucasian blood to the importance of their racial preservation?[29] Or was the *World* making fun of Negroes? A trivialization of argument was perhaps not the least of the fruits of postwar nativism.

The International Jew

Of all the European groups that lay outside of the charmed Nordic circle none was subjected to quite so much hatred as the Jews. They had always played a special role in the American imagination, but until the postwar period anti-Jewish sentiment, though unique in kind, probably did not exceed in degree the general level of feeling against other European nationalities. The fear of a Jewish money-power during the 1890's and Georgia's emotional debauch at the height of the Frank Case in 1914 were merely preludes to the much more widespread and tenacious anti-Semitism that developed after the World War. No pogrom has ever stained American soil, nor did any single anti-Jewish incident in the 1920's match the violence of the anti-Italian riot in southern Illinois. Nevertheless the Jews faced a sustained agitation that singled them out from the other new immigrant groups blanketed by racial nativism—an agitation that reckoned them the most dangerous force undermining the nation.

During a period of a general weakening in democratic values social discrimination against Jews would undoubtedly have spread even if no new ideological attack on them had occurred. After the war a flood of Jewish students into private eastern colleges resulted in restrictions on admission similar to those earlier adopted by preparatory schools and college fraternities. Beginning in 1919, New York University instituted stringent restrictions. Columbia soon cut the number of Jews in her incoming classes from 40 to 22 per cent. At Harvard, where Brahmin students feared that the university was becoming a new Jerusalem, President Lowell in 1922 moved, with unseemly frankness, to raise the bars.[30] At the same time job opportunities were continuing to shrink. By the end of the twenties one informed estimate indicated that Jews were excluded from 90 per cent of the jobs available in New York City in general office work.[31]

What was startling, however, was not so much the steady growth of discrimination as the rise of a new anti-Semitic nationalism. On the whole the wartime spirit of fraternity had repressed and inhibited anti-Semitic ideas. Nevertheless, the seeds of a new movement against Jews were to be found in the 100 per cent Americanism of the war years. The more wealthy and prominent Jews in the United States were of German background. Certain 100 per centers, therefore, applied to the Jews the suspicion of all things German. Among some of the bitter, overwrought men who believed that the Wilson administration was dealing laxly, perhaps treasonably, with traitors within and enemies without, dark rumors circulated concerning German-Jewish influence in high places.

Henry Cabot Lodge and others whispered about secret ties between Wilson and Germany through Paul Warburg, a recent Jewish immigrant who sat on the Federal Reserve Board. "The government," a Texas businessman exploded, "seems to be permeated with the atmosphere of different kinds of Jews." [32]

The growth of anti-radical nativism during the war opened another channel for anti-Semitic feelings—one that broadened enormously after the armistice. Morris Hillquit's remarkably strong showing as the Socialist, anti-war candidate for mayor of New York City in 1917 gave a good many people a glimpse of the radical ferment at work in Lower East Side tenements. Leon Trotsky's departure for Russia in 1917, after a brief stay in New York, and the sympathy with which other Russian Jews in the United States greeted the Bolshevik revolution sharpened an emerging image of the Jew as a subversive radical. In September 1918, Brooklyn witnessed the debut of a periodical "Devoted to the Defense of American Institutions Against the Jewish Bolshevist Doctrines of Morris Hillquit and Leon Trotsky." [33]

The Big Red Scare turned these surreptitious by-products of the war into a thriving anti-Jewish agitation. Most commonly, of course, the nativists of 1919 identified radicalism with foreigners generally, so that anti-Semitism remained a subordinate aspect of an attack upon the larger immigrant community. Nevertheless, the Jew offered the most concrete symbol of foreign radicalism, and his significance as such increased very greatly when 100 per cent Americanism burst through the confining dikes of wartime unity. Stories circulated about the streets of New York to the effect that every Jewish immigrant would become a soldier in the revolutionary army assembling in America. A Methodist clergyman testified before a Senate committee that Bolshevism in Russia was drawing much of its inspiration and support from the Yiddish sections of New York. The same doctrine that Bolshevism was a Jewish movement echoed from public meetings and from the pulpits of many churches. A powerful propaganda organization of conservative businessmen in the Midwest, the Greater Iowa Association, spread word throughout the state that Russian Jewish peddlers were disseminating Bolshevik literature.[34]

This was the atmosphere in which the most important anti-Semitic document of the early twentieth century came to America, and gained a certain credence. After Lenin seized power in Russia, Czarist sympathizers introduced into western Europe and the United States a spurious concoction, usually known as "The Protocols of the Elders of Zion," produced by the Russian secret police at the beginning of the century. The "Protocols" revealed a conspiratorial plan for establishing a Jewish world dictatorship. Purportedly drawn up by the leaders of world Jewry, the plan involved financial monopoly, chaos, war, and revolution.[35] Everywhere the intrigues of the Elders were advanced as an explanation for the downfall of Russia and the spread of Bolshevism. The "Protocols" reached America in 1918 through Czarist army officers who had come to this country on a military mission, notably through Lieutenant Boris Brasol. Brasol foisted upon the Military Intelligence Division of the United States Army an English translation of the "Protocols" and started typewritten copies circulating in other influential circles in Washington, D. C. A renegade associate, one Casimir Pilenas, tried to extort $50,000 for the manuscript from the American Jewish Committee.[36]

Although Brasol failed to influence governmental policy, he did get the "Protocols" before a larger public through the aid of two organizations engaged in 100 per cent American propaganda. One of these, the National Civic Federation, had adopted a nationalist line (in place of its original program of collaboration between capital and labor) too recently to give Brasol more than a little, covert support; the director, Ralph Easley, was forced to edit all anti-Semitism from Brasol's contributions to N.C.F. propaganda.[37] But the American Defense Society, the very quintessence of 100 per cent Americanism, took the White Russian and the "Protocols" under its wing. (Brasol had been in close contact with the chairman of the society even before the war ended.) Apparently under its subsidy, a small publishing house issued an American edition of the "Protocols" in August 1920. The American Defense Society then distributed copies among its members. Other copies of the book, which included much supplementary data on the responsibility of the Jews for Bolshevism, were sent to many Congressmen.[38] Shortly thereafter one of the society's most active members, the well-known publisher, George Haven Putnam, put out an American edition of *The Cause of World Unrest*, a British polemic based upon the "Protocols." [39]

Up to this point the anti-Semitic movement had fed largely on the Red Scare, reflecting the conditions of 1917-1919 rather than the newer anxieties emerging in 1920. At the very time, however, when anti-Semitism was coming into the open and the "Protocols" were beginning to play a small part in molding public opinion, anti-radical nativism was subsiding. Instead of collapsing with it, the anti-Jewish strain in 100 per cent Americanism outlived that early phase and passed on from a time of war and revolution to one of depression and disillusion. The importance of anti-Semitism actually increased in the course of this transition, because in 1920 it came out from under the shadow of the Red Scare; it became in its own right one of the major nativisms of the early twenties.

Far from interfering with this shift, the "Protocols" presented revolution merely as one instrument by which the Jew sought mastery of the world; they could be read in other lights aside from the glare of Bolshevism. Although fear of Jewish radicalism remained an important element in the anti-Semitic complex, the character of the assault broadened significantly. The Bolshevik theme fused with an onslaught on Jewish capitalism and a supplementary attack on Jewish morality; and over all of these clashing charges hovered an image of the Jew as a peculiarly and supremely international force.

Though the "Protocols" served to substantiate the menace of the "International Jew," his entry into the stream of American nativism was largely independent of such exotic documents. Twice before 1920 this world-wide power, conspiring against all nations, had invaded American imaginations: once during the "battle of the standards" in the 1890's, again (on a more limited scale) during the Frank Case on the eve of the World War. At both times factors that reappeared in 1920 had contributed to the concept. Both the nineties and 1914 were periods of depression, in which the countryside suffered at least as much as the city from impersonal economic forces of international proportions. When hard times struck again in 1920, they bore down especially heavily on the agricultural areas. Townsfolk and rural people who had followed Bryan and Watson in the nineties now saw their wartime gains wiped out and the subjugation of their agrarian society confirmed. Also, the twenties repeated a second characteristic of the 1890's, namely, a strong, diffuse nationalism not confined to a single foreign adversary but rather distrustful of a whole outside world. The isolationist reaction evident in 1920 pressed home the danger of world entanglements in a more conscious and articulate way than ever before. Whereas imperialism had swallowed up the free-floating jingoism of the nineties, and hyphenism had absorbed the assorted anti-foreign movements of 1914, the disillusion that followed the war left nationalists with no alternative to a thoroughgoing revulsion from all global crusades or encounters. Thus, while economic distress aroused old resentments at an alien money-power, isolation seemed a last defense against a threatening world.

It may be significant too that the very disillusion responsible for the recoil from international engagements closed in upon democratic reform as well. Though convinced that things had gone terribly wrong at home and abroad, men lacked the confidence to renew the progressive spirit of the prewar years. Their sense of social malaise, unallayed by substantial institutional reconstruction, found more shadowy and less rational objects. All of the xenophobias rampant in postwar America benefited from this failure of democratic morale, for it meant that the chief ideological check on the nativist traditions in the Progressive era was now relaxed. As far as anti-Semitism is concerned, the decline of progressivism helps to explain why the kind of sentiment that Tom Watson had incited during the Frank Case became much more widespread in the early twenties. Watson had appealed to rural or small-town progressives whose faith in concrete reform was already foundering and whose hatred of the trusts could be partially deflected to world conspiracies, Catholic and Jewish. Under the impact of the far greater disillusion of the postwar period, many more of the same kind of people found a substitute for reform in tilting at an international enemy, half banker and half Bolshevik.

The new anti-Semitism secured its standard-bearer and its prophet in one of the commanding figures of the day, Henry Ford. In the *Dearborn Independent*, a general magazine which he published and distributed through his thousands of dealerships, Ford, in May 1920, launched an offensive against the International Jew which continued off and on for several years. Then and after, the "Flivver King" was enormously popular (and not a little feared) as America's greatest industrialist, as a folk philosopher, and as a potential politician. In 1923 he was one of the most popular and widely discussed candidates for the next Presidential nomination. That he was a food faddist, a suspicious factory-master, a man of mercurial mood swings and dogmatic opinions, and a quixotic crusader who once sent a boatload of pacifists to Europe to stop the World War, counted for little in the public eye. To millions he embodied the old pioneer virtues: a farm-bred simplicity contemptuous of elegance or intellect, a rugged individualism, a genius for practical achievement.

Ford carried over into the industrial field not only the personal traits but also the social ideas typical of his rustic background. The son of Michigan tenant farmers, he looked upon big cities as cesspools of iniquity, soulless and artificial. He hated monopoly and special privilege. He jealously guarded his enterprises from banker influence and was regarded, in the words of the Detroit *News*, as "the recognized crusader against the money changers of Wall Street." [40] In short, Ford, for all of his wealth, typified some of the key attitudes for which Watson had stood. It is hardly surprising that in Ford and in many others with an agrarian background, nativism took a violently anti-Semitic turn at a time of depression, isolation, and disillusion.

Each of the factors that apparently impelled the extension of anti-Semitism after the Red Scare affected Henry Ford in an acute and special way. The economic slump of 1920 hit him hard and early. Swallowing his scruples, he had borrowed $75,000,000 in 1919 from eastern bankers in order to buy out his partners. The decline of sales in 1920 left him loaded with debts and unsold cars. His anti-Jewish campaign began in the midst of this crisis, and at first his propaganda presented the International Jew solely in the role of financier. Jewish bankers, according to the *Dearborn Independent*, operating through a vast international network, dominate the American economy. The great struggle of the hour lies between the contending forces of "international Finance" and "creative Industry," and apparently the latter cannot triumph until control of the world is wrested from the Jewish money-kings.[41]

Ford's plunge into anti-Semitism resulted at least as much from political disillusion as it did from economic difficulties. He registered in a remarkably dramatic manner the general collapse of Wilsonian idealism. His assault on a Jewish world-conspiracy coincided with an abrupt reaction on his part from an idealistic international outlook to a suspicious, somewhat cynical isolationism. After the failure of his "peace ship" in the winter of 1915-16, Ford had swung over to a Wilsonian position and had run for the Senate in 1918 as an avowed supporter of the League of Nations. Although his Americanization policies revealed a 100 per cent American streak, his outlook on the whole was liberal. To the horror of many business interests, the *Dearborn Independent* persisted throughout 1919 in championing the league, a world made safe for democracy, and "internationalism." At the same time the journal criticized the Red-hunters for intolerance and for serving selfish material interests, looked forward to a new era of partnership between labor and capital, and proposed such reforms as currency inflation and government ownership of the railroads.[42] But in the early months of 1920 a sour note crept in. The war has not brought forth a better world, the Ford editorials confessed, first sadly, then in a dark and bitter spirit. "The world is sick. The world is showing foretokens of delirium. And the worst of all is that there are no doctors skilled in this kind of disease. . . . We shall have to save ourselves before we can hope to save any one else. Americanism still has a mission to the world." [43] Thereafter no more was said about the league, Ford lost interest in reform, and "internationalism" became an anti-Semitic epithet.

Ford himself repeatedly attributed his Jew-hatred to something he learned on his ill-fated peace expedition. As early as December 1919, he was muttering privately, "I know who makes wars. The International Jewish bankers arrange them so they can make money out of them. I know it's true because a Jew on the peace ship told me." [44] Whoever did plant the seed in Ford's mind, the fact that he afterward connected the failure of his peace efforts with the Jewish question (when in fact a Jewish pacifist had inspired the peace ship idea!) indicates how deeply the acid of postwar disillusion affected him.

Soon the "Protocols" came to the attention of the *Independent's* editors, who proceeded to draw heavily upon them. Brasol and other reactionaries flocked to offer their services, and in time the paper exposed Jewish control of everything from the Versailles Treaty to Tammany Hall, from baseball to Bolshevism. The subject gripped Ford so obsessively that he would burst into sudden harangues upon it among Detroit business associates, who wondered at times if he was becoming mentally unbalanced.[45]

Hardly any other reputable magazine or newspaper openly backed the agitation. It lacked the respectability which the broader Anglo-Saxon tradition had secured in the course of a long, indigenous development; it rested on too insubstantial an intellectual foundation. Whereas native-born liberals directed only a scattering fire at the Nordic doctrine, they retorted massively to the new anti-Semitic ideology. The Federal Council of the Churches of Christ, a meeting of four hundred Protestant ministers in Chicago, the Wisconsin state legislature, and a group of 119 distinguished Americans headed by Woodrow Wilson and William Howard Taft issued slashing denunciations.[46] This opposition may have had some effect on Ford. The *Independent's* crusade slackened toward the end of 1921, perhaps because Ford was persuaded that it was endangering his Presidential prospects.[47]

Nonetheless, the anti-Jewish campaign excited nation-wide attention and met much *sotto voce* approval. A popular writer reported that scarcely a day passed without bringing him letters claiming that the Jews were plotting to control the world, and in a luridly advertised series of articles the general magazine, *World's Work*, elaborately explained that the real menace was not the International Jew but rather the Polish Jew.[48] Although social discrimination was bitterest in the urban centers, which felt the pressure of a large and growing Jewish population, apparently the ideological attack emanated more from the hinterlands of the West and South. There the agricultural depression revived an old, thwarted hostility toward international finance, and a cultural isolation intensified political isolationism. The *Dearborn Independent* itself appealed chiefly to a countrified audience. Hardly an issue came out without one or more articles of specifically rural interest, from the aspirations of the Farm Bloc to the profits that might be made growing pecans.[49] And constantly the *Independent* sang the values of that way of life.

Another index of the locus and relative importance of the anti-Semitic theme may be found in the chief organization that fostered it, the Ku Klux Klan. Since all of the xenophobias of the 1920's flowed into this central apotheosis of a tribal spirit, the Klan furnishes a kind of litmus-paper test of rural nativism. Significantly, the Klan's home was not in the great cities. Its strength came chiefly from the towns, from the villages, and from the ordinarily tranquil countryside. Through the theory and practice of a "noble Klannishness," anti-Semitism achieved, for the first time in American history, substantial organizational expression.

Klan propaganda echoed the Ford attack on the Jewish banker-Bolshevik, adding a special emphasis on vice that reflected the powerful strain of evangelical morality in the organization. To the Klan the Jew stood for an international plot to control America and also for the whole spectrum of urban sin—for pollution of the Sabbath, bootlegging, gambling, and carnal indulgence. Thus Klan publications described the Jew as a subversive radical, a Shylock seeking power through money, and a "Christ-killing" monster of moral corruption. All of these destructive forces radiated from the centers of population, and Klansmen had the assurance—in the words of one Oregon spellbinder—that in some cities "the Kikes are so thick that a white man can hardly find room to walk on the sidewalk." [50]

Still, later generations of Americans, remembering the Hitlerite groups of the 1930's, can easily exaggerate the part that anti-Semitism played in the organized nativism of the postwar decade. The Jew occupied, on the whole, a distinctly secondary rank in the Klan's demonology. On the level of ideas, other passions outweighed, other hatreds outreached the attack on the Jew. As for direct action, he suffered largely from sporadic economic proscriptions. In southern as well as western towns boycotts harassed long-established Jewish merchants; sometimes enterprising Klansmen launched their own proudly labeled "100 per cent American" clothing stores. [51] But personal violence was quite rare. Klan energies found larger outlet in the older, more massive traditions of American nativism. It is time to turn to the whole range of the Klan's operations, and to its central meaning.

The Klan Rides

In Atlanta on October 16, 1915, exactly two months after the Leo Frank lynching and at a time when excitement over the case still ran high in Georgia, William J. Simmons conjured into being the Invisible Empire of the Knights of the Ku Klux Klan and anointed himself its Imperial Wizard. For a number of years Simmons had made a living in the rural South as a salesman and organizer of national fraternal orders. He had promoted, or at least belonged to, more than a dozen of them, including Masonry, the Knights Templar, and the Woodmen of the World; in the latter he held the rank of colonel. As befitted a southern "colonel," he had cultivated a majestic presence and a grand manner that belied his village origin. Now Colonel Simmons was launching a secret order of his own.

The idea was not wholly spontaneous. The Frank lynchers had called themselves the "Knights of Mary Phagan," and Tom Watson was currently writing about the need for a new Ku Klux Klan.[52] In the same year a tremendously successful historical film (*The Birth of a Nation*) glorified the long-defunct Klan which ex-Confederates had organized in the Reconstruction era to intimidate Carpetbaggers and Negroes. Simmons was just the man to revive a vanished sectional institution as an instrument of modern American nationalism. His cloudy wits spun with the myths and history of the South; his heart exuded southern sentiment as a plum does juice. From his father, a small-town doctor and an ex-officer in the original Klan, Simmons heard bewitching tales of how it saved white civilization. Undoubtedly he knew also about the subsequent tradition of night-riding, by which rural bands often masked in white caps meted out informal justice upon their neighbors. He liked to trace his original inspiration to a vision that came upon him at the turn of the century not long after he returned from serving in the Spanish-American War—a vision that turned the clouds one day into white-robed horsemen galloping across the sky.

Simmons supplemented these romantic traits with an evangelical piety, a fine dramatic sense and, above all, the gift of the word. Converted by "the old-time religion" at a camp meeting, he had tried his hand at preaching before turning to the more lucrative field of fraternal work, and he remained a mellifluous orator. His first acts as Imperial Wizard were to draw up the high-sounding ritual of the Kloran, create a galaxy of Kleagles, Kligrapps, Cyclops, Geniis, and Goblins, and summon his little band of followers to Stone Mountain, where they dedicated themselves before a flaming cross and a flag-draped altar to uphold Americanism, advance Protestant Christianity, and eternally maintain white supremacy.

In modeling his little society fairly closely on the Klan of yore, Simmons had in mind the same social objective of controlling the Negroes, who were (he believed) getting "uppity" again. Even at the outset, however, there were important differences between the two organizations, and they grew more sharp as the new Klan evolved. The latter, unlike its predecessor, was formed partly as a money-making scheme; Simmons, who was half visionary and half promoter, designed his own Klan as a fraternal order in the hope of enriching himself by selling insurance benefits to the membership.[53] Although the Klan failed to develop along such lines, it always remained something of a racket.

More importantly, it differed from the first Klan in being an avowedly *patriotic* fraternal order. Apparently the Colonel did not begin with an overtly nativist program, but his venture reflected a strong nationalist impulse. It embodied the twentieth century fusion of primitive race-feelings with Anglo-Saxon nationalism. The nineteenth century Klan, a product of sectional strife, had championed white supremacy (and white supremacy only) at a time when southern race-feelings clashed directly with nationalism. The new Klan reflected the coalescence of racial and national loyalties. Simmons' organization dramatized what the more diffuse movements of the early twentieth century had already revealed: the South was pushing into the forefront of American nativism. Thus in contrast to the first Klan, which admitted white men of every type and background, the second Klan accepted only native-born Protestant whites and combined an anti-Negro with an increasingly anti-foreign outlook. Always Anglo-Saxon nationalism remained one of the main pillars of its strength.

For five years after its founding, the Invisible Empire was far more invisible than imperial. It recruited during that time a maximum of five thousand members and attracted practically no public attention. Part of its weakness came from Simmons' impracticality. He wasted money, kept careless accounts, and generally showed no business sense. A greater impediment, however, was the temporary subsidence of racial nationalism just at the time when the Klan was forming. The war period offered very little occasion for and indeed inhibited the Klan's *raison d'être*. Significantly, the order seems to have made what little progress it did by adapting itself to the typical pattern of wartime 100 per cent Americanism. Simmons joined an auxiliary of the American Protective League, turned his followers to spy-hunting, and began to envisage the Klan not as a benevolent order but as a vast secret service agency. One of the early, if not the first, public appearances of the Klan occurred late in the war in Montgomery, Alabama, when a hundred hooded Klansmen paraded through the main streets warning slackers and spies to get out of town and demanding that all others aid the Red Cross and buy their share of Liberty bonds.[54] Thereafter, wherever the Klan went and whatever it did, it persistently worked to enforce the 100 per cent American ethic of coercive conformity. The success of the Klan awaited, however, the return of a climate of opinion congenial to its own distinctive background.

The period of expansion began in the summer of 1920. Simmons joined forces with a pair of hard-boiled publicity agents, dour-faced Edward Y. Clarke and his plump partner, Mrs. Elizabeth Tyler. Both had long experience in fund-raising drives. They took over the actual management of the Klan, entering a contract with Simmons that guaranteed them $8 out of every $10 initiation fee collected by their organizers. Clarke and Tyler then launched an impressive membership campaign, operating partly through newspaper publicity, more largely through agents who usually started in a community by soliciting at the Masonic lodges.[55] In the next sixteen months they brought in about ninety thousand members. For this accomplishment Clarke and Tyler have generally received the whole credit. The secret of their success, however, lay essentially in the mood and circumstances of 1920. The whole complex of factors—depression, prohibition, and immigration; disillusion, isolationism, and reaction—that shunted 100 per cent Americanism into the older nativistic channels contributed to the Klan's growth. Never before had a single society gathered up so many hatreds or given vent to an inwardness so thoroughgoing.

Among the special circumstances stimulating the Klan's initial surge, not least was the agricultural depression that began in 1920. As cotton prices plunged catastrophically, desperate farmers in half a dozen states resorted to the old practice of night-riding in order to check the sale of cotton. All through the fall and winter of

1920-21 masked bands roamed the countryside warning ginneries and warehouses to close until prices advanced. Sometimes they set fire to establishments that defied their edict. Occasionally there was shooting.[56] Klan officials disavowed and apparently disapproved of this wave of economic terrorism, which indeed was soon suppressed by law enforcement officials. Like previous nativist organizations, the Klan had no economic program and rarely functioned in economic terms except to enforce a pattern of discrimination. Nevertheless the gin-burners frequently wore Ku Klux garb,[57] and their nocturnal exploits drew attention to the potentialities of the hooded order. Night-riding of a different kind flourished within the Klan, and it seems hardly doubtful that the organization diverted farmers' economic frustrations into more socially acceptable types of aggression.

The first acknowledged public appearances of the Klan in the postwar period reflected its underlying racial spirit. On the eve of the election of 1920, Klansmen paraded in many southern towns as a silent warning against Negro voting.[58] A large number of anti-Negro outrages were committed in the next few months under Klan auspices, provoked partly by fear that a "New Negro" had emerged from the war. (In point of fact, Negro veterans returning from France in 1919 and 1920 were often determined to stand militant and upright.) The men in white bludgeoned employers into downgrading or discharging Negro employees, intimidated Negro cotton-pickers into working for wages they would not otherwise accept, forced Negro residents out of a part of South Jacksonville coveted by whites, and branded the letters "KKK" on the forehead of a Negro bellboy.[59] In these early months of expansion the organization presented itself very largely as a means for keeping "the nigger in his place."

White supremacy remained an important theme even when the Klan spread into the North, but it would be a mistake to regard the Negro issue as the mainspring of its career. Fear of the "New Negro" rapidly declined as he either accepted his old place or moved to northern cities. By mid-1921 the Klan was specializing in attacking white people, and thereafter the great bulk of its disciplinary activities in all parts of the country had to do with whites.[60] This shift of emphasis by no means indicated a slackening of the racial imperative. To a considerable degree, however, it suggested that race-thinking was more and more taking a nativistic and nationalistic direction. The Klan's snowballing advance in the early twenties paralleled the upthrust of racial nativism in public opinion generally. And within the order an insistence on preserving the superiority of the old Anglo-Saxon stock over foreigners of every description became pronounced. Edward Y. Clarke exemplified this trend in 1922 by defining the Klan's mission as one of creating national solidarity by protecting "the interest of those whose forefathers established the nation." [61] Other Klan leaders, in particularizing on the old stock's interest, called immigration restriction the most momentous legislative issue of the day, asserted that only Anglo-Saxons or Nordics had an inherent capacity for American citizenship, damned "the cross-breeding hordes" of the new immigration, and trembled lest the "real whites" fail to keep the nation "free from all mongrelizing taints." [62] This emphatic Anglo-Saxonism did not, of course, prevent the same men from ranting loudly at foreigners as such, on the plea that America must be made safe for Americans.

If the Ku Klux Klan had mobilized only this much of the emotional ferment of the period, if it had functioned only through an Anglo-Saxon version of 100 per cent Americanism and through related fears of Jews and of foreigners generally, it would have incarnated a very large part of the current tribal spirit. Yet the Klan had another big side. By embracing the anti-Catholic tradition along with the racial tradition and the new anti-Semitism, it comprehended the whole range of post-1919 nativism. Anti-Catholicism did not prevail as widely in American public opinion as did the Anglo-Saxon ideas reflected in the organization; an urban, materialistic culture had stifled in too many Americans the religious feelings on which Protestant xenophobia fed. Due, however, to the semirural base of the Klan, within its ranks anti-Catholicism actually grew to surpass every other nativistic attitude. In fact, a religious impulse, perverted but not devoid of idealistic implications, accounts for much of the Klan's distinctive energy, both as a nativist organization and as an agent of other kinds of repressions too.

Although the Klan was Protestant from the day its first cross burned on Stone Mountain, an anti-Catholic emphasis came into the order only in the course of its expansion in 1920 and 1921.

Simmons, Clarke, and Tyler had not at first expected to sell the organization as a bulwark against Rome. The Klan's stress on religious nativism, even more than the parallel expansion of its Anglo-Saxon agitation, reflected the passions of the people who joined it.[63] By 1920 the anti-Catholic crusade that had appeared in the South and West after 1910 was reasserting itself more powerfully than ever. Under a prohibitionist governor, Alabama pointed the way as early as 1919. While laying plans for inspecting convents, the state also challenged Catholic (and secular) sentiment by requiring daily Bible reading in the public schools, thus reviving a trend begun in Pennsylvania in 1913.[64] The following year the tide came in strongly. Tom Watson's Senatorial campaign spread about Georgia an impression that President Wilson had become a tool of the Pope; Governor Sidney J. Catts stomped up and down Florida warning that the Pope planned to invade the state and transfer the Vatican there; an able journalist reported that anti-Catholicism had become "second only to the hatred of the Negro as the moving passion of entire Southern communities"; Michigan and Nebraska debated constitutional amendments banning parochial schools; and in Missouri the once-mighty anti-Catholic weekly, *The Menace*, revived under a new name, *The Torch*.

Sentiment of this kind amounted to a standing invitation to secret societies. The first to respond prominently was not the Klan but rather the True Americans, a local southern organization. The T.A.'s acquired such influence in Birmingham in 1920 that they dominated the city administration and secured a purge of Catholic municipal employees.[65] Before long Ku Kluxers eclipsed and very likely absorbed the True Americans. Klan propaganda, reviving all of the old stories about arms stored in Catholic church basements, began to lay special stress on the menace of Rome to the nation. Instead of relying entirely on professional organizers, the Klan engaged itinerant preachers as heralds of its message. Increasingly its arrival in a new area was signaled by public lectures on popish conspiracies to destroy *"the only truly Christian nation . . . where prophecy is being fulfilled."* [66] As if to demonstrate that the hatred transcended rhetoric, in the summer of 1921 a Methodist minister who belonged to the Klan shot to death a Catholic priest on his own doorstep, and incendiaries destroyed a

Catholic church in Illinois two hours after a monster Klan initiation.[67]

The storm of anti-Catholic feeling, for which the Klan proved a wonderfully sensitive barometer, was closely related to the growth of fundamentalism. This militant repudiation of a liberalized gospel and a secularized culture was making itself felt in the closing years of the Progressive era, but only after the World War did it become a major force in American Protestantism. In truth, fundamentalism owed so much to the emotional aftermath of the war that one may almost define it as the characteristic response of rural Protestantism to the disillusion following America's international crusade. The wartime hope for a new and beatific world had produced nothing but crime, moral chaos, and organized selfishness on a grander scale than before. Surely here was proof that the nation had misplaced its faith, that the only true salvation for a sinful society lay in blotting out the whole spirit of innovation and returning to the theological and moral absolutism of an earlier day. Insistence on a Biblical Christianity naturally sharpened the historic lines of Protestant-Catholic cleavage, but the vigor of anti-Catholicism in the twenties could only result from the affiliations between fundamentalism and 100 per cent Americanism. The fundamentalist determination to fix and purify a Protestant orthodoxy followed the same channels and obeyed the same laws that governed the course of 100 per cent Americanism. Both epitomized a kind of crusading conformity, reacted to a common disillusion, and represented an urge for isolation from an evil world. Who can wonder that the two movements intermingled in rural areas, or that fundamentalism energized a religious version of postwar nationalism? [68]

Simmons' religiously tinged imagination had given the Klan an appropriate structure for the anti-Catholic spirit that it absorbed and magnified. The flaming crosses burning on hillsides, the altars erected at meetings, and the kneeling posture of suppliants at initiation ceremonies were central in the Klan's symbolism. Every klavern, or local unit, had a kludd, its chaplain, who opened each meeting with a prayer; the closing ritual consisted of a "kloxology." As the Klan grew, it emphasized increasingly its militant Protestantism. Well-known hymns were modified and adopted as Klan songs. It became common practice for Klansmen to march in a silent body into a Protestant church in the middle of a Sunday service and hand the minister a donation.[69] The organization took a close interest in compulsory Bible reading in the public schools, and in several states it lent strong support to Bible-reading bills.[70] "Patriotism and Christianity," said one Exalted Cyclops, "are pre-eminently the moving principles of the Knights of the Ku Klux Klan." Another boasted: "The Klan stood for the same things as the Church, but we did the things the Church wouldn't do." [71]

The things that the church would not do included general boycotts of Catholic businessmen, bringing pressure against Catholic public officials, and intimidation of many Catholic individuals. It would be futile, however, to try to estimate how much of this strong-arm activity applied to Catholics as opposed to foreigners, Jews, Negroes, and plain old-stock Americans. Contemporary accounts seldom identified the background of the Klan's victims, a circumstance which in itself suggests how manifold the proscriptions were. The significant fact was that the crusading, evangelical spirit behind the Klan turned it into a general instrument for moral regulation. Quite possibly (since it centered in areas where its foreign and Catholic enemies constituted only a small minority), most of the Klan's coercions affected other native white Protestants. Certainly it differed from prewar nativist societies not only in embracing a variety of xenophobias but also in ranging far beyond nativistic limits. Somewhat like the wartime American Protective League, the Klan watched everybody.

In its function as censor and policeman of local morality, the Klan brought to a head the 100 per cent American heritage as it survived into the twenties. Impatient of legally constituted authority yet dedicated to the maintenance of law and order, local Klans saw themselves as agents for accomplishing what government was failing to do: they would work a moral regeneration by compelling all deviants or backsliders to adhere to the ancient standards of the community. Hardly any infraction of the village code seemed too petty for intervention. An undertaker refused the use of his hearse to a bereaved family unable to pay cash in advance; Klansmen drove him out of town. A businessman failed to pay a debt or practiced petty extortions; Klansmen tarred and feathered him. A husband deserted his family, or failed to support it, or maintained illicit relations with women, or gambled too much; Klansmen paid him a minatory call. A widow of doubtful virtue scandalized the neighbors; Klansmen flogged her and cut off her hair.[72] Prohibition especially drew the order's vigilance. Its most spectacular clean-up campaign occurred in Herrin, Illinois, where lax law enforcement permitted wide-open saloons and flagrant vice, and where the large Italian Catholic population was held chiefly at fault. There the Klan carried out mass raids on homes and roadhouses, engaged in pitched battles with the bootlegging faction, and temporarily seized the city government by force. The chaos extended over a two-year period, brought twenty deaths, and subsided finally in a great religious revival.[73]

Throughout this regulatory activity runs the war-born urge for conformity that had passed from anti-hyphenism, Americanization, and Palmer raids into fundamentalism and prohibition. No less important here is the other side of the 100 per cent American spirit, its crusading idealism. Ku Kluxers repeatedly justified their programs of action in terms of reform, though the reform consisted essentially of stabilizing the old order of things; and when first organized in a community, the Klan usually had the support of some of the "best people," intent partly on improving the local situation.[74] In the generation before the war this evangelical zeal for reform had poured into progressivism. The war directed it partly toward an international crusade, partly toward the maintenance of homogeneity. When the disillusion that followed the war choked off any large international or progressive outlet for moral idealism, about all that remained of it in small-town America turned inward, in a final effort to preserve the values of the community against change and against every external influence. Professor Frank Tannenbaum has summed up a good part of the Klan spirit as "an attempt to destroy the 'evil' that stands in the way of the millennial hope—a hope made vivid to many souls who actually believed that the war would usher in a 'world fit for heroes to live in.'"[75] Perhaps, in the pageant of American history, the white-robed Klansman should stand in the place of Santayana's genteel New Englander as the Last Puritan.

It was ironical but inevitable that the Klan crusade to purify and stabilize spread contamination and strife everywhere it went. The secrecy with which the order operated served to cloak many an act of private vengeance. With poetic justice it was held responsible for crimes and cruelties that others committed in its name. Still worse, the Klan rent families, communities, and states, turning husband against wife, neighbor against neighbor, and man against man, until it compacted an opposition as lawless as itself. And while hatred bred hatred outside its ranks, the poison of corruption worked within.

In 1921 the Klan crossed the Mason and Dixon Line and began to attract nation-wide attention. By the end of the year it claimed to be operating in forty-five states and enrolling a thousand members a day.[76] Nineteen twenty-two saw a tremendous expansion, demonstrated by great public ceremonies at which a thousand or more initiates would be sworn in at once.[77] At the same time, like its nineteenth century predecessors, the organization entered politics, not with any positive program but simply to show its strength by winning elections. In Georgia the Klan was instrumental in putting a very friendly governor in the state capitol. In Texas it spent lavishly in money and effort to send Earl Mayfield to the United States Senate. In Oregon Klan sentiment wrought a virtual political revolution, defeating a governor who had tried to suppress its activities and installing a legislature that proceeded to enact several anti-Catholic measures.[78] Hundreds of candidates for local offices in many states were indebted to the Klan vote.

Political power greatly increased the divisive effects of the organization, partly because the Klan itself became an issue in elections, partly because law enforcement officials often dared not curb its terrorism. Thus in the latter part of 1922 local authorities in Morehouse Parish, Louisiana, proved helpless in the face of a near-civil war between the Klan-infested parish seat of Bastrop and the more leisurely and aristocratic town of Mer Rouge. Bastrop was Dry and Baptist; Mer Rouge held the Klan and all its ways in contempt. A series of whippings culminated in the abduction and murder of a well-known Mer Rouge planter's son and his companion. For months thereafter troops sent by the governor kept order while the pro-Klan sheriff and district attorney stood idle. Twice the Morehouse grand jury refused to admit that a crime had been committed.[79]

Meanwhile internecine strife rocked the Invisible Empire. While its national officials exercised very little control over the local klaverns, an authoritarian constitution gave the members practically no control over their national leaders. For many of the latter the organization had an attraction quite different from that which drew its followers. It was immensely lucrative, and the profits to be extracted from membership fees and political corruption incited constant turmoil at the top. Clarke levied upon the Klan royally; Simmons, who was drunk or sick much of the time, was putty in his hands. When news got around in the fall of 1921 that Clarke was living with his confederate, Mrs. Tyler, this affront to Klan morality strengthened a group endeavoring to unseat him, but Simmons clung to Clarke and banished his principal enemies. Clarke held on against mounting opposition until November 1922, when a coalition of state leaders got rid of him by intimidating Simmons into retiring to an honorary position. Simmons retained a following and later tried to regain control, but the national headquarters had passed definitely into the hands of a moon-faced Texas dentist, Hiram Wesley Evans. Ultimately Simmons sold out his interest in the Klan to the Evans group for a sum which they announced as $90,000 but which he said should have been $146,000.[80] Evans regularized financial practices somewhat, but still the money flowed richly into many pockets.[81]

The Klan torrent rolled onward through 1923, reaching a high point late in the year. By that time the organization had enrolled an aggregate membership probably close to three million. Arkansas and Oklahoma fell vassal to it, and a spectacular expansion in the Midwest made Indiana and Ohio the leading Klan states in the nation. Except for Colorado, the order touched the Rocky Mountain states only negligibly; it left no considerable impression on the Atlantic seaboard outside of Pennsylvania and upstate New York.[82] In Indiana and Texas, however, it could organize vast public gatherings attended by seventy-five thousand people.

The tremendous midwestern expansion in 1923 threw a new demagogue into the limelight and opened another chapter in the struggle within the Klan. D. C. Stephenson emerged as the dominant figure in the northern Klans. He could corrupt a legislator as effectively as he could organize a membership drive, and with equal ease he could convince the rural masses that the President of the United States was leaning on him for advice. He lived in bacchanalian style on an estate in Indianapolis; his political ambitions were boundless. As his power grew, he strove to wrest the national headquarters from Evans. All through 1923 the fight for control went on behind the scenes, with Stephenson perhaps partly in alliance with the disinherited Simmons faction. In November an Evans henchman murdered Simmons' attorney, supposedly to prevent an impending exposé. Somehow, that may have turned the tables against Stephenson. He surrendered his position in the national hierarchy of the Klan, but he rather than Evans retained paramount influence in Indiana.[83]

While this internal struggle raged, opposition was mounting on all sides. All along, the urban press and urban liberals had denounced the Klan with singular unanimity. Now it was also rousing a more formidable popular resistance. Old-stock conservatives, horrified at the chaos that the Klan bred, rallied against it. So did the miscellaneous corruptionists and enraged minorities it attacked. In the winter of 1922-23 the conservative governor of Kansas opened a drive against the organization by bringing suit to restrain it from all public appearances or activities. New York, under its Catholic governor, Al Smith, took a series of legal steps that inhibited Klan operations there. Minnesota, Iowa, and Michigan passed laws forbidding the wearing of masks in public.[84]

Oklahoma's flamboyant governor, John Walton, cast legality to the winds in trying to crush the hooded order. Although elected by a farmer-labor coalition in 1922, he soon showed greater friendliness toward grafters and big oil interests. The Klan supposedly controlled the state legislature and the Tulsa local government. Walton, in August 1923, took advantage of a series of floggings to put Tulsa County under martial law (later extended to the whole state). He imposed censorship on the leading Tulsa newspaper, forbade Klan meetings, established military courts to try Klan vigilantes, and used the National Guard to prevent the legislature from convening. When the legislature did succeed in assembling in November, it promptly impeached the governor.[85]

At the same time, anti-Klan mobs were beginning to lash back at the organization in areas where the immigrants were strongly entrenched. A bomb wrecked the offices of the Klan newspaper in Chicago. In a suburb of Pittsburgh an angry throng pelted a white-robed parade with stones and bottles, killing one Klansman and injuring many others. In the small industrial city of Steubenville, Ohio, a mob of three thousand attacked a meeting of one hundred

Klansmen. In Perth Amboy, New Jersey, a mob six-thousand-strong, led by Jews and Catholics, closed in on a Klan meeting place, overwhelmed the entire police and fire departments, and fell upon some five hundred Ku Kluxers, kicking, stoning, and beating them as they fled.[86]

Such, from the West Frankfort riots of 1920 to the collapse of civil government in Oklahoma three years later, from the triumphant demonstrations of racist scholarship to the nightmares of Henry Ford, were some of the fruits of nativism in a postwar world neither brave nor new.

Chapter Eleven

Closing the Gates

NORDIC VICTORY IS SEEN IN DRASTIC RESTRICTIONS
—Los Angeles *Times* headline, April 13, 1924

The general terms of the great immigration restriction laws of the early twenties stare up at us from the pages of every textbook in American history. We realize that these measures brought to culmination a legislative trend extending back to the 1880's. It is not so obvious perhaps that they belonged equally to a cascade of anti-foreign statutes that began during the war. From the passage of the Espionage Act in 1917 through the tribal reaction of the twenties, state and national governments legislated almost ceaselessly against the successive dangers that seemed to arise from America's foreign population. Immigration restriction marked both the climax and the conclusion of an era of nationalistic legislation.

During the war and its immediate aftermath, interest focused not on the old objective of restriction but rather on new policies of repression, Americanization, and deportation. By 1920, however, about as much official coercion as the United States would tolerate had been undertaken; for some time to come further attempts to impose internal conformity would rest more completely in private hands. By 1920, also, the policies of Americanization and deportation, as massive ventures, were suffering general discredit. Political nativism shifted again toward its traditional goals, by the same maneuver that turned nativist thinking back into racial and religious channels. With new momentum the two main prewar trends in legislation revived: economic discriminations against aliens, and immigration restriction. In respect to the former, the early twentieth century movement to exclude aliens from a wide range of white-collar jobs went forward again as soon as the war ended, and in the first half of the 1920's these proscriptions accumulated more rapidly and extensively than ever before. Licensing acts in many states barred aliens from practicing medicine, surgery, chiropractic, pharmacy, architecture, engineering, and surveying, from operating motor buses, and from executing wills.[1] These state enactments paralleled the adoption by Congress of a more general kind of restriction: a human blockade sufficiently drastic to be generally considered at the time a permanent solution of the immigration question. And, in truth, the principles then adopted remain the foundation of our immigration law.

Restriction Reconsidered

The whole atmosphere in which the new restriction acts took shape was different from the atmosphere of similar debates in earlier decades. From the establishment of federal regulation in the 1880's until the World War, the main division in attitudes lay between those who wanted a general qualitative and quantitative restriction and those who held to essentially unrestricted European immigration. A large but diminishing middle group remained indifferent or undecided. The restrictionists won only with the enactment of the literacy test on the eve of American entry into the war. Then the new nationalism of 1917 and 1918 changed the terms of discussion. At least in native American opinion, the issue after the armistice no longer concerned the desirability of restriction but simply the proper degree and kind. The war virtually swept from the American consciousness the old belief in unrestricted immigration. It did so, very simply, by creating an urgent demand for national unity and homogeneity that practically destroyed what the travail of preceding decades had already fatally weakened: the historic confidence in the capacity of American society to assimilate all men automatically. And with the passing of faith in the melting pot there perished the ideal of American nationality as an unfinished, steadily improving, cosmopolitan blend. Once almost everyone except immigrant spokesmen tacitly conceded that immigration might overtax the natural processes of assimilation, supporters of a "liberal" policy had to retire from grounds of fundamental principle to an uneasy, relative position.

Partly as a result of acquiescence in the premise of restriction, the dwindling company of progressive thinkers and writers lacked the will (even if they had retained the means) to play a significant part in the legislative controversy. They might, and sometimes did, rather querulously criticize specific restrictive proposals as irrational or prejudiced, but the leading journal of progressive opinion, the *New Republic*, as early as 1916 made the momentous confession: "Freedom of migration from one country to another appears to be one of the elements in nineteenth-century liberalism that is fated to disappear. The responsibility of the state for the welfare of its individual members is progressively increasing. The democracy of today . . . cannot permit . . . social ills to be aggravated by excessive immigration." [2]

The one real effort on the part of liberals to define a clear-cut alternative to the main drift of postwar restriction revealed the distance that American opinion had traveled in a few short years. The Reverend Sidney L. Gulick, a former Protestant missionary in Japan, had advanced in 1914 a "nondiscriminatory" quota scheme designed to eliminate differential treatment of the Japanese by applying a uniform principle to all immigrant nationalities. Briefly, he proposed quotas for each nationality proportionate to the number of naturalized citizens and their American-born children already drawn from that nationality. Each year a federal commission would fix the total allowable immigration at a certain percentage, 10 or less, of those first and second generation citizens. In adopting the rate of naturalization as a standard, Gulick admitted that some nationalities were assimilated more easily than others and argued: "The proved capacity for genuine Americanization on the part of those already here from any land should be the measure for the further immigration of that people." [3] This criterion would substantially reduce the new immigration, as Gulick pointed out. Nevertheless he enlisted a good deal of liberal support for his plan when he organized a National Committee for Constructive Immigration Legislation in 1918. When fully constituted, the committee included such prominent liberals as Norman

Hapgood, Frederic C. Howe, Robert E. Park, Louis F. Post, James Harvey Robinson, Vida D. Scudder, Oswald Garrison Villard, and Lillian D. Wald.[4] Even this modest dissent from prevailing views lost force after 1920, and the committee disappeared from sight.

While native-born progressives surrendered to the restrictionist trend, big business maintained a tenacious opposition. Rooted in self-interest, the industrialists' clamor against increasingly stringent legislation continued well into the twenties. After the war manpower shortage, corporations looked forward greedily to a revival of heavy immigration, expecting that it would beat down an inflated wage scale and curb the increased power of the unions. Through the Inter-Racial Council, the National Association of Manufacturers, and other trade organizations, business leaders even advocated repeal of the literacy test.[5] Nevertheless, they too had actually retreated some distance from their prewar views. Wartime emotions had worked upon their national consciousness, and the Red Scare frightened many of them at least temporarily. While few industrialists favored more rigid limitations on immigration, most of them now acknowledged the importance of some restrictive controls, on patriotic grounds. The National Association of Manufacturers confessed that immigration might endanger the nation and agreed with the nativists that policy must rest on "the needs and interest of America first." The *Commercial and Financial Chronicle* looked about for a middle ground that would satisfy business needs but also ensure both racial preservation and "protection against the poisonous agents and agencies of anarchy."[6]

These alterations in progressive and business thinking left the immigrants themselves pretty much isolated as uncompromising enemies of any general limitation on transatlantic movement. Doggedly, the immigrants set themselves to keep the gates of America as open as possible for their fellow countrymen. Still, the golden Irish voice of Bourke Cochran rose in the House of Representatives to oppose all restriction except on the criminal, the diseased, or the imbecile. Still, scrappy little Adolph Sabath, renowned in the greenhorn sections of every American city as the immigrant's Congressman, protested in Bohemian accents at any modification of a historic American principle. On this issue the immigrant vote

continued to outweigh the labor vote in major urban centers; *
toward the end of the struggle twenty out of the twenty-two
members of the New York state Democratic delegation in the
House of Representatives issued an angry declaration excoriating
the pending legislation.[7]

Meanwhile immigrant writers appealed constantly to the democratic and cosmopolitan strains in the American heritage. Franz
Boas continued to lead the attack on ideas of racial superiority.
Some minority spokesmen still described the American people as
an ever evolving, composite nationality, or America as a home
of the oppressed.[8] There was much rhapsodizing over "immigrant
gifts," with the Knights of Columbus sponsoring a series of books
on the "racial contributions" of various immigrant groups.[9] One
Jewish intellectual, Horace Kallen, developed a radically new theory of American nationality in defense of minority cultures. Reacting violently against the dominant 100 per cent American outlook, Kallen argued that true Americanism lay in the conservation and actual fostering of group differences, not in melting them
down or "contributing" them. At the time, his doctrine of cultural
pluralism made little impression outside of Zionist circles.[10] Indeed, the whole immigrant counteroffensive hardly dented the
massive phalanx of native American opinion. Nor did the outcries
of the new immigrants rouse any appreciable sympathy among
their brethren from northern Europe. The Germans, by the end of
1920 once more restored to favor through another swift reversal of
judgment, were doubtless relieved that the lightning struck elsewhere. The Scandinavians showed their undiluted Americanism
by joining in the cry for higher bars against the new immigration.[11]

If the enfeeblement of the opposition illustrates the new temper
of discussion, the radical demands of postwar restrictionists bring
us to the heart of the revolution in opinion. Agitation for legislation did not await the events of 1920; it burst forth immediately
upon the signing of the armistice in 1918. And from the very first,
the new drive for restriction had a drastic quality inconceivable
in the decades before the war. Nativists now demanded nothing

* Historians who have attributed immigration restriction primarily to
agitation from the trade unions have not considered that the Congressmen
most exposed to A.F.L. pressure were often precisely the ones who felt
more strongly the anti-restrictionist pressure exerted by the immigrants.

less than total suspension of all immigration for periods ranging from two to fifty years.

In its severity the idea had little precedent; in its appeal, none. Only during a few of the most excited moments of the 1890's had the immigrants' critics broached so extreme a proposal, and then not with the force they now commanded. Yet the reopening of the immigration debate on an exclusionist note is only another indication of how much the war altered the temper of American nationalism. It should occasion little surprise that both of the two main groups inaugurating the suspension campaign moved under the influence of 100 per cent Americanism.

Organized pressure came first from the American Federation of Labor. During the last week in December 1918, a special A.F.L. committee on postwar problems met with Samuel Gompers at the organization's headquarters in Washington, D. C., and decided to push for a law stopping immigration for at least two years. Within a few days a bill containing the A.F.L. proposal came before the House Committee on Immigration, and the federation's Canadian-born secretary, Frank Morrison, testified in its behalf. The following summer, when the members of the A.F.L. first got a chance, at their annual convention, to approve this new line of action, they did so overwhelmingly.[12]

The union leaders justified their position primarily on the ground that demobilization would create great unemployment. Certainly this fear of economic dislocations and of the immigrants' economic competition weighed obsessively on organized labor; Gompers announced to the press in December 1918 that unemployment and wage reductions would form the principal dangers of the postwar era.[13] But the economic threat of immigrant labor was an old story. It had always been the burden of the unions' complaint against the foreign-born, yet never before had the A.F.L. advanced so severe a remedy. Why did labor now react so strongly? Could the war have injected a new consideration into its thinking?

Significantly, the A.F.L. urged a second reason for suspension, apart from economics. Immigration, it believed, had exceeded the nation's capacity to unify and Americanize. This explicit appeal to national homogeneity had not graced official A.F.L. declarations before the war period. Gompers and the men around him had argued along strictly materialistic lines until about 1916, when the A.F.L. president in supporting the literacy test vented an impassioned plea for developing "American character and national unity." "America," he wrote, "has not yet become a nation. It is still a conglomerated mass of various and diverse ethnic groups . . . honeycombed with 'foreign groups' living a foreign life." Thereafter wartime emotions tugged harder and harder at Gompers, so that in 1917 he thought the A.F.L. convention "honeycombed" with German spies. When peace broke out, the Bolshevik danger kept him in a nervous state; no small part of his desperate fear of postwar unemployment was due to a belief that it would breed revolutionary sentiment.[14] Evidently the storm of nationalism lashing the whole country was affecting labor's response to immigration, even when the unions rationalized their proposals in economic terms.

The second group initiating the exclusionist agitation consisted of out-and-out 100 per centers—newspaper editors, politicians, and leaders of patriotic societies. Often, as in the case of the American Defense Society, they had not the slightest sympathy with their allies in organized labor.

At first the super-patriots commonly addressed themselves to the prospect of a deluge of murderous Huns. A month after the armistice the National Civic Federation queried: "Shall we permit the bestial hordes who ravished Belgium [sic] women and bayonetted little children to make their homes where American womanhood is held sacred and where innocent childhood is loved?"[15] But speedily the 100 per centers' trepidations swung to the Red menace. How could the United States really guarantee itself against foreign radicalism without cutting off all immigration? Accordingly, the House Committee on Immigration reported a suspension bill to Congress early in 1919 with the argument that revolutionists and Bolsheviks could be kept out of the country only by keeping everybody out. At least one ardent exclusionist, who apparently was more contemptuous than frightened of communism, had still another consideration in mind. Madison Grant commented wryly: "When the Bolshevists in Russia are overthrown, which is only a question of time, there will be a great massacre of Jews and I suppose we will get the overflow unless we can stop it."[16]

In March 1919, when the Republicans took control of Congress, the chairmanship of the House Committee on Immigration passed into the hands of an unusually energetic and vehement nativist, Albert Johnson, who provided from that day forward most of the political leadership that the restriction movement was to have. The foreign danger was the governing passion of his whole Congressional career. First elected to Congress in 1912 on a restriction platform, he kept talking and working on the subject until the voters retired him twenty years later. He was not the incisive commander that Henry Cabot Lodge had once been. He had an ordinary intellect, a certain opportunism made him vacillate at times, and some of his more earnest associates thought he drank too much. But he exuded a certain crude vigor, people liked him, and above all he embraced the two bitterest aversions of his timber-rich constituency in southwestern Washington—a hatred of the Wobblies and a hatred of the Japanese.[17] Consequently Johnson could spark with equal enthusiasm the anti-radical nativism of 1919 and the wave of racial nativism that followed.

Nevertheless, the exclusion drive made no headway after the first few months of 1919. Congressional interest in the idea actually diminished so much as the year wore on that Johnson and his committee decided not to press their suspension bill.[18] The fact was that the anticipated torrent of immigration failed to materialize. Instead, labor unrest and internal radicalism absorbed all of the attention that Congress could spare from peace-making. Far from being inundated, the country witnessed a mounting exodus of foreigners. Meanwhile the House Committee on Immigration found headlines easier to capture by investigating alleged "coddling" of Red deportees at Ellis Island than by crusading for exclusion. Johnson plunged headlong into the Red Scare, ending up as the chief instigator of impeachment proceedings against Louis F. Post. What energy Johnson could spare for legislation was given to securing more sweeping laws for deporting aliens;[19] the issue of keeping them out had to rest for the moment.

So matters stood while the Red Scare ran its course, while the Americanization movement continued, while the flush of postwar prosperity lasted. So they stood until the nation lumbered into the summer of 1920.

The First Percentage Law

Now the transatlantic tide was turning. Now transportation lines were fully operative once more, a better time had come in Europe, and she was sending forth again her teeming humanity. Now the literacy test got its first real trial.

The test proved a fairly coarse sieve. When first proposed in the 1880's, this criterion undoubtedly would have effected a substantial reduction. Then it barred anyone unable to read and write. During the confident years of the early twentieth century, Congress watered it down to a simple reading test, and in that form it became law. In the meantime the literacy rate in Europe had steadily risen. The postwar inrush of immigrants who could pass the test showed every sign of soon equalling the size of the indiscriminate, prewar movement. Net alien arrivals in the latter half of 1920 averaged fifty-two thousand monthly, and by February 1921, the jam at Ellis Island had become so great that immigration authorities were hastily diverting New York-bound ships to Boston.[20]

The fresh influx was caught up immediately in the whole seething readjustment in American conditions and attitudes. Most obviously the immigrants collided with an unemployment problem that developed in the last months of 1920, along with a general business depression. Newspaper cartoonists sketched the picture: a deluge of foreigners pouring from ships while crowds of idle American workers stood watching.

The concurrent ideological changes were less immediately apparent, but one may doubt if they were any less deeply felt. The declining Red Scare left an afterglow of vague suspicion that the immigrants harbored subversive designs; yet the passing of the mood of 1919 ended hopes that any quick internal therapy could cure the nation's ills. The collapse of the Americanization movement, which had seemed to many the most positive way to deal with immigration, suggested that only preventive action could preserve the nation; and the failure of the Americanizers to transform the alien seemed ample evidence of his unassimilable nature.[21] In a climate gray with disillusion, a racial nativism pinpointed on the new immigration was coming back in fashion. A growing isolationism poisoned the atmosphere still further, and for many the

Jews were becoming a special bogey. When Congress reassembled in November 1920, the occasion had arrived (in the words of a representative from Minnesota) for "a genuine 100 per cent American immigration law." [22]

Without troubling with extended hearings, Johnson's committee refurbished and reintroduced its two-year suspension bill, softening it somewhat by exempting close relatives of resident aliens. Admittedly, the proposal was a stopgap, designed as such to meet the dread crisis at Ellis Island and allow Congress time to work out a permanent policy. The House of Representatives acted swiftly. It cut the period of suspension to one year and, within the space of a week, passed the bill by an immense bipartisan majority of 296 to 42. All but one of the negative votes came from industrial areas between Chicago and Boston. [23]

Congressional restrictionists knew that public opinion upheld them, even if some of the big city newspapers remained critical. Consequently the supporters of the bill felt little need to engage in elaborate justifications. Was it not enough to realize that a terrible emergency had befallen the nation? The vision of hungry Europe inundating jobless America provided, therefore, the main theme of debate, and enough of the spirit of the Red Scare endured to furnish supplementary reflections on the immigrants' Bolshevistic and disloyal propensities. Apparently the doctrines of racial nativism had not yet regained a wide enough currency to play much part in the discussion. On the other hand, a considerable strain of anti-Semitism was present.

A postwar wave of persecution in central and eastern Europe was bringing the United States 119,000 Jews during the fiscal year 1920-21, and the sponsors of the suspension bill made as much of this condition as they dared. From an official in the State Department known as a pronounced anti-Semite, Johnson secured a report paraphrasing comments by American consuls overseas on the pernicious character and gigantic proportions of Jewish emigration. According to this document, America faced an inundation of "abnormally twisted" and "unassimilable" Jews—"filthy, un-American, and often dangerous in their habits." The House Committee on Immigration appended these comments to its own report in favor of the suspension bill and used them to suggest that the present immigration was largely Jewish. This strategy made a strong impression. It left a conviction in various quarters that the chief purpose of the immigration law of 1921 was to keep out the Jews.[24]

Before the Johnson bill could become law, however, it had to clear the Senate and receive executive approval. The Senate proved less responsive than the House to nativist influence. The Republican leadership in the Senate heeded solicitously the counsels of business interests, and prospects of a suspension of immigration, even on a temporary basis, filled employers of foreign labor with dismay. The Senate Committee on Immigration was dominated by eastern Republicans like its chairman, Le Baron Colt of Rhode Island, who kept both the interests of the businessman and the votes of his foreign-born employees in mind. Refusing to grant that a calamity impended, Colt's committee opened leisurely hearings at which southwestern cotton growers, Colorado beet producers, building contractors, the National Federation of Construction Industries, and the National Association of Manufacturers protested against exclusion. For a while it seemed that all action might be postponed.[25]

Public pressure was too strong to flout, however, and the great majority of Senators shared the popular desire at least to cut down on the new immigration. A moderate restrictionist, Senator William P. Dillingham of Vermont, offered a plan designed to do just that. His scheme would not affect existing arrangements which excluded most Asiatic immigration, nor would it interfere with the unrestricted movement of Canadian and Latin American labor into the United States. But it would limit European immigration during the coming year to 5 per cent of the number of foreign-born of each nationality present in the United States at the time of the last available census, that of 1910. This percentage plan would hold the new immigration to an annual maximum of a quarter of a million without reducing the normal flow from northwestern Europe.[26]

Dillingham, who headed the old prewar United States Immigration Commission, had presented a similar bill back in 1913. The idea probably originated with his able secretary, William Walter Husband, who came to Washington with Dillingham early in the century. Husband had served as executive secretary for the Immigration Commission and was probably responsible for the inclusion, among the commission's recommendations in 1911, of the first vague formulation of a percentage plan.[27] But the country was not ready for it until the twenties.

The Dillingham bill passed the Senate with practically no opposition except from southern and western Senators who wanted complete suspension. The House of Representatives then abandoned its suspension plan in favor of the quota system but persuaded the Senate to reduce the quotas from 5 per cent to 3 per cent of the 1910 census. This would restrict European immigration to a maximum of about 350,000 and assign most of that total to northwestern Europe.[28] So the bill came before Woodrow Wilson in his last days in office. Supported by the adverse recommendation of Secretary of Labor William B. Wilson, the President simply ignored the bill, allowing it to die by withholding his signature. The ailing, rejected chief of state never explained his silent scorn, and his available papers provide no clue to it.[29] Did he still remember his iron-clad promises to the immigrants in 1912? Did his mind turn back to the cosmopolitan ideals that echoed through his earlier vetoes of the literacy test? Whatever the case, Wilson's disapproval was an anachronism in the world of 1921. It may stand as the inarticulate swan song of unrestricted immigration.

This last Presidential veto made no real difference. The die was cast. The new chief executive, Warren G. Harding, was summoning a special session of Congress, and Harding was a different sort of fellow. The bill that Wilson had blocked was reintroduced in both houses, Johnson now supporting it rather than his own suspension plan. The measure cleared the House in a matter of hours without a record vote, passed the Senate by 78 to 1, and became law in May.[30]

Although adopted as very temporary legislation, the law of 1921 proved in the long run the most important turning-point in American immigration policy. It imposed the first sharp and absolute numerical limits on European immigration. It established a nationality quota system based on the pre-existing composition of the American population—an idea which has survived in one form or another through all subsequent legislation. It ensured especially that the new immigration could not reach more than a small fraction of its prewar level. Above all, the policy now adopted meant that in a generation the foreign-born would cease to be a major factor in American history.

Deadlock, 1921-1923

One may doubt that a grave emergency existed before the passage of the new law; immigration was already slackening in the early months of 1921, reflecting somewhat tardily the business decline. On the other hand, the law most certainly created an emergency. Since no more than one-fifth of a nation's annual quota could be used in any single month, steamship companies made a rush to land their human cargoes early in June. During the first few days of the month twelve ships docked at New York and Boston. They overflowed the Italian quota for the month, nearly exhausted the Polish and Rumanian quotas, and filled more than half the month's quotas for several other countries. The surplus was held on board ship while the authorities wondered what to do. In Boston harbor a thousand half-hysterical Italians jammed the steerage in one hapless ship.

Much to Congressman Johnson's disgruntlement, the Secretary of Labor allowed the Italians to land temporarily, under an escape clause in the law permitting him in special circumstances to distribute excess immigrants over future monthly quotas. But similar scenes were re-enacted regularly. The steamship lines competed fiercely for the reduced immigrant traffic, and the first of each month saw a frantic race for Ellis Island. On the last day of a quota period ocean liners—sometimes a dozen or more—anchored just outside the port of New York, waiting until midnight when they would make a dash for the harbor. Gradually administrative policy tightened, fewer exemptions were allowed, and whole boatloads of heartsick immigrants were sent back across the Atlantic.[31]

In the face of these difficulties, the Congressional restrictionists scarcely knew which way to turn. While the "emergency" law created harsh injustices, it also demonstrated that a workable act would require very careful thought and involve many technical considerations. Above all, the present law was effecting a great and satisfying decrease in immigration, and one must beware lest humane amendments should in any way weaken it. Better let present hardships continue a while longer than take a false step. With little fuss, therefore, Congress in May 1922 extended the life of the temporary law for two more years.[32]

Meanwhile Albert Johnson and his committee were busily gathering ideas for a permanent restriction policy. More or less from the outset they aimed not just for a more practical law but also for a stricter one. They could not, it was now clear, bring about total exclusion. Although the A.F.L., the American Legion, and many southern Congressmen kept doggedly urging such a policy,[33] it seemed unattainable in the face of diplomatic and economic objections. On the other hand, the committee would not rest content with a quota system that still admitted more than 150,000 from southern and eastern Europe annually. This determination reflected, of course, the general spirit of 100 per cent Americanism, but it also showed something more. Through the whole movement, from 1921 on, for more drastic curbs on the new immigration ran an increasingly assertive racial nativism. Out of the rising vigor of the racial tradition in the early twenties came one plea after another for an immigration law designed specifically to keep the old stock from becoming "hopelessly bogged down in the mire of mongrelization." [34] The House Immigration Committee, dominated by southern and western Congressmen, proved a sensitive barometer to the trend of opinion.

Johnson's own contacts with leading race-thinkers went back a long way. He knew Prescott F. Hall of the Immigration Restriction League before the war, and he consulted often with the league's lobbyist after assuming the chairmanship of the House Committee. By 1920 Hall was sinking into a fatal illness, and others were stepping into the role that the Immigration Restriction League had played for so long. By then Madison Grant was in active correspondence with Johnson,[35] who was much impressed by the thesis of Grant's book, *The Passing of the Great Race*. The rough-and-tumble politician from the West Coast became fairly well acquainted with the fastidious Park Avenue socialite, for they met together both at the Capitol and in New York.[36]

Perhaps partly through Grant's intercession, other patrician easterners joined the circle around Johnson as time went on. Lothrop Stoddard came to testify. Kenneth Roberts practically camped in the committee's offices while working on his immigration series for the *Saturday Evening Post*.[37] Johnson was especially pleased to enlist the cooperation of a leading eugenicist, Harry H. Laughlin, who was Charles B. Davenport's right-hand man at the genetics laboratories at Cold Spring Harbor, Long Island. Laughlin supervised the Eugenics Record Office, which Davenport had established there in 1910 to study the hereditary traits of the American population. Laughlin gave the House Committee, and through it the American people, an extensive education in the importance of basing immigration policy on scientifically racial rather than economic considerations. After Laughlin's first appearance before the committee in 1920, it appointed him its "expert eugenics agent." In this capacity he testified from time to time on the bad breeding stock that was entering the country and spoiling its inborn national qualities. His most highly publicized report to the committee presented statistics on the inmates of American mental hospitals, jails, and poorhouses, to show that the new immigration contained a disproportionate percentage of "inborn socially inadequate qualities." [38] Johnson always treated Laughlin with great deference, and apparently the esteem was reciprocal. In 1923 the Eugenics Research Association at Cold Spring Harbor elected Albert Johnson its president. [39]

While Laughlin gave the committee's deliberations scientific prestige, Johnson got more practical advice and encouragement from another member of New York's nativist elite, John B. Trevor. Trevor was a well-to-do lawyer, a member of the best clubs, an old friend of Charles Stewart Davison, who headed the American Defense Society, and a fellow trustee with Madison Grant of the American Museum of Natural History. During the war Trevor became an Army captain, and he proudly retained the title for the rest of his life. As the commanding officer of the Military Intelligence Division in New York City immediately after the war, he acquired a lively interest in the radical movement on the Lower East Side. The Jews bothered him especially, but the whole subject of immigration became a pressing concern. He went to Washington voluntarily in January 1921 to tell Congress what he had learned in the Army about the overwhelmingly foreign character of New York radicals, [40] and he made a strong impression on Johnson. Before long Trevor was drawn into intimate association with the committee. He sat in on informal meetings of the restrictionist majority, fed ideas to it, and contributed to the drafting of reports, all on a voluntary, unpaid basis.

With this talent at its disposal, the committee by the fall of 1922 was developing its fundamental strategy. It would keep the percentage system but reduce the quotas from 3 per cent to 2 per cent. Furthermore, it would change the census base from 1910 to 1890, when the new immigration constituted only a tiny part of the American population. By calculating quotas on the basis of the number of foreign-born in the United States in 1890, the government could not only reduce the total annual immigration but also choke off all but a trickle from southern and eastern Europe. The committee drew up an elaborate bill to this effect in the hope that Congress would approve it before adjourning in March 1923.[41]

Then a change in the course of events suddenly threw the restrictionists on the defensive, stalling their bill completely and even threatening for a time to roll back the nativist tide. The economic indices were turning upward. The depression that struck in 1920 was clearly breaking up by the latter part of 1922, and tidings of a new age of prosperity were abroad in the land. As markets opened up and unemployment shrank, businessmen felt the pinch of a labor shortage again. Unskilled labor became especially tight, because the war had converted so much raw manpower into skilled labor and because immigration was now rigidly limited. Consequently, wages soared. By the spring of 1923 common laborers received an unheard-of $6.50 per day, bricklayers twice as much or more.[42] Industrialists who had acquiesced grudgingly in the law of 1921 now clamored for its liberalization. During the winter and spring of 1922-23, steel corporations, construction industries, and copper mining and smelting interests took the lead in a powerful and widespread business campaign to soften the attitude of Congress and of the administration. James Emery, lobbyist for the National Association of Manufacturers, was never busier in the corridors of the Capitol on matters of immigration; the United States Chamber of Commerce proposed adding another 2 per cent to the present quotas "on a selective basis"; and Judge Gary, head of the United States Steel Corporation, announced bitterly at a stockholders' meeting: the present law is "one of the worst things that this country has ever done for itself economically." [43] The business protests also received considerable support from big farmers appalled at the exodus of their hired hands to the cities.[44]

Briefly this pressure had some effect, notably among administration Senators. Chairman Colt of the Senate Immigration Committee introduced in behalf of the N.A.M. a bill retaining the quota system but permitting the entry of additional immigrants in periods of labor shortage. (The N.A.M. regarded this as a first step toward a genuinely flexible policy.)[45] Another eastern Republican, David A. Reed of Pennsylvania, developed a compromise between business and nativist demands, designed to increase the total allowable immigration while reducing the southeastern European share of it. His plan sounded appealing to conservative Senators, but it came up against the stubborn fact that northwestern Europeans were using only half of their present quotas. Thus any decrease in the new immigration would, from a business point of view, simply make matters worse. And all of this furor failed to budge the nativist leaders in the House of Representatives from their draconic intentions.

The result was a stand-off. Johnson's bill clearly had no chance in the Senate, and the A.F.L. refused even to support it in the House for fear of crippling amendments.[46] On the other hand, the corporations had won nothing but a breathing spell. Their proposals for relaxing the policy of 1921 met little sympathy in public opinion. The *Saturday Evening Post* was growling at the manufacturers for being unwilling to adjust their businesses to the well-being of the nation, and the majority of the urban press received Judge Gary's outburst against the new immigration policy with cold hostility.[47] The Republican leaders in both houses decided to defer the whole issue to 1924. A weary Congress adjourned for its first long vacation in several years, with nothing settled, with no one satisfied, and with only one certainty ahead. Something would have to be done when the legislators met again, lest the temporary act lapse with no new barriers to replace it.

The Nordic Victory

The air had wonderfully cleared by the time Congress reassembled in December 1923. Industry had passed through another season of restricted immigration unscathed by the economic chaos its spokesmen sometimes predicted during the preceding winter. Wages were still spiraling upward, to be sure, but so were production and profits, even more dramatically. In large measure the industrial boom arose from tremendous advances in mechanization.

Efficiency and standardization accelerated as never before; machines replaced muscles on an unprecedented scale. To the extent that the decline of immigration after the war encouraged capital investments in machinery, restriction probably stimulated the whole upward trend. In any event businessmen were discovering that the iron men, combined with growing migration of black men from the rural South, were emancipating industry from its historic dependence on European manpower. Business journals began to assure their readers that a permanent solution of the immigration problem had arrived. "Machinery," one business editor wrote, " 'stays put.' It does not go out on strike, it cannot decide to go to Europe, or take a job in the next town." [48]

While such reassurances allayed employers' economic worries, the pressure of racial nativism beat steadily upon them. Instead of turning back the current of race-thinking, industrialists found their own ranks increasingly infected by it. In December 1923, the National Industrial Conference Board, a research and publicity agency for thirty-one leading industrial associations, held a big conference on immigration at the Hotel Astor in New York. Over a thousand businessmen attended, and their discussions revealed a paralyzing uncertainty. On the one hand, most of them disliked the prospect of further restrictions on immigrant labor. On the other hand, there was much concern over the effects "of mixture of races upon the virility and social progress of our nation." In opening the conference the N.I.C.B.'s director conceded that immigration was "essentially a race question—a question of the kind of citizenship and national life we desire to develop in the United States." One delegate unwittingly summed up the dilemma in business thinking by proposing this as a guiding principle: "Immigration from, and emigration to countries peopled by races with which inter-marriage gives deteriorated (or 'half-breed') and unsatisfactory results— races socially and politically unassimilable—should be permitted by all governments concerned only for commercial purposes." [49]

In this frame of mind the big employers lacked the resoluteness and conviction to wage another fight. The National Association of Manufacturers and the United States Chamber of Commerce recommended early in 1924 that the quotas of 1921 be retained rather than reduced,[50] but neither organization brought any pressure to bear upon Congress to that end. In contrast to the commotion a year earlier, industrialists looked on passively, with little complaint, as the politicians proceeded to raise the barriers against European immigration still higher.[51] The business withdrawal made the passage of a more stringent law relatively easy, because no hand was now raised against it except that of the immigrants who suffered from it.

For them the fight went on to the bitter end. Since the brunt of the restrictionist attack was aimed more than ever at the supposedly racial qualities of the new immigration, it stung the Jews, the Italians, the Slavs, and the Greeks deeply. The concentration of these nationalities in the manufacturing states of the Northeast and Midwest meant that some of the same Senators responsive to big business had to take the new immigrant vote into account too. The nativists, therefore, still had to deal with a cautious attitude among an influential group of Senators, as well as angry opposition in the House from a small body of immigrant representatives. The hour had grown too late, however, for this lingering resistance to divert the nativists from their general course. Even the approach of a Presidential election did not, for the first time since the beginning of the restriction movement, delay its advance. The country took for granted the enactment of a stringent restriction law in the spring of 1924; consequently, the question attracted much less popular interest than the more controversial issues of tax reduction and the Harding scandals.[52] All that really remained was for Congress to translate the prevailing nationalist spirit into a specific legislative design.

Without exercising any real leadership or endorsing any definite restrictive scheme, the new Coolidge administration gave the cause its general blessing. President Coolidge's first annual message to Congress called for some action in order that America might be kept American. Unofficially, Coolidge had already lent his name to the Nordic theory in a popular article on immigration published in 1921. Biological laws, Coolidge or his ghost writer had averred, show us that Nordics deteriorate when mixed with other races.[53] Secretary of Labor James J. Davis took an especially lively interest in restriction and had an ardent attachment to Nordic nationalism. To Davis, a Welsh iron puddler by birth and background, the difference between old and new immigrations seemed roughly equivalent to a difference between the beaver type that built up America and the rat-men trying to tear it down; and obviously rats could never become beavers.[54] Davis toured Europe in the summer of 1923 in an effort to work out a plan for consular inspections of prospective immigrants and their family backgrounds (an idea that Laughlin also recommended on eugenic grounds), but the House Committee on Immigration thoroughly overhauled the proposals that Davis submitted to it.[55]

The direction of affairs still rested with Albert Johnson and the men around him. Johnson's purpose was fixed. He wanted to put European immigration on 2 per cent quotas computed from the 1890 census, thereby cutting the Italian quota from 42,000 to about 4,000, the Polish from 31,000 to 6,000, the Greek from 3,000 to 100.[56] Also, if possible, he wanted to exclude completely the Japanese, sweeping aside the Gentlemen's Agreement of 1907. Some members of the House Committee doubted the wisdom of flouting a treaty obligation, but the passions of the southern and western committeemen carried the day. Since other Orientals were already barred, they argued, it was no discrimination to treat the Japanese like the rest of their race.[57]

But what about discrimination between Europeans? Was it not unfair and discriminatory to shift to an antique census base in order to favor the old immigration at the expense of the new? Johnson knew that his bill would face this charge, and it worried him. His concern at this point was significant. Despite the committee's actual determination to discriminate against southeastern Europe, it could not admit to any but equitable intentions. Despite the prevalence of racial nativism, Johnson could not openly justify his bill on grounds of Nordic superiority. The use of the 1890 census would have to be rationalized as a way of treating all Europeans by a principle of true equality. That much tribute, at least, America's democratic creed demanded. Only a minority went the whole way of racism with Madison Grant, explicitly repudiating democratic ideals and Christian values in the interest of a Nordic philosophy. In popular thought, if not in the minds of an *avant-garde* of intellectuals, American nativism still had to live side by side with the spirit of democracy and the instinct of fair play and come to some terms with them.

Johnson's unofficial adviser, Captain Trevor, supplied a brilliant solution. Trevor saw that if the aim of the Johnson bill (shifting the quota base from 1910 to 1890) was to keep the new immigration from encroaching on the dominant position of the Great Race that founded and developed America, then the bill amounted to an effort to preserve the racial status quo. What, then, was the present racial situation in America, and how did the proposed quotas jibe with it?

The great bulk of the American people, Trevor realized, derived from northwestern Europe. If one could work out a statistical picture of the hereditary backgrounds of the present population, quotas based on a past census might be shown to correspond fairly with (and therefore perpetuate) the existing racial balance. In other words, any census, past or present, could be construed as racially fair for restriction purposes if it yielded quotas roughly proportionate to the present ratio between the old stock and the new immigrant stock in the whole American population.

With these assumptions, Trevor formulated an attack on the percentage scheme adopted in 1921, and in doing so he completely turned the tables on the charge of discrimination leveled against Johnson's proposal. Clearly, quotas based on the number of foreign-born of various nationalities in the United States in 1910 did *not* reflect the racial status quo: by 1910 northwestern Europeans had lost the preponderant position among the foreign-born which their descendants still retained among the native-born. By a racial yardstick, the existing law could be charged with actually discriminating against the *old stock*, because it gave northwestern Europeans a smaller share in the annual quota immigration than they had in the total American population. *Thus the use of the 1910 census really favored southeastern Europeans!* Congress should base quotas on an earlier census, when the old immigration furnished the vast majority of America's foreign-born, in order to do justice to everybody's ancestors.

The argument depended, of course, on a statistical breakdown of the origins of the present American population, against which the present and proposed quota systems might be compared. Clinton Stoddard Burr had attempted such a breakdown a couple of years before in *America's Race Heritage*. Trevor may have known of Burr's work, though it would not do to use Burr's explicitly Nordic and non-Nordic categories. Accordingly Trevor prepared for Johnson's committee a statement on the quota problem, using figures on national origins to make an approximate "racial analysis" of the current population of the United States.

The analysis sought to prove that quotas based on the census of 1890 would not discriminate either against the old immigration or against the new. By relying on a recent census monograph that reflected a similar curiosity about the ancestry of the American people, and by making several assumptions, Trevor was able to argue that about 12 per cent of the American people derived from southern and eastern Europe; yet on the basis of the census of 1910 those countries were allocated about 44 per cent of the total quota immigration. They would have 15 per cent if the 1890 census were applied. Consequently Johnson's bill would give the new immigration justice tempered by liberality.

In reporting the bill to the House of Representatives, the Immigration Committee relied heavily on Trevor's brief. The committee adopted verbatim as its key argument Trevor's introductory comments on the necessity of maintaining the "racial preponderance" of "the basic strain of our population," and his statistics were attached to the committee report to show that this could be accomplished with fairness to all.[58]

Congressmen from new-immigrant constituencies might rage at such reasoning as hypocritical and denounce the racial assumptions behind the bill, but the opposition never had a ghost of a chance to amend it. After a week of flamboyant oratory, a landslide of southern, western, and rural votes passed the measure intact. Its champions now largely ignored the economic arguments they had advanced in behalf of the first quota law three years before. Instead, they talked about preserving a "distinct American type," about keeping America for Americans, or about saving the Nordic race from being swamped.[59] The Ku Klux Klan, which was organizing a vigorous letter-writing campaign in support of the Johnson bill, probably aided and abetted this swell of racial nativism,[60] but Klan backing made no material difference. Congress was expressing the spirit of the nation. Even the American Federation of Labor, which at first was mildly critical of the discriminatory aspect of the House measure, ended by endorsing it as a way of maintaining America's dominant racial characteristics; Gompers, for the first time in his long restrictionist fight, openly (though with a certain reluctance) embraced the idea that European immigration endangered America's racial foundations.[61]

In contrast to the decisive action in the House, the Senate floundered for a while in uncertainty. Senator Colt, the chairman of the Immigration Committee in the upper house, was adamant against any change in the census base. A number of his colleagues agreed that a shift to 1890 smacked of discrimination, and Secretary of State Charles Evans Hughes lent discreet support to their view. The committee, therefore, reported a bill to keep the 1910 census as a base but fix quotas at 2 (rather than 3) per cent. Colt being in feeble health and essentially unsympathetic toward greater restriction, Senator David A. Reed took charge of the measure.[62]

Reed himself was far from satisfied with this alternative to the Johnson bill. He appreciated the essential artificiality of shifting the census base back to 1890, and he recognized the force of the objections against such a change, but he wanted to accomplish the purpose that the House had in mind. Like Trevor, his thoughts were turning toward the preservation of the racial status quo. Could not a way be found to relate quotas directly to the composition of the whole American population instead of merely counting the foreign-born at the time of some past census? Reed was mulling over the problem at the same time that Trevor was developing his statistical defense of the 1890 scheme. Their minds were converging, and apparently the two men reached the same conclusion just about simultaneously. Why not apportion quotas directly according to the contribution of each national stock to the present American population? [63]

This "national origins" principle had numerous attractions. It would be every bit as restrictive as any census-based plan because the law could set an absolute maximum for the annual quota immigration, this figure to be divided in accordance with the origins of the whole white population. Practically, such a system would yield results quite similar to the use of the 1890 census, in that both devices would admit about six or seven times as many immigrants from northwestern Europe as from southern and eastern Europe. Yet Reed's proposal would rest squarely upon and serve to maintain what Johnson's bill guarded only by indirection: America's racial status quo. And by counting everybody's ancestors (instead of the number of foreign-born at some arbitrarily chosen census date), equal justice would be done to one and all. In short, the national origins system offered a direct implementation of racial nationalism and an answer to all charges of discrimination. It gave expression to the tribal mood, and comfort to the democratic conscience.[64]

Without Trevor's statistical tables to show how national origins quotas might work out in practice, Reed would never have succeeded in persuading the Senate of their feasibility. Even so, many doubted the essential accuracy of the calculations. The melting pot had simmered quite long enough to melt most of its original ingredients. Any effort to discover where the 100,000,000 people in the United States in 1920 had really come from was bound to be a very crude approximation at best. Reed granted that careful estimates would require some time to compile. Johnson was impatient of the complexities and uncertainties in such a scheme and induced the House to reject it when it was offered as an amendment to his bill. In the Senate, however, the idea prevailed through Reed's able sponsorship. Henry Cabot Lodge, quickly sensing the significance of the new scheme, encouraged Reed to push it and lent his own prestige to it.[65] Thus the gentleman from Massachusetts, who had given up his place on the Senate Immigration Committee in 1917 and who had played little part in restriction controversies for many years, entered in the evening of his Congressional career into the fulfillment of the movement he had done so much to initiate.

The Senate rejected its committee's original proposal for retaining the 1910 census base and adopted the national origins principle with the stipulation that it would not go into effect until 1927, so that the government could have ample time to formulate the exact quotas. For the interim, the Senate accepted the House proposal for 2 per cent quotas based on the 1890 census. In this double-barreled form the measure passed the upper house with only six negative votes. Two of the most liberal Senators, Thomas J. Walsh of Montana and Magnus Johnson of Minnesota, though opposed to the nativist feeling behind the bill, yielded to the pressure of public opinion and joined the majority.[66] As finally agreed upon by both houses, the prospective law contained all of the important modifications which the Senate had made in the original Johnson bill. At the eleventh hour immigrant leaders pleaded for a White House hearing at which they might argue for a Presidential veto, but Coolidge declined to see them [67] and signed the bill on May 26, 1924.

The Johnson-Reed Act carried the policy of immigration restriction as far as Congress was destined to take it. The act did not accomplish all that a 100 per center might demand. It still allowed an average of 287,000 immigrants per year to enter during the late twenties, chiefly because it continued the exemption of Canada and Latin American countries from the quota system. Nevertheless, together with the provisions of the law of 1917 which still remained in effect, the new statute erected a formidable wall. It prohibited Japanese immigration, thereby perfecting the structure of Oriental exclusion and precipitating a diplomatic crisis with Japan. As for European immigrants, the law established a certain amount of inspection overseas and also ended the chaos of the Emergency Act by requiring the intending immigrant to secure a special "immigration visa" from an American consul abroad; quotas were to be filled by counting the number of visas issued instead of waiting to count the immigrants after their arrival at an American port. Until 1927 quotas were limited to 2 per cent of the number of foreign-born residents of each nationality in 1890. Family exemptions from these quotas were permitted only for the wives and minor children of American *citizens*, not for the wives or children of aliens. And after 1927 a total quota of 150,000 would be parceled out in ratio to the distribution of national origins in the white population of the United States in 1920.

Actually the national origins clause came into effect only in 1929, after two postponements and much quarreling; but the great struggle was over. As Captain Trevor wrote in a pamphlet explaining the new law: "The passage of the Immigration Act of 1924 marks the close of an epoch in the history of the United States." [68]

Ebb Tide

Nativists greeted the event with joy and thanksgiving. To the Native Sons of the Golden West the passage of the act proved that Congress was still composed of red-blooded Americans. The Chicago *Tribune* foresaw a new dawn for the spirit of American nationality and a guarantee that America's future would rest safely in the hands of the American people. A business journal predicted that the law would stimulate greater efficiency and better production methods; it was glad to see America kept American. Two years later Professor Lee Roy Henry, president of the Nordic League, declared that due to the Johnson Act a number of cities had already "gone into the Nordic column." And when the measure had been in operation for no more than a year, the Commissioner of Immigration at Ellis Island reported that virtually all immigrants now looked exactly like Americans.[69]

Yet a final word remains to be said. To leave the nativists on the crest of the wave that had borne them upward for a generation would be false to the longer rhythms of American history. The nativists had won, indeed, a culminating victory. But they could not savor it for long without vitiating their own spirit and values. Nativism lived through compulsive anxiety and sleepless vigilance; it could not afford to relax. In 1924 it faced a peril to itself graver than any foreign influence: an inner sense of relief.

Leading nativists knew that they dared not rest and chafed to accomplish unfinished tasks. The quota system, they agreed, must be extended to the countries of the Western Hemisphere. The considerations that prevented such a step in 1921 and 1924—Pan-American good will and regional economic needs—must yield to the racial danger of Latin America's "colored blood." Also, all aliens must be required to register annually, and stricter deportation laws must be enacted.[70]

Surely this amounted to a modest program compared with the achievements of the early twenties. Nevertheless, through the rest of the decade it all remained undone, and such further restriction as was secured in the heartbreak years of the early thirties came about by administrative changes under existing statutes. Meanwhile, the restrictionists, thrown on the defensive by a long-drawn wrangle over application of the national origins proviso, had to give much of their energy to defending the gains of 1924. The legislative victory that year had come none too soon. Enacted a couple of years later, the law might have been considerably milder.

In all of its manifestations 100 per cent Americanism in the mid-twenties was losing its driving force. Muscular patriots kept hammering on the dangers to the nation and the crisis of the hour, but it all sounded less and less real, more and more tinny. By 1925

Will Rogers, the greatly beloved cracker-barrel philosopher of the decade, was beginning to hoot and jibe at people who called themselves 100 per cent American. The United States has nothing to be concerned about, Rogers declared happily. "The next time a Politician gets spouting off about what this Country needs, either hit him with a tubercular Tomato or lay right back in your seat and go to sleep. Because THIS COUNTRY HAS GOT TOO BIG TO NEED A DAMN THING." [71]

Leading 100 per centers could not help but feel the change in public opinion that Rogers' remark reflected. In 1925 the National Americanism Commission of the American Legion bewailed the greater difficulty it faced every year in selling the legion's ideals to the country. "Americans have become apathetic to the monotonous appeal of the patriotic exhorter. The utmost ingenuity is frequently necessary to obtain publicity." About the same time the *Dearborn Independent* noted bitterly "a constant, calculated and somewhat concentrated campaign" against the term 100 per cent Americanism and the ideals connected with it. To make matters worse, according to the *Independent*, the attack (which came of course chiefly from the Jews) included a "program of belittling and besmirching everything 'Nordic.' " [72]

Actually the important change was not an outspoken offensive against the premises or results of the new nationalism but rather a swing away from its emotional tone. The idea remained while the energy drained away. Although no general revulsion disturbed the principles of 100 per cent Americanism, its spirit deflated.

Undoubtedly the triumphs of the early twenties helped to alter the public mood. Immigration restriction gave many nativists an enervating satisfaction, and the operation of the new laws progressively reduced a major irritant. On the whole, the relatively small number of immigrants who came through Ellis Island in 1925 and thereafter probably did look appropriately Nordic. But plenty of foreign influence survived on the American scene for nationalism to feed upon, if it had kept a hungry and aggressive appetite. The surfeit it displayed reflected changes in public opinion that began before the passage of the Johnson-Reed Act and extended far beyond the limits of the immigration problem. Not only the restriction movement, but each of the nativist currents that had swelled from strength to strength since the late Progressive period, was subsiding.

In the intellectual world the slackening of nativist impulses after 1924 brought a marked decrease in race-thinking. Henry Pratt Fairchild's *The Melting-Pot Mistake* in 1926 proved as much an epitaph to this school of thought as a qualified summation of it. Although Fairchild's book received respectful and on the whole favorable reviews, when Madison Grant returned to the fray a few years later with *The Conquest of a Continent*, he met a chorus of critical jeers. One reviewer expressed surprise that such books were still being written.[73] Meanwhile, interest in eugenics declined steadily, and the movement shrank to the status of a dedicated but ineffectual cult. Similarly, old-guard literary critics largely abandoned the struggle to rescue American literature from alien-minded writers.

On a popular level Henry Ford's contribution to American xenophobia collapsed with a resounding smash. In 1924-1925, the *Dearborn Independent* broke out in a long series of articles attacking Jewish exploitation of the American farmer, whereupon Aaron Sapiro, general counsel for the American Farm Bureau Federation, filed a libel suit against the magazine. For the next couple of years, while the suit pended, the incidence and intensity of anti-Semitic comment in the *Independent* gradually diminished. When the case came to trial in the spring of 1927, all hostile references to Jews ceased.[74] In June, Ford sent two emissaries to Louis Marshall, head of the American Jewish Committee. They reported that the automobile magnate was convinced of the injustice of the charges he had sponsored and wanted to make some amends. Marshall asked for complete retraction, full apology, and a pledge that Ford would never again indulge in such activities. The latter dutifully signed a statement that Marshall prepared for him and released it promptly to the Hearst press.[75]

The most impressive sign of a change of mood occurred well before Ford did his belated penance, and it produced far greater reverberations. In 1924 and 1925 the Invisible Empire of the Knights of the Ku Klux Klan fell apart. In 1923, when it reached its high point, the growing strength of the opposition to it was already apparent. The next year saw the Klan on the defensive in most states. Either because of a desire to achieve respectability or out of a simple loss of vigor, it very generally gave up tactics of terrorism and lawlessness. In fact Klansmen now meted out less violence than their enemies inflicted on them.[76]

Politically, the organization still presented a façade of great strength in many areas. It seemed strong enough nationally to become a considerable issue in the Presidential election of 1924. The Democrats, meeting in the most bitterly divided nominating convention since 1896, defeated an anti-Klan plank for the party's platform by the slimmest of majorities, and the kind of sentiment that the Klan represented prevented the nomination of Al Smith, a Wet and a Catholic from the slums of New York, as the Democratic candidate for President.[77] In a few states the political power of the Klan lasted intact through the fall elections—in Colorado, for example, and especially in Indiana, where D. C. Stephenson dominated the Republican party and a Klan ticket swept into office.[78] Elsewhere, however, the elections of 1924 gave the organization its first great setback. Oklahoma's revulsion enabled the battered Klan-fighter, former Governor John Walton, to win the Democratic nomination for Senator. Louisiana elected a governor who promised to make all fraternal organizations file annual membership lists and drop the use of masks in public places; the legislature quickly did his bidding. Texas witnessed so complete an overturn that within a few months after "Ma" Ferguson's election as Governor the Klan had virtually disappeared from sight.[79]

As disintegration set in, the internal strife endemic in the order from its beginnings got out of hand. Once the golden flow of new initiation fees slackened, many Klansmen began to wonder where all the money had gone. Ugly charges of corruption and dishonesty, leveled at state and national leaders, spread far and wide in 1925. There were schisms, secessions, and exposés, which the leaders fought with the full venom and terror at their disposal. Imperial Wizard Hiram Evans held tight, backing up his loyal kleagles and dragons by bringing court action against the dissidents. The suits resulted in still more unsavory publicity. The worst blowup happened in Indiana. In a hotel room with D. C. Stephenson, a girl who accused him of abducting and assaulting her took poison and died; Stephenson was tried and convicted of second-degree murder. He said he was framed, and in revenge he gave the newspapers a sordid accounting of the state officials who had worked with and for him. The Indiana Klan was literally drowned in slime.[80]

The anti-Catholic spirit that the order embodied flared up violently again in the election of 1928, when the Democratic candidate, Al Smith, seemed almost the Pope incarnate. But that campaign failed to revive an organized nativist movement. The really significant fact was that 100 per cent Americanism had receded enough so that a Catholic with a progressive record could win a Presidential nomination.

In some respects the waning of American nativism after the early twenties was a familiar phenomenon. Anti-foreign movements had surged and subsided time and again in American history. Each time the stresses that fostered them had eased in a few years, the agitators had sunk into obscurity, the secret societies had dissolved in factional strife, and the people had recovered their tempers and their aplomb.

The forces that contributed to this down-swing in the twenties were also not entirely unfamiliar; for some of the underlying conditions that had curbed the nativist impulse in earlier periods reasserted themselves. In the mid-1920's, as in the 1860's and in the late 1890's, a billowing prosperity washed over and helped to smooth the emotional turmoil of the preceding years. The fabulous economic boom from 1923 to 1929 swept more and more Americans into a hectic kind of confidence in their institutions. If the self-assurance was somewhat more forced and less natural than it once had been, temporarily it had much the same effect. Furthermore, one can scarcely doubt that again, as in previous eras, a democratic balance-wheel, working deep inside the national culture, partially counteracted the nativist movements. Even at the height of the Nordic craze, Congressional nativists could not embrace its premises with an entirely good conscience. And although America felt too well satisfied with itself after 1924 to sheer openly and consciously in another direction, the nation's traditional values undoubtedly exercised a quiet brake on xenophobia.

Whereas both prosperity and democracy had restrained nativism at the turn of the century, a third factor operating in the twenties took the United States all the way back to the atmosphere of the age of confidence. As opposed to 1898, when an exhilarating new issue diverted the crusading impulse, Coolidge's America relapsed into a general indifference toward all big problems, international and internal alike. After more than three decades of practically incessant crusading—for reform, for empire, for world salvation, and for national unity—the time had come for a moral holiday. The related missionary ventures of the postwar era, prohibition and fundamentalism, shared in the desiccation that nativism underwent, and no mass movement, no grander vision, appeared to take their places. If any popular ideal dawned in the late 1920's, it was the cozy image of two chickens in every pot and two cars in every garage. Isolation seemed guaranteed by statesmen's promises never to resort to war again; and the radio blared "It Ain't Gonna Rain No More." Thus, America reverted to the spirit of the early 1880's in bidding farewell to that passion for uplift which stirred both liberal and illiberal movements from the days of the Populist party to those of the Ku Klux Klan.

Still, the real burden of the nativist story transcends its cyclical theme. History may move partly in cycles but never in circles. With every revolution some new direction opens, and some permanent accretion is carried into the next phase. Each upthrust of nativism left a mark on American thought and society. The consequences of the anti-foreign wave that flowed without pause for two decades in the early twentieth century are still too recent to be clearly evident; yet who can doubt their primary significance?

Although that wave resembled its predecessors in some ways and incorporated much of their heritage, it must stand alone in its persistence, in its complexity, and in the massiveness of its institutional deposit. Earlier nativist episodes produced only marginal changes in American life; but now the country would never be the same again, either in its social structure or in its habits of mind. Although immigration of some sort would continue, the vast folk movements that had formed one of the most fundamental social forces in American history had been brought to an end. The old belief in America as a promised land for all who yearn for freedom had lost its operative significance. And the new equation between national loyalty and a large measure of political and social conformity would long outlive the generation that established it.

Afterword: Reflections on the Life of *Strangers in the Land*

Strangers in the Land was my first book, the child of my youth, and it has enjoyed as fortunate a life as any parent could wish for a well-behaved offspring. It was clearly a professional historian's book—not a potential best seller, as my understanding publisher gently reminded me when I complained of the book's slow start. But it was born at the right time. Beginning life in 1955 amid the salutes of godparents and friends, it gathered influence and readership year by year. First it brought me to the attention of immigration policymakers. Then it went into a small library of Americana at the White House and appeared in the citations of at least one Supreme Court opinion. Without a shred of advertising beyond the original, modest announcement, and without being displayed at historical meetings, it eventually justified a second hardcover edition and has sold over 116,000 copies in paperback.[1] Most remarkably, it has never come under sustained criticism from any of the schools of historiography that have arisen since its publication, nor has it been superseded by wider syntheses or by a deeper penetration of its subject. *Strangers in the Land* remains to this day a hardy, solitary perennial—an academic phenomenon with a history of its own that begs for explanation.

Looking back to the formative questions and concerns that gave this book its particular character, I can make out three objectives

[1] Lawrence McIntyre, Atheneum Publishers, to Christina Blake, Rutgers University Press, May 27, 1986.

that led me to the endeavor. For one, I wanted to probe the roots of prejudice and ethnic diversity in American society. Here I was addressing the immediate world in which I had grown up. Secondly, I sought historical perspective on modern nationalism. Here I was asking what the study of history could tell us about the direction in which the world was moving. Finally, I wanted to try my hand at writing a kind of intellectual history that could encompass and synthesize political, social, and economic change. Here I was joining in the exciting methodological discourse that accompanied the rising interest of American historians in intellectual history.

As I recall the grandiosity of these aims—my desire simultaneously to stretch the form of historical writing and to shape the future of the United States—I marvel at their innocence. For a young person in the 1940s and early 1950s, however, objectives as ambitious as mine were less extraordinary than they now seem. What is remarkable, I believe, is that a book produced by such vaulting aspiration should remain alive long after the underlying objectives have lost much of the appeal they had in the 1940s.

The most obvious of my goals—exposing injustice to ethnic minorities—remains a continuing challenge, still recognized (albeit reluctantly) as one of the unfinished tasks of American civilization. Nevertheless, the luster of this task has dimmed in recent years, along with many other liberal causes; and the other two objectives that set me going have faded more completely. Nationalism, which weighed so heavily on sensitive minds in the immediate aftermath of two world wars, no longer impresses us as a transforming force in most parts of the world. In the study of American history it never became a major focus of research. Similarly, my expectations for intellectual history—that it could provide the key to synthesis and thus unlock the deepest secrets of the past—have proved overblown. Intellectual historians have retracted their generalizing claims and have largely adjusted to the cautious role of specialists. Yet *Strangers in the Land*, which claimed to be "a general history of the anti-foreign spirit . . . at every social level and in every section where it left a mark,"[2] somehow endures. How that happened I

---

[2] *Strangers in the Land: Patterns of American Nativism, 1860–1925* (New Brunswick, N.J., 1955), ix–x.

shall try to explain. But first something more should be said about the three objectives that shaped my book.

The concern with prejudice was closest to my own experience. It arose from the disparity between what I heard at home as a boy and what I met outside. I grew up in a modest, middle-class suburb of New York City, where everyone was from somewhere else. My school friends, who were very largely of Jewish, Irish, Italian, or German descent, with an occasional Greek or Norwegian thrown in, lived in Queens because their parents had climbed out of more narrowly ethnic neighborhoods in Manhattan or Brooklyn. I lived there because a truck company in Detroit sent my father east as a salesman. We knew some other old-stock Protestants, but they occupied a higher class level than my plain midwestern family. Where I belonged wasn't clear to me. But I knew that the uncomplimentary things my parents said about people who voted Democratic or fed spaghetti and wine to infants didn't do justice to my cosmopolitan friends; and somehow my parents realized that too. They didn't feel entirely comfortable with their prejudices, nor I with my scorn for their provincialism. All of us were displaced, all of us haunted by ghosts and shadows.

The problem of prejudice did not attract me academically, however, until I had fixed on nationalism as the larger subject I wanted to study. In college in the late 1930s I had become convinced, by reading European history and the antiwar novelists of that period, that nationalism was the bane of the modern world; and I was concerned that an awareness of its destructive force had as yet made little imprint on the writing of American history.[3] My choice of a subject for a dissertation was therefore not so much personal as ideological. I was drawn to the kind of progressive thought—distinctly socialist rather than communist—that looked forward to a fraternity of peoples rather than the solidarity of a class. In the ideological battles of the late thirties I attached myself to the liberal isolationism of Norman Thomas and opposed as best I could American entrance into the Second World War. In my revulsion from power politics, I had no wish to study international relations. So

---

[3] One exception that impressed me was Albert K. Weinberg's *Manifest Destiny* (Baltimore, 1935).

I decided after the war to concentrate on the internal history of nationalism, especially its social sources and its ideological development. In choosing antiforeign feeling as the subject for a dissertation I was selecting a manageable and suitably repugnant strand in the mottled pattern of American nationalism.

I received important encouragement in this choice from my major professor at the University of Wisconsin, Merle Curti. A veteran pacifist, Curti had published a pioneering history of American patriotism, *The Roots of American Loyalty* (1946), just before I returned to graduate school from military service. Curti helped me immeasurably in coping with the social complexity my theme presented. But none of us who were awakening in the 1940s to the depth of racial and national antipathies in American history knew how to explain those antipathies satisfactorily within the framework of the historiographical tradition we had inherited. Progressive history, as laid out especially by Charles A. Beard, featured an ongoing struggle between the great mass of the people and an overly powerful economic class. Like most historians of his generation, Beard had been insensitive to ethnic divisions; progressive history had played down religious and racial conflicts.[4] For my generation those issues of group rights and civil liberties had acquired a preeminent importance. Thus, without quite realizing it, I had stumbled into an enormous conceptual problem. How could the many-sided differences between cultural groups—races, nationalities, and religions—be integrated into the simpler social dualism our historiographical heritage prescribed?

Several answers emerged during the 1950s. One approach, best exemplified by C. Vann Woodward's *Origins of the New South*, kept the progressive framework intact. Here acute racial strife was explained as a displacement of antagonisms grounded in economic conflict. Through frustration, popular protest against a ruling class was twisted into racial persecution.[5] Another approach, not yet fully clarified when my book was under way, was appearing in the writings of Oscar Handlin and was best stated in a collection of his articles, *Race and Nationality in American Life* (1957). This view dis-

---

[4] Ellen Nore, *Charles A. Beard: An Intellectual Biography* (Carbondale, Ill., 1983), 66, 118–120.

[5] *Origins of the New South, 1877–1913* (Baton Rouge, 1951).

carded the progressive framework altogether. No single polarity had directed the course of American history. Instead of assuming a fundamental division between "haves" and "have-nots," Handlin celebrated the diversity of American society. The major outbursts of racial and ethnic prejudice he traced to diffuse psychological stresses, such as loneliness and alienation, produced by the breakdown of tradition.

I followed what proved to be a middle course. On one hand, I held to the dialectical structure of progressive history and to an accompanying conviction that deep social crises provide the pivot of change. In progressive style my history projected two opposing sides, the nativists and their adversaries; but while I featured class conflict when I found it, I did not insist on it. The crisis of the Great War seemed as important for the later stage of my story as the class crisis of the nineties was for the earlier stage. Moreover, the basic dualism that I traced was not between the dominant class and an exploited class; it was between two ideas, two versions of the meaning of America. In effect (although I could not have said this so explicitly at the time) I was trying to loosen and enlarge the pattern of progressive history in order to allow a semiautonomous scope for beliefs and emotions. In doing so I was making cautious use of the psychological theories on which Handlin and other innovative historians were drawing more heavily.

In conceiving of my book as an intellectual history, I thought that I was making a methodological experiment. American intellectual history had just come into prominence in the interwar period; its early practitioners still smarted from the condescension of colleagues with more conventional interests. What this new genre could accomplish was a matter of lively debate. Some intellectual historians practiced an elegant, sharply focused study of leading thinkers and refined ideas. Call the "internal" approach, this sort of intellectual history implied that creative thought is the most notable if not the most powerful force in history. Others practiced an "external" approach, which tended to present ideas as the instruments of socioeconomic groups and forces. This second approach lent itself to a broadly based study of popular attitudes.[6] As an under-

---

[6] John Higham, "Intellectual History and Its Neighbors," *Journal of the History of Ideas* 15 (1954): 339–347.

graduate at Johns Hopkins, I had come under the influence of both of these perspectives: the first embodied in the awesome presence of a recently retired but still very active professor of philosophy, Arthur O. Lovejoy; the second represented most grandly by Charles A. Beard himself.[7] In graduate school Curti further expanded my vision of an inclusive, socially conditioned intellectual history; but I would not give up altogether a more intellectualistic history of ideas. I wanted them both—the original ideas that defined a choice as well as the cruder emotions and myths that permeate a broad historical movement. Too often in progressive historiography, ideas seemed little more than reflections of a reality located outside the mind. Too often in Lovejoy's kind of intellectual history they dwelled in an autonomous realm of their own. So, in the preface to *Strangers in the Land* I declared that I was examining opinion—public opinion—as an all-embracing medium in which "events, institutions, and ideas meet and blend in a single historical process."[8]

This way of stating my approach sounds as if I was writing as an idealist. Actually, in striving to be comprehensive without being reductionistic, I tried to combine a materialist perspective on some parts of the subject with an idealist perspective on others. On the most general level, external situations played a determining role in the story I told. But I took pains to try to demonstrate the power of certain new ideas to transcend the specific contexts that produced them. Thus I devoted a special chapter to the internal history of Nordic racism, from its beginnings in the romantic nationalism of the early nineteenth century to its culmination in the physical anthropology of the early twentieth. Although I now regard this chapter as only partly successful in analyzing the scientific ideas that affected race-thinking, I did take science seriously enough to escape the trivializing condescension that progressive scholars sometimes displayed toward thoroughly discredited theories. The book also attained a transcontextual sweep in dealing with some

---

[7] Beard was a visiting professor at Johns Hopkins during my junior year (1939–40). My first scholarly publication, written under the guidance of Eric F. Goldman, was a highly Beardian study of Southern nationalism, "The Changing Loyalties of William Gilmore Simms," *Journal of Southern History* 9 (1943): 210–223.

[8] *Strangers*, ix.

popular attitudes, notably with 100 percent Americanism during and after World War I. By treating the 100 percent American impulse as the culmination of a crusading fervor that had been continuously active in one form or another since the 1890s, I felt able to show that wartime emotions were not a mere product of the war and could therefore shift rapidly to different objectives in the postwar years.

The initial challenge that *Strangers in the Land* had to meet from new approaches to American history came during the first decade after its publication. Tendencies already evident in Handlin's work coalesced into a sweeping repudiation of progressive historiography. In contrast to the bitter conflicts my book featured, historians were increasingly writing about the sunny side of American life, the success of American institutions, the common bonds of an American national character.[9] If climates of opinion were simple and uniform, a work as negative as mine should have lost favor. Certainly the consensus mood of the late 1950s and early 1960s did not encourage the writing of more books like mine. In fact, the whole genre of immigration history, which looked so promising when I ventured into it, failed to flourish. During the consensus years the process of assimilation was in actuality proceeding rapidly and widely in American society—so much so that the enduring significance of ethnic differences seemed more doubtful than some of us had supposed. I myself found the ethnic theme less interesting than I had a decade earlier, and moved away from it.[10]

Nevertheless, professors assigned my book, and students read it. The paperback revolution, which hit the college market in a major way in the late 1950s, created a voracious demand for reprint rights to books that could be assigned in undergraduate courses. The conservative temper of the time may very well have delayed the full impact of *Strangers*, since it did not go into paperback until 1963, eight years after the original hardcover publication. Paperback sales

[9] I first took explicit notice of this trend in "Anti-Semitism in the Gilded Age: A Reinterpretation," *Mississippi Valley Historical Review* 43 (1957): 559–562. For the general trends in historiography postulated in the present memoir see John Higham, *History: Professional Scholarship in America*, 2d ed. (Baltimore, 1983).

[10] John Higham, "The Mobilization of Immigrants in Urban America," *Norwegian-American Studies* 31 (1986): 5–6.

reached a high volume—two printings per year—only in 1965.[11]
Yet interest was obviously building throughout the consensus era.
What special appeal did my story have?

The answer, I think, is plain to see. *Strangers in the Land* treated an
obvious, overwhelming anomaly in the consensus paradigm. Whatever improvements were occurring in racial and ethnic relations in
the mid-twentieth century, no one could—or really tried—to deny
the depth of those divisions in the past. Even if the melting pot was
now working overtime, moral involvement in issues of race and
ethnicity was alive and growing. The enormous success of Woodward's *Strange Career of Jim Crow* testified to that. Published the
same year that my book came out, Woodward's was much more
programmatic and hopeful; but he, too, focused on dramatic
changes in a pattern of ethnic injustice. Woodward showed how
influential a critical study of race relations could be in the very heyday of consensus history.[12]

It is moreover conceivable that young professors and students
who chose not to dwell in their own writing on the darker side of
American history may have discovered in *Strangers in the Land* an inescapable personal lesson. Without explicitly making the point,
the book doubtless brought home to them how much things had
changed for the better since the 1920s. By the time my book was
published, the elaborate structure of discrimination that had severely curtailed the appointment of Blacks or Jews to the faculties
of American colleges and universities was breaking up. As higher
education ceased to guard the privileged sanctuaries of a Protestant
social elite, Jews especially were opening doors that many of them
had never thought they could pass through. This experience surely
encouraged the warm view of America that the consensus school
was spelling out, for most of the pioneers of consensus history were
second-generation Americans. But nothing could expunge the bitter memories of the obstacles to social advancement and acceptance
their families had come up against before World War II. So the
holistic image of America that was beginning to prevail allowed a
partial exception for race and ethnicity, and many young historians

[11] *Strangers in the Land* (New York, 1985), copyright page.
[12] Woodward, *Thinking Back: The Perils of Writing History* (Baton Rouge,
1986), 81–99.

of foreign parentage read my book as a poignant reminder of a past they dared not forget and as a measure of the distance they had come.

The personal relevance of *Strangers in the Land* certainly sustained its readership among the third-generation Americans who poured into the colleges and universities during the 1960s and 1970s. Now, however, the book entered a radically transformed intellectual environment. The consensus paradigm evaporated. With it went all the reluctance historians had manifested in the early 1960s toward studying social conflict. The record of struggle, suffering, and injustice was exactly what the new historiography of the late sixties and seventies insisted on reclaiming. For the New Left, history was once more, as it had been for progressive historians, a battleground. Since *Strangers in the Land* was rooted in a progressive inheritance and additionally infused with my own animus against American nationalism, it acquired for rebellious students in the 1960s a broad intellectual relevance matching the specific personal meaning it had for the children and grandchildren of immigrants. It is little wonder that the paperback edition reached its peak sales from 1965 to 1974.

A special segment of the expanding audience I found in those years materialized in ethnic studies programs and in courses on the history of American minorities. The ethnic revival of the 1970s demanded a new past in which pluralism superseded the earlier expectation that ethnic differences were inexorably fading. Ethnic history became interesting again because its outcome was once more in doubt. *Strangers in the Land* responded to that interest, although it ventured no prediction concerning ethnic survival. Instead, it seems to have served as a means of broadening the historical consciousness of black and Hispanic students by helping to put their own struggles in a comparative perspective. Young college teachers of ethnic studies have occasionally told me how much my book meant to them when they were students.

While acknowledging the affinities between *Strangers in the Land* and the ethos of the 1970s, I must add that the fit was far from perfect. Mine was a liberal book rather than a radical one. Whereas young scholars often implied that the whole system was at fault and that reformers were especially to blame for victimizing minority groups, I had described an alternative tradition that sometimes made possible a fruitful rapport between old-stock reformers and minority groups. This cosmopolitan strain in American nationalism, dating back to the Enlightenment and nourished by the country's long history of immigration, was submerged at times but never obliterated. Since the cosmopolitan strain was present in the Progressive movement, I tried to render a nuanced but generally sympathetic judgment on progressivism rather than a decidedly negative one.

Having survived consensus history in the first decade of its life and radical history in the second, *Strangers in the Land* has in its third decade faced the most serious challenge to date. Nothing hurts more than a loss of interest in one's subject; and there is little doubt that the great boom in ethnic studies that started in the 1960s has subsided in the 1980s. Diminished also in the Reagan era is the deep moral engagement that people of many ethnic backgrounds used to feel in problems of racial prejudice and discrimination. These changes have unquestionably contributed to a decline in sales during the last several years.

Nevertheless, another printing in 1985 suggests that the book is still working in some fashion. Is it possible that the design of the book has now become critical in extending its life? More than at any time since the 1950s, historians today are calling for large-scale narrative syntheses. For a generation, most social and intellectual historians turned away from big thematic narratives. The best talent of the profession went into microstudies of everyday experience, usually viewed from below. In the 1980s the failure of this specialized work to produce a connected vision of social change set off a reaction. Influential voices are urging a return to narrative, particularly the kind of narrative that centers on "a continuing contest among social groups and ideas for the power to define public culture, thus the nation itself."[13] *Strangers in the Land* was written as such a story. The definition of the nation is its subject; the pace and direction of change is its center of attention. *Strangers in the Land* was never a model of narrative history, and its social portraiture is quite thin compared to what would be possible today. But it is a serious attempt to tell what happened to and between different kinds

---

[13] Thomas Bender, "Wholes and Parts: The Need for Synthesis in American History," *Journal of American History* 73 (1986): 126.

of people who took part in the making of modern America. In that sense the book belongs to a genre that is in demand.

In looking back over this convoluted course from 1955 to the present—this tacking and trimming through the crosscurrents of a fickle historiography—can we discern any general lesson? Can the fate of *Strangers in the Land* teach us anything about the survivability of historical writing? One lesson, essential and obvious, must be that sales are not a sufficient measure of worth. My brief chronicle inevitably brings to mind other books on American history with bolder interpretations or more imposing erudition, which are no longer read. On the positive side, however, a different lesson appeals to me. It concerns the virtue of mediation.

Strangers in the Land has survived dramatic shifts in historical interpretation partly because it never belonged to any single school. It was designed to mediate between rival approaches to intellectual history and also between opposing theories of prejudice, one economic and external, the other psychological and subjective. One set of affiliations linked my project to the progressive school; the other set exposed it to challenges from the emerging consensus paradigm. I like to think that a grounding in progressive scholarship saved the book from the more vulnerable features of consensus history, while an openness to postprogressive ideas enabled it to take a wide variety of causes and relationships into account. Divided origins helped *Strangers in the Land* speak to successive audiences. Between those audiences it played a mediating role by containing its own antinomies within the multicausal texture of a narrative.

To end the story here would imply that a work of scholarship lives entirely on the winds of opinion. Let us remember that every scholarly creation must also rest upon, and within, a larger corpus of knowledge growing around it. How the course of research has altered the problems addressed in *Strangers in the Land* bears vitally on the career of the book. But the task of exploring the impact of subsequent inquiry must be left mostly to others, who have indeed already done that in good measure.[14] Here I shall touch only on a major difficulty I left unresolved, which my successors have not yet cleared up.

[14] See the varied articles collected in *American Jewish History* 76, no. 2 (December 1986), especially James M. Bergquist, "The Concept of Nativism in Historical Study Since *Strangers in the Land*," 125–141.

The difficulty arose from the centrality I assigned to nationalism in conceptualizing my subject. The kind of nationalism I concentrated upon—a fervid demand for a new level of national unity—gained explosive force from major social crises in which ethnic divisions were only one dimension. I dwelled on two national crises, the first in the decade from 1886 to 1896 and the second in the period of World War I, separated from one another by a marked downswing in nativism during the buoyant years around the turn of the century. I showed how the immigration restriction movement was a major indicator of nativist feeling.

Critics have noticed certain problems this focus entailed. Some asked if immigration restriction resulted fundamentally from specific social crises or if it was rather an inescapable concomitant of the growth of the state in the twentieth century. Nathan Glazer, for example, suggested in an interesting review of my book that an underlying desire for a more fixed and stable society may have been more important than crisis-provoked hysteria in spurring immigration restriction.[15] My concentration on the psychology of nationalism did not allow a full examination of big structural changes in institutions and world population movements.

Others, among whom I include myself, have wished that *Strangers in the Land* told more about the cultures that were contending for ascendancy or simply for survival in America. My strategy was to distinguish between three ideological variants of American nativism (anti-Catholic, anti-radical, and racial) and to locate individuals and groups in relation to these ideological themes. I was able in this way to explore quite extensively the rhetoric of American nationalism and the social landscapes in which it resonated; I necessarily gave less attention to the daily interaction of ethnic groups, the distinctive strategies that people of different heritages and classes employed in coping with one another, and the slow changes that occurred in their ways of life. At the time when I wrote, American

---

[15] Nathan Glazer, "Closing the Gates," *Commentary* 21 (1956): 587–589. Examining immigration restriction as a strategy of state-building, Aristide R. Zolberg offers a cogent alternative to my approach in "International Migration Policies in a Changing World System," in *Human Migration: Patterns and Policies*, ed. William H. McNeill and Ruth S. Adams (Bloomington, Ind., 1978), 241–286.

historiography was unready for a cultural history of ethnic and race relations. Scholars have not yet produced such a history, but the great advance in the study of immigration, race, and ethnicity since the 1950s has been in this area. Patiently and affectionately, historians have described the behavior and values of dozens of ethnic groups in specific locales in America and in their homelands. In some cases we also have illuminating comparative studies of different groups in the same environment and even a broad, new synthesis of certain commonalities in immigrant experience.[16] What is still lacking is a persuasive theory of how ethnic identities have been constructed, preserved, altered, and abandoned.

In writing *Strangers in the Land* I was aware that cultural differences affected the ethnic conflicts I was examining. That is why I took some care to spell out the stereotypes white Protestant Americans held of the minorities in their midst. I characterized these stereotypes as "the cultural subsoil" in which nativism grew. But American nationalism of a certain kind was my subject. In order to keep it in the center of attention I treated the ethnocentric attitudes displayed in stereotypes as a relatively stable precondition for the much more volatile passions of nativism. Although this distinction between stereotypes and the driving force of nationalism helped to maintain a strong thematic control over a sprawling topic, it privileged the role of ideology at the expense of a wider cultural perspective.

A striking indication of how the book suffered from this constric-

[16] For specific comparisons, see various articles in *Harvard Encyclopedia of American Ethnic Groups*, ed. Stephan Thernstrom (Cambridge, Mass., 1980); also Stephan Thernstrom, *The Other Bostonians: Poverty and Progress in the American Metropolis, 1880–1970* (Cambridge, Mass., 1973); Olivier Zunz, *The Changing Face of Inequality: Urbanization, Industrial Development, and Immigrants in Detroit, 1880–1920* (Chicago, 1982); Victor R. Greene, *American Immigrant Leaders, 1800–1910: Marginality and Identity* (Baltimore, 1987); Thomas Sowell, *Ethnic America: A History* (New York, 1981); John Bodnar, Roger Simon, and Michael P. Weber, *Lives of Their Own: Blacks, Italians, and Poles in Pittsburgh, 1900–1960* (Urbana, Ill., 1982); Walker Connor, ed., *Mexican-Americans in Comparative Perspective* (Washington, D.C., 1985); Thomas Kessner, *The Golden Door: Italian and Jewish Immigrant Mobility in New York City, 1880–1915* (New York, 1977); Josef Barton, *Peasants and Strangers: Italians, Rumanians, and Slovaks in an American City, 1890–1950* (Cambridge, Mass., 1975). For an impressive new synthesis, see John Bodnar, *The Transplanted: A History of Immigrants in Urban America* (Bloomington, Ind., 1985).

tion of its subject is in the virtual absence of both the Chinese and
the Mexicans from my story. Some sympathetic readers have supposed that I bypassed anti-Chinese and anti-Mexican prejudice
because there was, at the time I wrote, too little monographic literature to start from. The truth is that I excluded these topics because
a cursory examination of the anti-Chinese movement and of the discussion of Mexican immigration in Congress suggested that those
groups were not widely perceived as a national threat. Their impact was localized, and the feeling against them was ethnocentric
and racial without being markedly nationalistic.[17] I now realize
that by leaving them out I missed an opportunity to test critically
the preeminent importance that *Strangers in the Land* ascribed to
nationalism.

In view of the proliferation of ethnocultural studies since the
1960s, many of the gaps in the context that I provided are now easily recognized. But how has the book held up as a contribution to
its own proper subject—the history of American nationalism? To
ask the question is to realize with a shock that my account of the
intensification of nationalism in the period from 1886 to 1924 has
not yet been seriously challenged. Surely this is not a consequence
of the invulnerability of my analysis but rather a by-product of a
loss of scholarly interest in the whole subject. As scholars threw
themselves into the multiple histories of particular groups and localities, questions about the molding of an American nationality,
which had seemed urgent to some of us in the 1950s, faded away.
After the failure of McCarthyism in the mid-fifties, Americans
gradually lowered the pitch of nationalistic rhetoric, relaxed the coercions and conformities that had operated on the widest levels of
public opinion, and moved toward a generally pluralistic world
view. Nationalism, although still vigorous, has become curiously
routinized. For historians and social scientists who study less-
developed countries, especially in the Third World, nationalism remains a vital issue; but Americanists influenced by contemporary
priorities have been content to let it slip from their research

[17] See p. 170, above. For my distinction between ethnocentrism and nativism see pp. 24–27.

agendas.[18] Because I wrote about nationalism from a critical perspective at the end of its heyday, my interpretation of that receding era has been easily— perhaps indulgently—received. This lack of scholarly resistance to the core of the book must be counted among the reasons for its longevity.

Impressed by the durability of *Strangers in the Land*, some colleagues in ethnic studies have called it a "classic." I do not think that is correct. To me a classic in the human sciences is a work that people still read after the kernel of its argument has been rejected or substantially revised. *Strangers in the Land* has not yet met that test. After thirty years it seems overdue.

---

[18] In contrast to earlier interpretations by Carlton J. H. Hayes, Hans Kohn, and Karl Deutsch, the most stimulating recent overviews of nationalism have come from authorities on the Third World. See Ernest Gellner, *Nations and Nationalism* (Ithaca, 1983); Benedict Anderson, *Imagined Communities: Reflections on the Origin and Spread of Nationalism* (London, 1983). In American studies there are valuable exceptions to the neglect of the topic, among them Charles C. Alexander's *Here the Country Lies: Nationalism and the Arts in Twentieth-Century America* (Bloomington, Ind., 1980).

Notes

NOTES TO CHAPTER ONE

1. Quoted in Sister M. Evangeline Thomas, *Nativism in the Old Northwest, 1850-1860* (Washington, 1936), 131. On terminology see Mitford M. Mathews, *A Dictionary of Americanisms on Historical Principles* (Chicago, 1951), II, 1113.
2. Popular among Catholic historians, this view was summed up most forcefully by Ray Allen Billington, *The Protestant Crusade, 1800-1860: A Study of the Origins of American Nativism* (New York, 1938).
3. Max Savelle, *Seeds of Liberty: The Genesis of the American Mind* (New York, 1948), 568-73; Sister Mary Augustina (Ray), *American Opinion of Roman Catholicism in the Eighteenth Century* (New York, 1936).
4. Reprinted in Peter G. Mode, *Source Book and Bibliographical Guide for American Church History* (Menasha, 1921), 466-69. See also W. Darrell Overdyke, *The Know-Nothing Party in the South* (Baton Rouge, 1950), 86-87; Allan Nevins, *Ordeal of the Union* (New York, 1947), II, 328-31, 398-400, 465-68.
5. Louis Hartz, "American Political Thought and the American Revolution," *American Political Science Review*, XLVI (1952), 321-42.
6. John C. Miller, *Crisis in Freedom: The Alien and Sedition Acts* (Boston, 1951).
7. "Immigration," *North American Review*, XL (1835), 461; Cephas Brainerd and Eveline Warner Brainerd, eds., *The New England Society Orations* (New York, 1901), I, 315.
8. Carl Wittke, *Refugees of Revolution: The German Forty-Eighters in America* (Philadelphia, 1952), 183-86, 215; William G. Bean, "An Aspect of Know-Nothingism—The Immigrant and Slavery," *South Atlantic Quarterly*, XXIII (1924), 328-29. See also Alfred B. Ely, *American Liberty, Its Sources, Its Dangers, and the Means of Its Preservation* (New York, 1850), 26.
9. Samuel Kliger, *The Goths in England: A Study in Seventeenth and Eighteenth Century Thought* (Cambridge, 1952); Hans Kohn, *The Idea of Nationalism: A Study in Its Origins and Background* (New York, 1944), 206-208, 518, 645-46; Arthur O. Lovejoy, "The Meaning of Romanticism for the Historian of Ideas," *Journal of the History of Ideas*, II (1941), 257-78.
10. "The Anglo-Saxon Race," *North American Review*, LXXIII (1851), 34-71; "The Anglo-Saxon Race," *American [Whig] Review*, VII (1848), 28-46; George Ripley and Charles A. Dana, eds., *The New American Cyclopaedia* (New York, 1858), I, 573-75. For a somewhat

special version see George Perkins Marsh, *The Goths in New England* (Middlebury, 1843). Until Turner began to write at the turn of the century, the term Anglo-Saxon referred simply to a language, not to a race. See *Encyclopaedia; or, a Dictionary of Arts, Sciences, and Miscellaneous Literature* (Philadelphia, 1798), II, 7.

11. Albert K. Weinberg, *Manifest Destiny: A Study of Nationalist Expansionism in American History* (Baltimore, 1935), 163, 360-61; New York *Herald*, April 6, 1850; *The Writings of James Russell Lowell* (Boston, 1890), IX, 55; Samuel J. Bayard, *A Sketch of the Life of Com. Robert F. Stockton* (New York, 1856), appendix, 83. See also the anonymous Yankee quoted in Richard Lyle Power, "A Crusade to Extend Yankee Culture, 1820-1865," *New England Quarterly*, XIII (1940), 647.

12. Horace Bushnell, "The True Wealth or Weal of Nations," Clark S. Northrup and others, eds., *Representative Phi Beta Kappa Orations* (Boston, 1915), 14; Frederick Saunders, *A Voice to America; or, The Model Republic* (New York, 1855), 83-95; Edith Abbott, *Historical Aspects of the Immigration Problem: Select Documents* (Chicago, 1926), 773.

13. "Anglo-Saxon Race," *North American Review*, LXXIII (1851), 56; "The Anglo-Saxons and the Americans: European Races in the United States," *American Whig Review*, XIV (1851), 193.

Notes to Chapter Two

1. Otto Eisenschiml and Ralph Newman, eds., *The American Iliad: The Epic Story of the Civil War as Narrated by Eyewitnesses and Contemporaries* (Indianapolis, 1947), 333; Thomas Wentworth Higginson, *Book and Heart: Essays on Literature and Life* (New York, 1897), 162-63.

2. Order of United Americans, "Scrapbook 1849-1886" (Manuscript Division, New York Public Library), 1861-1862; Harry J. Carman and Reinhard H. Luthin, "Some Aspects of the Know-Nothing Movement Reconsidered," *South Atlantic Quarterly*, XXXIX (1940), 232; Albert C. Stevens, *The Cyclopaedia of Fraternities* (New York, 1899), 311-17. The general effects of the Civil War on the status of the foreign-born are sketched in Marcus Lee Hansen, *The Immigrant in American History* (Cambridge, 1942), 141-42. See also Ella Lonn, *Foreigners in the Union Army and Navy* (Baton Rouge, 1952), 581-82.

3. Florence E. Gibson, *The Attitudes of the New York Irish Toward State and National Affairs, 1848-1892* (New York, 1951), 157-58, 168; Allan Nevins and Milton Halsey Thomas, eds., *The Diary of George Templeton Strong* (New York, 1952), III, 335, 340-43, 352.

Strong, an outraged gentleman who could hardly contain his loathing for the rioters, nevertheless observed that a revived Know-Nothingism would be under the disadvantage of having to discriminate between Irish and Germans since the latter had behaved so well. "A mere anti-Hibernian party would have no foundation on principle, would seem merely vindictive and proscriptive, and would lead to no lasting result, I fear" (p. 343). (Quoted by permission of The Macmillan Company.)

It is also suggestive that *Harper's Weekly*—a bitter critic of the Irish in the 1870's—defended their loyalty on this occasion.

4. Bertram Wallace Korn, *American Jewry and the Civil War* (Philadelphia, 1951), 121-88. Although allowance must be made for an excess of zeal and for certain methodological limitations, the evidence that this study presents is still impressive.

5. Quoted in William B. Hesseltine, *Lincoln and the War Governors* (New York, 1948), 364.

6. Emerson D. Fite, *Social and Industrial Conditions in the North During the Civil War* (New York, 1910), 188-94.

7. "Our Country's Future," September 28, 1864, in Chicago Tribune, *A Century of Tribune Editorials* (n.p., 1947), 28.

8. *Reports of the Immigration Commission: Immigration Legislation* (61 Cong., 3 Sess., Senate Document No. 758, Washington, 1911), 362-64.

9. United States Bureau of the Census, *Historical Statistics of the United States, 1789-1945* (Washington, 1949), 26, 32; United States Bureau of the Census, *Immigrants and Their Children, 1920*, Census Monograph No. 7 (Washington, 1927), 25-26; Oscar Handlin, *The Uprooted: The Epic Story of the Great Migrations That Made the American People* (Boston, 1951), 63.

10. Census Bureau, *Historical Statistics*, 33-34; Edward W. Bemis, "The Distribution of Our Immigrants," *Andover Review*, IX (1888), 588; Joseph Edgar Chamberlin, "The Foreign Elements in Our Population," *Century Magazine*, XXVIII (1884), 762-64; Frederick A. Bushee, *Ethnic Factors in the Population of Boston* (New York, 1903), 63-67.

11. Carl Wittke, *We Who Built America: The Saga of the Immigrant* (New York, 1946), 262-99; Iris Saunders Podea, "Quebec to 'Little Canada': The Coming of the French Canadians to New England in the Nineteenth Century," *New England Quarterly*, XXIII (1950), 365-80. For the unique agricultural emphasis of the Scandinavians see *United States Census, 1870*, Vol. III: *Wealth and Industry*, 833.

12. Edith Abbott, *Historical Aspects of the Immigration Problem: Select Documents* (Chicago, 1926), 356-57.

13. Paul Wallace Gates, *The Illinois Central Railroad and Its Colonization Work* (Cambridge, 1934), 171-214; Richard C. Overton, *Burlington West: A Colonization History of the Burlington Road* (Cambridge, 1941), 158-61, 291-368, 445; James B. Hedges, "The Colonization Work of the Northern Pacific Railroad," *Mississippi Valley Historical Review*, XIII (1926), 311-42; C. T. Hopkins, *Common Sense Applied to the Immigrant Question . . .* (San Francisco, 1869), 47. Italics in original.

14. *Second Annual Report of the Immigration Association of California, 1883*, pp. 3-7. See also Merle Curti and Kendall Birr, "The Immigrant and the American Image in Europe, 1860-1914," *Mississippi Valley Historical Review*, XXXVII (1950), 210 n.

15. *United States Census, 1870*, Vol. III: *Wealth and Industry*, 830, 841; *United States Census, 1880*, Vol. I: *Population*, 723, 735; *United States Census, 1890*, Vol. I: *Population*, Part 2, cxvii; Census Bureau, *Immigrants and Their Children, 1920*, 273-74.

16. Abbott, *Historical Aspects*, 854.

17. Edward Young, *Special Report on Immigration* (Bureau of Statistics, Treasury Department, Washington, 1872), ix; Edward Self, "Why They Come," *North American Review*, CXXXIV (1882), 351; William H. Rideing, "The Immigrant's Progress," *Scribner's Monthly*, XIV (1877), 587; "The Immigration Movement," *Banker's Magazine*, XXX (1875), 177; Andrew Carnegie, *Triumphant Democracy, or Fifty Years' March of the Republic* (New York, 1886), 34. See also "The Political Economy of Immigration," *The American*, IV (1882), 262-63; "A National Need and Its Business Supply," *Manhattan*, II (1883), 60-66; Horace Greeley, *Essays Designed to Elucidate the Science of Political Economy* (Boston, 1870), 306-22.

18. Kirk H. Porter, ed., *National Party Platforms* (New York, 1924), 82-83. For other federal plans to aid immigration see George M. Stephenson, *A History of American Immigration, 1820-1924* (Boston, 1926), 139-40.

19. Ernest Correll, ed., "The Congressional Debates on the Mennonite Immigration from Russia, 1873-1874," *Mennonite Quarterly Review*, XX (1946), 183-216; C. Henry Smith, *The Story of the Mennonites* (Berne, Ind., 1941), 641-43, 659. Railroads offered extraordinary favors to the Mennonites; merchants and officials in Topeka feted them.

20. Gates, *Illinois Central*, 169-70; Theodore C. Blegen, "The Competition of the Northwestern States for Immigrants," *Wisconsin Magazine of History*, III (1919), 3-29; Maurice G. Baxter, "Encouragement of Immigration to the Middle West During the Era of the Civil War," *Indiana Magazine of History*, XLVI (1950), 25-38; Bert James Loewenberg, "Efforts of the South to Encourage Immigration, 1865-1900," *South Atlantic Quarterly*, XXXIII (1934), 363-85. A thorough compilation of federal and state enactments is contained in *Reports of the Immigration Commission* (61 Cong., 3 Sess., Senate Doc. No. 758).

21. William G. Bean, "Puritan Versus Celt, 1850-1860," *New England Quarterly*, VII (1934), 70-89.

22. Eugene Lawrence, "The Romish Victory over the Common Schools," *Harper's Weekly*, XVI (1872), 974; Albert Bigelow Paine, *Th. Nast, His Period and His Pictures* (New York, 1904), 139, 190. See also Gibson, *Attitudes of New York Irish*, 235-75.

23. Charles W. Dilke, *Greater Britain: A Record of Travel in English-Speaking Countries During 1866 and 1867* (New York, 1869), 32; James Watson Gerard, *The Impress of Nationalities upon the City of New York* (New York, 1883), 31.

24. *Celebration of the 4th of July, 1877, by the Sons of Revolutionary Sires in San Francisco, California* (n.p., n.d.).

25. Gibson, *Attitudes of New York Irish*, 205.

26. George W. Julian, *Speeches on Political Questions* (New York, 1872), 113. For the democratic theme see also San Francisco *Alta California* quoted in *Asmonean*, IV (1851), 21.

27. *The Writings of James Russell Lowell* (Boston, 1890), V, 310-11; Elisha Mulford, *The Nation* (Boston, 1870), 397. For other applications of Christian and democratic values to the question of assimilation see *Nation*, II (1866), 648; George Mooar, "The Favorable References to the Foreign Element in the Hebrew History," *Bibliotheca Sacra*, XXVII

(1870), 622-24; Henry Ward Beecher, *Patriotic Addresses in America and England, from 1850 to 1885* (New York, 1887), 825-26.

28. Quoted in Merle Curti, *The Growth of American Thought* (New York, 1943), 233.

29. Merle Curti, *The Roots of American Loyalty* (New York, 1946), 70-72, 202; Floyd Stovall, ed., *Walt Whitman: Representative Selections* (New York, 1934), 314-17; Herman Melville, *Redburn, His First Voyage* (New York, 1924), 191.

30. Henry Ward Beecher, "The Advance of a Century," New York *Tribune Extra*, July 4, 1876, p. 38; William M. Evarts, "What the Age Owes to America," *ibid.*, p. 9; New York *Tribune*, March 11, 1881, p. 4. Earlier evidence is in Abbott, *Historical Aspects*, 751, and "Sources from Which Great Empires Come," *De Bow's Review*, XVIII (1855), 698.

31. Charles Darwin, *The Descent of Man, and Selection in Relation to Sex* (New York, 1872), I, 172; Allan Nevins, ed., *America Through British Eyes* (New York, 1948), 355.

32. *Sixteenth Annual Report of the Board of Directors of the St. Louis Public Schools*, 1870, p. 177; William T. Harris, "On the Relation of Education to the Individual, to Society, and to the State," *Wisconsin Journal of Education*, IV (1874), 1-11; Fulmer Mood, ed., *The Early Writings of Frederick Jackson Turner* (Madison, 1938), 22-23; Frederick Jackson Turner, *The Frontier in American History* (New York, 1920), 23.

33. Self, "Why They Come," 366-67; Carnegie, *Triumphant Democracy*, 35-36; *Proceedings of the National Conference of Charities and Correction*, 1886, pp. 253-55, 258.

34. Hans Kohn, *The Idea of Nationalism: A Study in Its Origins and Background* (New York, 1944), 273-75, 290-94, 320-25; Howard Fast, ed., *The Selected Work of Tom Paine and Citizen Tom Paine* (New York, 1943), 20, 31. See also Robert Ernst, "The Asylum of the Oppressed," *South Atlantic Quarterly*, XL (January, 1941), 1-10.

35. Dilke, *Greater Britain*, 29; *How to Become a Member of the United American Mechanics, Together with the Laws of the Life Insurance Department* (New York, 1882), 4; Gerard, *Impress of Nationalities*, 32; Porter, *Platforms*, 62, 70; Abbott, *Historical Aspects*, 843.

36. *The Poems of Emma Lazarus* (Boston, 1889), I, 202-203.

37. Chamberlin, "Foreign Elements," 770.

38. *Journal of the Knights of Labor*, XX (October, 1900), 1; Elmer C. Sandmeyer, *The Anti-Chinese Movement in California* (Urbana, 1939); Jules Alexander Karlin, "The Anti-Chinese Outbreaks in Seattle, 1885-1886," *Pacific Northwest Quarterly*, XXXIX (1948), 103-30.

39. Rowland Tappan Berthoff, *British Immigrants in Industrial America, 1790-1950* (Cambridge, 1953), 130-42; Bushee, *Ethnic Factors*, 153; Kirk Munroe, "Some Americans from Overseas," *Harper's Monthly*, XCVI (1898), 440.

40. Herman J. Deutsch, "Yankee-Teuton Rivalry in Wisconsin Politics of the Seventies," *Wisconsin Magazine of History*, XIV (1931), 262-82, 403-18; Philip Kinsley, *The Chicago Tribune: Its First Hundred Years* (Chicago, 1946), II, 182; J. J. Lalor, "The Germans in the West,"

Atlantic Monthly, XXXII (1873), 459-70; E. V. Smalley, "The German Element in the United States," *Lippincott's Magazine*, XXXI (1883), 356-57.

41. Smalley, "German Element," 359.

42. James Anthony Froude, "Romanism and the Irish Race in the United States," *North American Review*, CXXIX (1879), 519-36, and CXXX (1880), 31-50; Kenneth R. Rossman, "The Irish in American Drama in the Mid-Nineteenth Century," *New York History*, XXI (1940), 46-47; *Life*, XIII (1889), 26, 127; Henry Cabot Lodge quoted in Edward N. Saveth, *American Historians and European Immigrants, 1875-1925* (New York, 1948), 56-57. A distinction should be noted between the German reputation for conviviality and the Irish reputation for drunkenness; see Lalor, "Germans in the West," 462.

43. Henry Seidel Canby, *American Memoir* (Boston, 1947), 22-24; Hutchins Hapgood, *A Victorian in the Modern World* (New York, 1939), 10; Robert Morss Lovett, *All Our Years* (New York, 1948), 20. Boyhood battles with other nationalities seem to have been infrequent, although Theodore C. Blegen mentions a Yankee-Norwegian episode in *Grass Roots History* (Minneapolis, 1947), 99.

44. West Side Association of the City of New York, "Minutes 1879-1885" (New-York Historical Society), May 24, 1879, February 21, 1880, and May 23, 1885; Lady Duffus Hardy, *Through Cities and Prairie Lands* (New York, 1881), 66-67.

45. William Dean Howells, *Three Villages* (Boston, 1884), 15, 43; Beecher, *Patriotic Addresses*, 831; George Campbell, *White and Black: The Outcome of a Visit to the United States* (London, 1879), 13; Edward A. Freeman, *Some Impressions of the United States* (London, 1883), 141; Philip H. Bagenal, *The American Irish and Their Influence on Irish Politics* (London, 1882), 67.

46. Oscar Handlin, "American Views of the Jew at the Opening of the Twentieth Century," *Publications of the American Jewish Historical Society*, XL (1951), 325-26; Henry Morgenthau, *All in a Lifetime* (New York, 1922), 9.

47. Nina Morais, "Jewish Ostracism in America," *North American Review*, CXXXIII (1881), 269-70; *Saturday Evening Gazette* quoted in *Jewish Messenger*, XLVI (August 1, 1879), 2; Alice Hyneman Rhine, "Race Prejudice at Summer Resorts," *Forum*, III (1887), 525. See also the cartoons in *Life*, XIII (1889), 258-59, 334-35.

48. Anna Laurens Dawes, *The Modern Jew: His Present and Future* (Boston [1884]), 29-30. See also the references cited in note 47 above. On the Seligman incident see Lee M. Friedman, *Jewish Pioneers and Patriots* (New York, 1943), 269-78.

49. Robert H. Lord and others, *History of the Archdiocese of Boston in the Various Stages of Its Development, 1604 to 1943* (New York, 1944), III, 64-78; Alvin Packer Stauffer, Jr., "Anti-Catholicism in American Politics, 1865-1900" (Ph.D. thesis, Harvard University, 1933), 41-45; *Harper's Weekly*, XVI (1872), 974, and XVIII (1874), 918.

50. Charles Richard Williams, *The Life of Rutherford Birchard Hayes* (Boston, 1914), I, 397-401; William B. Hesseltine, *Ulysses S. Grant, Politician* (New York, 1935), 390-91. The speech is reprinted in Ed-

ward McPherson, *Hand-book of Politics for 1876* (Washington, 1876), 155-56.

51. *Congressional Record*, 44 Cong., 1 Sess., 5589.
52. *Ibid.*, 175, 181, 5189-91, 5453-54, 5594; *Nation*, XXI (1875), 383. On the religious issue in New Jersey see William Edgar Sackett, *Modern Battles of Trenton* (Trenton, 1895), 112-17.
53. James M. King, *Facing the Twentieth Century: Our Country, Its Power and Peril* (New York, 1899), 268-70; Williams, *Hayes*, I, 485; Lord, *History of Archdiocese of Boston*, III, 79.
54. *Report of the Joint Special Committee to Investigate Chinese Immigration* (44 Cong., 2 Sess., Report No. 689, Washington, 1877), 1041; *Harper's Weekly*, XVI (1872), 717-18, 974; Henry Martyn Scudder, *The Catholics and the Public Schools* (New York, 1873), 8-9; Charles Eliot Norton, ed., *Orations and Addresses of George William Curtis* (New York, 1894), III, 114-15.
55. Order of the American Union, *The Future Conflict: An Address* [Cleveland, 1878], 25; Henry C. Robinson to Henry Baldwin, April 9, 1888, in Henry Baldwin Papers (Manuscript Division, New York Public Library); Stauffer, "Anti-Catholicism," 60-61; New York *Herald*, May 6, 1878, pp. 3, 6.
56. George L. Cherry, "American Metropolitan Press Reaction to the Paris Commune of 1871," *Mid-America*, XXXII (1950), 3-12.
57. "Why the Commune Is Possible in America," May 24, 1874, in Chicago Tribune, *Century of Editorials*, 43; Foster Rhea Dulles, *Labor in America, A History* (New York, 1949), 116.
58. William Roscoe Thayer, *The Life and Letters of John Hay* (Boston, 1908), II, 1-2; New York *Herald*, May 20, 1878, p. 6; Kinsley, *Chicago Tribune*, II, 277. See also *American Annual Cyclopaedia and Register of Important Events*, 1877, p. 428; Charles Terry Collins, *The Modern Migration of Nations; or The Danger and the Duty of the Hour* (New York [187?]), 8-14; Beecher, *Patriotic Addresses*, 819-20; *Thirteenth Annual Report of the [Massachusetts] Bureau of Statistics of Labor*, 1882, p. 369.
59. San Francisco *Argonaut*, December 1-29, 1877, and September 11, 1886; George T. Clark, *Leland Stanford, War Governor of California, Railroad Builder and Founder of Stanford University* (Stanford, 1931), 154, 433.
60. *Harper's Weekly*, XX (1877), 618; *Nation*, XXVI (1878), 302, 318; *Commercial and Financial Chronicle*, XXV (1877), 73-74; W. M. Grosvenor, "The Communist and the Railway," *International Review*, IV (1877), 585-99.
61. *Nation*, XXV (1877), 68-69. See also New York *Herald*, May 8, 1878, p. 6.
62. Freeman, *Impressions*, 17-19, 25; Matthew Arnold, *Discourses in America* (New York, 1924), 69-70; William T. Harris, "Professor Seeley on the British Race," *Journal of Education*, XIV (1881), 5-6; William Henry Poole, *History, the True Key to Prophecy: In Which the Saxon Race Is Shown to Be the Lost Tribes of Israel* (Brooklyn, 1880). On the reaction of American intellectuals see Saveth, *American Historians*,

16-42, 51-67, and Howard Mumford Jones, *The Theory of American Literature* (Ithaca, 1948), 79-117.

63. Oscar Handlin, ed., *This Was America* (Boston, 1949), 244; W. Fraser Rae, *Columbia and Canada: Notes on the Great Republic and the New Dominion* (London, 1877), 168, 182; Norton, *Orations of G. W. Curtis*, I, 245-46, 381-90, 395-97; Pacific Coast Association of the Native Sons of Vermont, *Report*, 1879-80, p. 19.

64. Joseph Parrish Thompson, *Church and State in the United States* (Boston, 1873), 165. The impact of Darwinism on race-thinking is considered more closely in Chapter VI following.

65. *The Personal Letters of John Fiske* (Cedar Rapids, 1939), 689; Fiske to his mother, June 4, 1880, in Letters of John Fiske, 1867-1896 (Division of Manuscripts, Library of Congress); John Spencer Clark, *The Life and Letters of John Fiske* (New York, 1917), II, 413-15, 433. Like his master Freeman, Fiske abjured the term "Anglo-Saxon," insisting on the "English race" as the properly designated and peculiarly endowed subdivision of the Teutonic race; see John Fiske, *American Political Ideas Viewed from the Standpoint of Universal History* (Cambridge, 1911), 96-97.

66. Fiske, *American Political Ideas*, 97; Chamberlin, "Foreign Elements," 761, 770. The best summary of race-thinking in this period is Dexter Arnold Hawkins, *The Anglo-Saxon Race: Its History, Character, and Destiny* (New York, 1875), esp. p. 26. Other evidence is in *The Poetical Works of Bayard Taylor* (Boston, 1907), 344, read in connection with Richmond C. Beatty, *Bayard Taylor: Laureate of the Gilded Age* (Norman, 1936), 158-59; Abbott, *Historical Aspects*, 346; Thompson, *Church and State*, 152, 163-165; Gerard, *Impress of Nationalities*, 3, 6, 21, 30; Carnegie, *Triumphant Democracy*, 11-12, 25-29, 34.

NOTES TO CHAPTER THREE

1. M. A. Hardaker, "A Study in Sociology," *Atlantic Monthly*, L (1882), 215, 219.

2. New York *Tribune*, March 31, 1884, p. 4; *History of Cincinnati and Hamilton County, Ohio: Their Past and Present* (Cincinnati, 1894), 367-71.

3. Henry David, *The History of the Haymarket Affair* (New York, 1936), 6-10, 18-20; Dixon Wecter, *The Saga of American Society, 1607-1937* (New York, 1937), 215-32. For reports of wage reductions see Philadelphia *Public Ledger* during December 1884.

4. New York *Tribune*, July 2, 1881, p. 5. For suggestive comments on "closed space" see James C. Malin, "Space and History," *Agricultural History*, XVIII (1944), 65-74, 107-26.

5. Josiah Strong, *Our Country: Its Possible Future and Its Present Crisis* (New York, 1885), 40-45, 57, 92-130, 143. Strong's well-known Anglo-Saxon imperialism did not enter into his fear of immigration. He expected no change in America's racial composition because of immigration, and he was convinced that Christianity could not only solve the other social problems but also easily Americanize the immigrant; *ibid.*, 148-49, 171, 210.

6. Samuel Lane Loomis, *Modern Cities and Their Religious Problems* (New York, 1887), 73-76, 81-82, 99-100. For evidence of interest in this book see Henry May, *Protestant Churches and Industrial America* (New York, 1949), 117.

7. Jacob A. Riis, *How the Other Half Lives: Studies Among the Tenements of New York* (New York, 1890), 1-5, 21-22, 296-97. For descriptions of similar conditions at mid-century see Oscar Handlin, *Boston's Immigrants, 1790-1865: A Study in Acculturation* (Cambridge, 1941), 93-127, and Robert Ernst, *Immigrant Life in New York City, 1825-1863* (New York, 1949), 37-60. For the use of Riis's book by immigration restrictionists see Henry Cabot Lodge, "The Restriction of Immigration," *North American Review*, CLII (1891), 34; Francis A. Walker, *Discussions in Economics and Statistics* (New York, 1899), II, 447-48.

8. Richard T. Ely, *The Labor Movement in America* (New York, 1886), v, viii, 288-93, 308-11; John J. Lalor, ed., *Cyclopaedia of Political Science, Political Economy, and of the Political History of the United States* (Chicago, 1883), 89-90. For Ely's critical views of immigration see his *Problems of To-Day: A Discussion of Protective Tariffs, Taxation, and Monopolies* (2nd ed., New York, 1890), 74-78.

9. Edward W. Bemis, "Restriction of Immigration," *Andover Review*, IX (1888), 251-64; Richmond Mayo-Smith, *Emigration and Immigration: A Study in Social Science* (New York, 1890), 1-8 and *passim*; Richard T. Ely, "Scrapbook: American Economic Association, 1885-1906" (State Historical Society of Wisconsin), 27, 32.

10. *Journal of the Knights of Labor*, X (June 19, 1890), 2. See also Mary Earhart, *Frances Willard, From Prayer to Politics* (Chicago, 1944), 190; Kirk H. Porter, ed., *National Party Platforms* (New York, 1924), 146, 171.

11. Charles Eliot Norton, ed., *Orations and Addresses of George William Curtis* (New York, 1894), III, 78-79; Allan Nevins, *Abram S. Hewitt, with Some Account of Peter Cooper* (New York, 1935), 512-16; New England Society in the City of New York, *Anniversary Celebration*, 1887, pp. 52-53; New York *Tribune*, May 5, 1888, p. 5; *Public Opinion*, V (1888), 313. See also William Howe Tolman, *Municipal Reform Movements in the United States* (New York, 1895), 48-49, 100-103.

12. Henry George, *Social Problems* (reprint, New York, 1886), 40-46, 161-62. On the rise of land reform see Roy M. Robbins, *Our Landed Heritage* (Princeton, 1942), 271-74, 295.

13. Strong, *Our Country*, 137; Thomas P. Gill, "Landlordism in America," *North American Review*, CXLII (1886), 60. Lee Benson's ingenious but tenuous argument that the immigration and land questions first coalesced in 1891 reflects an overemphasis on C. Wood Davis as the source of the concept of an exhausted domain; Lee Benson, "The Historical Background of Turner's Frontier Essay," *Agricultural History*, XXV (1951), 73.

14. *Congressional Record*, 49 Cong., 1 Sess., 7831; 49 Cong., 2 Sess., 2319-20; *Public Opinion*, I (1886), 124-25; *American Standard* (San Francisco), April 6, 1889, p. 8; *Prohibiting Aliens from Acquiring Title to Lands in the United States* (51 Cong., 1 Sess., House Report No. 2388,

Washington, 1890), 1, 3. The text of the 1887 measure is in *United States Statutes at Large*, XXIV, 476-77.

15. Worthington C. Ford, "Regulating Immigration," *Epoch*, I (1887), 229-30; *Public Opinion*, III (1887), 98-99, and IX (1890), 151; *Commercial and Financial Chronicle*, XLIV (1887), 669.

16. L. L. Bernard and Jessie Bernard, *Origins of American Sociology: The Social Science Movement in the United States* (New York, 1943), 530-40; Edith Abbott, ed., *Historical Aspects of the Immigration Problem: Select Documents* (Chicago, 1926), 345, 651-56.

17. *Reports of the Immigration Commission: Immigration Legislation* (61 Cong., 3 Sess., Senate Document No. 758, Washington, 1911), 27-30, 339-61, 784-85. For further details on the state system see Ernst, *Immigrant Life in New York*, 25-31.

18. *Proceedings of the Conference of Charities*, 1876, p. 174; Samuel Royce, *Deterioration and the Elevation of Man through Race Education* (3rd ed., Boston, 1880), I, 52, 70; Frank D. Watson, *The Charity Organization Movement in the United States* (New York, 1922), 174.

19. *Reports of the Immigration Commission* (61 Cong., 3 Sess., Senate Doc. No. 758), 30-32, 97-98; Conference of Charities, *Proceedings*, 1876, pp. 162-70; 1890, p. 279; New York *Tribune*, January 19, 1878, p. 8, January 25, 1878, p. 1, and April 5, 1882, p. 2; *Cong. Rec.*, 47 Cong., 1 Sess., 5106-08, 5113. An anti-Chinese law in 1875 included general provisions forbidding the "importation" of prostitutes and the immigration of convicts. This is often taken as the beginning of federal regulation of immigration, but it was apparently a dead letter. The law excited no debate in Congress or discussion in the eastern press. *Cong. Rec.*, 43 Cong., 2 Sess., 1599, 2161; Philadelphia *Public Ledger*, March 4, 1875. The law in 1882 was entirely divorced from the Chinese question.

20. Isaac Aaronovich Hourwich, *Immigration and Labor: The Economic Aspects of European Immigration to the United States* (2nd ed., New York, 1922).

21. Robert Ernst, "Economic Nativism in New York City during the 1840's," *New York History*, XXIX (1948), 170-86; John R. Commons, ed., *History of Labor in the United States* (New York, 1921), II, 117-18.

22. *Cong. Rec.*, 47 Cong., 1 Sess., 5574; *The American: An Exponent of True Americanism & Devoted to the Interests of the Jr. O.U.A.M.* (Pittsburgh), January 24, 1891, p. 1; Wisconsin Bureau of Labor and Industrial Statistics, *Third Biennial Report*, 1887-1888, pp. 1-14.

23. Chester G. Vernier, *American Family Laws* (Stanford, 1931-1938), V, 375.

24. Rodman W. Paul, "The Origin of the Chinese Issue in California," *Mississippi Valley Historical Review*, XXV (1938), 181-96; Josiah Royce, *California from the Conquest in 1846 to the Second Vigilance Committee in San Francisco: A Study of American Character* (New York, 1948), 282-85; Frederic J. Stimson, *American Statute Law* (Boston, 1886), I, 663. Early provisions on the licensing of auctioneers in Michigan and Minnesota refer to citizens of the state or to legal voters, but the phraseology does not suggest discriminatory intent; *Compiled*

Laws of Michigan, 1857, p. 334, and *General Statutes of Minnesota,* 1866, p. 232.

25. *Cong. Rec.,* 49 Cong., 1 Sess., 6995; *Labor Laws of the United States* (Second Special Report of the Commissioner of Labor, Washington, 1896), 229, 242, 1178.

26. Wisconsin Bureau of Labor and Industrial Statistics, *Second Biennial Report,* 1885-1886, p. 437.

27. Peter Roberts, *The Anthracite Coal Industry* (New York, 1901), 103-105, 174-82; Jules I. Bogen, *The Anthracite Railroads: A Study in American Railroad Enterprise* (New York, 1927), 54.

28. Local Pennsylvania newspaper quoted in New York *Times,* February 18, 1884, p. 2; see also *Times* editorial, June 2, 1874, p. 4.

29. *American Annual Cyclopaedia and Register of Important Events,* 1874, p. 682; *Testimony Taken by the Select Committee of the House of Representatives to Inquire into the Alleged Violation of the Laws Prohibiting the Importation of Contract Laborers, Paupers, Convicts, and Other Classes* (50 Cong., 1 Sess., House Miscellaneous Document No. 572, Washington, 1888), 603-604. For the general reception of the immigrants in the coal region see Peter Roberts, *Anthracite Coal Communities* (New York, 1904), 37.

30. Philadelphia *Public Ledger,* September 2 and December 10, 1884; New York *Times,* February 18, 1884.

31. *Cong. Rec.,* 48 Cong., 1 Sess., 5349-50; *To Prohibit the Importation of Foreign Contract Labor into the United States* (48 Cong., 1 Sess., House Report No. 444, Washington, 1884), 7-9.

32. T. V. Powderly, *Thirty Years of Labor* (Columbus, 1889), 442-47; Porter, *Platforms,* 114-15, 118, 126, 134; *Cong. Rec.,* 48 Cong., 2 Sess., 1785; Victor Safford, *Immigration Problems: Personal Experiences of an Official* (New York, 1925), 213-14.

33. *Testimony Taken by the Select Committee* (50 Cong., 1 Sess., House Misc. Doc. 572), 392, 501, 506; *Journal of United Labor,* X (September 26, 1889), 2; *Report of the Select Committee on Immigration and Naturalization* (51 Cong., 2 Sess., House Report No. 3472, Washington, 1891), 706-709; *Investigation of Labor Troubles* (52 Cong., 2 Sess., Senate Report No. 1280, Washington, 1893), 216.

34. Hourwich, *Immigration and Labor,* 330-33, 552; Frederick A. Bushee, *Ethnic Factors in the Population of Boston* (New York, 1903), 83; San Francisco *Argonaut,* April 3, 1886, p. 1.

35. Powderly, *Thirty Years,* 429; Samuel Gompers, *Seventy Years of Life and Labor: An Autobiography* (New York, 1925), II, 30-31. See also *Proceedings of the General Assembly of the Knights of Labor,* 1885, p. 18.

36. *Commercial and Financial Chronicle,* XLIV (1887), 669, 796. Independently of my own research, Morrell Heald has carefully examined this whole subject in "Business Attitudes Toward European Immigration, 1880-1900," *Journal of Economic History,* XIII (1953), 291-304.

37. Philadelphia *Public Ledger,* January 18-February 22, 1886; Senate Report No. 1280 (52 Cong., 2 Sess., Washington, 1893), 158-59.

38. *American Manufacturer and Iron World* (Pittsburgh), January 22-29 and March 5, 1886; *Bradstreet's,* XIII (1886), 369.

39. *Proceedings of the Nineteenth Annual Meeting of the National Board of Trade*, 1888, pp. 138-41; Wisconsin Bureau of Labor, *Second Biennial Report*, 1885-1886, pp. 416-30. The two polls are not strictly comparable, since the employers were asked for their views on restriction, whereas the employees were asked the narrower question of whether they believed immigration was injuring their trade. Still, a comparison is suggestive. Whereas 428 workers felt that immigration injured them as against 291 who did not, employers divided 460 to 63 on the issue of restriction. No answer was received from 150 workers and from 272 employers. Among the 460 pro-restrictionist employers, 70 favored total prohibition.

40. Chamber of Commerce of the State of New York, *Report of a Special Committee on the Proposed Legislation by Congress to Restrict Immigration into the United States* (New York, 1888), 4-6; *Commercial and Financial Chronicle*, XLVI (1888), 557-58, and XLVIII (1889), 143.

41. David, *Haymarket Affair*, 109-22.

42. The first quotation comes from Harry Barnard, *"Eagle Forgotten": The Life of John Peter Altgeld* (Indianapolis, 1938), 133. The rest are drawn from *Public Opinion*, I (1886), 82-86, III (1887), 49, and V (1888), 432.

43. Mayo-Smith, *Emigration and Immigration*, 88; Tolman, *Municipal Reform Movements*, 103; Hjalmar H. Boyesen, "Dangers of Unrestricted Immigration," *Forum*, III (1887), 533, 540-41, and "Immigration," *National Perils and Opportunities* (New York, 1887), 67; *Public Opinion*, V (1888), 432. See also National Educational Association, *Journal of Proceedings and Addresses*, 1888, pp. 145-47; San Francisco *Argonaut*, January 9, 1886, p. 1.

44. *Railway Conductor's Monthly*, IV (1887), 372; V (1888), 613-14. For a sketch of the union see Lloyd G. Reynolds and Charles C. Killingsworth, *Trade Union Publications* (Baltimore, 1945), I, 48-51.

45. P. D. Wigginton, *America for Americans: Declaration of Principles of the American Party, with a Speech, Delivered by Hon. P. D. Wigginton, at Fresno City, on May 27, 1886* (Fresno, 1886), 1-2. For details see John Higham, "The American Party, 1886-1891," *Pacific Historical Review*, XIX (1950), 37-46.

46. *American Standard* (San Francisco), 1889: May 25, p. 1; July 6, pp. 4-5; October 5, p. 2; October 19, p. 2.

47. New York *Tribune*, August 23, 1887, p. 4; *Cong. Rec.*, 50 Cong., 1 Sess., 58-59; Winfield J. Davis, *History of Political Conventions in California, 1849-1892* (Sacramento, 1893), 538.

48. Mary R. Dearing, *Veterans in Politics: The Story of the G.A.R.* (Baton Rouge, 1952), 408.

49. Order of United American Mechanics, National Council, *51st Annual Convention Souvenir*, 1896; *Junior Order United American Mechanics* [Circular, 1886], 2-4.

50. *J.O.U.A.M.* [Circular], 8; *The American: An Exponent of True Americanism & Devoted to the Interests of the Jr. O.U.A.M.* (Pittsburgh), October 12, 1889, p. 4; O.U.A.M., *51st Convention Souvenir*; Albert C. Stevens, *The Cyclopaedia of Fraternities* (New York, 1899), 302 ff.

51. Patriotic Order Sons of America, *Camp News*, XVI (1883), 264; F. W.

Hendley to Henry Baldwin, February 27, 1888, and January 21, 1891, in Henry Baldwin Papers (Manuscript Division, New York Public Library); Agatha Beamer to Baldwin, n.d., *ibid.*

52. *J.O.U.A.M.* [Circular], 3-4; Patriotic Order Sons of America, *A Sketch of the Origin, Progress and Work of the Fraternity with Its Platform of Principles* (n.p. [189-?]), 12.

53. *The Council Chat: A Journal Devoted to the Jr. O.U.A.M. and Kindred Orders*, I (1890), 533, 539, 542-43.

54. Charles L. Hoyt to Henry Baldwin, November 10, 1887, in Baldwin Papers.

55. *American Citizen* quoted in *American Standard*, May 11, 1889, p. 10; Henry J. Browne, *The Catholic Church and the Knights of Labor* (Washington, 1949), 275-78, 287-88, 299.

I have assumed throughout this section that organized nativist groups fairly reflect the social concentration of nativist sentiment. On the social composition of the whole organized nativist movement see G. G. Minor to Henry Baldwin, September 14, 1889, and Henry Baldwin to John W. Hoyt, October 22, 1891, in Baldwin Papers.

56. J. Edward Johnson to Henry Baldwin, September 1, 1889, in Baldwin Papers.

57. Harry J. Sievers, "The Catholic Indian School Issue and the Presidential Election of 1892," *Catholic Historical Review*, XXXVIII (1952), 136-41; Daniel F. Reilly, *The School Controversy (1891-1893)* (Washington, 1943), 31-48; Gerald Shaughnessy, *Has the Immigrant Kept the Faith? A Study of Immigration and Catholic Growth in the United States, 1790-1920* (New York, 1925), 166.

58. Robert H. Lord and others, *History of the Archdiocese of Boston in the Various Stages of Its Development, 1604 to 1943* (New York, 1944), III, 110-33; National Educational Association, *Proceedings*, 1891, pp. 294-95, 393-98; Louise P. Kellogg, "The Bennett Law in Wisconsin," *Wisconsin Magazine of History*, II (1918), 3-25; Anson Phelps Stokes, *Church and State in the United States* (New York, 1950), II, 733.

59. James M. King, *Facing the Twentieth Century: Our Country, Its Power and Peril* (New York, 1899), 519-24; *First Annual Report of the General Secretary of the National League for the Protection of American Institutions* [1890]. Exceptional among anti-Catholic organizations in its upper-class background, the league was too genteel to attract a mass following. A nativist critic complained that "they will circulate a little printed stuff and then drop off in their easy chairs—and say they are too old for political work"; Andrew Powell to Henry Baldwin, September 3, 1889, in Baldwin Papers.

60. Justin D. Fulton, *Washington in the Lap of Rome* (Boston, 1888); Lord, *History of Archdiocese of Boston*, III, 103-104.

61. Alvin Packer Stauffer, Jr., "Anti-Catholicism in American Politics 1865-1900" (Ph.D. thesis, Harvard University, 1933), 93-108; Adolph Kraus, *Reminiscences and Comments* (Chicago, 1925), 65.

62. Stauffer, "Anti-Catholicism," 163-65, 169-70; G. G. Minor to Henry Baldwin, August 28 and November 25, 1889, in Baldwin Papers.

63. "Collection of Newspaper Clippings Relating to the Situation of the Roman Catholic Church in America" (New York Public Library), I,

55; Stevens, *Cyclopaedia of Fraternities*, 290-92; United Order of Native Americans, *By-Laws* (San Jose, 1888); *Ritual and Full Information Concerning the American Patriotic League* (n.p., n.d.); Get There American Benefit Association, *Constitution and By-Laws* (Newburyport, Mass., 1890). For details on the Red, White and Blue see S. M. Douglas to Henry Baldwin [1887], and Baldwin to I. A. Heald, April 20, 1891, in Baldwin Papers.

64. Clipping from *St. George Journal and American British World*, January 1, 1891, in Baldwin Papers; "Collection of Clippings," II, 452-53; Rowland Tappan Berthoff, *British Immigrants in Industrial America, 1790-1950* (Cambridge, 1953), 189-200.

65. F. W. Hendley to Henry Baldwin, February 27, 1888, in Baldwin Papers.

66. John Higham, "The Mind of a Nativist: Henry F. Bowers and the A.P.A.," *American Quarterly*, IV (1952), 16-24.

67. Donald L. Kinzer, "The American Protective Association: A Study of Anti-Catholicism" (Ph.D. thesis, University of Washington, 1954), 78-81. There is supplementary information, drawn from Walliker's personal recollections, in Ruth Knox Stough, "The American Protective Association" (M.A. thesis, University of Nebraska, 1931), 1-3.

68. Stauffer, "Anti-Catholicism," 184-87; Stough, "A.P.A.," 5, 18, 34; H. F. Bowers to Baldwin, December 22, 1890, and W. J. Traynor to Baldwin, March 3, 1891, in Baldwin Papers.

69. *Public Opinion*, V (1888), 432. See also Bemis, "Restriction," 252.

70. New York *World*, October 29, 1886.

71. New York *Times*, June 23, 1891, p. 4. For pro-immigrant sentiment in western and southern papers see *Public Opinion*, III (1887), 98, 337; VIII (1889), 284; IX (1890), 151.

72. Chester D. Schaper to Henry Baldwin, March 26, 1888, in Baldwin Papers.

73. *Nation*, LII (1891), 108; *Public Opinion*, VIII (1889), 240.

74. *United States Census, 1880*, Vol. I: *Population*, 468, 472, 492-95, 541; Lady Duffus Hardy, *Through Cities and Prairie Lands* (New York, 1881), 66.

75. Allan Nevins and Milton Halsey Thomas, eds., *The Diary of George Templeton Strong* (New York, 1952), I, 94 (quoted by permission of The Macmillan Company); *The Personal Letters of John Fiske* (Cedar Rapids, 1939), 172; Emerson quoted in Arthur A. Ekirch, Jr., *The Idea of Progress in America, 1815-1860* (New York, 1944), 92; Paul Wallace Gates, *The Illinois Central Rail-road and Its Colonization Work* (Cambridge, 1934), 318-19. See also Mark Twain, *The Innocents Abroad* (New York, 1911), I, 39-40, 209, 271.

76. United States Bureau of Labor, *The Italians in Chicago: A Social and Economic Study* (55 Cong., 1 Sess., Senate Document No. 138, Washington, 1897), 25-29; Robert F. Foerster, *The Italian Emigration of Our Times* (Cambridge, 1919), 376-90.

77. *Chinese Immigration* (51 Cong., 2 Sess., House Report No. 4048, Washington, 1891), 1-5, 44, 55; George J. Manson, "The 'Foreign Element' in New York City," *Harper's Weekly*, XXXIV (1890), 817.

78. Appleton Morgan, "What Shall We Do With the 'Dago'?" *Popular*

Science Monthly, XXXVIII (1890), 177; William Foote Whyte, "Race Conflicts in the North End of Boston," *New England Quarterly*, XII (1939), 629. As early as 1882 the New York *Tribune* editorialized indignantly on the Italians' addiction to mayhem; see issue of July 23, 1882, p. 6.

79. New York *Tribune*, June 13, 1882, p. 8. See also the characterization and comparison of Italians and Jews in *Testimony Taken by the Select Committee* (50 Cong., 1 Sess., House Misc. Doc. 572), 216.

80. Riis, *How the Other Half Lives*, 106-107; *American Hebrew*, XXX (1887), 36; Louis Wirth, *The Ghetto* (Chicago, 1928), 180-81. See also Z. Ragozin, "Russian Jews and Gentiles," *Century Magazine*, XXIII (1882), 919.

NOTES TO CHAPTER FOUR

1. *Manufacturer's Gazette*, XVII (January 31, 1891), 6; *Commercial and Financial Chronicle*, LV (1892), 162; *Proceedings of the Twenty-Second Annual Meeting of the National Board of Trade*, 1892, pp. 126-28, 272-73. See also *Bradstreet's*, XX (1892), 6; *Iron Age*, LI (1893), 81.

2. New York *Journal of Commerce*, December 13, 1892, p. 2. See also Frick's statement in New York *Tribune*, April 5, 1891, p. 2, and for the proposals for limiting naturalization instead of immigration, Gustav H. Schwab, "A Practical Remedy for Evils of Immigration," *Forum*, XIV (1893), 813-14; *Manufacturer's Gazette*, XVII (May 23, 1891), 7.

3. National Board of Trade, *Proceedings*, 1894, pp. 51-63, 69-88, 131; James M. Swank, *Notes and Comments on Industrial, Economic, Political and Historical Subjects* (Philadelphia, 1897), 181; *Iron Age*, LIII (1894), 722-23.

4. J. R. Leeson, President, Boston Merchants Association, to Grover Cleveland, February 20, 1897, in Grover Cleveland Papers (Division of Manuscripts, Library of Congress); *Publications of the Immigration Restriction League*, No. 18, pp. 3-4.

5. *Proceedings of the General Assembly of the Knights of Labor*, 1892, pp. 4-5, 86. In 1896 the Knights endorsed the literacy test; *ibid.*, 1896, pp. 39-40.

6. *Proceedings of the Eleventh Annual Convention of the American Federation of Labor*, 1891 (Bloomington, Ill., 1905), 15; Samuel Gompers, *Seventy Years of Life and Labor* (New York, 1925), II, 154, 158. On the cigarmakers see *Testimony Taken by the Select Committee of the House of Representatives to Inquire into the Alleged Violation of the Laws Prohibiting the Importation of Contract Laborers, Paupers, Convicts, and Other Classes* (50 Cong., 1 Sess., House Miscellaneous Document No. 572, Washington, 1888), 363-64, 394-95.

7. John Swinton, *Striking for Life: Labor's Side of the Labor Question* (n.p., 1894), 39-57; *American Federationist*, I (1894), 216-17, and III (1897), 233-35. See also *Public Opinion*, XIX (1895), 735, and the numerous references after 1893 in Lloyd G. Reynolds and Charles C. Killingsworth, *Trade Union Publications* (Baltimore, 1945), II, 349 ff.

8. A.F.L., *Proceedings*, 1897, pp. 88-91; *The Carpenter*, XVII (1897), 11, 14; Boston Central Labor Union to Cleveland, February 9, 1897, in Cleveland Papers.

9. A.F.L., *Proceedings*, 1894, p. 47, 1896, pp. 81-82, and 1897, pp. 88-91; *Congressional Record*, 54 Cong., 2 Sess., 72-73; F. E. Wolf, *Admission to American Trade Unions* (Baltimore, 1912), 100-101, 111 n. The more important groups on record for restriction were the Central Labor Union of New York, United Brotherhood of Carpenters and Joiners, Glass Bottle Blowers' Association, Horseshoers' International Union, Atlantic Coast Seaman's Union, and National Association of Hat Makers. The American Railway Union hedged in 1894 by demanding a ban on "Chinese and similar classes." Ray Ginger, *The Bending Cross: A Biography of Eugene Victor Debs* (New Brunswick, 1949), 116.

10. *Laws of the State of New York*, 1894, ch. 622, p. 1569; *Labor Laws of the United States* (Second Special Report of the Commissioner of Labor, Washington, 1896), 993.

11. *Reports of the Immigration Commission: Immigration Legislation* (61 Cong., 3 Sess., Senate Document No. 758, Washington, 1911), 635; Frank Julian Warne, *The Slav Invasion and the Mine Workers* (Philadelphia, 1904), 87-88.

12. *Pennsylvania State Reports*, 1898, Vol. 187, pp. 193-97; Christopher G. Tiedeman, *A Treatise on State and Federal Control of Persons and Property in the United States* (St. Louis, 1900), I, 331.

13. *Western Rural and American Stockman*, XXVIII (1890), 657; XXIX (1891), 311. Partly as a bid for labor support, the Populist party in 1892 endorsed restriction, but its candidate for President took a directly contrary view. Avery Craven and others, eds., *A Documentary History of the American People* (Boston, 1951), 556; James B. Weaver, *A Call to Action: An Interpretation of the Great Uprising, Its Source and Causes* (Des Moines, 1892), 281-82.

14. *Public Opinion*, XIV (1892), 297; *Cong. Rec.*, 51 Cong., 2 Sess., 2741, 2948, 2954, 2958; *Alien Immigration: Reports to the Board of Trade* (British Parliamentary Papers, Vol. 71, c. 7113, London, 1893), 102.

15. Kansas City *Sunday Star*, January 20, 1895; *Public Opinion*, XXIII (1897), 261; *Cong. Rec.*, 53 Cong., 2 Sess., 8239-40, 54 Cong., 1 Sess., 58, 1028, 5421, and 54 Cong., 2 Sess., 1823.

16. *Publications of the Immigration Restriction League*, No. 18, p. 3. On fresh efforts to attract outsiders to Montana and South Dakota see *American Annual Cyclopaedia and Register of Important Events*, 1896, pp. 497, 707.

17. Rowland T. Berthoff, "Southern Attitudes Toward Immigration, 1865-1914," *Journal of Southern History*, XVII (1951), 345, 351, 353; Bert James Loewenberg, "Efforts of the South to Encourage Immigration, 1865-1900," *South Atlantic Quarterly*, XXXIII (1934), 382; J. L. M. Curry cited in Merle Curti, *The Social Ideas of American Educators* (New York, 1935), 269.

18. *Cong. Rec.*, 54 Cong., 2 Sess., 247, 1677, 2946-47. I have tabulated the vote in March 1897 on overriding President Cleveland's veto of the literacy test. On southern immigration societies in the nineties see Berthoff, "Southern Attitudes," 338-39, 341; C. Vann Woodward, *Origins of the New South, 1877-1913* (Baton Rouge, 1951), 298; *American Annual Cyclopaedia*, 1893, p. 465.

19. Sydney G. Fisher, "Alien Degradation of American Character," *Forum,*
XIV (1893), 613-14; *Cong. Rec.,* 54 Cong., 1 Sess., 5429-30; Rena
Michaels Atchison, *Un-American Immigration; Its Present Effects and
Future Perils: A Study from the Census of 1890* (Chicago, 1894), 11,
131; Rhoda Gale, "Immigration Evils," *Lippincott's Magazine,* LVIII
(1896), 231-36.

20. *Sons of the Revolution, New York* [private pamphlet, 1890], 11; National Society of the Sons of the American Revolution, *Addresses Made
at the Banquet, Given . . . by Dr. Wm. Seward Webb* (New York,
1890), 16, 19, 21-22. On flag ceremonies see Mary R. Dearing, *Veterans
in Politics: The Story of the G.A.R.* (Baton Rouge, 1952), 402-408,
471-76; and National Educational Association, *Journal of Proceedings
and Addresses,* 1891, pp. 103-10, and 1892, pp. 61-64.

21. Colman Barry, *The Catholic Church and German-Americans* (Milwaukee, 1953), 119, 163, and *passim;* Edward Bellamy, *Looking Backward,
2000-1887* (Boston, 1888), 354-55.

22. The view presented here converges with and has profited from Richard
Hofstadter's brilliant essay, "Manifest Destiny and the Philippines," in
Daniel Aaron, ed., *America in Crisis* (New York, 1952), 173-200. I am
not, however, persuaded that the jingoist impulse as a general phenomenon in the 1890's may be traced *chiefly* to radical and reformist sources
—a conclusion which perhaps may be too easily drawn from Professor
Hofstadter's analysis of the Spanish-American War.

23. *Outlook,* LIII (1896), 505-506; Edward W. Bemis, "Restriction of Immigration," *Andover Review,* IX (1888), 260.

24. *Nation,* LVI (1893), 43; New England Society in the City of New
York, *Anniversary Celebration,* 1893, pp. 73-75; William D. P. Bliss,
The Encyclopaedia of Social Reforms (New York, 1897), I, 714.

25. T. N. Carver, "Immigration and the Labor Problem," *American Journal of Politics,* III (1893), 80-81; *Nation,* LII (1891), 104; *Public Opinion,* XIII (1892), 369, 426, and XV (1893), 222; *Review of Reviews,* X
(1894), 141; *Railway Conductor,* XI (1894), 189, 413; A. F. Schauffler,
"Taking Strongholds: Christian Work for Our Foreign Population,"
Missionary Review, XX (1897), 169.

26. Roscoe C. Martin, *The People's Party in Texas: A Study in Third Party
Politics* (Austin, 1933), 106; *Investigation of the Employment of Pink-
erton Detectives in Connection with the Labor Troubles at Homestead,
Pa.* (52 Cong., 1 Sess., House Miscellaneous Document No. 335, Washington, 1892), 141; Senate Report No. 1280 (52 Cong., 2 Sess., Washington, 1893), 205.

27. John Tracy Ellis, *The Life of James Cardinal Gibbons, Archbishop of
Baltimore, 1834-1921* (Milwaukee, 1952), I, 707, and *passim; American
Annual Cyclopaedia,* 1893, p. 673; Gustavus Myers, *History of Bigotry
in the United States* (New York, 1943), 223, 237.

28. J. C. Burrows, "The Need for National Legislation Against Anarchism,"
North American Review, CLXXIII (1901), 727-45, reports the fate of
repeated legislative attempts to exclude anarchists beginning in 1888.

29. See note 20 above, and S.A.R., *Addresses,* 19-20; *Proceedings of the
Second Annual Congress of the Sons of the American Revolution,* 1891,
p. 8; *American Historical Register and Monthly Gazette of the Patri-*

otic-Hereditary Societies of the United States of America, I-II (1895), 474, 902, 1069; Society of Colonial Wars, *Constitution and By-Laws, Membership*, 1893, p. 53; New England Society, *Anniversary Celebration*, 1895, p. 38.

30. Donald L. Kinzer, "The American Protective Association: A Study of Anti-Catholicism" (Ph.D. thesis, University of Washington, 1954), 123-28, 156-59.

31. Albert C. Stevens, *The Cyclopaedia of Fraternities* (New York, 1899), 303; *Immigration Investigation* (52 Cong., 1 Sess., House Report No. 2090, Washington, 1892), 693-94; Board of Officers, J.O.U.A.M. of Pennsylvania, to Grover Cleveland, March 2, 1897, in Cleveland Papers.

32. Ruth Knox Stough, "The American Protective Association" (M.A. thesis, University of Nebraska, 1931), 6-7; Alvin Packer Stauffer, Jr., "Anti-Catholicism in American Politics, 1865-1900" (Ph.D. thesis, Harvard University, 1933), 318-19; *A.P.A. Magazine*, I (1895), 45-46, 155.

33. Humphrey J. Desmond, *The A.P.A. Movement* (Washington, 1912), 8-9, 63-67; Kinzer, "A.P.A.," 133-50.

34. *Nation*, LVII (1893), 347; New York *Tribune*, November 13, 1893, p. 5, and November 14, 1893, p. 2.

35. My estimate of total A.P.A. strength, based on an extrapolation of various state claims, falls midway between Kinzer's very severe calculation and Stauffer's somewhat incautious one. On the society's growth see also "Immigration Clippings Collected by Prescott F. Hall" (Widener Library, Harvard University), I, 6; *A.P.A. Magazine*, I (1895), 161-62; New York *Tribune*, February 9, 1894, p. 5, and March 21, 1895, p. 9.

36. Traynor to Henry Baldwin, March 3, 1891, in Baldwin Papers (Manuscript Division, New York Public Library); Hall, "Immigration Clippings," I, 6; Kinzer, "A.P.A.," 197 ff.

37. Stauffer, "Anti-Catholicism," 326-27; Washington Gladden, "The Anti-Catholic Crusade," *Century Magazine*, XLVII (1894), 790.

38. New York *Tribune*, March 9, 1894, p. 1; Stough, "A.P.A.," 33-34; Chris Evans, *History of United Mine Workers of America from the Year 1860 to 1900* (Indianapolis, 1918-20), II, 257, 269-70.

39. *A.P.A. Magazine*, I (1895), 135-36, 173-74; Sister Mary Callista Hynes, "The History of the American Protective Association in Minnesota" (M.A. thesis, Catholic University of America, n.d.), Appendix II B.

40. Desmond, *A.P.A.*, 38-43; *Public Opinion*, XVII (1894), 139.

41. *A.P.A. Magazine*, I (1895), 35, 170, 175; Burton Ames Huntington, *The Coming American Civil War* (Minneapolis, 1893), 172; Boston *Advertiser*, May 15, 1896. The A.P.A.'s immigration bill, introduced by Linton, was buried in committee; *Index to the Congressional Record*, 53 Cong., 3 Sess., H.R. 8774.

42. Richard Wheatley, "The American Protective Association," *Harper's Weekly*, XXXVIII (1894), 1017; H. H. Boyesen, "The Scandinavian in the United States," *North American Review*, CLV (1892), 528, 531.

43. Hynes, "A.P.A. in Minn.," 102; New York *Tribune*, May 4, 1894, p. 4, and May 9, 1895, p. 7; Stauffer, "Anti-Catholicism," 193-99, 336.

44. Fritiof Ander, "The Swedish American Press and the American Protective Association," *Church History*, VI (1937), 173-77.

45. Kinzer, "A.P.A.," 93-98, 178, 301-91; *Nation*, LVII (1893), 389; *Public Opinion*, XVII (1894), 139, 615, and XIX (1895), 203; Stevens, *Cyclopaedia*, 297.

46. Myers, *Bigotry*, 230-41; New York *Tribune*, September 20, 1893, p. 1, and January 19, 1894, p. 4.

47. Reuben Maury, *The Wars of the Godly* (New York, 1928), 206-11; New York *Tribune*, April 4-5, 1894, p. 1. On the third affair, occurring in East Boston on July 4, 1895, see Robert H. Lord and others, *History of the Archdiocese of Boston in the Various Stages of Its Development, 1604 to 1943* (New York, 1944), III, 145-56.

48. Huntington, *Coming Civil War*, 39-42, 172; Desmond, *A.P.A.*, 19-20.

49. *Cong. Rec.*, 53 Cong., 2 Sess., 6003; Elbert Hubbard, "A New Disease," *Arena*, X (1894), 78-79; Hynes, "A.P.A. in Minn.," 115; Gladden, "Anti-Catholic Crusade," 792-93.

50. Kinzer, "A.P.A.," 339-48, 366-67, 414-38; New York *Tribune*, March 9, 1894, p. 2; *A.P.A. Magazine*, I (1895), 178.

51. Ander, "Swedish American Press," 175-77; Hynes, "A.P.A. in Minn.," 102-03, 120.

52. Wheatley, "A.P.A.," 1017-18; Edward Sculley Bradley, *Henry Charles Lea: A Biography* (Philadelphia, 1931), 172-73.

53. Rev. B. W. Williams, "Our Attitude Toward Foreigners," *American Magazine of Civics*, VIII (1896), 65-66; John M. Schick, "The Immigrant Problem," *Reformed Church Review*, I (1897), 484-95; New England Society, *Anniversary Celebration*, 1893, p. 62.

54. New York *Tribune*, June 14, 1895, p. 1; Stough, "A.P.A.," 6, 63.

55. Victor Safford, *Immigration Problems: Personal Experiences of an Official* (New York, 1925), 46; United States Bureau of the Census, *Historical Statistics of the United States, 1789-1945* (Washington, 1949), 33.

56. Census Bureau, *Historical Statistics*, 32; Warren Thompson and P. K. Whelpton, *Population Trends in the United States* (New York, 1933), 63.

57. Carl Wittke, studying immigrant stereotypes on the American stage, found no references to Slavs; "The Immigrant Theme on the American Stage," *Mississippi Valley Historical Review*, XXXIX (1952), 232.

58. The *Manufacturer's Gazette*, XVII (May 9, 1891), 6, reported that 70 per cent of the strikers were foreigners, half of whom could not speak English. See also *Testimony Taken by the Select Committee* (50 Cong., 1 Sess., House Misc. Doc. 572), 604. The general background of the strike is reported by Frick himself in *Investigation of Labor Troubles* (52 Cong., 2 Sess., Senate Report No. 1280, Washington, 1893), 159.

59. New York *Tribune*, 1891: March 31, p. 1; April 3, p. 1; April 4, p. 1. For indications of how widely and unfavorably the affair was publicized see Creston (Iowa) *Daily Gazette*, March 31 and April 2, 1891; *Review of Reviews*, III (1891), 331; *American Annual Cyclopaedia*, 1891, p. 717.

60. New York *Tribune*, April 5-7, 1894, p. 1, and May 25, 1894, p. 1; Evans, *United Mine Workers*, II, 352-61. The *Tribune* regarded the "fiendish crimes" of these "desperate gangs of imported criminals" as incontest-

able proof of the need for immigration restriction; see issue of April 6, p. 6.

61. New York *Tribune*, September 11-12, 1897, pp. 1, 3.

62. *Public Opinion*, XI (1891), 126; *Il Progresso Italo-Americano* quoted in *The Illustrated American*, XIV (1893), 629; letter to editor in Boston *Herald*, July 16, 1894.

63. John Bassett Moore, *A Digest of International Law* (Washington, 1906), VI, 837-49; Philadelphia *Public Ledger*, August 3-4, 1891, p. 1; New York *Tribune*, March 14, 1895, p. 1.

64. John E. Coxe, "The New Orleans Mafia Incident," *Louisiana Historical Quarterly*, XX (1937), 1067-1110.

65. Henry Baldwin to Andrew Powell, April 15, 1891, in Henry Baldwin Papers (Manuscript Division, New York Public Library); George L. Curtiss, "Duty of This Nation and the Church Toward Immigration," *Methodist Review*, LI (1891), 723; *Public Opinion*, X (1891), 616; *Literary Digest*, II (1891), 693; J. A. Karlin, "The Italo-American Incident of 1891 and the Road to Reunion," *Journal of Southern History*, VIII (1942), 242-46.

66. New York *Tribune*, April 2, 1891, p. 2; John Chetwood, Jr., *Immigration Fallacies* (Boston, 1896), 146-47; *Review of Reviews*, III (1891), 331.

67. *Review of Reviews*, III (1891), 443, 449; John Hawks Noble, "The Present State of the Immigration Question," *Political Science Quarterly*, VII (1892), 232; Baldwin to I. A. Heald, April 26, 1891, in Baldwin Papers; *Nation*, LII (1891), 312, 354-55; W. H. Wilder, "The Evil of Immigration," *Methodist Review*, LI (1891), 719-20; Rev. George W. Cutter, *The Mafia and Foreign Immigration: A Sermon* (Newport, R. I., 1891). See also New York *Times*, April 27, 1891.

68. What was probably the first magazine article describing this ferment was friendly and sympathetic; Ida Van Etten, "Russian Jews as Desirable Immigrants," *Forum*, XV (1893), 172-82.

69. *American Hebrew*, XXX (1887), 123; Natchez *Daily Democrat*, January 20, 1893; *Oesterreichische Wochenschrift*, X (1893), 88; *Allgemeine Zeitung des Judentums*, LVII (December 8, 1893), appendix, 4. Cf. Woodward, *Origins of New South*, 188.

70. Louis Wirth, *The Ghetto* (Chicago, 1928), 180-81; Edna Ferber, *A Peculiar Treasure* (New York, 1939), 50; New York *Tribune*, June 29, 1899, p. 11.

71. Philadelphia *Public Ledger*, September 19-22, 1891, p. 2; *Hazefirah*, XVIII (1891), 910.

72. Letter to editor, New York *Sun*, March 24, 1895; Edward N. Saveth, *American Historians and European Immigrants, 1875-1925* (New York, 1948), 65-89; *Cong. Rec.*, 54 Cong., 1 Sess., 5215; *Outlook*, LIII (1896), 291.

73. Anon., *The Talmud-Jew: A True Exposure of the Doctrines and the Aims of Judaism* (New York, 1892), 5-10; *Hamagid l'Israel*, III (1894), 317.

74. James A. Barnes, *John G. Carlisle: Financial Statesman* (New York, 1931), 390-91, 397; Oscar Handlin, "American Views of the Jew at the Opening of the Twentieth Century," *Publications of the American*

Jewish Historical Society, XL (1951), 329-34; Thornton Anderson, *Brooks Adams, Constructive Conservative* (Ithaca, 1951), 60.

75. Fisher, "Alien Degradation," 615. The principal organization opposed to southern and eastern European immigration, the Immigration Restriction League, publicly dissociated itself from groups fostering religious bigotry; Boston *Transcript,* October 27, 1894.

76. Francis A. Walker, "The Tide of Economic Thought," *Publications of the American Economic Association,* VI (January-March, 1891), 37; Henry Cabot Lodge, "The Restriction of Immigration," *North American Review,* CLII (1891), 27-32; *Cong. Rec.,* 51 Cong., 2 Sess., 2956. For a fuller discussion of the rise of Anglo-Saxon nativism see Chapter VI.

77. Henry Cabot Lodge, *Early Memories* (New York, 1913), 203-209; *The Education of Henry Adams* (New York, 1931), 353, 419-20; *Essays in Anglo-Saxon Law* (Boston, 1876), 55-119.

78. Henry Cabot Lodge, *Speeches* (Boston, 1892), 45-47.

79. James Morton Smith, "The Enforcement of the Alien Friends Act of 1798," *Mississippi Valley Historical Review,* XLI (1954), 85-104.

80. For impressive reaffirmations of the cosmopolitan tradition see Charles W. Eliot, *American Contributions to Civilization and Other Essays and Addresses* (New York, 1897), 30, 34; Rev. W. G. Puddefort, "Is the Foreigner a Menace to the Nation?" *American Magazine of Civics,* IX (1896), 10-11; Lyman Abbott, *Christianity and Social Problems* (Boston, 1896), 358-59, 369-70; Frederick H. Gillett, *George Frisbie Hoar* (Cambridge, 1934), 190-92.

81. A. Cleveland Coxe, "Government by Aliens," *Forum,* VII (1889), 607; C. C. Bonney, "Naturalization Laws and Their Enforcement," *New Englander,* XIII (1888), 324-26; *Nation,* LVI (1893), 43; Office of Commissioner-General of Immigration, *Report of the Immigration Investigating Commission to the Honorable the Secretary of the Treasury* (Washington, 1895), 39. See also note 2 above.

82. Frederic J. Stimson, *American Statute Law* (Boston, 1886), I, 59; Leon E. Aylsworth, "The Passing of Alien Suffrage," *American Political Science Review,* XXV (1931), 114.

83. James Bryce, *The American Commonwealth* (2nd ed., London, 1891), II, 29-36; Frederic C. Howe, *The Confessions of a Reformer* (New York, 1925), 3, 64.

84. New York *Tribune,* December 23, 1887, p. 4; *Reports of the Immigration Commission* (61 Cong., 3 Sess., Senate Doc. 758), 37-38.

85. Mayo-Smith, *Emigration,* 222-25; John Lombardi, *Labor's Voice in the Cabinet; A History of the Department of Labor from Its Origins to 1921* (New York, 1942), 123-24; *Reports of the Immigration Commission* (61 Cong., 3 Sess., Senate Doc. 758), 39.

86. *Annual Report of the Secretary of the Treasury,* 1890, pp. 790-91.

87. *Reports of the Immigration Commission* (61 Cong., 3 Sess., Senate Doc. No. 758), 40; *Reports of the Industrial Commission* (57 Cong., 1 Sess., House Document No. 184, Washington, 1901), XV, xviii; Safford, *Immigration Problems,* 182-95. In 1893 another administrative statute prescribed the content of the steamship examination by requiring the companies to submit extensive data on each of their passengers.

88. Safford, *Immigration Problems*, 163-67; *Review of Reviews*, VI (1892), 263; *Alien Immigration (British Parliamentary Papers*, Vol. 71), 48-49.
89. *Review of Reviews*, VII (1893), 3; *Reports of the Immigration Commission* (61 Cong., 3 Sess., Senate Doc. 758), 42, 931; *Cong. Rec.*, 52 Cong., 2 Sess., 290, 717, 750-52.
90. Roy L. Garis, *Immigration Restriction: A Study of the Opposition to and Regulation of Immigration into the United States* (New York, 1927), 41-42; *Report of a Special Committee of the Chamber of Commerce of the State of New York on the Proposed Legislation by Congress to Restrict Immigration into the United States* (New York, 1888), 3-4.
91. *Immigration Investigation* (52 Cong., 1 Sess., House Report 2090), 681-694; *Cong. Rec.*, 53 Cong., 2 Sess., 7756, 8216-17, 8235-37, 8244.
92. Bemis, "Restriction," 263; *Cong. Rec.*, 51 Cong., 2 Sess., 2956; Lodge, "Restriction," 36; Lodge, "Lynch Law and Unrestricted Immigration," 612; Senate Report No. 1333 (52 Cong., 2 Sess., Washington, 1893), ii, 143-45, 199.
93. "Records of the Executive Committee of the Immigration Restriction League," May 31, 1894, and December 10, 1895, in Files of the Immigration Restriction League (Houghton Library, Harvard University); "Immigration Clippings Collected by Prescott F. Hall," I, 114, 132, 195-97. For the background of the founders see *Harvard University Directory* (Cambridge, 1913).
94. Mrs. Prescott F. Hall, *Immigration and Other Interests of Prescott Farnsworth Hall* (New York, 1922), xiii-xxvii, 119-22; Prescott F. Hall, "Musical Development," *Harvard Advocate*, XLVI (1888), 55-56.
95. On Ward see *Dictionary of American Biography*, XIX, 436; "Records of the Executive Committee I.R.L.," June 12, 1913. For other early members see Immigration Restriction League, *Annual Report of the Executive Committee*, 1895; and *The Personal Letters of John Fiske* (Cedar Rapids, 1939), 635.
96. *Publications of the Immigration Restriction League*, Nos. 1-9; I.R.L. to members, October 23, 1895, in Files of the I.R.L., Box 2; Boston *Globe*, October 8, 1894.
97. Hall, "Immigration Clippings," I, 210, and II, 33; *Cong. Rec.*, 54 Cong., 1 Sess., 2817 ff., 5477.
98. New York *Tribune*, April 14, 1896, p. 5, and April 24, 1896, p. 3; Philadelphia *Public Ledger*, May 21, 1896, p. 9; Bliss, *Encyclopaedia*, 714.
99. Boston *Transcript*, April 11 and 15, 1896; Philadelphia *Public Ledger*, April 13, 1896; *Cong. Rec.*, 54 Cong., 1 Sess., 5418, 5478-85.
100. Philadelphia *Public Ledger*, June 6, 1896, p. 17, and December 7, 1896, p. 1; *Cong. Rec.*, 54 Cong., 1 Sess., 6248-49.
101. Philadelphia *Public Ledger*, December 9, 1896, p. 1; *Cong. Rec.*, 54 Cong., 2 Sess., 1125; Henry Cabot Lodge to Prescott F. Hall, December 24, 1896, in Files of the I.R.L., Box 3.
102. *Nation*, LXIII (1896), 359; *Bradstreet's*, XXIV (1896), 741; *Cong. Rec.*, 54 Cong., 2 Sess., 372-73.
103. *Cong. Rec.*, 54 Cong., 2 Sess., 372-73; J. H. Semmes to John Carlisle, February 18, 1897, in Cleveland Papers; Philadelphia *Public Ledger*, February 18, 1897, p. 13.

104. James D. Richardson, *A Compilation of the Messages and Papers of the Presidents, 1789-1897* (Washington, 1898), IX, 758-59. On the Canadian issue see Boston *Transcript*, February 20, 1897; Parke, Davis & Company to Cleveland, February 20, 1897, and John B. Riley to Cleveland, February 24, 1897, in Cleveland Papers.

Notes to Chapter Five

1. "Records of the Executive Committee of the Immigration Restriction League," January 10, 1898, in Files of the Immigration Restriction League (Houghton Library, Harvard University); *Congressional Record*, 55 Cong., 2 Sess., 689.

2. Chicago *Post*, January 10, 1898; New York *Times*, January 16, 1898; Boston *Globe*, January 14, 1898; Washington *Sentinel*, January 22, 1898; Prescott F. Hall, *Immigration and Its Effects Upon the United States* (New York, 1906), 268-69.

3. *Outlook*, LVIII (1898), 509, and LX (1898), 990; Carl Schurz, "Restricting Immigration," *Harper's Weekly*, XLII (1898), 27; Boston *Herald*, February 12, 1898; *Hearings: Violations of Free Speech and Rights of Labor* (Senate Committee on Education and Labor, 76 Cong., 3 Sess., Washington, 1940), part 54, pp. 19819-20.

4. Jules Cambon quoted in *Nationalism: A Report by a Study Group of Members of the Royal Institute of International Affairs* (Oxford, 1939), 124; *Educational Review*, XVI (1898), 204.

5. "Records of the Executive Committee I.R.L.," May 11, 1898; I.R.L. to members, November 25, 1899, in Files of the I.R.L., Box 2; Prescott F. Hall, "Present Status of Immigration Restriction," *Gunton's Magazine*, XVIII (1900), 305-306; *Nation*, LXIX (1899), 293-94.

6. A. P. C. Griffin, *List of Books (with References to Periodicals) on Immigration* (Washington, 1907), 59-61; Edward S. Deemer, national secretary J.O.U.A.M., to Henry Baldwin, September 27, 1899, in Baldwin Papers (Manuscript Division, New York Public Library).

7. See, for a partial indication, A. P. C. Griffin, *Select List of References on Anglo-Saxon Interests* (Washington, 1906). Racial nationalism is treated more extensively in Chapters VI and VII following.

8. See, for example, Albert J. Beveridge, *Americans of To-Day and To-Morrow* (Philadelphia, 1908), 122-23; F. Dumont Smith, "The Anglo-Saxon and His Conquests," in *Transactions of the Kansas State Historical Society*, 1901-1902, pp. 292-96.

9. National Education Association, *Proceedings*, 1900, pp. 586-87; Kate Holladay Claghorn, "Our Immigrants and Ourselves," *Atlantic Monthly*, LXXXVI (1900), 546-48.

10. Edward A. Ross, *Social Control: A Survey of the Foundations of Order* (New York, 1924), 16-22, 32-35, 439-40, and *Seventy Years of It: An Autobiography* (New York, 1936), 93, 331-33.

11. Edward A. Ross, "The Value Rank of the American People," *Independent*, LVII (1904), 1061-63, and *Social Psychology: An Outline and Source Book* (New York, 1923), 140, 241-43. See also Ross's "The Causes of Race Superiority," *Annals of the American Academy of Political and Social Science*, XVIII (1901), 85-86.

12. *Outlook,* LXXIX (1905), 219; Professor W. J. McGee quoted in Daniel T. Pierce, "Americans of the Future: An Optimistic Estimate of the Effect of Immigration," *World To-day,* XI (1906), 738; Herbert N. Casson, "The Americans in America," *Munsey's Magazine,* XXXVI (1907), 432. See also F. Spencer Baldwin, "What Ireland Has Done for America," *New England Magazine,* XXIV (1901), 85; Bliss Perry, *The American Mind* (Boston, 1912), 72; New York Society, Order of the Founders and Patriots of America, *Banquet Addresses,* 1906, p. 27.

13. See the convenient graph in Roy F. Garis, *Immigration Restriction: A Study of the Opposition to and Regulation of Immigration into the United States* (New York, 1927), 206.

14. Broughton Brandenburg, *Imported Americans* (New York, 1904), 225.

15. Emma Goldman, *Living My Life* (New York, 1931), I, 312.

16. My judgment of public opinion rests on the contemporary statements collected in: *Public Opinion,* XXXI (1901), 390; Charles E. Benedict, comp., *William McKinley: Character Sketches of America's Martyred Chieftain; Sermons and Addresses* (New York [1902]); Rt. Rev. Samuel Fallows, *Life of William McKinley Our Martyred President* (Chicago [1901]); Grand Army of the Republic, Thirty-Fifth National Encampment, *Reports of the Citizens Committees Together with the Addresses Made at the Two McKinley Meetings Held in Cleveland on September 12 and 19, 1901.* See also Charles Johnston, "The Anarchists and the President," *North American Review,* CLXXIII (1901), 440-42; General Lew Wallace, "Prevention of Presidential Assassinations," *North American Review,* CLXXIII (1901), 721-26.

17. Fallows, *McKinley,* 432; *Regulation of Immigration* (57 Cong., 2 Sess., Senate Document No. 62, Washington, 1902), 469. On the provisions and legislative history of the bill see also *Reports of the Immigration Commission: Immigration Legislation* (61 Cong., 3 Sess., Senate Document No. 758, Washington, 1911), 50-55.

18. "Records of the Executive Committee I.R.L.," October 2 and November 20, 1901; "I.R.L. Contributors," in Files of the I.R.L., Box 1.

19. Boston *Journal,* December 16, 1901; "Records of the Executive Committee I.R.L.," January 25 and December 13, 1902; office memorandum, January 20, 1902, in Files of the I.R.L., Box 3; *Regulation of Immigration* (57 Cong., 2 Sess., Senate Doc. 62), 327-85.

20. *Regulation of Immigration* (57 Cong., 2 Sess., Senate Doc. 62), 470-76; *Report of the Proceedings of the Twenty-Third Annual Convention of the American Federation of Labor,* 1903, pp. 25-26; *The Works of Theodore Roosevelt* (National Edition, New York, 1926), XV, 96; *Proceedings of the Thirty-Second Annual Meeting of the National Board of Trade,* 1902, pp. 174-77; 1903, pp. 208-209.

21. "Records of the Executive Committee I.R.L.," May 24, 1902; *Cong. Rec.,* 57 Cong., 1 Sess., 5829; Frank Julian Warne, "The Real Cause of the Miners' Strike," *Outlook,* LXXI (1902), 1053-57; New York *Times,* May 20, 1902, p. 1.

22. *Selections from the Correspondence of Theodore Roosevelt and Henry Cabot Lodge, 1884-1918* (New York, 1925), I, 545; William B. Shattuc to Prescott F. Hall, March 3, 1903, in Files of the I.R.L., Box 3; New

York *Tribune*, December 11, 1902, p. 5, and December 15, 1902, p. 7. A list of 110 pro-restrictionist newspapers compiled at the time included only seven papers west of Omaha and only ten papers in the South. "Papers in Favor of Restriction," in Files of the I.R.L., Box 2. I have judged the apathy of the East toward the measure from the very slight reports of it in the New York *Tribune*.

23. Henry Cabot Lodge, "Efforts to Restrict Undesirable Immigration," *Century Magazine*, XLV (1904), 469.

24. Edward Corsi, *In the Shadow of Liberty: The Chronicle of Ellis Island* (New York, 1935), 184-85.

25. *Correspondence of Roosevelt and Lodge*, II, 77-79; William I. Thomas, "The Psychology of Race Prejudice," *American Journal of Sociology*, IX (1904), 611; H. G. Wells, *The Future in America* (New York, 1906), 138. After failing to influence either national party convention in 1904, the Immigration Restriction League again suspended; "Records of the Executive Committee I.R.L.," September 30, 1904.

26. Colorado State Board of Immigration, *First Annual Report*, 1910, pp. 24-25. See also National Civic Federation, *Facts on Immigration* (n.p., 1907), 121-23.

27. Rowland T. Berthoff, "Southern Attitudes Toward Immigration, 1865-1914," *Journal of Southern History*, XVII (1951), 329, 331, 334-35; Boston *Transcript*, July 25, 1905; *Cong. Rec.*, 59 Cong., 1 Sess., 9169-70. See also C. Vann Woodward, *Origins of the New South, 1877-1913* (Baton Rouge, 1951), 308, 406-407, 415.

28. William Garrott Brown, "The White Peril: The Immediate Danger of the Negro," *North American Review*, CLXXIX (1904), 824-25, 833-35; Robert DeCourcy Ward, "Immigration and the South," *Atlantic Monthly*, XCVI (1905), 613-14; *Cong. Rec.*, 59 Cong., 2 Sess., 3029.

29. *Literary Digest*, XXXI (1905), 646; H. B. Grose, *Aliens or Americans?* (New York, 1906), 113; *Harper's Weekly*, XLVIII (1904), 1980; Berthoff, "Southern Attitudes," 333-34, 341.

30. Berthoff, "Southern Attitudes," 331, 334, 339-40, 357; *Literary Digest*, XXIX (1904), 898, XXX (1905), 810-11, XXXIII (1906), 794, and XXXIV (1907), 448; *Cong. Rec.*, 57 Cong., 1 Sess., 5773-74.

31. Peter Roberts, *The New Immigration: A Study of the Industrial and Social Life of Southeastern Europeans in America* (New York, 1913), 73-74; *Reports of the Immigration Commission: Abstracts* (61 Cong., 3 Sess., Sen. Doc. No. 747, Washington, 1911), I, 321-22. See also Walter E. Weyl and A. M. Sakolski, "Conditions of Entrance to the Principal Trades," *Bulletin of the United States Bureau of Labor*, XIII (1906), 681-780.

32. Roberts, *New Immigration*, 75; William M. Leiserson, *Adjusting Immigrant and Industry* (New York, 1924), 92-93.

33. National Board of Trade, *Proceedings*, 1903, pp. 208-209; 1904, pp. 174-75; 1907, p. 153; 1910, pp. 186-87.

34. *Commercial and Financial Chronicle*, LXXXVI (1903), 409; *Literary Digest*, XXVI (1903), 644; *National Civic Federation Review*, II (September-October, 1905), 17; New York *Commercial Bulletin*, December 11, 1905.

35. *National Civic Federation Review*, II (September-October, 1905), 17; Philadelphia *Public Ledger*, June 26, 1906; Boston *Transcript*, July 17, 1905.

36. *National Civic Federation Review*, II (June, 1905), 1-7, 16, and II (January-February, 1906); Arthur P. Kellogg, "The National Conference on Immigration," *Charities*, XV (1905), 372-76. One of the labor executives of the federation is reported to have warned the secretary to go no further into work that would disrupt it; "Records of the Executive Committee I.R.L.," October 9, 1905.

37. National Association of Manufacturers, *Proceedings of the Twelfth Annual Convention*, 1907, pp. 24-25, 198.

38. Walter Johnson, *William Allen White's America* (New York, 1947), 55.

39. *Proceedings of the National Conference of Charities and Correction*, 1905, pp. 364-370; John R. Commons, *Races and Immigrants in America* (New York, 1907), 154-59.

40. Commons, *Races and Immigrants*, 1-7, 179; Edward A. Ross, "The Outlook for Plain Folk," *Everybody's Magazine*, XIX (1908), 755, and "The Tendencies of Natural Values," *Yale Review*, II (1893), 192-93.

41. Ernest Crosby, "The Immigration Bugbear," *Arena*, XXXII (1904), 596-602; Finley Peter Dunne, *Observations by Mr. Dooley* (New York, 1902), 51-52.

42. Lincoln Steffens, *The Shame of the Cities* (New York, 1904), 4-5; Frederic C. Howe, *The Confessions of a Reformer* (New York, 1925), 92, 115, and *The City, the Hope of Democracy* (New York, 1905), 62, 73; *Proceedings of the National Municipal League*, 1909, p. 43. See also *Literary Digest*, XXVII (1903), 158; *Outlook*, LXXX (1905), 360.

43. United States Department of Labor, *Historical Sketch of Naturalization in the United States* (Washington, 1926), 8-12; Oscar S. Straus, *Under Four Administrations: From Cleveland to Taft* (Boston, 1922), 232; Boston *Transcript*, January 20, 1905.

44. Some evidence of this disinterest may be found in Elwood P. Lawrence, "The Immigrant in American Fiction, 1890-1920" (Ph.D. thesis, Western Reserve University, 1943), 194, 202, 209-26, 456-59. On the estrangement of immigrants and progressives see Oscar Handlin, *The Uprooted: The Epic Story of the Great Migrations That Made the American People* (Boston, 1951), 218-21.

45. Henrietta O. Barnett, *Canon Barnett: His Life, Work, and Friends* (London, 1919), I, 307-12; Jane Addams and others, *Philanthropy and Social Progress: Seven Essays* (New York, 1893), 2-3, 15-16, 23; Jane Addams, "Hull House: An Effort toward Social Democracy," *Forum*, XIV (1892), 226.

46. Frank D. Watson, *The Charity Organization Movement in the United States* (New York, 1922), 329-36; Frank J. Bruno, *Trends in Social Work as Reflected in the Proceedings of the National Conference of Social Work, 1874-1946* (New York, 1948), *passim.*

47. *Charities*, VIII (1902), 325-30, XII (1904), 420-24, 457-63, and XIII (1904), 189-266; National Conference of Charities, *Proceedings*, 1906, pp. 279-324, 1909, pp. 224-35, and 1912, pp. 236-38; Lillian D. Wald, *The House on Henry Street* (New York, 1915), 290.

48. I refer to the Americanization movement; see pp. 238-41.

49. Addams, *Philanthropy*, 35-38; Jane Addams, *Twenty Years at Hull House* (New York, 1910), 36-37; Jane Addams, *Newer Ideals of Peace* (New York, 1907), 18-19, 49, 214-17; Wald, *House on Henry Street*, 66, 184, 310.

50. Jane E. Robbins, "The Foreign-Born American," *Outlook*, LXXXIII (1906), 891; *Charities*, XIII (1904), 197.

51. Julius Drachsler, *Democracy and Assimilation: The Blending of Immigrant Heritages in America* (New York, 1920), 32; National Conference of Charities, *Proceedings*, 1914, p. 407; Republican National Committee, *Republican Campaign Text-Book*, 1916, p. 141; Frank B. Lentz, ed., *Immigration—Some New Phases of the Problem* (San Francisco, 1915), 62-63.

52. In 1900, for example, the Presbyterian Board of Home Missions was maintaining 121 schools, only three of which served the foreign-born; *Missionary Review*, XXII (1899), 709. See also *Literary Digest*, II (1891), 693; and George H. Schodde, "The Religious Work Among the Immigrants," *Missionary Review*, XIII (1890), 419-21.

53. Elias B. Sanford, ed., *Federal Council of the Churches of Christ in America: Report of the First Meeting*, 1908, pp. 256-57, 260-61; Grose, *Aliens*, 196-97; Charles Stelzle, *American Social and Religious Conditions* (New York, 1912), 117-19; National Conference of Charities, *Proceedings*, 1909, p. 236; Anon., *New Americans for a New America* (n.p., 1913), 2-4.

54. William Chauncy Langdon, *The Celebration of the Fourth of July by Means of Pageantry* (New York, 1912), 7-9.

55. Carl Wittke, *German-Americans and the World War (with Special Emphasis on Ohio's German-Language Press)*, (Columbus, 1936), 89; John C. Murphy, *An Analysis of the Attitudes of American Catholics Toward the Immigrant and the Negro, 1825-1925* (Washington, 1940), 104; J. C. Monaghan, "Immigration Problems," *Catholic World*, LXXIX (1904), 298; *Cong. Rec.*, 59 Cong., 1 Sess., 7772-74, and 62 Cong., 3 Sess., 2032.

56. *Cong. Rec.*, 59 Cong., 1 Sess., 7774, 62 Cong., 3 Sess., 2032, and 63 Cong., 3 Sess., 3025; Max Kohler, *Immigration and Aliens in the United States* (New York, 1936), 79; Oscar Straus, *The American Spirit* (New York, 1913), 284.

57. Israel Zangwill, *The Melting-Pot: A Drama in Four Acts* (New York, 1909). For background see *Literary Digest*, XLVIII (1914), 424. Others occasionally used the melting-pot metaphor long before Zangwill, but he gave it general currency. For other immigrant writers presenting similar ideas in this period see the long series of books which Edward A. Steiner issued extolling the redemptive power of his adopted country; and see also Robert Stauffer, ed., *The American Spirit in the Writings of Americans of Foreign Birth* (Boston, 1922).

58. Mary Antin, *The Promised Land* (Boston, 1912), xi.

59. Franz Boas, *Changes in Bodily Form of Descendants of Immigrants*, in *Reports of the Immigration Commission* (61 Cong., 2 Sess., Senate Document No. 208, Washington, 1911), 2-7; *Literary Digest*, XL (1910), 43, and XLIII (1911), 237. The *Survey* regarded this study as the most

distinctive contribution of the Immigration Commission; *Survey*, XXV (1911), 519. For Boas's related ideas see his *Race and Democratic Society* (New York, 1945), esp. 87-92, 168-71.

60. Elting E. Morison, ed., *The Letters of Theodore Roosevelt* (Cambridge, 1951-1954), III, 254-55; Marcus Braun to Samuel S. Koenig, September 13, 1911, in William Howard Taft Papers, Presidential Series 2, File 77 (Division of Manuscripts, Library of Congress).

61. Arthur Koppell to Taft, January 29, 1912, and J. C. Delaney to C. D. Hilles, January 15, 1912, in Taft Papers, File 423; Robert E. Park, *The Immigrant Press and Its Control* (New York, 1922), 377-411.

62. *Who Was Who in America, 1897-1942*, p. 1024; Charles Bernheimer, ed., *The Russian Jew in the United States* (Philadelphia, 1905), 257-63; Philip Cowen, *Memories of an American Jew* (New York, 1932), 190-91, 257-58; Philadelphia *Public Ledger*, June 22, 1906, p. 16; Morison, *Letters of Theodore Roosevelt*, III, 411, 659 n. For an indication of how the Republicans won Jewish support by anti-Russian diplomatic gestures see Tyler Dennett, *John Hay: From Poetry to Politics* (New York, 1934), 396-97.

63. "William R. Hearst the Democratic Candidate," *Outlook*, LXXXIV (1906), 402; New York *Evening Journal*, July 8, 1912; William Z. Ripley, "Races in the United States," *Atlantic Monthly*, CII (1908), 751; *Collier's Weekly*, XLVII (June 10, 1911), 10.

64. Morison, *Letters of Theodore Roosevelt*, V, 439-40, 453-54.

65. Edward Lauterbach, "Keeping the Door Open: The Story of the National Liberal Immigration League," *American Citizen*, I (1912), 286-88; *Immigration: Address of L. J. Ellis of New York Representing the National Liberal Immigration League Before the Immigration Association of Missouri* (n.p., 1906), 2-3.

66. Oscar Straus to Cyrus Adler, May 28, 1906, and to Cyrus Sulzberger, June 14, 1906, in Oscar Straus Papers (Division of Manuscripts, Library of Congress). See also letters from William Russell, Adler, Edward Lauterbach, and Nathan Bijur in this period.

67. Morison, *Letters of Theodore Roosevelt*, V, 285-86, 360-61; Blair Bolles, *Tyrant from Illinois: Uncle Joe Cannon's Experiment with Personal Power* (New York, 1951), 71-72.

68. *Cong. Rec.*, 59 Cong., 1 Sess., 9152, 9156, 9195; Philadelphia *Public Ledger*, June 24, 1906, p. 11, and June 26, 1906, pp. 1, 8.

69. Bolles, *Tyrant*, 75-76.

70. M. F. Behar, *Our National Gates: Shut, Ajar or Open?* (New York, 1916), 6; *American Jewish Year Book*, 1907-08, p. 537.

NOTES TO CHAPTER SIX

1. Roy Harvey Pearce, *The Savages of America: A Study of the Indian and the Idea of Civilization* (Baltimore, 1953), 5-11, 20-26; Arnold J. Toynbee, *A Study of History* (London, 1934), I, 209-15.

2. Earl W. Count, "The Evolution of the Race Idea in Modern Western Culture During the Period of the Pre-Darwinian Nineteenth Century," *Transactions of the New York Academy of Sciences*, VIII (1946), 139-65; John C. Greene, "Some Early Speculations on the Origin of Hu-

man Races," *American Anthropologist*, LVI (1954), 31-41, and "The American Debate on the Negro's Place in Nature, 1780-1815," *Journal of the History of Ideas*, XV (1954), 384-96.

3. William Z. Ripley, "Geography as a Sociological Study," *Political Science Quarterly*, X (1895), 636-43.

4. Daniel C. Gilman, "Science in America," in Nathaniel S. Shaler, ed., *The United States of America: A Study of the American Commonwealth* (New York, 1894), II, 385; Stow Persons, ed., *Evolutionary Thought in America* (New Haven, 1950), 18, 273-74, 282-84. One exceptionally speculative American anthropologist, Daniel G. Brinton, championed the white race but made little effort to define particular branches of it; see his *Races and Peoples: Lectures on the Science of Ethnography* (New York, 1890).

5. *The Age of Steel* quoted in *Public Opinion*, I (1886), 355.

6. T. T. Munger, "Immigration by Passport," *Century Magazine*, XXXV (1888), 792-98. See also his *On the Threshold* (16th ed., Boston, 1885), 104-105; and (for the circumstances of the above article) Munger's letters to Richard Watson Gilder, September 17, 1886, and November 17, 1887, in The Century Collection (New York Public Library).

7. Josiah Strong, *Our Country: Its Possible Future and Its Present Crisis* (New York, 1885), 171; James K. Hosmer, *A Short History of Anglo-Saxon Freedom: The Polity of the English-Speaking Race* (New York, 1890), 313, 321-27. See also Charles Morris, *The Aryan Race: Origins and Achievements* (Chicago, 1888), 311-12. For unqualified paeans to racial fusion see *Public Opinion*, II (1887), 429; and New England Society, *Anniversary Celebration*, 1886, p. 29.

8. A. Cleveland Coxe, "Government by Aliens," *Forum*, VII (1889), 599-603; *Dictionary of American Biography*, IV, 484.

9. Edward N. Saveth, *American Historians and European Immigrants, 1875-1925* (New York, 1948), 42-48, 137-40; John W. Burgess, "The Ideal of the American Commonwealth," *Political Science Quarterly*, X (1895), 406-11; Henry Cabot Lodge, *Early Memories* (New York, 1913), 203-209; John H. Denison, "The Survival of the American Type," *Atlantic Monthly*, LXXV (1895), 16-28.

10. United States Bureau of the Census, *Immigrants and Their Children, 1920*, Census Monograph No. 7 (Washington, 1927), 14; Barbara Miller Solomon, "The Intellectual Background of the Immigration Restriction Movement in New England," *New England Quarterly*, XXV (1952), 47-59.

11. Barrett Wendell, *Stelligeri and Other Essays Concerning America* (New York, 1893), 16, 110; Mark De Wolfe Howe, ed., *Barrett Wendell and His Letters* (Boston, 1924), 107-109. See also the comment on Wendell in Oswald Garrison Villard, *Fighting Years: Memoirs of a Liberal Journalist* (New York, 1939), 90.

12. Nathaniel S. Shaler, "European Peasants as Immigrants," *Atlantic Monthly*, LXXI (1893), 647-55; Shaler, *United States of America*, II, 613. Shaler's general, Darwinian assumptions about race and environment are in his *Nature and Man in America* (New York, 1891).

13. Henry Cabot Lodge, *Speeches* (Boston, 1892), 45-47.

14. Lodge, "The Distribution of Ability in the United States," *Century Magazine*, XLII (1891), 687-94; *Congressional Record*, 54 Cong., 1 Sess., 2819. Cf. the transitional point of view that Lodge expressed in "The Restriction of Immigration" and "Lynch Law and Unrestricted Immigration," *North American Review*, CLII (1891), 27-35, 602-12.

15. *Cong. Rec.*, 54 Cong., 1 Sess., 2817-20; Gustave Le Bon, *The Psychology of Peoples* (reprint, New York, 1924).

16. Francis A. Walker, *Discussions in Economics and Statistics* (New York, 1899), II, 308-13, 317, 445-47; Francis A. Walker, "The Tide of Economic Thought," *Publications of the American Economic Association*, VI (January-March, 1891), 37. In attacking the natural selection argument, Walker was expanding an observation that Richmond Mayo-Smith had made in "Control of Immigration," *Political Science Quarterly*, III (1888), 76.

17. Walker, *Discussions*, II, 415-26. Curiously, this population theory was anticipated many years earlier by one M. J. Dee, "Chinese Immigration," *North American Review*, CXXVI (1878), 519-22, but the idea fell on barren ground and no one seemed to recall it when Walker's essay appeared.

18. A. P. C. Griffin, *Select List of References on Anglo-Saxon Interests* (Washington, 1906) provides a rough, chronological index to this astonishing outpouring.

19. Franklin H. Giddings, "Comments on the Foregoing," *Century Magazine*, LXV (1903), 690-91, and "The American People," *International Quarterly*, VII (1903), 287; "The World and His Wife: A Popular Explanation of the Affairs of To-Day," *Ladies' Home Journal*, XX (September, 1903), 14.

20. Albert Shaw, *Political Problems of American Development* (New York, 1907), 65-74; Frederick William Chapman, "The Changed Significance of 'Anglo-Saxon,'" *Education*, XX (1900), 364-69. See also Brander Matthews, *The American of the Future and Other Essays* (New York, 1910), 11-22; and Society of Mayflower Descendants in the State of Illinois, *Publication No. 1* (Chicago, 1900).

21. Albert K. Weinberg, *Manifest Destiny: A Study of Nationalist Expansionism in American History* (Baltimore, 1935), 314-18, 367-69; Thomas B. Wilson, "The Asiatic Giant," *Overland Monthly*, XLVI (1905), 39-41; and James E. Free, "A War Cloud," *Overland Monthly*, XLIX (1907), 137-38.

22. Charles E. Woodruff, *The Effects of Tropical Light on White Men* (New York, 1905), 143-54, 261-82, 320. For an indication of Woodruff's impact on one of the most popular writers of the day see Jack London, *Mutiny on the Elsinore* (New York, 1914), 148-49.

23. See note 31, Chapter VII.

24. George Edward Woodberry, *The Torch: Eight Lectures on Race Power in Literature Delivered Before the Lowell Institute* (New York, 1912), 4-6; Monroe Royce, *The Passing of the American* (New York, 1911); Albert Bushnell Hart, "Is the Puritan Race Dying Out?" *Munsey's Magazine*, XLV (1911), 252-55; *Literary Digest*, XLVI (1913), 767; Providence *Bulletin*, February 29, 1908, quoted in Files of the Im-

migration Restriction League, Box 1 (Houghton Library, Harvard University).

25. *Reports of the Industrial Commission* (57 Cong., 1 Sess., House Document No. 184, Washington, 1901), XV, 277; *Charities*, VIII (1902), 326-30; Robert DeCourcy Ward, "The Restriction of Immigration," *North American Review*, CLXXIX (1904), 235-36; Henry Pratt Fairchild, *Immigration: A World Movement and Its American Significance* (New York, 1913), 215-16. The first formal refutation was E. A. Goldenweiser, "Walker's Theory of Immigration," *American Journal of Sociology*, XVIII (1912), 342-51.

26. Edward A. Ross, "The Causes of Race Superiority," *Annals of the American Academy of Political and Social Science*, XVIII (1901), 85-88, and "The Value Rank of the American People," *Independent*, LVII (1904), 1061-63.

27. Henry F. Pringle, *Theodore Roosevelt* (New York, 1931), 471-72; Alfred Henry Lewis, ed., *A Compilation of the Messages and Speeches of Theodore Roosevelt, 1901-1905* (Washington, 1906), I, 548. A deeper insight into Roosevelt's mind is supplied in Elting E. Morison, ed., *The Letters of Theodore Roosevelt* (Cambridge, 1951-1954), V, 19-20, VI, 959-63.

28. *Harper's Weekly*, XLIX (1905), 419; M. S. Iseman, M.D., *Race Suicide* (New York, 1912), 5-6; Lydia Kingsmill Commander, *The American Idea: Does the National Tendency Toward a Small Family Point to Race Suicide or Race Development?* (New York, 1907). See also John R. Commons, *Races and Immigrants in America* (New York, 1907), 200-208; Robert Hunter, *Poverty* (New York, 1905), 302-308, 315; *Readers' Guide to Periodical Literature*, II (1905-1909), 1819-20.

29. William E. Leuchtenburg, "Progressivism and Imperialism: The Progressive Movement and American Foreign Policy, 1898-1916," *Mississippi Valley Historical Review*, XXXIX (1952), 483-504.

30. Morison, *Letters of Theodore Roosevelt*, I, 523, IV, 795, 832. For another example see Thornton Anderson, *Brooks Adams, Constructive Conservative* (Ithaca, 1951), *passim*.

31. Henry James, *The American Scene* (New York, 1907), 85-86, 125, 138. See also Elizabeth Robins, "Embryo Americans," *Harper's Monthly Magazine*, CIII (1901), 602; New England Society, *Anniversary Celebration*, 1903, pp. 43-45; Eliot Norton, "The Diffusion of Immigration," *Annals of the American Academy of Political and Social Science*, XXIV (1904), 163.

32. See the illuminating account of these trends in Richard Hofstadter, *Social Darwinism in American Thought, 1860-1915* (Philadelphia, 1945), 133-45.

33. Karl Pearson, *The Life, Letters and Labours of Francis Galton* (Cambridge, 1914-1930), IIIA, 217-42; Francis Galton, "Eugenics: Its Definition, Scope and Aims," *American Journal of Sociology*, X (1904), 1-25.

34. President's Research Committee on Social Trends, *Recent Social Trends in the United States* (Washington, 1933), 428.

35. Oscar Riddle, "Charles Benedict Davenport," in National Academy of Sciences, *Biographical Memoirs*, XXV (1949), 75-91; Charles B. Davenport, *Heredity in Relation to Eugenics* (New York, 1911), iv-v, 270-71;

Race Betterment Foundation, *Proceedings of the First National Conference on Race Betterment*, 1914, p. 455.

36. L. C. Dunn, ed., *Genetics in the 20th Century* (New York, 1951), 60-65; American Breeders' Association, *Report of the Meeting*, 1907, pp. 137-38.

37. Race Betterment Foundation, *Proceedings*, 1914, pp. 487-88; Robert DeCourcy Ward, "National Eugenics," *North American Review*, CXCII (1910), 59-64; Edward McNall Burns, *David Starr Jordan: Prophet of Freedom* (Stanford, 1953), 72-73. Davenport's own animus centered on the eastern European Jews; Davenport, *Heredity*, 216.

38. *Cong. Rec.*, 63 Cong., 3 Sess., 206; Thomas W. Salmon to Woodrow Wilson, January 16, 1915, in Woodrow Wilson Papers, File VI-B, sec. 292 (Division of Manuscripts, Library of Congress).

39. The latter phrase is in *Scientific American*, CVI (1912), 324. See also Portersville (California) *Messenger*, October 19, 1912; *Literary Digest*, LIII (1916), 887-88; *Cong. Rec.*, 63 Cong., 2 Sess., 2617, 2714.

40. Prescott Farnsworth Hall, *Immigration and Its Effects upon the United States* (New York, 1906), 99-101; National Conference of Charities, *Proceedings*, 1906, pp. 280-82.

41. "Records of the Executive Committee I.R.L.," March 30, 1908, December 14, 1911, May 9, 1912; *American Breeders Magazine*, III (1912), 20-25, 75; *Journal of Heredity*, V (1914), 297; Race Betterment Foundation, *Proceedings*, 1914, p. 542.

42. Ward, "National Eugenics," 56-67, and "Our Immigration Laws from the Viewpoint of National Eugenics," *National Geographic Magazine*, XXIII (1912), 38-41; *Immigration and Other Interests of Prescott Farnsworth Hall* (New York, 1922), 33, 52-66; *Reports of the Immigration Commission: Statements and Recommendations Submitted by Societies* (61 Cong., 3 Sess., Senate Document No. 764, Washington, 1911), 106-107.

43. Davenport, *Heredity*, 221-24. And see the nebulous statements in Edwin G. Conklin, *Heredity and Environment in the Development of Men* (Princeton, 1915), 416-18.

44. Alfred P. Schultz to Prescott F. Hall, July 21, 1911, in Files of the I.R.L., Box 7; Schultz, *Race or Mongrel* (Boston, 1908); Telemachus T. Timayenis, *The Original Mr. Jacobs: A Startling Exposé* (New York, 1888); Carlos C. Closson, "Social Selection," *Journal of Political Economy*, IV (1896), 449-66. Although Closson wrote several articles for reputable scholarly journals recapitulating the racist anthropology of the French scientist, G. Vacher de Lapouge, I cannot discover that anyone paid serious attention to him. Houston Stewart Chamberlain's *The Foundations of the Nineteenth Century* was belatedly translated into English (from German) in 1911 and made a strong impression on Prescott F. Hall; but according to Chamberlain's disciple Schultz, the book caused no more than a ripple. Thus the belief that many Americans were attentively reading European racist writers in the late nineteenth and early twentieth centuries seems unwarranted. Lodge stands out almost alone.

45. William Z. Ripley, *The Races of Europe: A Sociological Study* (reprint, New York, 1923), v, 121, 597. See also Ripley, "Geography," 636-55, and *National Cyclopaedia of American Biography*, XXXII, 65.

46. Ripley, "Races in the United States," 755. For the then existing state of knowledge on this question see J. Arthur Thomson, *Heredity* (New York, 1908), 125, 133-43, 524. There is an indication of the alarmed newspaper comment on Ripley's address in Arthur I. Street, ed., *Street's Pandex of the News*, November 28, 1908. See also Morison, *Letters of Theodore Roosevelt*, VI, 1435. On the new appreciation of reversion that resulted from Mendelian principles see American Breeders' Association, *Report*, 1907, p. 133.

47. New York *Times*, May 31, 1937, p. 15; New York *Times Magazine*, November 20, 1949, p. 15; Society of Colonial Wars, *Constitution and By-Laws, Membership*, 1893, p. 76.

48. Madison Grant to William Howard Taft, November 22, 1910, in Taft Papers, Presidential Series No. 2, File 77 (Division of Manuscripts, Library of Congress). Some of the sources of Grant's thinking are suggested in his *The Passing of the Great Race or The Racial Basis of European History* (New York, 1916), xx-xxi, 229-32, while a fuller indication is provided in the Supplement included in the 1921 edition.

49. In his private letters to Prescott F. Hall, Grant almost always got around to the Jews. See especially Grant to Hall, October 21 and December 19, 1918, in Files of the I.R.L., Box 1.

50. This conception of racism and its earlier appearance in European thought are elucidated by Ernst Cassirer, *The Myth of the State* (New Haven, 1946), 225-47, and with wayward brilliance by Hannah Arendt, *The Origins of Totalitarianism* (New York, 1951), 158-84 and *passim*. For an analysis and criticism of Grant as a political theorist see David Spitz, *Patterns of Anti-Democratic Thought* (New York, 1949), 137-62.

NOTES TO CHAPTER SEVEN

1. *United States Census, 1910*, Vol. I: *Population*, 174-75; Roy L. Garis, *Immigration Restriction: A Study of the Opposition to and Regulation of Immigration into the United States* (New York, 1927), 205.

2. New York *Tribune Index*, 1902, pp. 178-79. Out of 74 entries for the year under the heading "Italians," 55 are obviously accounts of crime and violence.

3. Robert E. Park and Herbert A. Miller, *Old World Traits Transplanted* (New York, 1921), 241-58; Arthur I. Street, ed., *Street's Pandex of the News*, 1908, pp. 30-31; *Hearings* (House Committee on Immigration and Naturalization, 60 Cong., 1 Sess., Washington, 1908), 10.

4. Theodore A. Bingham, "Foreign Criminals in New York," *North American Review*, CLXXXVIII (1908), 383-94; *American Jewish Year Book*, 1909-10, pp. 62-63.

5. The chief anti-Semitic incident of the period between 1896 and 1913 was a funeral riot on New York's East Side in 1902, an affair which apparently pitted Jews against Irish. Philip Cowen, *Memories of an American Jew* (New York, 1932), 289.

6. The best treatment is Abraham Cahan's novel, *The Rise of David Levinsky* (New York, 1917). For unfriendly comments see Burton J. Hendrick, "The Great Jewish Invasion," *McClure's Magazine*, XXVIII

(1907), 307-21; and Ralph Philip Boas, "The Problem of American Judaism," *Atlantic Monthly*, CXIX (1917), 147-51.

7. Norman Hapgood, "Jews and College Life" and "Schools, Colleges and Jews," *Harper's Weekly*, LXII (1916), 53-55, 77-79; Charles S. Bernheimer, "Prejudice Against Jews in the United States," *Independent*, LXV (1908), 1106-1107; Alexander Francis, *Americans: An Impression* (New York, 1909), 84-85, 187.

8. A. J. Severson, "Nationality and Religious Preferences as Reflected in Newspaper Advertisements," *American Journal of Sociology*, XLIV (1939), 541-43; Cyrus Adler, *Jacob H. Schiff: His Life and Letters* (New York, 1928), I, 363.

9. Park and Miller, *Old World Traits*, 51, 255.

10. *Compiled Laws of Michigan*, 1897, p. 439; *Session Laws State of Wyoming*, 1899, p. 60, and 1911, p. 61; *Session Laws of Arizona*, 1907, p. 138; *Laws of the State of New York*, 1908, I, 337, and 1909, II, 1324; *Callaghan's Michigan Digest*, I, 244; *Revised Laws of Minnesota: Supplement*, 1909, p. 622; *General Laws of Nebraska*, 1909, p. 2919; *A Digest of the Statutes of Arkansas*, 1921, p. 2151; *Digest of Pennsylvania Statute Law*, 1920, pp. 1117-18; *Acts and Resolves Passed by the General Court of Massachusetts*, 1910, p. 428.

11. "Records of the Executive Committee of the Immigration Restriction League," May 13, October 2, and November 16, 1905, and January 20, 1906, in Files of the Immigration Restriction League (Houghton Library, Harvard University); Boston *Herald*, December 18, 1905, and June 26, 1906.

12. This is frankly an impression of mine, rather than a statistical fact; but for suggestive data see William Z. Ripley, "Race Factors in Labor Unions," *Atlantic Monthly*, XCIII (1904), 306; Selig Perlman and Philip Taft, *A History of Labor in the United States, 1896-1932* (New York, 1935), 13-19.

13. *Report of Proceedings of the Twenty-fifth Annual Convention of the American Federation of Labor*, 1905, pp. 75-76, 101-102, 238; Philadelphia *Public Ledger*, June 4, 1906, p. 16; *Congressional Record*, 59 Cong., 1 Sess., 9171, 9189; *Selections from the Correspondence of Theodore Roosevelt and Henry Cabot Lodge, 1884-1918* (New York, 1925), II, 204. See also *The Carpenter*, January, 1906, pp. 9-10; *Machinists' Monthly Journal*, XVII (1905), 394, 1113; *Appeal to Reason* (Girard, Kansas), April 1, August 12, and September 2, 1905.

Of course the unions that did have a large number of new immigrants among their members were hesitant to join in the drive. The United Mine Workers, for example, clung to the old, equivocal distinction between voluntary and assisted immigration; *United Mine Workers' Journal*, August 23, 1906.

14. Samuel Gompers, *Seventy Years of Life and Labor* (New York, 1925), II, 167, 171; *Selections from Correspondence of Roosevelt and Lodge*, II, 158.

15. *Cong. Rec.*, 59 Cong., 1 Sess., 551-55, 7293-95. For a much later indication of Lodge's failure to realize how profoundly southern opinion on immigration was changing see Lodge to Theodore Roosevelt, May 10,

1912, in Theodore Roosevelt Papers, Box 286 (Division of Manuscripts, Library of Congress).

16. Asiatic Exclusion League, *Proceedings*, February, 1908, pp. 19, 71, and December, 1908, pp. 17, 19; James N. Davis to Robert DeCourcy Ward, January 10, 1914, in Files of the I.R.L., Box 7; *Cong. Rec.*, 59 Cong., 1 Sess., 9187, and 64 Cong., 1 Sess., 4782. For the vote in 1912 cast by Congressmen from Washington, Oregon, California, Nevada, Arizona, Utah, Idaho, and Montana, see *Cong. Rec.*, 62 Cong., 2 Sess., 5023, and 62 Cong., 3 Sess., 864. Anti-Japanese sentiment was, of course, very strong throughout the Rocky Mountain area.

17. Thomas A. Bailey, *Theodore Roosevelt and the Japanese-American Crises* (Stanford, 1934), 67-72, 108-109; Eleanor Tupper and George E. McReynolds, *Japan in American Public Opinion* (New York, 1937), 62-63.

18. *Cong. Rec.*, 62 Cong., 2 Sess., 5023, and 62 Cong., 3 Sess., 864. This was the first recorded vote on the literacy test since 1898, Cannon's maneuvers having prevented a recorded vote in 1906. For typical southern thinking about European immigration see *Cong. Rec.*, 59 Cong., 1 Sess., 9192, and 63 Cong., 2 Sess., 2623; *Reports of the Immigration Commission: Statements and Recommendations Submitted by Societies* (61 Cong., 3 Sess., Senate Document No. 764, Washington, 1911), 124.

19. John Higham, "The American Party, 1886-1891," *Pacific Historical Review*, XIX (1950), 38; San Francisco *Argonaut*, January 9 and April 3, 1886. For a typical example of how California's race-feeling dissociated the Chinese from European immigrants see C. T. Hopkins, *Common Sense Applied to the Immigrant Question* (San Francisco, 1869), esp. 20-22. In the twentieth century William Randolph Hearst perpetuated this old Californian combination of sympathy for European immigration and hatred for Oriental. See the platform of his Independence party in Kirk H. Porter, ed., *National Party Platforms* (New York, 1924), 292-93.

20. *Cong. Rec.*, 51 Cong., 2 Sess., 2948, and 55 Cong., 2 Sess., 583, and see the roll call vote, 55 Cong., 2 Sess., 689. The Anglo-Saxon nativism of a Knoxville lawyer, Joshua W. Caldwell, was exceptional. See his "The South Is American," *Arena*, VIII (1893), 610-15.

21. *Cong. Rec.*, 63 Cong., 2 Sess., 2624.

22. *Reports of the Immigration Commission: Abstracts* (61 Cong., 3 Sess., Senate Doc. 747), I, 645-53; *United States Census, 1910: Abstract*, 197. See also Jack London, *The Valley of the Moon* (New York, 1913).

23. Rowland T. Berthoff, "Southern Attitudes Toward Immigration, 1865-1914," *Journal of Southern History*, XVII (1951), 332-36; *United States Census, 1910: Abstract*, 197. In 1910 the new immigration constituted 1 per cent of the white population in the South and 5.6 per cent in the Pacific states.

24. Frank Tannenbaum, *Darker Phases of the South* (New York, 1924), 177-78; Ray Stannard Baker, *Following the Color Line* (New York, 1908), 295; Norman Walker, "Tallulah's Shame," *Harper's Weekly*, XLIII (1899), 779. Southern Congressmen repeatedly referred to the mixed blood of southern Europeans and pointed to the further mixing

of Latins and Negroes occurring in South America as an object lesson for the United States; *Cong. Rec.*, 59 Cong., 1 Sess., 9155, 9174.

25. Booker T. Washington, "Races and Politics," *Outlook*, XCVIII (1911), 264; Berthoff, "Southern Attitudes," 348.

26. A cross section of anti-Chinese sentiment can be studied in Elmer C. Sandmeyer, *The Anti-Chinese Movement in California* (Urbana, 1939), and in *Report of the Joint Special Committee to Investigate Chinese Immigration* (Report No. 689, 44 Cong., 2 Sess., Washington, 1877), esp. 1044-51.

27. C. Vann Woodward, *Origins of the New South, 1877-1913* (Baton Rouge, 1951), 324-26, 350-55. On the sectional response to imperialism see Richard Hofstadter, "Manifest Destiny and the Philippines," in Daniel Aaron, ed., *America in Crisis* (New York, 1952), 181, 187-189.

28. Paul H. Buck, *The Road to Reunion, 1865-1900* (Boston, 1937), 306-307.

29. *Hearings Relative to the Further Restriction of Immigration* (House Committee on Immigration and Naturalization, 62 Cong., 2 Sess., Washington, 1912), 49-50. See also *Cong. Rec.*, 59 Cong., 1 Sess., 9174; 63 Cong., 2 Sess., 2623-27; 63 Cong., 3 Sess., 3040.

30. Carey McWilliams, *Prejudice: Japanese-Americans, Symbol of Racial Intolerance* (Boston, 1944), 19; Bailey, *Roosevelt and the Japanese-American Crises*, 9-11; Tupper and McReynolds, *Japan in American Public Opinion*, 33. In this respect too the anti-Japanese movement contrasts with the older anti-Chinese movement. Neither China nor any other nation posed a direct, international threat to the secure and isolated America of the seventies and eighties.

31. Homer Lea, *The Valor of Ignorance* (New York, 1909), esp. 124-28. See also his *The Day of the Saxon* (New York, 1912). For all of his militarism and racial nationalism, Lea was no ordinary anti-Oriental bigot. He became a general in the Chinese army and showed no sympathy for the popular indignities inflicted on the Japanese in America.

32. Joan London, *Jack London and His Times: An Unconventional Biography* (New York, 1939), 212-13; Jack London, *Revolution and Other Essays* (New York, 1910), 267-89, and *South Sea Tales* (Cleveland, 1946), 235-39.

33. Jack London, *Valley of the Moon*, 102-103, and *The Mutiny of the Elsinore* (New York, 1914), 197-201. See the comments on these books in Charmian London, *The Book of Jack London* (New York, 1921), II, 258, 274.

34. Charles B. Barnes, *The Longshoremen* (New York, 1915), 8-9; William M. Leiserson, *Adjusting Immigrant and Industry* (New York, 1924), 71-72.

35. Ira Kipnis, *The American Socialist Movement, 1897-1912* (New York, 1952), 278-88. Ernest Untermann of Idaho was apparently the moving spirit. For another indication of the infectiousness of the anti-Oriental movement see an article by an eastern physician, Albert Allemann, "Immigration and the Future American Race," *Popular Science Monthly*, LXXV (1909), 586-96.

36. Philadelphia *Public Ledger*, June 27, 1906; *Harper's Weekly*, XLVIII (1904), 1980; Ernest Hamlin Abbott, "Sectional Misapprehension," *Out-*

look, LXXX (1905), 237-41; John Hope Franklin, *From Slavery to Freedom* (New York, 1948), 435-36.

37. *Outlook,* LXXXI (1905), 956; John R. Commons, *Races and Immigrants in America* (New York, 1907), 3-17, 39-62; *Christian Science Monitor,* September 27, 1913.

38. National Council, Junior Order United American Mechanics, *Official Proceedings,* 1907, p. 57, and 1914, p. 168; *Cong. Rec.,* 62 Cong., 2 Sess., 3531. The Junior Order's nearest competitor, the Patriotic Order Sons of America, was still surviving in the East in 1912 but was much less active; *ibid.,* 3531, 3535.

39. *Cong. Rec.,* 59 Cong., 1 Sess., 9174; Asiatic Exclusion League, *Proceedings,* February, 1908, pp. 55, 57; *Hearings* (House Committee on Immigration, 62 Cong., 2 Sess.), 6, 16.

40. The most nativistic of progressive intellectuals, Edward A. Ross, may also be understood in part as a product of the Far West. His fascination with the immigration issue dates from his turbulent years at Stanford University, and his first polemic on the subject was an attack on the Oriental. Edward Alsworth Ross, *Seventy Years of It: An Autobiography* (New York, 1936), 69-70.

41. *The Tradesman* (Chattanooga), July 15, 1905; "Immigration Clippings Collected by Prescott F. Hall" (Widener Library, Harvard University), VI, 220.

42. *Cong. Rec.,* 61 Cong., 1 Sess., 1526; *Hearings* (House Committee on Immigration, 62 Cong., 2 Sess.), 3-23; *Mississippi Union Advocate,* June 15, 1910; *The National Field,* January 15, 1914.

43. Francis Butler Simkins, *Pitchfork Ben Tillman, South Carolinian* (Baton Rouge, 1944), 490; *Acts and Joint Resolutions of the General Assembly of the State of South Carolina,* 1909, pp. 14, 194; National Liberal Immigration League, *Proceedings of the General Meeting* (New York, 1908), 9; *Cong. Rec.,* 62 Cong., 2 Sess., 3536.

Those writers (Berthoff, Handlin, and others) who have maintained that the immigration promotion activities of the southern states were brought to an end by their inherent failure or by adverse federal regulations are, I am convinced, mistaken. It is true that the immigration law of 1907 and a new administrative ruling of the same year narrowed somewhat the possible functions of the state bureaus by forbidding them to pay an immigrant's passage with privately donated funds or to promise him a specific job, but the states were still free to advertise for immigrants and to subsidize immigration with public money. It was the rise of popular opposition within the South that stopped them from doing so. *Annual Report of the Commissioner-General of Immigration,* 1907, pp. 66-67, and 1908, p. 133.

44. For an indication of how lightly the most ardent nativist could take the danger of immigrant radicalism in the mid-1900's see Prescott F. Hall, *Immigration and Its Effects upon the United States* (New York, 1906), 183-87.

45. Scrapbook entitled "Johnson Politics, 1912" (Hoquiam Public Library, Washington), 64-65, 72, and *passim.* For additional biographical facts see "One Who Must Be Shown," *Saturday Evening Post,* CXCV (May 19, 1923), 92, 97.

46. J. H. Patten to Executive Committee, December 10, 1913, in Files of the I.R.L., Box 7; Johnson scrapbook entitled "Personal 1913" (Hoquiam Public Library), 61, 66, 84. Johnson was urging Asiatic exclusion and total suspension of European immigration except for close relatives of American residents.

47. *Cong. Rec.*, 62 Cong., 2 Sess., 4793-94. See also *ibid.*, 3538-40, and 63 Cong., 3 Sess., 741, 3056; *Literary Digest*, XLVII (1913), 197; *Christian Science Monitor*, June 13, 1912; David F. Houston, *Eight Years with Wilson's Cabinet, 1913 to 1920* (New York, 1926), I, 128. For background on the Lawrence strike and on the I.W.W. approach to immigrants see William M. Leiserson, *Adjusting Immigrant and Industry* (New York, 1924), 179-83, 203-205; *The Strike at Lawrence, Mass.* (Hearings, House Committee on Rules, 62 Cong., 2 Sess., Washington, 1912), 34-35, 75, 155; *Solidarity*, April 11, 1914.

48. Washington Gladden, "The Anti-Papal Panic," *Harper's Weekly*, LIX (July 18, 1914), 55-56; Jeremiah J. Crowley, *Romanism: A Menace to the Nation* (Aurora, Mo., 1912); J. W. Gibson and E. E. Miller, *Modern Americanism* (Chicago, 1911), 105-107.

49. William G. Bean, "Puritan Versus Celt, 1850-1860," *New England Quarterly*, VII (1934), 70-89.

50. *Watson's Magazine*, IV (1910), 277-82. For further complications in the "Fairbanks incident," involving Theodore Roosevelt, see *The New International Year Book*, 1910, pp. 635-36.

51. *Watson's Magazine*, XX (1914-15), 338-39; see also pp. 110, 193, and *passim*. C. Vann Woodward's excellent biography, *Tom Watson, Agrarian Rebel* (New York, 1938), underestimates, I think, the persistence in Watson of a radical impulse.

52. Walter B. Stevens, *Missouri The Center State, 1821-1915* (Chicago, 1915), III, 514-17, IV, 536; *The Menace*, November 25 and December 9, 1911, April 20, 1912, and November 15, 1913; *N. W. Ayer & Son's American Newspaper Annual and Directory*, 1914, p. 497.

53. *The Menace*, January 27, 1912; Charles W. Ferguson, *Fifty Million Brothers: A Panorama of Lodges and Clubs* (New York, 1937), 302-307. Apparently this oath made its debut in 1912 in a pamphlet entitled *The Church of Rome in American Politics*; *Literary Digest*, XLV (1912), 152-53.

54. *The Menace*, November 25, 1911, January 13, June 8, October 19, and November 23, 1912, and April 12, 1913.

55. Knights of Columbus, *Report of Commission on Religious Prejudices*, 1915, pp. 11, 17, 19-20, and 1916, pp. 30-31; New York *Times*, October 29, 1914, p. 10.

56. Although a careful sociological analysis of the Know-Nothing movement is yet to be made, two studies of New York state agree: "In the country districts . . . nativism had no enduring basis in general public sentiment." Louis D. Scisco, *Political Nativism in New York State* (New York, 1901), 252; Whitney R. Cross, *The Burned-Over District: The Social and Intellectual History of Enthusiastic Religion in Western New York, 1800-1850* (Ithaca, 1950), 231-32.

57. Knights of Columbus, *Report*, 1916, pp. 11-12; *The Menace*, January 27, 1912, and circulation figures in the issue of November 15, 1913.

58. Watson was anti-clerical and attacked Protestant foreign missions; *The Menace* started out with Protestant religious overtones, but before long it was appealing explicitly to agnostics as well as believers; *The Menace,* November 30, 1912.

59. J. G. Crites, Secretary Democratic Central Committee, Ransom County, North Dakota, to Woodrow Wilson, February 12, 1915, in Woodrow Wilson Papers, File VI-B, sec. 292 (Division of Manuscripts, Library of Congress). On the character of progressivism I am indebted especially to Woodward, *New South,* 371-95, and George E. Mowry, *The California Progressives* (Berkeley, 1951), 86-104.

60. Knights of Columbus, *Report,* 1915, pp. 22-23; B. O. Flower, ed., *The Patriot's Manual: Dealing with the Irrepressible Conflict Between Two Mutually Exclusive World Theories of Government* (Fort Scott, Kan., 1915), 224-32.

61. *The Menace,* January 20 and March 23, 1912; *Independent,* LXXIII (1912), 103-104; *Reveille: Lieut. Gen. Nelson A. Miles to All Guardians of Liberty* [New York, 1915]; Form letter from Committee on Lecturers, National Court, Guardians of Liberty, n.d. (Wisconsin Historical Society).

62. New York *World,* December 28, 1914, quoted in *Solidarity,* January 9, 1915.

63. New York *Times,* December 5, 1914, p. 16, and March 2, 1915, p. 1; Christopher G. Tiedeman, *A Treatise on State and Federal Control of Persons and Property in the United States* (St. Louis, 1900), I, 331; Thomas Reed Powell, "The Right to Work for the State," *Columbia Law Review,* XVI (1916), 99-114.

64. Knights of Columbus, *Report,* 1915, pp. 21-22; *The Menace,* March 20 and April 17, 1915. Eventually the hysterical propaganda campaign *The Menace* launched to "defend" itself came under the direction of Benjamin O. Flower, a reformist editor who had labored for many causes, including populism and Christian socialism.

65. *Current Opinion,* LVIII (1915), 347-48.

66. The campaign may be followed in the New York *Times,* esp. October 27, 1914, p. 18, and November 7, 1914, p. 6; *The Menace,* October 24, 1914; Theodorus Van Wyck, Headquarters, American party, to Theodore Roosevelt, June 26, 1914, in Roosevelt Papers.

67. Charles H. Watson, "Need of Federal Legislation in Respect to Mob Violence in Cases of Lynching of Aliens," *Yale Law Journal,* XXV (1916), 561-67. For an absorbing account of the region's earlier feuds between natives and attacks on Negro strikebreakers see Paul M. Angle, *Bloody Williamson: A Chapter in American Lawlessness* (New York, 1952).

68. New York *Times,* February 18, 1914, p. 3, June 23, 1915, p. 10, and August 20, 1915, p. 4. For a general account see C. P. Connolly, *The Truth About the Frank Case* (New York, 1915).

69. Atlanta *Georgian,* November 1, 1913; *B'nai B'rith News,* VI (April, 1914), 5; New York *Times,* February-May, 1914.

70. New York *Times,* August 20, 1915, p. 4; Woodward, *Tom Watson,* 437-42; *Watson's Magazine,* XX (1915), 139-63, 278.

71. New York *Times*, June 22-26, 1915; *Watson's Magazine*, XXI (1915), 296.
72. *Watson's Magazine*, XXI (1915), 293, 296. Before this belated outburst of generalized, race-conscious anti-Semitism, Watson's attitudes were somewhat mixed. In January 1915, he had called Frank a "typical young libertine Jew." In March he said that every race and nation has men like Frank, who "was false to the higher standards of his race." Although the Frank articles boosted Watson's circulation greatly, it is worth noting that anti-Catholicism remained his principal issue. The presumption is strong that Watson was following public opinion on the Frank Case more than he was making it.
73. Anon., *White American* [San Francisco, 1914].
74. Henry Weismann, "Immigration: Its Value to the Country," *American Industries*, XII (1912), 30-31; *Cong. Rec.*, 62 Cong., 3 Sess., 2311, and 63 Cong., 3 Sess., 3062; Youngstown *Vindicator*, January 13, 1915.
75. National Liberal Immigration League to Members, December 8, 1913, in Gustav Scholer Papers (Manuscript Division, New York Public Library); *Cong. Rec.*, 63 Cong., 3 Sess., 3045-47. See also various league pamphlets in the Wisconsin Historical Society.
76. *The American Leader*, I (February 29, 1912), 32-33, 58; File 77, Presidential Series No. 2, William H. Taft Papers (Division of Manuscripts, Library of Congress).
77. *Hearings Relative to the Dillingham Bill, S. 3175* (House Committee on Immigration and Naturalization, 62 Cong., 2 Sess., Washington, 1912); *Cong. Rec.*, 62 Cong., 3 Sess., 2032, 3268-69, 3420-21, and 63 Cong., 3 Sess., 3022-23; *Literary Digest*, XLIV (1912), 1089; Telegram to President Taft, May 8, 1912, File 77, Taft Papers.
78. *Cong. Rec.*, 62 Cong., 3 Sess., 2027, 2305-06; T. J. Brennan, "The Literacy Test," *Catholic World*, CV (1917), 224-28.
79. Prescott F. Hall, "The Recent History of Immigration and Immigration Restriction," *Journal of Political Economy*, XXI (1913), 737-40, 747-50; "Records of the Executive Committee I.R.L.," July 2, 1907, in Files of the I.R.L.; Elting E. Morison, ed., *The Letters of Theodore Roosevelt* (Cambridge, 1951-1954), VI, 1096-97; John Lombardi, *Labor's Voice in the Cabinet: A History of the Department of Labor from Its Origins to 1921* (New York, 1942), 125-27, 131.
80. Lombardi, *Labor's Voice*, 60, 144-46; Gompers, *Seventy Years*, II, 167-69; Hall, "Recent History," 742.
81. A.F.L., *Proceedings*, 1911, pp. 66-67; *Cong. Rec.*, 62 Cong., 1 Sess., 3709-10, and 62 Cong., 2 Sess., 3531, 3536, 10418; Prescott F. Hall to John L. Burnett, June 24, 1912, and Burnett to Hall, July 16, 1912, in Files of the I.R.L., Box 7.
82. *Cong. Rec.*, 62 Cong., 3 Sess., 2302; Tacoma *Ledger*, October 22, 1912; New York *Sun*, July 29, 1912; *Campaign Contributions: Testimony* (Senate Subcommittee of the Committee on Privileges and Elections, 62 Cong., 3 Sess., Washington, 1913), I, 404.
83. Arthur S. Link, *Wilson: The Road to the White House* (Princeton, 1947), 382-87, 493-99; *Cong. Rec.*, 63 Cong., 3 Sess., 1546-47, 1550.
84. Frank J. Bruno, *Trends in Social Work as Reflected in the Proceedings of the National Conference of Social Work, 1874-1946* (New York,

1948), 221-22; Porter, *Platforms*, 347-48; letters from Frances Kellor to Theodore Roosevelt, 1911-1913, in Boxes 269-70, Roosevelt Papers.

85. John Palmer Gavit, *American by Choice* (New York, 1922), 354. An anti-Roosevelt circular distributed by the Junior Order on election eve is enclosed in William B. Griffith to Elihu Root, January 9, 1913, in Elihu Root Papers, Box 258 (Division of Manuscripts, Library of Congress). For further evidence on Roosevelt's appeal to new immigrant voters see Link, *Wilson*, 499-500; Louis Hammerling to President Taft, August 28, 1912, in Taft Papers, File 77; Mary Kingsbury Simkhovitch, *Neighborhood: My Story of Greenwich House* (New York, 1938), 175.

86. Taft to Theodore E. Burton, February 10, 1913, in Taft Papers, File 77; Taft to A. Lawrence Lowell, November 6, 1910, in Files of the I.R.L., Box 7; Hall, "Immigration Clippings," X, 73.

87. Otto Heller, ed., *Charles Nagel: Speeches and Writings, 1900-1928* (New York, 1931), I, xiii-xxii; Walter B. Stevens, *St. Louis: History of the Fourth City, 1763-1909* (Chicago, 1909), II, 72-73; Henry Steele Commager, ed., *Documents of American History* (New York, 1946), No. 387.

88. See maps in Frank Julian Warne, *The Tide of Immigration* (New York, 1916), 292-94; and also *Publications of the Immigration Restriction League*, No. 63.

89. *Cong. Rec.*, 63 Cong., 2 Sess., 2590-96; New York *Times*, February 3-5, 1914.

90. Undated clippings in Archives of the American Jewish Committee, Box 63 (New York); Madison Grant to George Shiras, February 6, 1914, and to Prescott F. Hall, December 13, 1913, in Files of the I.R.L., Box 7; John L. Burnett to Hall, February 11, 1914, *ibid*.

91. Woodrow Wilson to E. D. Smith, March 5, 1914, and to John Sharp Williams, January 7, 1915, in Wilson Papers, sec. 292.

92. New York *Times*, March 11, 1914, p. 10, and March 13, 1914, p. 11; Chicago *Post*, March 19, 1914; Brooklyn *Standard-Union*, August 23, 1914; "Records of the Executive Committee I.R.L.," May 1, September 24, and October 9, 1914, in Files of the I.R.L.

93. *Cong. Rec.*, 63 Cong., 3 Sess., 261-62, 787; Cyrus Adler to Roland S. Morris, December 10, 1913, and N. I. Stone to Cyrus Adler, February 23, 1914, in A.J.C. Archives, Boxes 61 and 63. On Wilson's interest in this phase of the question see Charles P. Nixon to Joseph Tumulty, January 27, 1915, in Wilson Papers, sec. 292; and *Outlook*, CIX (1915), 321.

94. Commager, *Documents*, No. 404.

95. *Cong. Rec.*, 63 Cong., 3 Sess., 3077-78; Boston *Transcript*, January 28, 1915; "Records of the Executive Committee I.R.L.," January 29, 1915, in Files of the I.R.L.

Notes to Chapter Eight

1. One Progressive, Harold Ickes, in criticizing Wilson for pusillanimity, wrote: "Our people just now are stale on questions of industrial justice and social betterment: they simply aren't interested. . . . I find

that my chief interest at this time is in the relationship of the United States to the present European situation. I feel ashamed for my own country and I don't like to feel that way. . . . This nation has got to set to work to rebuild its own character. . . . There is a great depth of moral indignation in the country today that must find expression along moral and altruistic lines"; Ickes to Theodore Roosevelt, December 17, 1915, in Roosevelt Papers, Box 261 (Division of Manuscripts, Library of Congress). On some of the links between progressive idealism and anti-Germanism see Ralph H. Gabriel, *The Course of American Democratic Thought* (New York, 1940), 357-65; and Robert Endicott Osgood, *Ideals and Self-Interest in America's Foreign Relations: The Great Transformation of the Twentieth Century* (Chicago, 1953).

2. The estimate of the Census Bureau in 1917 was 2,349,000; New York *Times*, June 18, 1917, p. 9. See also United States Bureau of the Census, *Historical Statistics of the United States, 1789-1945* (Washington, 1949), 32.

3. Frederick A. Bushee, *Ethnic Factors in the Population of Boston* (New York, 1903), 154; H. B. Woolston, "Rating the Nations," *American Journal of Sociology*, XXII (1916), 381-90. See also Josiah Flynt, "The German and the German-American," *Atlantic Monthly*, LXXVIII (1896), 655-64; Kate Holladay Claghorn, "Our Immigrants and Ourselves," *Atlantic Monthly*, LXXXVI (1900), 536; *Harper's Weekly*, XLVIII (1904), 857-58; H. B. Grose, *Aliens or Americans?* (New York, 1906), 126; Price Collier, *Germany and the Germans from an American Point of View* (New York, 1913), x-xi.

4. Acting Commissioner of Labor Statistics to Assistant Secretary of Labor, December 5, 1917, in General Records of the Department of Labor, File 16/595 (National Archives); *Reports of the Immigration Commission: Abstracts* (61 Cong., 3 Sess., Senate Document No. 747, Washington, 1911), I, 468-69.

5. Clifton James Child, *The German-Americans in Politics, 1914-1917* (Madison, 1939), 4-7, 43-55.

6. New York *Times*, February 1, 1915, p. 8. A succession of revealing letters to the editor follows in the issues of February 5, 7, 11, 17, and 20. For indications of the very widespread character of similar comments see *Independent*, LXXXI (1915), 265-66; *Literary Digest*, L (1915), 299-301; *Nation*, C (1915), 134.

7. New York *Times*, August 11, 1915, p. 5, and August 25, 1915, p. 10; Child, *German-Americans*, 87-88, 90-94, 178.

8. *Literary Digest*, LI (1915), 944. See also George Creel, "The Hopes of the Hyphenated," *Century Magazine*, XCI (1916), 350-63.

9. Theodore Roosevelt, *America for Americans* (n.p., 1916), 3, 11, 15; *The Works of Theodore Roosevelt* (National Ed., New York, 1926), XVIII, 278-79; Elting E. Morison, ed., *The Letters of Theodore Roosevelt* (Cambridge, 1951-1954), VIII, 897. The last phrase quoted is from Roosevelt to Charles Evans Hughes, August 11, 1916, in Hughes Papers (Division of Manuscripts, Library of Congress). On Roosevelt's attitudes in the nineties see *Works*, XIII, 20-24.

10. Frederick L. Paxson, *American Democracy and the World War* (Bos-

ton, 1936-1939), I, 335, 348-50, 359; Child, *German-Americans*, 143-49; Morison, *Letters of Theodore Roosevelt*, VIII, 1099, 1111, 1121.

11. John Bach McMaster, *The United States in the World War* (New York, 1918-1920), I, 133-36, 233; Paxson, *American Democracy*, I, 199-202, 248. In 1913 Gardner ran for governor of Massachusetts largely on the issue of immigration restriction; *Congressional Record*, 63 Cong., 3 Sess., 3073-74.
       For insight into the ideology of preparedness see Osgood, *Ideals and Self-Interest*, 130-38, 199-222.

12. Ray Stannard Baker and William E. Dodd, eds., *The Public Papers of Woodrow Wilson: The New Democracy* (New York, 1926), I, 423-25; Walter Millis, *Road to War: America 1914-1917* (Boston, 1935), 237-39. It is true, as Frederick L. Paxson has pointed out, that Wilson spoke of hyphens in May 1914, but not, I think, in a significant way. The term was an old one, and Wilson's emphasis at the time was on the success of the melting pot.

13. Millis, *Road to War*, 304-305.

14. *The Menace*, April 17 and May 8, 1915, and subsequent issues; Knights of Columbus, *Report of Commission on Religious Prejudices*, 1916, p. 27. See also Michael Williams, *The Shadow of the Pope* (New York, 1932), 121-22.

15. Aleš Hrdlička, "Study of Old Americans," *Journal of Heredity*, VI (1914), 509, and "The Old White Americans," *Proceedings of the Nineteenth International Congress of Americanists*, 1915, pp. 582-601; Madison Grant, *The Passing of the Great Race, or The Racial Basis of European History* (New York, 1916), 200. The *Book Review Digest* lists only three reviews at the time of publication.

16. Mercer Green Johnston, *Patriotism and Radicalism: Addresses and Letters* (Boston, 1917), 179-85; Frank Perry Olds, "Kultur in American Politics," *Atlantic Monthly*, CXVIII (1916), 384; Hartley Burr Alexander, *Liberty and Democracy and Other Essays in War-Time* (Boston, 1918), 155-65 (an essay written in 1916).

17. G. Stanley Hall, *Life and Confessions of a Psychologist* (New York, 1923), 565-67.

18. Kate Holladay Claghorn, *The Immigrant's Day in Court* (New York, 1923), 308-309, 315-16. On the evolution of these provisions see *Cong. Rec.*, 62 Cong., 2 Sess., 2081, and 63 Cong., 2 Sess., 2596, 2610; Tacoma *News*, December 29, 1913.

19. Frank Julian Warne, *The Tide of Immigration* (New York, 1916), 327-41; Colorado Springs *Gazette*, April 7, 1916; *Cong. Rec.*, 64 Cong., 1 Sess., 12763. For statistics see *Survey*, XXXV (1916), 524; United States Census Bureau, *Historical Statistics*, 33.

20. *Immigration Journal*, I (1916), 20; *World's Work*, XXXI (1916), 601; Fall River *Globe*, June 30, 1916; *Cong. Rec.*, 64 Cong., 1 Sess., 11792; Chicago *Tribune*, January 11, 1917.

21. *Cong. Rec.*, 64 Cong., 1 Sess., 12767, 12923-44; Boston *Journal*, August 23, 1916. The bill had passed the House in March.

22. *Cong. Rec.*, 64 Cong., 2 Sess., 316, 2443, 2456, 2629; *Literary Digest*, LIV (1917), 392; *Policies of the Chamber of Commerce of the United States of America* [Washington, 1925], 43-44.

23. Roy L. Garis, *Immigration Restriction: A Study of the Opposition to and Regulation of Immigration into the United States* (New York, 1927), 123-38. On the Oriental provision see New York *Times*, February 3, 1914, p. 2, and February 4, 1914, p. 14.

24. "Records of the Executive Committee of the Immigration Restriction League," February-March, 1917, in Files of the Immigration Restriction League (Houghton Library, Harvard University).

25. McMaster, *U. S. in World War*, I, 351.

26. H. L. Mencken, *The American Language* (New York, 1946), 174, names Theodore Roosevelt as the inventor or at least the propagator of this potent phrase. I have not found in Roosevelt's published writings any evidence that he ever used the phrase, though he embraced a good deal of the point of view it connoted.

27. In education this point of view resulted in the belief that the war had supplied America with one all-purpose criterion by which every school subject might henceforth be evaluated. Arthur D. Dean, *Our Schools in War Time—and After* (Boston, 1918), 17. For a scornful account of the submission of Christianity to nationalism see Ray H. Abrams, *Preachers Present Arms: A Study of the War-Time Attitudes and Activities of the Churches and the Clergy in the United States, 1914-1918* (Philadelphia, 1933).

28. Roosevelt, *Works*, XIX, 181-82, 254-55; *Education*, XXXVIII (1918), 793-94; Dean, *Schools in War Time*, 44.

29. Lafayette Young, ed., *Fifteen Patriotic Editorials from the Des Moines Capital* (n.p., n.d.).

30. During the war the word "propaganda" was first coming into widespread use, testifying to a wholly new respect for the susceptibility of the average mind to the manipulations of the trained opinion-maker.

31. Henry Landau, *The Enemy Within: The Inside Story of German Sabotage in America* (New York, 1937), 310; Carl F. Wittke, *German Americans and the World War (with Special Emphasis on Ohio's German-Language Press)* (Columbus, 1936), 128-42.

32. Frederick Palmer, *Newton D. Baker: America at War* (New York, 1931), I, 100-102; Wittke, *German-Americans*, 144. A friend has reported to me that his mother, a Texan, affirms the ground-glass story to this day.

33. New York *Times*, March 31, 1918, p. 16; *World's Work*, XXXV (1918), 237; Emerson Hough, *The Web* (Chicago, 1919), 63-69.

34. Minute Mayor's Advisory Committee, April 20, 1917, in Gustav Scholer Papers (Manuscript Division, New York Public Library); *Literary Digest*, LVII (May 11, 1918), 12; McMaster, *U. S. in World War*, II, 67.

35. *Literary Digest*, LVI (March 30, 1918), 29-31; United States Bureau of Education, *Biennial Survey of Education*, 1916-18, I, 120-21; Wittke, *German-Americans*, 181-86; *The American Defense Society: History, Purpose and Accomplishments* (New York [1918]). Theodore Roosevelt was the honorary president of the society; Madison Grant was one of its trustees.

36. Roosevelt characteristically coupled this recommendation with a warning that loyal Americans must not be discriminated against because of

their national origin; *Letters of Theodore Roosevelt*, VIII, 1207-1208.

37. Abrams, *Preachers Present Arms*, 120-22; Wittke, *German-Americans*, 188-96; National Civil Liberties Bureau, *War-Time Prosecutions and Mob Violence* (New York, 1919), 6-12.

38. Thomas W. Gregory to T. V. Taylor, April 15, 1918, in Gregory Papers (Division of Manuscripts, Library of Congress); G. H. Walker and Sterling E. Edmonds to National Directors, American Protective League, April 3 and 5, 1918, in General Records of the Department of Justice, File 186751 (National Archives). See also George Creel, *How We Advertised America* (New York, 1920), 444.

39. Zechariah Chafee, Jr., *Free Speech in the United States* (Cambridge, 1941), 36-39, 45-49.

40. W. C. Hunter, "Alien Rights in the United States in Wartime," *Michigan Law Review*, XVII (1918-19), 33-39; James W. Garner, "Treatment of Enemy Aliens," *American Journal of International Law*, XII (1918), 38-42, 54; *Annual Report of the Attorney General of the United States*, 1917, p. 56.

41. Chafee, *Free Speech*, 39-41, 50-79; Homer Cummings and Carl McFarland, *Federal Justice: Chapters in the History of Justice and the Federal Executive* (New York, 1937), 424-26. It is worth noting that the growth of the government's repressive powers caused no general alarm or even uneasiness. James R. Mock, *Censorship 1917* (Princeton, 1941), 45-54.

42. *Annual Report of the Attorney General*, 1918, pp. 27-35, 39, 746-47; 1919, p. 25.

43. Thomas W. Gregory to Fred Feigl, July 18, 1917, and to A. M. Briggs, November 16, 1917, in Justice File 186751; Abrams, *Preachers Present Arms*, 119-20.

44. Hough, *The Web*, passim. (Quoted from pp. 441-42 by permission of The Reilly and Lee Company.) This extraordinary book is the best single revelation of the 100 per cent mind. On the quality of A.P.L. reports see A. Mitchell Palmer to James M. Cox, April 30, 1919, in Justice File 186751. On the number of A.P.L. units see A. B. Bielaski to John L. O'Brian, November 5, 1917, *ibid.*

45. See various reports in Justice File 186751; Gregory to Woodrow Wilson, September 9, 1918, in Gregory Papers; *The Spy Glass*, January 25, 1919. For a vivid portrait of strong-arm tactics suggestive of the A.P.L. see Edward A. Steiner's novel, *Sanctus Spiritus and Company* (New York, 1919), 289-96.

46. *Annual Report of the Attorney General*, 1918, p. 15.

47. New York *Times*, June 18, 1917, p. 9; Niles Carpenter, *Immigrants and Their Children, 1920* (United States Bureau of the Census Monograph No. 7, Washington, 1927), 262.

48. Acting Commissioner of Labor Statistics to Assistant Secretary of Labor, December 5, 1917, in Labor File 16/595; Franklin H. Martin, *Digest of the Proceedings of the Council of National Defense During the World War* (73 Cong., 2 Sess., Senate Document No. 193, Washington, 1934), 346.

49. Samuel Hopkins Adams, "Invaded America," *Everybody's Magazine*, XXXVII (March, 1918), 55-56.

50. Leon E. Aylsworth, "The Passing of Alien Suffrage," *American Political Science Review*, XXV (1931), 114-16. President Wilson wished to stop enemy aliens from voting by executive order but found that he lacked the authority to do so; see Justice File 72-100-4.

51. National Americanization Committee, *Memorandum to the Advisory Commission of the Council of National Defense Concerning a War Policy for Aliens* (New York, 1917), 9, 28; *Cong. Rec.*, 65 Cong., 1 Sess., 6379, 6492, and 2 Sess., 745, 3881; *Second Report of the Provost Marshal General . . . on the Operations of the Selective Service System* (Washington, 1919), 93.

52. *Hearings: Proposed Deportation of Aliens Who Surrendered Their First Papers in Order to Escape Military Service* (House Committee on Immigration and Naturalization, 66 Cong., 1 Sess., Washington, 1919).

53. Palmer, *Baker*, II, 162.

54. W. D. Jones to Thomas W. Gregory, April 25, 1917, in Gregory Papers; W. S. Sutton, "The Assault on the University of Texas," *Educational Review*, LIV (1917), 390-409.

55. Elin Anderson, *We Americans: A Study of Cleavage in an American City* (Cambridge, 1937), 183-84. See also Lee Levinger, *A Jewish Chaplain in France* (New York, 1921), 214. For a perceptive comment on a similar condition in World War II see W. Lloyd Warner, *Democracy in Jonesville: A Study in Quality and Inequality* (New York, 1949), 288.

56. Robert M. Yerkes, ed., *Psychological Examining in the United States Army*, Memoirs of the National Academy of Sciences, Vol. 15 (Washington, 1921), 693. The difference was due to the higher percentage of young males in the immigrant than in the native-born population.

57. Reproduced in Thomas Burgess, *Foreign Born Americans and Their Children: Our Duty and Opportunity for God and Country from the Standpoint of the Episcopal Church* (New York, 1923), 17. See also J. B. W. Gardiner, "Our Share in the Military Victory," *World's Work*, XXXVII (1919), 271; *Second Report of Provost Marshal General*, 86; Creel, *How We Advertised*, 171-73, 177-78; National Conference of Social Work, *Proceedings*, 1918, pp. 450-51.

58. George Creel, *Rebel at Large: Recollections of Fifty Crowded Years* (New York, 1947), 201; New York *Times*, July 5, 1918, p. 1; Wittke, *German-Americans*, 153-54. And see Roosevelt, *Works*, XIX, 303-304.

59. *Missionary Review of the World*, XLI (1918), 803.

60. Thomas G. Masaryk, *The Making of a State: Memories and Observations, 1914-1918* (New York, 1927), 218-24, 235-62; New York *Times*, June 7, 1918, p. 12, and June 30, 1918, sec. 2, p. 2; Robert E. Park, *The Immigrant Press and Its Control* (New York, 1922), 201, 207-10.

61. *Literary Digest*, LV (December 29, 1917), 21-22; Ray Stannard Baker and William E. Dodd, eds., *The Public Papers of Woodrow Wilson: War and Peace* (New York, 1927), I, 19-20, 140.

62. *America: A Catholic Review of the Week*, XIX (1918), 636.

63. Cf. Madison Grant, *The Passing of the Great Race, or The Racial Basis of European History* (2nd ed., New York, 1918), 83, 88, 231-32, with first edition; William S. Sadler, *Long Heads and Round Heads or What's the Matter with Germany* (Chicago, 1918); *The American*

Weekly, June 2, 1918. Osborn, the president of the American Museum of Natural History, was a close friend of Grant's.

64. Mock, *Censorship,* 148-51; Frank B. Kellogg to Theodore Roosevelt, April 6, 1918, in Roosevelt Papers, Box 270.

65. See especially James A. B. Scherer, *The Nation at War* (New York, 1918); Hough, *The Web;* and *Hearings: Brewing and Liquor Interests and German and Bolshevik Propaganda* (Senate Subcommittee on the Judiciary, 66 Cong., 1 Sess., Washington, 1919).

66. "The I.W.W. Develops into a National Menace," *Current Opinion,* LXIII (1917), 153-54; George L. Bell to Council of National Defense, July 19, 1917, in Labor File 20/77. For background see John S. Gambs, *The Decline of the I.W.W.* (New York, 1932), 35-38.

67. Bell to C.N.D., July 19, 1917, in Labor File 20/77; Thomas W. Gregory to Charles Warren, July 11, 1917, and Gregory to United States Attorneys, July 17, 1917, in Justice File 186701; National Civil Liberties Bureau, *War-Time Prosecutions,* 38; Gambs, *Decline of I.W.W.,* 26-27; Claghorn, *Immigrant's Day in Court,* 336-40.

68. Scherer, *Nation at War,* 161; *Grizzly Bear,* XXV (July, 1919), 5; Arnon Lyon Squiers, ed., *One Hundred Per Cent American: Addresses Delivered by Famous Patriots* (New York, 1918), 53.

69. Claghorn, *Immigrant's Day in Court,* 315-16, 339-42; *Cong. Rec.,* 65 Cong., 2 Sess., 8107-27, 8938-40, 11037. The genesis of this statute may be followed in Justice File 192538.

70. *The American City,* XX (1919), 319.

71. New York *Times,* 1918: July 7, p. 12, July 28, sec. 4, p. 4, August 11, sec. 2, p. 2, August 29, p. 5, September 9, p. 4, and September 15-21; *Hearings: Brewing and Liquor Interests* (Senate Subcommittee on Judiciary, 66 Cong., 1 Sess.), II, 2669 ff., and III, *passim.*

72. Clayton R. Lusk, "Radicalism under Inquiry," *American Review of Reviews,* LXI (1920), 167-68; *Literary Digest,* LXIII (November 22, 1919), 15; *Cong. Rec.,* 66 Cong., 1 Sess., 3367-68; Interchurch World Movement of North America, *Public Opinion and the Steel Strike* (New York, 1921), 98-99, 109-10. When Attorney General Palmer's home was bombed in June 1919, an Anti-Saloon League official advanced the theory that the act "was inspired by Germans with wet tendencies"; George McGinnis to A. Mitchell Palmer, June 12, 1919, in Justice File 202600.

73. See various correspondence in Justice File 186751, November, 1918-March, 1919, and in Records of the Immigration and Naturalization Service, File 27671-6184 (National Archives).

74. Richard Seelye Jones, *A History of the American Legion* (Indianapolis, 1946), 23-29, 40; Marcus Duffield, *King Legion* (New York, 1931), 156-71, 193-222. Membership rose to 845,186 in 1920—a point which it did not reach again until 1930; Dorothy Culp, *The American Legion: A Study in Pressure Politics* (Chicago, 1942), 1.

75. *Investigation Activities of the Department of Justice* (66 Cong., 1 Sess., Senate Document No. 153, Washington, 1919), 12-13; New York *Times,* December 31, 1918, p. 4; Frederick Lewis Allen, *Only Yesterday: An Informal History of the Nineteen-Twenties* (reprint, New York, 1946), 61-67.

76. James Oneal and G. A. Werner, *American Communism: A Critical Analysis of Its Origin, Development and Programs* (New York, 1947), 43-45, 52-53; Jerome Davis, *The Russian Immigrant* (New York, 1922), 173.
77. William M. Leiserson, *Adjusting Immigrant and Industry* (New York, 1924), 74-75, 204; Claghorn, *Immigrant's Day in Court*, 271-72, 278-81; New York *Times*, January 20, 1919, pp. 8-9; Interchurch World Movement, *Public Opinion*, 95 ff.
78. Emerson Hough, "Round Our Town," *Saturday Evening Post*, CXCII (February 21, 1920), 102; New York Legislature, Joint Committee Investigating Seditious Activities, *Revolutionary Radicalism: Its History, Purpose and Tactics* (Albany, 1920), III, 3098; Jerome Davis, *The Russians and Ruthenians in America* (New York, 1922), 109; Claghorn, *Immigrant's Day in Court*, 272-76, 414.
79. New York *Times*, February 7-11, 1919; John M. Blum, *Joe Tumulty and the Wilson Era* (New York, 1951), 206.
80. Arthur Wallace Dunn, "The 'Reds' in America," *Review of Reviews*, LXI (1920), 166; Lynn Ford, "The Growing Menace of the I.W.W.," *Forum*, LXI (1919), 70; Hough, "Round Our Town," 106; "Dealing with the 'Red' Agitators," *Current History*, XII (1920), 703.
81. Claghorn, *Immigrant's Day in Court*, 359, 388-89, 416-17; Eldridge Foster Dowell, *A History of Criminal Syndicalism Legislation in the United States* (Baltimore, 1939), 48-50, 147-48; L. L. Thompson to Louis F. Post, April 3, 1920, in Labor File 167/255.
82. *Review of Reviews*, LXI (1920), 123; *Investigation Activities* (66 Cong., 1 Sess., Senate Doc. 153), 6-8.
83. National Society of the Daughters of the American Revolution, *Report*, 1919-20, p. 21; Farmers National Congress to A. Mitchell Palmer, November 12, 1919, in Justice File 202600; *Cong. Rec.*, 65 Cong., 3 Sess., 3116; Nelson Van Valen, "The Bolsheviki and the Orange Growers," *Pacific Historical Review*, XXII (1953), 49.
84. Claghorn, *Immigrant's Day in Court*, 340-45; memorandum for the Assistant Secretary, February 28, 1918, and Louis F. Post to L. L. Thompson, December 10, 1919, in Labor File 167/255. On the origin of the 1918 law in the Immigration Bureau and for an indication of Secretary Wilson's vagueness about its provisions see Justice File 192538.
85. New York *Times*, February 10, 1919, p. 1; *Literary Digest*, LX (March 1, 1919), 16.
86. New York *Times*, June 29, 1919, p. 1; New York *World*, November 25, 1919.
87. William T. Ellis, "The 'Fighting Quaker' of the Cabinet," *American Review of Reviews*, LXI (1920), 35-38; Donald Wilhelm, "If He Were President," *Independent*, CII (1920), 65.
88. Louis F. Post, *The Deportations Delirium of Nineteen-Twenty: A Personal Narrative of an Historic Official Experience* (Chicago, 1923), 36-40, 48-49; Robert D. Warth, "The Palmer Raids," *South Atlantic Quarterly*, XLVIII (1949), 2-3.

89. Claghorn, *Immigrant's Day in Court*, 359-73; Harriet Stanton Blatch to Newton D. Baker, January 1, 1921, and W. B. Wilson to Newton D. Baker, January 6, 1921, in Labor File 167/255A.
90. *New Republic*, XXII (1920), 260.
91. Frederick R. Barkley, "Jailing Radicals in Detroit," *Nation*, CX (1920), 136.
92. *Annual Report of the Commissioner General of Immigration*, 1920, pp. 32-34, 1921, p. 14; William B. Wilson to Joe Tumulty, January 17, 1921, in Labor File 167/255A; Francis F. Kane, "The Communist Deportations," *Survey*, XLIV (1920), 143. Wilson took heart in May and decided that the Communist Labor party did not fall under the prohibitions of the deportation law; his action resulted in automatic release of about three hundred of those arrested in January.
93. New York *Times*, 1920: April 16, p. 4, May 1, p. 12, May 8, p. 24; *Literary Digest*, LXV (May 22, 1920), 25.
94. Inter-Racial Council, *Proceedings National Conference on Immigration* (New York, 1920), 9, 12; T. Coleman du Pont, "Does America Want Immigration or Emigration?" *Current Opinion*, LXIX (1920), 179; William H. Barr, "Plain Facts About Immigration," *Blast Furnace and Steel Plant*, VIII (1920), 422; *The American Citizen*, June 1, 1921.
95. Chafee, *Free Speech*, 168-69, 269-82; New York *Times*, 1920: January 13, p. 2, January 17, p. 11, January 23, p. 3.
96. Warth, "Palmer Raids," 20; *The New International Year Book*, 1920, pp. 697-98; *United States Statutes at Large*, XLI, 1008-1009; *Saturday Evening Post*, CXCVI (March 22, 1924), 28. For a survey of editorial reaction to the May Day episode see *Dearborn Independent*, XX (May 29, 1920), 6.

NOTES TO CHAPTER NINE

1. John T. Buchanan, "How to Assimilate the Foreign Element in Our Population," *Forum*, XXXII (1902), 691. See also Lawrence A. Cremin, *The American Common School: An Historic Conception* (New York, 1951), 44-47.
2. New York City, which undoubtedly had the most extensive program, was teaching 1,376 foreign students in special evening classes in 1879 and 36,000 in 1905; Gustave Straubenmueller, "The Work of the New York Schools for the Immigrant Class," *Journal of Social Science*, XLIV (1906), 177. See also Charles Hirschfeld, *Baltimore, 1870-1900: Studies in Social History* (Baltimore, 1941), 112.
3. In this chapter I pass over as a separate matter the occasional Americanizing activities conducted by immigrant organizations among their own nationalities. The most extensive of these organizations was probably the Educational Alliance, a Jewish agency operating in New York's Lower East Side from 1891 on. For an amusing picture of Jewish children in the classrooms of the alliance, singing patriotic songs while waving little American flags in each hand, see H. G. Wells, *The Future in America* (New York, 1906), 148-50. See also Paul Abelson, "The Education of the Immigrant," *Journal of Social Science*, XLIV (1906), 163-72.

4. See Chapter V, note 49; University Settlement Society, *Report*, 1896, p. 26, 1898, pp. 27-28; *Hull-House Bulletin*, I (October 15, 1896), 1-2, 7; Hale House, *Eleventh Annual Report*, 1908, p. 10.

5. *Report of the National Society of the Daughters of the American Revolution*, 1898-1900, pp. 156-57, 196-97, 213, and 1905-06, p. 23; *American Monthly Magazine*, XXVI (1905), 407.

6. Edward G. Hartmann, *The Movement to Americanize the Immigrant* (New York, 1948), 31-36; *Immigrants in America Review*, I (1915), 63; Records of the Immigration and Naturalization Service, Americanization Section, File 27671-1828 (National Archives).

7. D.A.R., *Report*, 1905-06, p. 23; Sons of the American Revolution, *National Year Book*, 1902, pp. 174-80, and 1914, pp. 137-38.

8. Kirk H. Porter, ed., *National Party Platforms* (New York, 1924), 347-48.

9. R. L. Duffus, *Lillian Wald: Neighbor and Crusader* (New York, 1939), 147.

10. Leroy Hodges, "The Church and the Immigrants: A Record of Failure and the Remedy," *Missionary Review*, XXXV (1912), 167-72; H. B. Grose, *The Incoming Millions* (New York, 1906), 106-17; Mrs. D. B. Wells and others, *Conservation of National Ideals* (New York, 1911), 105-22; Charles Stelzle, *American Social and Religious Conditions* (New York, 1912), 112-16; *New Americans for a New America* [n.p., 1913], 7.

11. Hartmann, *Movement*, 28-29; *Immigrants in America Review*, I (1915), 18-23.

12. See, for example, Peter Roberts, *The New Immigration* (New York, 1913), viii, 306-307; Elias B. Sanford, ed., *Federal Council of the Churches of Christ in America: Report of the First Meeting*, 1908, p. 98; Wells, *Conservation*, 12, 103.

13. Helen Christine Bennett, *American Women in Civic Work* (New York, 1915), 167-70; Elting E. Morison, ed., *The Letters of Theodore Roosevelt* (Cambridge, 1951-1954), V, 523-24.

14. Among Frances Kellor's early writings see especially "New Spirit in Party Organization," *North American Review*, CXCIX (1914), 879-92; "Who is Responsible for the Immigrant?" *Outlook*, CVI (1914), 912-17; *Straight America: A Call to National Service* (New York, 1916). For her admiration of Roosevelt see Kellor to Roosevelt [December, 1912], in Theodore Roosevelt Papers, Box 269 (Division of Manuscripts, Library of Congress).

15. Hartmann, *Movement*, 53-55, 68-71; Lillian D. Wald, *The House on Henry Street* (New York, 1915), 293; *Immigrants in America Review*, II (July, 1916), 3.

16. Hartmann, *Movement*, 38-49, 56-63; and see the *Annual Reports* of North American Civic League for Immigrants, 1908-1912.

17. N.A.C.L., *Annual Report*, 1912-13, p. 6, 1913-14, p. 4, and 1914-15, pp. 9-10, 16; *Immigrants in America Review*, I (1915), 16-17. For an illuminating report of how N.A.C.L. agents broke a strike see *Immigration Journal*, I (1916), 69-70.

18. Hartmann, *Movement*, 71-87; *Proceedings of the National Conference of Social Work*, 1919, pp. 753-55, and 1921, p. 474.

19. Immigrants' Protective League, *Annual Report*, 1916, p. 10.

20. *Immigrants in America Review*, I (1915), 3-4, 15; Frances Kellor and Joseph Mayper, *Recommendations for a Federal Bureau of Distribution Department of Labor* (New York [1914]); Hartmann, *Movement*, 97-101.

21. Frank Julian Warne, *The Tide of Immigration* (New York, 1916), 358-59. (Quoted by permission of Appleton-Century-Crofts, Inc.)

22. This story is best followed in *Immigrants in America Review*, June-September, 1915.

23. Hartmann, *Movement*, 124-29; National Security League, *Proceedings of the National Security Congress*, 1916, p. 202; Kellor, *Straight America*, *passim*.

24. For business views of Americanization see Frances A. Kellor, "Engineers and the New Nationalism," *Engineering Record*, LXXIV (1916), 12-13; Chamber of Commerce of the United States of America, *Immigration Committee Bulletin*, April 1, 1916, p. 2; Chamber of Commerce, *Fifth Annual Meeting . . . 1917: Report of Committee on Immigration*, 2; *American Industries*, XVI (October, 1915), 26; *Proceedings of the National Conference on Americanization in Industries*, 1919, pp. 28-32; Board of Education of the City of Chicago Cooperating with the Chicago Association of Commerce, *A Year of Americanization Work, July 1918-July 1919* (n.p., n.d.). On the initial effort in Detroit see Gregory Mason, "'Americans First,'" *Outlook*, CXIV (1916), 193-201; National Education Association, *Proceedings*, 1916, pp. 910-17.

25. "A Three Minute Talk on Americanization," in Records of the Council of National Defense, File 13J-A3 (National Archives); Howard C. Hill, "The Americanization Movement," *American Journal of Sociology*, XXIV (1919), 613-16, 642.

26. George Creel, *Rebel at Large: Recollections of Fifty Crowded Years* (New York, 1947), 198-99. (Quoted by permission of G. P. Putnam's Sons.)

27. Hartmann, *Movement*, 188-215; Hill, "Americanization," 624-27; James R. Mock and Cedric Larson, *Words That Won the War: The Story of the Committee on Public Information, 1917-1919* (Princeton, 1939), 216-30. See also the wry comment in the General Report of the Department of Educational Propaganda, September 11, 1918, in the Records of the Council of National Defense, File 13J-A3: ". . . the work is still vague and ineffective notwithstanding the progress made in organizing it. We, with the State Councils Section, are only pushing the plan of the Bureau of Education, and that plan is not well worked out."

28. Quoted in John Dewey, *Characters and Events: Popular Essays in Social and Political Philosophy* (New York, 1929), II, 466.

29. Mason, "'Americans First,'" 197; N.E.A., *Proceedings*, 1916, p. 915; *Independent*, LXXXV (1916), 294.

30. Arthur D. Dean, *Our Schools in War Time—and After* (Boston, 1918), 22; *The Survey*, XLII (1919), 279; Creel, *Rebel at Large*, 197.

31. Kate Holladay Claghorn, *The Immigrant's Day in Court* (New York, 1923), 300-304; Peter Roberts, *The Problem of Americanization* (New York, 1920), 77; William A. Bond, *Practical Americanization: A Business Man's View* [n.p., 1919], 7.

32. *Immigration Journal*, I (March, 1916), 8; *Congressional Record*, 65 Cong., 2 Sess., 745.
33. National Americanization Committee, *Memorandum to the Advisory Commission of the Council of National Defense Concerning a War Policy for Aliens* (New York, 1917), 20-22; Memo from N.A.C., January 7, 1918, in Roosevelt Papers, Box 272; Frances Kellor, *Neighborhood Americanization* (New York, 1918), 7-8.
34. N.E.A., *Proceedings*, 1916, pp. 185, 937; John Erskine, *Democracy and Ideals: A Definition* (New York, 1920), 34-58. On Dewey and Addams see Paul Arthur Schlipp, ed., *The Philosophy of John Dewey* (Evanston, 1939), 29-30. For other examples of the liberal theory of Americanization see Horace J. Bridges, *On Becoming an American* (Boston, 1918), 131-48; National Federation of Settlements, *Eighth Conference*, 1918, p. 25.
35. James A. Beebe, "The Christianization of Patriotism," *Methodist Review*, LXXVIII (1918), 236; Walter Lippmann, *The Stakes of Diplomacy* (New York, 1915), 173-79; Shailer Mathews, *Patriotism and Religion* (New York, 1918), 41-43; W. B. Pillsbury, *The Psychology of Nationality and Internationalism* (New York, 1919), 278-309.
36. N.E.A., *Proceedings*, 1917, pp. 125-28; National Conference of Social Work, *Proceedings*, 1918, pp. 441-54, and 1919, pp. 730-33; Charles Alvin Brooks, *Christian Americanization: A Task for the Churches* (n.p., 1919), 8-10.
37. Ray Stannard Baker and William E. Dodd, eds., *The Public Papers of Woodrow Wilson: War and Peace* (New York, 1927), I, 319-21, II, 77-79, 368-69, 389, 400.
38. Horace M. Kallen, *Culture and Democracy in the United States: Studies in the Group Psychology of the American Peoples* (New York, 1924), 140-42; National Conference of Social Work, *Proceedings*, 1919, p. 477; Cleveland Americanization Committee of the Mayor's War Board, *Americanization in Cleveland* (Cleveland, 1919).
39. Mock and Larson, *Words That Won the War*, 221-30; Creel, *Rebel at Large*, 195-201.
40. The tone of the Carnegie Americanization Studies may be judged from the first and best volume in the series: Robert E. Park and Herbert A. Miller, *Old World Traits Transplanted* (New York, 1921). Howe's essay, "The Alien," is in Harold E. Stearns, ed., *Civilization in the United States: An Inquiry by Thirty Americans* (New York, 1922), 337-50.
41. Hartmann, *Movement*, 254-58; M. E. Ravage, "The Immigrant's Burden," *New Republic*, XIX (1919), 211.
42. Eric F. Goldman, *Rendezvous with Destiny: A History of Modern American Reform* (New York, 1952), 299-303.
43. In 1916 the United States Bureau of Education was able to find only fourteen institutions which had special courses in immigration. By 1921 almost every university and teachers college was offering training in some phase of Americanization. *Immigration Journal*, I (1916), 110; N.E.A., *Proceedings*, 1921, p. 656.

44. *American Legion Weekly*, II (January 30, 1920), 10; N.E.A., *Proceedings*, 1919, pp. 553-54; Charles S. Thomas, "The Evils in Our Democracy," *Forum*, LXI (1919), 51-52.

45. New York Legislature, Joint Committee Investigating Seditious Activities, *Revolutionary Radicalism: Its History, Purpose and Tactics* (Albany, 1920), III, 2283-92; *Investigating Strike in Steel Industries* (66 Cong., 1 Sess., Senate Report 289, Washington, 1919), 27.

46. National Security League, *The Flying Squadron of Speakers* (New York, 1919), 4; New York *Times*, December 2, 1918, p. 9.

47. National Security League, *A Square Deal for the Public: A Working Program for Crushing the Radical Menace* (New York, 1919); National Security League, *Annual Report of Charles D. Orth, President*, 1920; National Security League to Secretary of Labor William B. Wilson, February 1920, in Records of the Immigration and Naturalization Service, File 27671-4618 (National Archives).

48. American Legion, *Summary of Proceedings of the National Convention*, 1919, pp. 39-42, 46.

49. "Constitutional Government League," Records of the Immigration and Naturalization Service, File E-10428; *Foreign-Born*, July 29, 1920; Elizabeth C. Barney Buel, *Manual of the United States for the Information of Immigrants and Foreigners* (rev. ed., n.p., 1923), 10-11, 17, 20, 52-55.

50. *American Citizen*, April 1, 1921; National Conference on Americanization in Industries, *Proceedings*, 1919, pp. 8-9 and *passim;* Bond, *Practical Americanization*, 10; John E. Otterson, "Decreased Immigration—Less Production," *Iron Age*, CV (1920), 1133.

51. Hartmann, *Movement*, 101 n, 225-26.

52. Frances Kellor to Theodore Roosevelt, November 27 and December 18, 1918, in Roosevelt Papers, Box 272; *Hearings: Presidential Campaign Expenses* (Senate Privileges and Elections Committee, 66 Cong., 3 Sess., Washington, 1921), II, 2682.

53. T. Coleman du Pont, "Does America Want Immigration or Emigration?" *Current Opinion*, LXIX (1920), 179. The anatomy and policies of the I.R.C. are best explained in *Hearings: Proposed Restriction of Immigration* (House Committee on Immigration and Naturalization, 66 Cong., 2 Sess., Washington, 1921), 90-121, but see also *Literary Digest*, LXII (July 26, 1919), 96.

54. Miss Kellor declared in 1919 that she was not seeking to dictate editorial policies but only to disseminate "pro-American" advertisements paid for by the Inter-Racial Council. Nevertheless at least one immigrant editor charged in 1920 that propaganda articles were being forced on the foreign-language papers, and du Pont acknowledged that this was indeed the intention. Cf. Robert E. Park, *The Immigrant Press and Its Control* (New York, 1922), 451-57; *Foreign-Born*, January-February, 1920, p. 20; *Hearings: Presidential Campaign Expenses* (66 Cong., 3 Sess.), II, 2683-84.

55. *Cong. Rec.*, 66 Cong., 2 Sess., 1650-51; *Hearings: Americanization Bill* (Senate Committee on Education and Labor, 66 Cong., 1 Sess., Washington, 1919); Hartmann, *Movement*, 229-32. The National Education Association came out for the compulsory idea; see its *Proceedings*, 1919, p. 25.

56. Hartmann, *Movement*, 233-52.
57. Harry Rider, "Americanization," *American Political Science Review*, XIV (1920), 111-14; *Laws State of New York*, 1918, p. 749.
58. *New Republic*, XXII (1920), 262; André Siegfried, *America Comes of Age* (New York, 1927), 65; *Harvard Law Review*, XXXV (1922), 469. The Oregon School Law, aimed especially at parochial schools, grew out of the new wave of anti-Catholic nativism as well as the declining spirit of Americanization.
59. Robert T. Hill, "From Americanization to Adult Education," *Survey*, LXII (1929), 366-67; National Conference of Social Work, *Proceedings*, 1924, p. 577. The National Education Association changed its Department of Immigrant Education into a Department of Adult Education in 1924; N.E.A., *Proceedings*, 1924, p. 566.
60. Sons of the American Revolution, *National Year Book*, 1919, p. 122; American Legion, *Summary*, 1919, p. 42; Bessie Louise Pierce, *Citizens' Organizations and the Civic Training of Youth* (New York, 1933), 52-55; N.E.A., *Proceedings*, 1921, pp. 38-42, 760; *Literary Digest*, LXIV (February 21, 1920), 90.
61. *Literary Digest*, LXV (May 8, 1920), 52; *Nation*, CX (1920), 128; *Athletes' Americanization League* (n.p., n.d.). In an unpublished paper Edwin Layton has shown that the Americanization Fund of Los Angeles was actually a subsidiary of the Better America Federation, a propaganda organization of ultra-conservative businessmen.
62. N.E.A., *Proceedings*, 1922, pp. 953-55, 968; Hartmann, *Movement*, 265.
63. *Saturday Evening Post*, CXCIII (May 14, 1921), 20; Arthur Sweeney, M.D., "Mental Tests for Immigrants," *North American Review*, CCXV (1922), 609-10; Prescott F. Hall, "Immigration and the World War," *Annals of the American Academy of Political and Social Science*, XCIII (1921), 192; Clinton Stoddard Burr, *America's Race Heritage* (New York, 1922), 6; David Starr Jordan quoted in *American Jewish Year Book*, 1922-23, p. 54.
64. Emerson Hough, "Round Our Town," *Saturday Evening Post*, CXCII (February 21, 1920), 102.

NOTES TO CHAPTER TEN

1. New York *Times*, August 6-8, 1920.
2. Although West Frankfort is just north of the Williamson County line, this event would have fit well into Paul M. Angle's *Bloody Williamson: A Chapter in American Lawlessness* (New York, 1952).
3. Carey McWilliams, *Prejudice: Japanese-Americans, Symbol of Racial Intolerance* (Boston, 1944), 57-61.
4. C. Vann Woodward, *Tom Watson, Agrarian Rebel* (New York, 1938), 463-74; Charles P. Sweeney, "Bigotry in the South," *Nation*, CXI (1920), 585; *General Laws of the Legislature of Alabama*, 1919, pp. 881-83.
5. Jacob Zeitlin and Homer Woodbridge, *Life and Letters of Stuart P. Sherman* (New York, 1929), II, 476, 482-83; *Saturday Evening Post*, CXCIII (May 7, 1920), 20.

6. "The New Tide of Immigration," *Current History*, XII (1920), 704-705; *Literary Digest*, LXII (July 26, 1919), 96, LXV (June 5, 1920), 32, LXVI (September 11, 1920), 18, LXVII (December 18, 1920), 9, and LXVII (December 25, 1920), 14.
7. *Literary Digest*, LXIII (December 27, 1919), 14.
8. Frank Bohn, "The Ku Klux Klan Interpreted," *American Journal of Sociology*, XXX (1925), 399; Stanley Frost, "When the Klan Rules," *Outlook*, CXXXVI (1924), 262; Pauli Murray, ed., *States' Laws on Race and Color* (n.p., 1950), 123, 259, 290, 378, 423, 504, 524. Without attempting a systematic coverage, this volume contains the Wyoming statute and similar ones passed by six other states, all within the period 1921-1925.
9. Thomas A. Bailey, *Woodrow Wilson and the Great Betrayal* (New York, 1945), 47, 153, 201-204, 225-26, 266, 273-74, 289-90; John M. Blum, *Joe Tumulty and the Wilson Era* (Boston, 1951), 254.
10. On anti-alien legislation see Chapter XI, note 1. Good examples of the connection between anti-League and anti-foreigner attitudes are in Ira E. Bennett, *Editorials from The Washington Post 1917-1920* (Washington, 1921), 420, 569-75; *Grizzly Bear*, XXV (September, 1919), 6, and XXVI (April, 1920), 5.
11. New York *Times*, May 31, 1937, p. 15.
12. *Ibid.*, February 20, 1921, p. 2; *Saturday Evening Post*, CXCIII (May 7, 1920), 20.
13. *American Industries*, XX (October, 1919), 18; American Constitutional Association, *American Ideals* (Charleston, W. Va. [1924]), 5; Albert Greene Duncan, *The Spirit of America* (University of Rochester Bulletin, Ser. XVI, No. 3, November, 1920), 15; James M. Beck, *The Constitution of the United States, Yesterday, Today—and Tomorrow?* (New York, 1924), 206-209, 288-309.
14. "Aristocracy and Politics," *Journal of Heredity*, X (1919), 166. Hall was deeply impressed by Grant's book, though he had already come to roughly the same point of view through his own studies of European racist literature. Grant, in turn, thought well of Hall and was an active member of Hall's Immigration Restriction League as early as 1905. The relation between the two men may be traced in the Files of the Immigration Restriction League (Houghton Library, Harvard University).
15. Harry Huntington Powers, *The American Era* (New York, 1920), 184; Frances Rumsey, "Racial Relations in America," *Century Magazine*, XCVII (1919), 786; Theodore Lothrop Stoddard, *The Revolt Against Civilization: The Menace of the Under Man* (New York, 1922).
16. *The Rising Tide of Color Against White World Supremacy* (New York, 1920), 166 and *passim*.
17. Charles W. Gould, *America, A Family Matter* (New York, 1920); Clinton Stoddard Burr, *America's Race Heritage* (New York, 1922), 208; Kenneth Lewis Roberts, *Why Europe Leaves Home* (Indianapolis, 1922), 22. On Roberts see also John Tebbell, *George Horace Lorimer and the Saturday Evening Post* (New York, 1948), 90-91.
18. Paul Popenoe and Roswell Hill Johnson, *Applied Eugenics* (New York, 1918), 300-306, 424-27.

19. *Scientific Papers of the Second International Congress of Eugenics* (Baltimore, 1923), I, 1-4, II, 1-6, 41-61, 175-88. The press featured the relevance of this discussion to immigration restriction and ignored the papers of two Jewish eugenicists who argued that intermarriage of Jewish and non-Jewish populations positively improves the "human breed"; New York *Times*, September 25-28, 1921.

20. Ellsworth Huntington, *The Character of Races as Influenced by Physical Environment, Natural Selection and Historical Development* (New York, 1924); Edward M. East, *Mankind at the Crossroads* (New York, 1923). There were also such popular eugenicist tracts as A. E. Wiggam's *The Fruit of the Family Tree* (Indianapolis, 1924), or (still more vulgar) Feri Felix Weiss's *The Sieve or Revelations of the Man Mill* (Boston, 1921). Wiggam believed that he was descended from Nordic Vikings.

21. Robert M. Yerkes, ed., *Psychological Examining in the United States Army*, Memoirs of the National Academy of Sciences, XV (Washington, 1921), 693. Contemporaneous civilian studies are summarized in William McDougall, *Is America Safe for Democracy?* (New York, 1921), 56-68. For background see Gardner Murphy, *Historical Introduction to Modern Psychology* (New York, 1949), 351-62.

22. Carl C. Brigham, *A Study of American Intelligence* (Princeton, 1923), vi, 192; Robert M. Yerkes, "Testing the Human Mind," *Atlantic Monthly*, CXXXI (1923), 364-65; McDougall, *Is America Safe?* On the popular discussion of the Army intelligence tests see Arthur Sweeney, "Mental Tests for Immigrants," *North American Review*, CCXV (1922), 600-12; *Literary Digest*, LXXVII (June 2, 1923), 27-28; William C. Bagley, "The Army Tests and the Pro-Nordic Propaganda," *Educational Review*, LXVII (1924), 179-87.

23. H. L. Mencken, *Prejudices: Second Series* (New York, 1920), 44-47, 143-50; *Prejudices: Third Series* (New York, 1922), 22-25, 34-36; *Prejudices: Fifth Series* (New York, 1926), 153-58. There are some interesting editorial comments on this controversy in the *Nation*, CXII (1921), 330.

24. Gertrude Atherton, "The Alpine School of Fiction," *Bookman*, LV (1922), 26-33; Brander Matthews, "The Anglo-Saxon Myth," *New York Times Book Review*, July 2, 1922, p. 11, and "The Mongrelian Language," *Scribner's Magazine*, LXVIII (1920), 219-21; John Farrar, "The American Tradition," *Bookman*, LVIII (1924), 609-14; Zeitlin, *Sherman*, II, 479-83. To another critic, writing from an independent point of view, it seemed that the Nordic aristocracy, for all of its superiority, had simply abdicated. Ernest Boyd, *Portraits: Real and Imaginary* (New York, 1924), 118-28.

25. See, for example, William S. Rossiter, "What Are Americans?" *Atlantic Monthly*, CXXVI (1920), 270-80; Ramsay Traquair, "The Caste System of North America," *Atlantic Monthly*, CXXXI (1923), 417-23; Charlotte Perkins Gilman, "Is America Too Hospitable?" *Forum*, LXX (1923), 1983-89; *World's Work*, XLVI (1923), 123; *Literary Digest*, LXVII (December 18, 1920), 9, and LXXXI (June 7, 1924), 15.

26. *Current Opinion*, LXXIV (1923), 399; Hiram W. Evans, *The Menace of Modern Immigration* [Dallas, 1923], 5, 12-15.

27. George Creel, "Close the Gates," *Collier's*, LXIX (May 6, 1922), 9.
28. Francis W. Coker, *Recent Political Thought* (New York, 1934), 322; New York *Times*, July 30, 1922, sec. 7, p. 8; *American Standard*, I (April 15, 1924), 18-19. On the Sacramento Church Federation see *New Republic*, XXXVIII (1924), 217.
29. New York *World*, January 13, 1924, p. 3.
30. *Nation*, CXIV (1922), 708; Harry Starr, "The Affair at Harvard," *Menorah Journal*, VIII (1922), 263-76; Harris Berlock, "Curtain on the Harvard Question," *Zeta Beta Tau Quarterly*, VII (May, 1923), 3-5.
31. Heywood Broun and George Britt, *Christians Only: A Study in Prejudice* (New York, 1931), 231-32.
32. Letter to Thomas W. Gregory, June 26, 1918, in Gregory Papers (Division of Manuscripts, Library of Congress); Henry Cabot Lodge to Theodore Roosevelt, January 15, 1915, in Roosevelt Papers, Box 286 (Division of Manuscripts, Library of Congress); Elting E. Morison, ed., *The Letters of Theodore Roosevelt* (Cambridge, 1951-1954), VIII, 1304.
33. *The Anti-Bolshevist*, I (September, 1918), 1. The whole pattern of the new anti-Semitic ideology appears here in embryo: the linking of German-Jewish bankers with Russian-Jewish Bolshevists, the charge that the Jews hastened American entry into the war and then treacherously prolonged it, the fear of international influences such as the League of Nations. On the identification of Jewry with Bolshevism see also New York *Times*, November 19, 1917, p. 2, and Jacob Schiff to Louis Marshall, August 19, 1918, in Archives of the American Jewish Committee, Box 72 (New York).
34. Benjamin Antin, *The Gentleman from the 22nd* (New York, 1927), 82; *Hearings: Brewing and Liquor Interests and German and Bolshevik Propaganda* (Senate Subcommittee on the Judiciary, 66 Cong., 1 Sess., Washington, 1919), III, 112 ff.; *Literary Digest*, LXI (April 19, 1919), 32, and LXV (May 8, 1920), 52; *Nation*, CXI (1920), 493; Harry Schneiderman to Cyrus Adler, December 29, 1919, and Herbert Hirsch to American Jewish Committee, January 9, 1920, in A.J.C. Archives, Box 132.
35. John S. Curtiss, *An Appraisal of the Protocols of Zion* (New York, 1942).
36. Statement by Dr. Harris A. Houghton, February 9, 1919, and Cyrus Adler to Louis Marshall, April 25, 1921, in A.J.C. Archives, Box 132; Stephen S. Wise to Thomas W. Gregory, December 3, 1928, and Gregory to Wise, December 10, 1928, in Gregory Papers. Correspondence with and about Pilenas is in A.J.C. Archives, Box 75.
37. Ralph Easley to J. P. Morgan, July 8, 1920, in Files of the National Civic Federation (Manuscript Division, New York Public Library); Norman Hapgood, "The Inside Story of Henry Ford's Jew-Mania," *Hearst's International*, XLII (September, 1922), 133-34.
38. Hapgood, "Inside Story," *Hearst's International*, XLII (August, 1922), 45, 119; Cyrus Adler to Louis Marshall, September 15, 1920, and Adolph Kraus to Henry B. Joy, October 20, 1920, in A.J.C. Archives, Box 132; *The Protocols and World Revolution* (Boston, 1920). See also Brasol to Theodore Roosevelt, September 13, 1918, in Roosevelt Papers, Box

188. Meanwhile this enterprising officer was writing an anti-Semitic work of his own, *The World at the Cross Roads* (Boston, 1921), and a theoretical critique of Marxism, *Socialism vs. Civilization* (New York, 1920). Later Brasol became an authority on criminology.

39. *The Cause of World Unrest* (New York, 1920). The depth of Putnam's own anti-Semitism is fully revealed in Putnam to Lee Weiss, March 13, 1922, and Schneiderman to Marshall, March 14, 1922, in A.J.C. Archives, Box 132.

40. *Literary Digest*, LXXVII (June 16, 1923), 8-9; Keith Sward, *The Legend of Henry Ford* (New York, 1948), 106-15, 185. For Ford's views on cities see Philadelphia *Public Ledger*, June 20, 1923, p. 10, and *Dearborn Independent*, May 1, 1920, p. 5.

41. *Dearborn Independent*, May 22, 1920, p. 1, and June 12, 1920, p. 3; Sward, *Legend*, 75-77. It seems doubtful that Ford had actual difficulties with Jewish bankers; at least his associates do not remember that he ever talked about his anti-Jewish campaign in such terms; William C. Richards, *The Last Billionaire: Henry Ford* (New York, 1949), 89.

Although Ford hired professional journalists to speak for him in the pages of the *Independent*, supplementary evidence consistently indicates that the views expressed there corresponded roughly to his own.

42. *Dearborn Independent*, November 1, 1919-January 31, 1920; Sward, *Legend*, 116-18, 141-44. On the business opposition to Ford see John D. Mangum to Will Hays, November 30, 1918, in Roosevelt Papers, Box 270.

43. *Dearborn Independent*, March 6, 1920, p. 3, and April 24, 1920, p. 3; Sward, *Legend*, 79.

44. Richards, *Last Billionaire*, 89-90; New York *Times*, December 5, 1921, p. 33; *Current Opinion*, LXX (1921), 501.

45. David A. Brown to Louis Marshall, September 14, 1920, in Marshall Papers, Box C, A.J.C. Archives; Hapgood, "Inside Story," *Hearst's International*, XLI (June, 1922), 17-18. The first reference to the "Protocols" appeared in the *Independent* on July 10, 1920, pp. 8-9.

46. *American Jewish Year Book*, 1921-22, p. 116; *Current Opinion*, LXX (1921), 501. The Wilson-Taft manifesto is reprinted in Samuel Walker McCall, *Patriotism of the American Jew* (New York, 1924), 259-62. See also the popular commentator, Dr. Frank Crane, in New York *Globe*, October 30, 1922.

47. Richards, *Last Billionaire*, 96-97.

48. Herbert Adams Gibbons, "The Jewish Problem," *Century Magazine*, CII (1921), 786; Burton J. Hendrick, "The Jews in America," *World's Work*, XLV (1922-23), 144-61, 266-86, 366-77; *American Jewish Year Book*, 1924-25, p. 625. For further evidence see *Current Opinion*, LXIX (1920), 842; *America: A Catholic Review of the Week*, XXV (1921), 65.

49. For further evidence of rural anti-Semitism see A. E. Rotter to Louis Marshall, March 17, 1921, and Marshall to Judge James C. Hume, August 28, 1922, in Marshall Papers, Box C, A.J.C. Archives. Hume was an Iowa judge so distraught by the agricultural collapse that he sprinkled a court opinion in a stock fraud case with references to the defendants as "three Yids," "Big Yous," etc.

50. "Memorandum on the Activities of the Ku Klux Klan in the State of Oregon," in General Records of the Department of Justice, File 198589 (National Archives); *The Imperial Night-Hawk*, June 27, 1923, p. 6; Bohn, "Klan Interpreted," 387-88.

51. See correspondence of October 25, 1921, May 16, 1922, and June 24, 1924, in Justice File 198589; Samuel Taylor Moore, "Consequences of the Klan," *Independent*, CXIII (1924), 534-35.

52. Woodward, *Tom Watson*, 443; New York *Times*, June 26, 1915, p. 4.

53. The best accounts of Simmons and of the Klan's early years are in Robert L. Duffus, "Salesmen of Hate: The Ku Klux Klan," *World's Work*, XLVI (1923), 31-33; *Hearings: The Ku Klux Klan* (House Committee on Rules, 67 Cong., 1 Sess., Washington, 1921), 67-69; Winfield Jones, *Knights of the Ku Klux Klan* (New York, 1941), 72-82; William G. Shepherd, "How I Put Over the Klan," *Collier's*, LXXXII (July 14, 1928), 5-7, 32-35.

54. William G. Shepherd, "Ku Klux Koin," *Collier's*, LXXXII (July 21, 1928), 8-9; New Orleans *Times-Democrat*, September 23, 1918.

55. C. Anderson Wright to Warren G. Harding, September 22, 1921, and "Memo on the Klan in Oregon," in Justice File 198589.

56. New York *Times*, 1920: October 7, p. 1, October 11, p. 1, October 28, p. 17, and November 1, p. 1; 1921: January 24, p. 1, and March 7, p. 15.

57. *Ibid.*, October 20, 1920, p. 12, and November 1, 1920, p. 27.

58. Walter F. White, "Election by Terror in Florida," *New Republic*, XXV (1921), 195; New York *Times*, October 31, 1920, p. 12.

59. Samuel D. Miller to Chief of Bureau of Investigation, September 25, 1921, Lena M. Clarke to Bureau of Investigation, October 17, 1921, and J. H. Williams to Department of Justice, September 8, 1921, in Justice File 198589; Charles P. Sweeney, "The Great Bigotry Merger," *Nation*, CXV (1922), 8; New York *Times*, April 3, 1921, p. 13.

60. *Literary Digest*, LXX (August 27, 1921), 12; Robert L. Duffus, "How the Ku Klux Klan Sells Hate," *World's Work*, XLVI (1923), 179.

61. *Literary Digest*, LXXIV (August 5, 1922), 52. Although Clarke's whole statement was somewhat more loosely phrased than I have suggested, this was his essential meaning.

62. Ku Klux Klan, *Papers Read at the Meeting of Grand Dragons . . .* (Asheville, 1923), 132-33; Hiram W. Evans, *The Menace of Modern Immigration* [Dallas, 1923], 20; *Imperial Night-Hawk* (Atlanta), May 25, 1923, p. 5, July 12, 1923, p. 2, August 15, 1923, p. 6, and January 23, 1924, p. 2; Chicago *Dawn*, June 2, 1923, p. 12.

63. Sweeney, "Great Bigotry Merger," 9.

64. Alvin W. Johnson and Frank H. Yost, *Separation of Church and State in the United States* (Minneapolis, 1949), 33.

65. Sweeney, "Bigotry in the South," 585-86. It is significant that in this 1920 article Sweeney, who later took part in the New York *World's* investigation of the Klan, does not mention the hooded order. On the movement against parochial schools in Michigan and Nebraska see *Foreign-Born*, December 1920, p. 42.

66. Duffus, "Klan Sells Hate," 180. Quotation is from *The Foreign Language Press: America's Greatest Menace* [n.p., 1924]. For other illustrations see S. L. Baugher to Attorney General, October 15, 1921, in

Justice File 198589; and Stanley Frost, *The Challenge of the Klan* (Indianapolis, 1924), 128-42.

67. Charles P. Sweeney, "Bigotry Turns to Murder," *Nation*, CXIII (1921), 232-33, and "Great Bigotry Merger," 8.

68. Norman F. Furniss, *The Fundamentalist Controversy, 1918-1931* (New Haven, 1954), 37-38, suggests caution in assuming a direct connection between the Klan and fundamentalism as organized movements. On the other hand, his careful study provides abundant evidence that they drew upon common attitudes.

69. Emerson H. Loucks, *The Ku Klux Klan in Pennsylvania* (Harrisburg, 1936), 118-24.

70. *American Standard*, I (May 20, 1924), 12-17; *Illinois Fiery Cross*, February 22, 1924, p. 5, and March 28, 1924, p. 1.

71. K.K.K., *Papers*, 124; Loucks, *Klan in Pennsylvania*, 39.

72. Many such instances are in Loucks, *Klan in Pennsylvania*, 40-43. See also Frost, "Klan Rules," 262; Max Bentley, "A Texan Challenges the Klan," *Collier's*, LXXII (November 3, 1923), 11, 22; C. M. Hughes to Attorney General, June 26, 1921, in Justice File 198589.

73. Angle, *Bloody Williamson*, 134-205.

74. Duffus, "Klan Sells Hate," 179; Henry Zweifel to Attorney General, July 22, 1921, in Justice File 198589; Edward T. Devine, "The Klan in Texas," *Survey*, XLVIII (1922), 10-11; Robert S. Lynd and Helen Merrell Lynd, *Middletown: A Study in Contemporary American Culture* (New York, 1929), 481.

75. Frank Tannenbaum, *Darker Phases of the South* (New York, 1924), 16-17. There are also perceptive comments in Loucks, *Klan in Pennsylvania*, 38-39; and Frederic C. Howe, *The Confessions of a Reformer* (New York, 1925), 17. One of the New York *World* investigators of the Klan reported in 1921 that in every case of violence which he had studied the victim was told that his punishment resulted from some violation of moral or statutory law; *Hearings: Ku Klux Klan* (House Committee on Rules, 67 Cong., 1 Sess.), 15.

76. Jones, *Klan*, 111-12. The chronology of the Klan's growth may be followed in the New York *Times Index*.

77. *Literary Digest*, LXXIV (August 5, 1922), 44-46.

78. *Ibid.*, LXXIII (June 10, 1922), 15, and LXXIV (August 5, 1922), 14; Waldo Roberts, "The Ku-Kluxing of Oregon," *Outlook*, CXXXIII (1923), 490-91; John W. Owens, "Does the Senate Fear the K.K.K.?" *New Republic*, XXXVII (1923), 113-14. On Georgia see New York *Times*, November 18, 1923, sec. 2, p. 1.

79. *Literary Digest*, LXXVI (January 13, 1923), 10-12, and (March 31, 1923), 10-11; Leonard Lanson Cline, "In Darkest Louisiana," *Nation*, CXVI (1923), 292-93; Duffus, "Klan Sells Hate," 174-77.

80. This story is best followed in the New York *Times*, September, 1921-February, 1924, supplemented by Loucks, *Klan in Pennsylvania*, 45-48, and Francis Ralston Welsh to Calvin Coolidge, December 28, 1923, in Justice File 198589.

81. Frost, *Challenge of the Klan*, 21-27; Jones, *Klan*, 143; Edgar Allen Booth, *The Mad Mullah of America* (Columbus, 1927), 133-36.

82. The most careful breakdown, presenting an estimate of cumulative membership through May 1923, is in Robert L. Duffus, "The Ku Klux Klan in the Middle West," *World's Work*, XLVI (1923), 363-64. I add a half million to Duffus' total because of the remarkable continuing growth in subsequent months in Indiana, Ohio, and probably elsewhere. See New York *Times*, November 1, 1923, p. 1, and November 8, 1923, p. 3; *Literary Digest*, LXXIX (November 24, 1923), 13-14.

83. Booth, *Mad Mullah*, 34-35, 90, 131-32, 300; John Bartlow Martin, *Indiana: An Interpretation* (New York, 1947), 189-94; New York *Times*, November 6, 1923, p. 1, and November 18, 1923, sec. 2, p. 2.

84. Duffus, "Klan in Middle West," 365-66; *Literary Digest*, LXXVII (June 9, 1923), 12-13; New York *Times*, 1923: April 10, p. 26, June 28, p. 2, July 26, p. 1, August 31, p. 10, and September 11, p. 19. On newspaper opposition to the Klan see *Literary Digest*, LXXIII (June 10, 1922), 15, and LXXIV (August 5, 1922), 49.

85. See the running account in the *Literary Digest*, September 22, 1923-December 8, 1923, and in *Outlook*, September 26, 1923-November 28, 1923; also Bruce Bliven, "From the Oklahoma Front," *New Republic*, XXXVI (1923), 202-205.

86. New York *Times*, 1923: April 7, p. 15, August 17, p. 1, August 26, p. 1, and August 31, p. 1.

NOTES TO CHAPTER ELEVEN

1. For examples see *Session Laws of Arizona*, 1921, p. 175; *Public Acts of Connecticut*, 1921, p. 3282; *Public Acts of Michigan*, 1919, p. 592, and 1925, p. 77; *Laws of New Mexico*, 1921, p. 198; *Cahill's Consolidated Laws of New York*, 1923, p. 711; *Wyoming Revised Statutes*, 1931, pp. 1234, 1830.

2. *New Republic*, VI (1916), 254. (Quoted by permission of the publishers.) The indecisive character of liberal opposition to the new restriction laws is suggested in *New Republic*, XXVII (1921), 314-15, and XXXVIII (1924), 30; *Nation*, CXII (1921), 331, and CXV (1922), 404. For the most part these journals preserved a discreet silence on the issue.

3. *Immigration Journal*, I (1916), 55-58; Sidney L. Gulick, *The American-Japanese Problem* (New York, 1914), 282-88.

4. *National Committee for Constructive Immigration Legislation* (n.p., n.d.); National Committee for Constructive Immigration Legislation, *Our Immigration and Naturalization Laws* [New York, 1919]; Sidney Gulick to William H. Johnston, June 25, 1918, in General Records of the Department of Labor, File 164/14 (National Archives).

5. *Moody's Investment Service* quoted in *Literary Digest*, LXI (May 24, 1919), 131-32, and New York *Journal of Commerce* quoted in *Literary Digest*, LXV (April 24, 1920), 12; *American Industries*, XX (October, 1919), 10; New York *Times*, October 16, 1918, sec. 2, p. 3; Inter-Racial Council, *Proceedings National Conference on Immigration*, p. 8.

6. *Commercial and Financial Chronicle*, CXI (1920), 2267; *Hearings: Immigration and Labor* (House Committee on Immigration and Naturalization, 67 Cong., 4 Sess., Washington, 1923), 337; John E. Otterson, "Decreased Immigration—Less Production," *Iron Age*, CV (1920),

1134; *Mining and Scientific Press* quoted in *Literary Digest,* LXX (August 13, 1921), 23.

7. *Congressional Record,* 67 Cong., 2 Sess., 2804, and 68 Cong., 1 Sess., 5647-58; New York *Times,* February 25, 1924, p. 1; Milton Lehman, "The Ageless Gentleman from Illinois," New York *Times Magazine,* January 21, 1951, p. 28.

8. Franz Boas, "What Is a Race?" *Nation,* CXX (1925), 91; New York *Times,* April 26, 1924, p. 17; Commonwealth Club of California, *Transactions,* XVIII (1923), 203; *Justice,* April 4, 1924, p. 2. See also Ludwig Lewisohn's agonized autobiography, *Up Stream: An American Chronicle* (New York, 1922), 234.

9. Ed. F. McSweeney, *The Racial Contribution to the United States* (Knights of Columbus Historical Commission, n.d.), 5-17. The series included George Cohen, *The Jews in the Making of America* (Boston, 1924); Frederick Franklin Schrader, *The Germans in the Making of America* (Boston, 1924); and W. E. B. Du Bois, *The Gift of the Black Folk* (Boston, 1924).

10. Kallen first broached his theory in 1915 and summed it up most fully and insistently in *Culture and Democracy in the United States* (New York, 1924). Kallen speaks of Louis D. Brandeis especially as a Zionist leader who drew on his theory. See *Brandeis on Zionism: A Collection of Addresses and Statements by Louis D. Brandeis* (Washington, 1942), 8-11, 13-19, 49-50.

11. *Literary Digest,* LXVIII (February 26, 1921), 7; petition in support of Johnson bill to Senator E. F. Ladd, April 1, 1924, in Records of the Senate Committee on Immigration (National Archives). The collapse of anti-Germanism in 1920 is carefully documented in an unpublished paper by Harry W. Madison, Jr. *America,* a leading Catholic weekly, illustrates the spread of restrictionist views in Catholic circles also. During and after the Red Scare *America* reversed its former position, and by 1923 it was referring to the new immigrants as a handicap to Catholicism and to the nation; XXIII (1920), 392, and XXIX (1923), 32, 55.

12. *American Federationist,* XXVI, Part 1 (1919), 136, 163; Gompers to Executive Council, January 4, 1919, in Samuel Gompers Papers (A.F.L. Building, Washington, D. C.); *Report of Proceedings of the Thirty-Ninth Annual Convention of the American Federation of Labor,* 1919, 364-68.

13. Statement prepared by President Gompers for Newspaper Enterprise Association, December 17, 1918, in Gompers Papers.

14. *American Federationist,* XXIII (1916), 253-54; *Literary Digest,* LV (December 1, 1917), 15; Gompers to Matthew Woll, February 11, 1919, and to Frank Morrison, February 20, 1919, in Gompers Papers.

15. *National Civic Federation Review,* IV (December 20, 1918), 11; New York *Times,* December 8, 1918, sec. 3, p. 3; *Literary Digest,* LX (February 8, 1919), 17-18.

16. Madison Grant to Prescott F. Hall, October 21, 1918, in Files of the Immigration Restriction League, Box 1 (Houghton Library, Harvard University); *Literary Digest,* LX (February 8, 1919), 18, and LXII (July 5, 1919), 28; New York *Times,* January 10, 1919, p. 4; *Hearings:*

Prohibition of Immigration (House Committee on Immigration and Naturalization, 65 Cong., 3 Sess., Washington, 1919).

17. See note 45, Chapter VII. Also I am indebted to various personal informants.

18. New York *Times*, November 13, 1920, p. 11.

19. *Literary Digest*, LXII (July 26, 1919), 96; *Hearings: Administration of Immigration Laws* (House Committee on Immigration and Naturalization, 66 Cong., 2 Sess., Washington, 1920); Louis F. Post, *The Deportations Delirium of Nineteen-Twenty* (Chicago, 1923), 223-32, 241-42. On Johnson's deportation act of 1920 see text, p. 233.

20. *Literary Digest*, LXV (June 5, 1920), 32, and LXVI (September 11, 1920), 18; New York *Times*, February 2, 1921, p. 24, and February 12, 1921, p. 2. Monthly statistics are available in Harry Jerome, *Migration and Business Cycles* (New York, 1926), 106.

21. *Literary Digest*, LXII (July 5, 1919), 29, LXVII (December 18, 1920), 8-9, and LXVII (December 25, 1920), 14; National Education Association, *Proceedings*, 1921, p. 760.

22. *Cong. Rec.*, 66 Cong., 3 Sess., 4550.

23. *Ibid.*, 285-86.

24. *Temporary Suspension of Immigration* (66 Cong., 3 Sess., House Report No. 1109, Washington, 1920); *World's Work*, XLI (1921), 329-30, and XLIV (1922), 144; D. F. Garland, "Immigration and the Labor Supply," *System: The Magazine of Business*, XLIII (1923), 589; *Cong. Rec.*, 66 Cong., 3 Sess., 178-79. On the origin of the State Department report see Louis Marshall to Charles Evans Hughes, April 27, 1921, in Marshall Papers, Box C (Archives of the American Jewish Committee); and *Hearings: Emergency Immigration Legislation* (Senate Committee on Immigration, 66 Cong., 3 Sess., Washington, 1921), 10.

25. *Hearings: Emergency Immigration Legislation*, 1921, pp. 37-39, 87, 117-28; New York *Times*, December 5, 1920, p. 16, and January 12, 1921, p. 14.

26. New York *Times*, December 13, 1920, p. 25. On the pressure for Senatorial action see issues of February 9, 1921, p. 8, February 10, 1921, p. 15, and February 18, 1921, p. 3; and *Literary Digest*, LXVIII (February 26, 1921), 7. Actually the percentage plan applied to Europe, Siberia, Asia Minor, Persia, Africa, Australia, and New Zealand. On the provisions of the law as enacted see Roy L. Garis, *Immigration Restriction: A Study of the Opposition to and Regulation of Immigration into the United States* (New York, 1927), 142-49.

27. *Reports of the Immigration Commission: Abstracts* (61 Cong., 3 Sess., Senate Document No. 747, Washington, 1911), I, 47. For Dillingham's bill two years later see Seattle *Post-Intelligencer*, December 9, 1913. Husband's son, Richard F. Husband, tells me that his father claimed to be the originator of the percentage idea "as well as the author of the law introduced by Senator Dillingham." The fact that Husband presented to the Senate Committee in January 1921 the key testimony explaining the Dillingham bill tends to support this claim. Soon after, the incoming Harding administration rewarded Husband for his long services as an immigration expert by appointing him commissioner of immigration. See *Hearings: Emergency Immigration Legislation*, 1921,

534-44, and the biographical sketch in *National Cyclopaedia of American Biography*, XXXIV, 264.

28. New York *Times*, February 20, 1921, p. 1, and April 7, 1921, p. 29.
29. Secretary of Labor William B. Wilson placed his own opposition to the bill on technical grounds: that no emergency justified it and that it would be exceedingly difficult to administer; William B. Wilson to President Wilson, March 1, 1921, in Labor File 164/14.
30. New York *Times*, March 29, 1921, p. 19; *Cong. Rec.*, 67 Cong., 1 Sess., 589, 968.
31. *Hearings: Admission of Aliens in Excess of Percentage Quotas for June* (House Committee on Immigration and Naturalization, 67 Cong., 1 Sess., Washington, 1921); *Hearings: Operation of Percentage Immigration Law for Five Months* (House Committee on Immigration and Naturalization, 67 Cong., 1 Sess., Washington, 1921); New Britain *Daily Herald*, November 9, 1923; *Cong. Rec.*, 68 Cong., 1 Sess., 5465-66.
32. New York *Times*, February 2, 1922, p. 16, and April 16, 1922, p. 23. Johnson had first asked for an extension of one year only, but under the urging of Gompers and others the Senate doubled the period; Gompers to Albert Johnson, February 25, 1922, and to members of the Senate Committee on Immigration, March 16, 1922, in Gompers Papers.
33. *Hearings: Restriction of Immigration* (House Committee on Immigration and Naturalization, 68 Cong., 1 Sess., Washington, 1924), 92-96; American Legion, *Summary of Proceedings of the National Convention*, 1923, pp. 25-26; *Cong. Rec.*, 68 Cong., 1 Sess., 6473. Johnson himself introduced an exclusion bill as late as December 10, 1921. New York *Times*, December 11, 1921, p. 21.
34. *Saturday Evening Post*, CXCIV (February 11, 1922), 22; New York *Times*, July 10, 1921, sec. 6, p. 8; *World's Work*, XLIV (1922), 581.
35. "Records of the Executive Committee of the Immigration Restriction League," 1919-20, in Files of the I.R.L. The league's vigor and membership had declined over the years, and after 1916 it gave up propaganda work. The last entry in the records that Hall kept was made in April 1920; he died a year later.
36. Peter F. Snyder to author, June 16, 1952. Mr. Snyder, who served as Johnson's private secretary and committee clerk for many years, is a storehouse of information on immigration restriction during those years.
37. *Hearings: Restriction*, 1924, pp. 608-20; Snyder to author, June 6, 1952.
38. *Hearings: Biological Aspects of Immigration* (House Committee on Immigration, 66 Cong., 2 Sess., Washington, 1921); *Hearings: Analysis of America's Modern Melting Pot* (House Committee on Immigration, 67 Cong., 3 Sess., Washington, 1923); *Hearings: Europe as an Emigrant-Exporting Continent and the United States as an Immigrant-Receiving Nation* (House Committee on Immigration, 68 Cong., 1 Sess., Washington, 1924).
39. *Eugenical News: Current Record of Race Hygiene*, VIII (1923), 53.
40. *Hearings: Emergency Immigration Legislation*, 1921, 293-300. This paragraph rests primarily on an interview with Captain Trevor on July 23, 1949. The only biographical sketch is in *Who's Who in America*, 1954-55, p. 2698.
41. House Report No. 1621 (67 Cong., 4 Sess., Washington, 1923). See

also *American Jewish Year Book*, 1923-24, p. 58. Professor Roy L. Garis apparently originated the idea of using the census of 1890 in "The Immigration Problem," *Scribner's Magazine*, LXXII (1922), 364-67.

42. *Literary Digest*, LXXV (November 18, 1922), 18; C. Coapes Brinley, "Shall We Let Down the Bars?" *Industrial Management*, LXV (1923), 247; Franklin Remington to Secretary James J. Davis, April 27, 1923, in Labor File 164/14E.

43. New York *Times*, August 28, 1922, p. 20, October 19, 1922, p. 6, February 21, 1923, p. 2, and May 20, 1923, sec. 7, p. 5; *Hearings: Immigration and Labor* (House Committee on Immigration, 67 Cong., 4 Sess., Washington, 1923); *Hearings: Alien Seamen—Insane Aliens—Statements on Various Immigration Problems* (House Committee on Immigration, 67 Cong., 4 Sess., Washington, 1923), 644-97; *Policies of the Chamber of Commerce of the United States of America* [Washington, 1925], 44. Gary's statement is in *Literary Digest*, LXXVII (May 5, 1923), 9.

44. *Literary Digest*, LXXVII (April 28, 1923), 14; New York *Times*, November 23, 1922, p. 10, and August 6, 1923, p. 10.

45. *Commercial and Financial Chronicle*, CXVI (1923), 557-58; New York *Times*, February 21, 1923, p. 2; *Hearings: Immigration and Labor*, 1923, p. 334.

46. *Hearings: Amendment to Immigration Law* (Senate Committee on Immigration, 67 Cong., 4 Sess., Washington, 1923); New York *Times*, February 21, 1923, p. 2, and May 20, 1923, sec. 7, p. 5; Samuel Gompers to Peter F. Snyder, October 30, 1922, in Gompers Papers.

47. *Saturday Evening Post*, CXCV (December 23, 1922), 20; *Literary Digest*, LXXVII (May 5, 1923), 10; *Commercial and Financial Chronicle*, CXVI (1923), 1856. See also *American Legion Weekly*, V (January 12, 1923), 12.

48. Brinley, "Shall We Let Down the Bars?" p. 248; Garland, "Immigration and the Labor Supply," 589-90; L. W. Moffett, "Keen Interest in Coming of Immigrants," *Iron Age*, CXI (1923), 1573; K. H. Condit, "Immigration—or Machinery?" *American Machinist*, LVIII (1923), 393-95.

49. National Industrial Conference Board, *Special Report Number 26: Proceedings of the National Immigration Conference Held in New York City December 13 and 14, 1923* (New York, 1924), 25-26, 76, and *passim; Commercial and Financial Chronicle*, CXVII (1923), 2722-23. See also statement by editors, *Industrial Management*, LXV (1923), 321-23.

50. *American Industries*, XXIV (April, 1924), 27-32; *Policies of C. of C.*, 44-45; "The Immigration Question Up to Date," *Nation's Business*, XII (April, 1924), 56.

51. Rodney Bean, "Official Washington," *Annalist*, XXII (1923), 789; L. W. Moffett, "Little Opposition to Immigration Bill," *Iron Age*, CXIII (1924), 1233-34.

52. New York *Times*, February 25, 1924, p. 1; Philadelphia *Public Ledger*, March 5, 1924, p. 10, and March 7, 1924, p. 10.

53. Calvin Coolidge, "Whose Country Is This?" *Good Housekeeping*, LXXII (February, 1921), 14. Coolidge's message to Congress in December 1923 is quoted in Garis, *Immigration Restriction*, 169-70.

54. James J. Davis, *The Iron Puddler: My Life in the Rolling Mills and What Came of It* (New York, 1922), 28, 61. See also Davis to Calvin Coolidge, May 29, 1924, in Coolidge Papers, File 133 (Division of Manuscripts, Library of Congress); James J. Davis, "Our Labor Shortage and Immigration," *Industrial Management*, LXV (1923), 322.

55. Davis's proposals for immigration legislation are discussed in New York *Times*, January 2, 1924, p. 2, and in *Annual Report of the Secretary of Labor*, 1923, pp. 141-46, and 1924, pp. 70-97. Objections to a thoroughgoing examination and selection of immigrants overseas came from European governments, from Congressional nativists who thought that too many bad ones would slip past the consuls, and from the Consular Service itself. See John Cable to Davis, September 4, 1923, in Labor File 164/14G; and Snyder to author, June 16, 1952.

56. Garis, *Immigration Restriction*, 157, 256-57. Johnson kept talking about the 2 per cent plan all through 1923. See New York *Times*, May 9, 1923, p. 7, September 26, 1923, p. 1, and December 3, 1923, p. 2.

57. *Restriction of Immigration* (68 Cong., 1 Sess., House Report No. 350, Washington, 1924), 8-9; Snyder to author, June 16, 1952. Johnson had urged this step for many years.

58. This reconstruction is based on interview with Captain Trevor, supplemented by *Restriction of Immigration* (68 Cong., 1 Sess., House Report 350), 14, 16, 26-27, Trevor's original brief reprinted in *Cong. Rec.*, 68 Cong., 1 Sess., 5469-5471, and the remarks of Congressman William Vaile, based on Trevor's calculations, in *Cong. Rec.*, 68 Cong., 1 Sess., 5643-47. I have no evidence that Trevor originated the concept of preserving the racial status quo, but the above committee report, in stating this as the objective of the proposed legislation, clearly reflected Trevor's thinking as set forth in his brief to the committee. The fact that the committee took its principal argument verbatim from Trevor was pointed out by Charles P. Howland, ed., *Survey of American Foreign Relations, 1929* (New Haven, 1929), 450-51.

59. *Cong. Rec.*, 68 Cong., 1 Sess., 5640, ff.; New York *World*, April 6, 1924, p. 7, and April 13, 1924, p. 4.

60. Philadelphia *Public Ledger*, April 7, 1924, p. 16; *Imperial Night-Hawk*, March 5, 1924, p. 8, and April 2, 1924, p. 5; *Illinois Fiery Cross*, April 4, 1924, p. 1.

61. *American Federationist*, XXXI, part 1 (1924), 314-15, 464. Compare with A.F.L. position in December 1923, as expressed in *Hearings: Restriction*, 1924, pp. 92-96. It should also be added that the A.F.L. did not work very hard for the 1924 legislation, perhaps anticipating its passage as a matter of course. Moffett, "Little Opposition," 1234.

62. New York *Times*, February 28, 1924, p. 3, and February 29, 1924, p. 8; New York *World*, February 29, 1924, p. 13; Philadelphia *Public Ledger*, April 18, 1924, p. 1.

63. In response to my inquiries, both Trevor and Reed claimed the sole authorship of the idea. On the available evidence it is impossible to determine definitely which of them thought of it first, although each certainly made an essential contribution to developing it. Reed declares that this was "one of the few wholly original ideas that I have ever had." Albert Johnson, on the other hand, telegraphed to President

Coolidge in 1926: "John B. Trevor . . . is originator National Origins idea which was built up to show reasons for use of eighteen ninety census in Immigration law." But Trevor himself told the Senate Immigration Committee on March 8, 1924, that Reed "had reached about the same idea that I had." Johnson to Coolidge, August 25, 1926, in Coolidge Papers, File 133; David A. Reed to author, June 11, 1952; *Hearings: Selective Immigration Legislation* (Senate Committee on Immigration, 68 Cong., 1 Sess., Washington, 1924), 89.

The chronological sequence of events suggests that Reed may have hit upon the idea first but felt convinced that it would work only after seeing Trevor's statistical report to the House Immigration Committee in defense of the 1890 census. Trevor's report, dated March 5, 1924, contained a column of figures showing what the quotas would be according to Reed's proposed "national origins" amendment to the immigration bill. Thus Trevor knew about Reed's idea before filing the report. On the following day Reed gave notice to the Senate of his intention to submit a certain amendment to the pending immigration bill, and on March 8, Reed introduced Trevor to the Senate Committee to testify in support of Reed's national origins amendment.

64. See Reed's defense of the idea in *Cong. Rec.*, 68 Cong., 1 Sess., 5467-68, and in New York *Times*, April 27, 1924, sec. 9, p. 3.

65. Reed to author, June 11, 1952; interview with Trevor. For the unfavorable action in the House on the national origins plan see *Cong. Rec.*, 68 Cong., 1 Sess., 6227-29.

66. *Cong. Rec.*, 68 Cong., 1 Sess., 6649; "Legislative File—Immigration," April-May, 1924, in Thomas J. Walsh Papers (Division of Manuscripts, Library of Congress); Philadelphia *Public Ledger*, April 19, 1924, p. 4.

67. Stephen S. Wise to President, May 16, 1924, and President's Secretary to Samuel Dickstein, May 19, 1924, in Coolidge Papers, File 133.

68. John B. Trevor, "An Analysis of the American Immigration Act of 1924," *International Conciliation*, no. 202 (September, 1924), 5. See also William S. Bernard, ed., *American Immigration Policy: A Reappraisal* (New York, 1950).

69. *Grizzly Bear*, XXXV (May, 1924), 1; *Literary Digest*, LXXXI (June 7, 1924), 15; *Industrial Management*, LXVII (June, 1924), 324; *The Citizen*, I (October, 1926), 28; Henry H. Curran, "The New Immigrant," *Saturday Evening Post*, CXCVIII (August 15, 1925), 25.

70. *World's Work*, XLIX (1925), 233-34; Madison Grant, "America for the Americans," *Forum*, LXXIV (1925), 346-55; Allied Patriotic Societies, *Report of the Committee on Immigration* (New York, 1925); *The American Coalition* [pamphlet, 1929].

71. Donald Day, ed., *The Autobiography of Will Rogers* (Boston, 1949), 107-11, 160-64. (Quoted by permission of the Houghton Mifflin Company.)

72. "Who Knocks the 100 Per Center?" *Dearborn Independent*, August 15, 1925, p. 14; Legion quoted in William Gellermann, *The American Legion as Educator* (New York, 1938), 83.

73. Henry Pratt Fairchild, *The Melting-Pot Mistake* (Boston, 1926); Madison Grant, *The Conquest of a Continent* (New York, 1933); *Book Review Digest*, 1926, pp. 221-22, and 1933, p. 376.

74. See especially *Dearborn Independent*, March 13, 1926, pp. 6-7, and April 2, 1927, pp. 6, 11.
75. Marshall to Julius Rosenwald, July 22, 1927, and memo, July 14, 1927, in Marshall Papers, Box C.
76. *Free Speech in 1924: The Work of the American Civil Liberties Union*, 4, 28.
77. Michael Williams, *The Shadow of the Pope* (New York, 1932), 145-68.
78. *Literary Digest*, LXXXIII (November 22, 1924), 16; John Bartlow Martin, *Indiana: An Interpretation* (New York, 1947), 193-95; Ben B. Lindsey, "My Fight with the Ku Klux Klan," *Survey*, LIV (1925), 271-74, 319-21.
79. *Independent*, CXIII (1924), 114; Max Bentley, "'Let's Brush Them Aside,'" *Collier's*, LXXIV (November 22, 1924), 21, 47; *Literary Digest*, LXXXII (September 6, 1924), 7-9; New York *Times*, January 19, 1925, p. 4.
80. Emerson H. Loucks, *The Ku Klux Klan in Pennsylvania* (Harrisburg, 1936), 165-96; *Independent*, CXVI (1926), 58-59; *New Republic*, XLV (1926), 310-11; Martin, *Indiana*, 184-89, 195-99.

Bibliographical Note

Foreign influences have touched American life at so many points that a comprehensive bibliography of materials relevant to the history of nativism would be impossible to compile and meaningless to use. My own research was necessarily selective, and many parts of this story still need careful monographic study.

Since my object was a comprehensive synthesis of a subject that had no clearly visible limits, I was compelled to deal with almost every type of historical source. Some—fiction, for example—proved too unwieldy to handle with justice. The foundations of the present book rest on the general American periodicals of the day and on the vast array of United States government documents pertinent to immigration. As patterns unfolded, it became evident that I could not rely exclusively on the standard periodical and document indexes as guides to these sources. Some had to be studied systematically, volume by volume, and to others I had to return time and again with fresh questions in mind. A more specialized kind of source, but one essential for an understanding of organized nativism, consists of such fugitive materials as tracts and reports of societies. The New York Public Library is very rich in these items; others turned up at the Wisconsin Historical Society and the Henry E. Huntington Library.

The following brief comments have two general purposes: to list, for interested scholars, the manuscript collections and the newspaper files that were consulted; and, for all who wish to read further, to call attention to the secondary sources that proved most important and helpful.

MANUSCRIPTS

Three collections bear directly on the history of nativism. The Henry Baldwin Papers, in the Division of Manuscripts of the New York Public Library, consist of a mass of letters and other documents on nativistic and hereditary patriotic organizations collected by a zealous antiquary in the late eighties and early nineties. The Archives of the American Jewish Committee, located in New York, are rich in correspondence and reports on anti-Semitism since the committee's establishment in 1906. The Files of the Immigration Restriction League, in the Houghton Library, Harvard University, not only furnish a detailed record of the activities of that important organization from 1894 to 1920 but also contain revealing letters from Congressmen and citizens whom the league approached.

For a broader view of the politics of immigration restriction one must turn to the correspondence of political leaders. In the Division of Manuscripts at the Library of Congress I found pertinent data in the papers of five Presidents: Grover Cleveland, Theodore Roosevelt, William H. Taft, Woodrow Wilson, and Calvin Coolidge. Since the Roosevelt Papers are an almost inexhaustible record of American life, a sampling of the post-Presidential file also opened important perspectives in social history. On restriction legislation there is supplementary material in the papers of Elihu Root, Oscar S. Straus, and Thomas J. Walsh. The Thomas W. Gregory Papers, located in the same great manuscript repository, helped to clarify federal policy toward aliens during the First World War. Letter-press copies of Samuel Gompers' immense outgoing correspondence are preserved in the A.F.L. Building, Washington, D. C.; consulted only for the years 1918-1920 and 1922-1924, they had some limited value in sharpening the outlines of A.F.L. policy.

Beginning with the First World War, when the federal government developed broad administrative and investigative interests in America's alien population, important parts of the story of nativism must be dug out of the National Archives. Although the Records of the Immigration and Naturalization Service tell little about the history of immigration restriction, the files of the Americanization Section reveal the expanding functions of the Bureau of Naturalization after 1914. The General Records of the Department of Justice are of prime importance in understanding anti-German and anti-radical activities and the evolution of deportation legislation. There is also a helpful file of reports and complaints on local Ku Klux Klan activities, resulting from a desultory investigation that the Justice Department launched in 1921. The General Records of the Department of Labor contain material on radical and anti-radical movements, deportation, industrial problems during the war, and immigration restriction after 1917. Finally, in connection with the Americanization movement, I made some use of the unwieldy Records of the Council of National Defense.

Future students of political nativism may hope to exploit many more unpublished sources, including some that were closed to me. Undoubtedly this would have been a better book if permission to consult the Henry Cabot Lodge Papers at the Massachusetts Historical Society had not been withheld. Also, I did not receive access to the main body of Justice Department records dealing with the Big Red Scare of 1919-1920.

NEWSPAPER FILES

A full bibliography of the specialized nativist press would run into hundreds of titles. Almost all of these papers had a local circulation and an ephemeral life; the great majority never reached a library. The following were the most useful of those examined: *American Standard* (San Francisco), 1888-1890; *The American: An Exponent of True Americanism & Devoted to the Interests of the Jr. O.U.A.M.* (Pittsburgh), 1889-1891; *A.P.A. Magazine* (San Francisco), 1895-1897; *American Citizen* (Boston), 1905-1913; *Watson's Magazine* (Thomson, Ga.), 1910, 1913-1915; *The Menace* (Aurora, Mo.), 1911-1915; *The Ford International Weekly: The Dearborn Independent* (Dearborn, Mich.), 1919-1927; *American Legion Weekly* (New York), 1919-1920, 1923-1924; *The Dawn* (Chicago), 1922-1924, succeeded by *Illinois Fiery Cross*, 1924; *Imperial Night-Hawk* (Atlanta), 1923-1924. Dates indicate the extent of my research, not necessarily the whole span of publication.

General newspapers, chosen in part for reasons of availability, yielded information and attitudes on almost every aspect of the subject; and they had the intangible advantage of putting nativistic developments in the perspective of other current events. The following were searched most systematically: New York *Tribune*, 1875-1881, 1884-1897, 1899, 1902; Philadelphia *Public Ledger*, 1884, 1886, 1891, 1895-1897, 1905-1906, 1923-1924; New York

Times, 1914-1924. Additional data on the course of immigration restriction came from the Boston *Herald*, 1905-1906, Los Angeles *Times*, 1920, 1924, and New York *World*, 1923-1924. The San Francisco *Argonaut*, a politico-literary weekly, was studied for 1877 and 1886-1888 because of its blatant nativism. Certain other papers were consulted for specific incidents.

I am also greatly indebted to nativists who assembled and preserved scrapbooks of newspaper clippings. The most important collection consists of eleven volumes in the Widener Library, Harvard University, entitled "Immigration Clippings Collected by Prescott F. Hall." This is a chronological file bearing chiefly on immigration restriction and covering the years from 1894 to 1920. It is preceded by "Immigration: Clippings Collected by Robert DeCourcy Ward," one volume on the period 1891-1894. The New York Public Library has a two-volume "Collection of Newspaper Clippings Relating to the Situation of the Roman Catholic Church in America," dealing with anti-Catholicism in the 1880's. Albert Johnson has left two scrapbooks of newspaper clippings on his early political career (1912-1914), now in the possession of the Public Library in Hoquiam, Washington.

For an understanding of anti-Semitism in nineteenth century America I resorted to several Jewish newspapers and periodicals, which may be studied with the aid of two indexes at the American Jewish Historical Society: one (very incomplete) of the American Jewish press, the other of European Jewish periodicals that had American correspondents. The same subject on the eve of the First World War was followed in the *B'nai B'rith News*, 1912-1915.

Secondary Sources

GENERAL STUDIES

Whereas historians have done relatively little first-rate work on American ethnic relations (except perhaps in connection with slavery), this whole field has become a major preoccupation of social scientists in recent years. Out of the inquiries of sociologists and social psychologists have come a set of challenging concepts and a mass of contemporary data, all of which can enrich the historical imagination. They can also confine our sense of the past if they are not used cautiously. Almost all of this social science literature forms part of a general intellectual revolt against 100 per cent Americanism. Much of it underplays the objective realities of group conflict, assuming that antipathies are largely prejudices referable to subjective, irrational processes. Perhaps the most fundamental problem for one who seeks a comprehensive understanding of human experience in this area (and in how many others!) is to find a meaningful balance between the ideas inside men's heads and the world outside.

Sociologists took a systematic interest in immigration at a relatively early date. Robert E. Park and Herbert A. Miller, *Old World Traits Transplanted* (New York, 1921) remains one of the best studies of the immigrants' community life. William Carlson Smith, *Americans in the Making: The Natural History of the Assimilation of Immigrants* (New York, 1939) describes the process of individual adjustment through which the immigrant typically passed. Elin Anderson, *We Americans: A Study of Cleavage in an American City* (Cambridge, 1937) is a penetrating analysis of ethnic and religious divisions in Burlington, Vermont. Gordon W. Allport, *The Nature of Prejudice* (Boston, 1954) sums up a generation of research by social psychologists. T. W. Adorno and others, *The Authoritarian Personality* (New York, 1950) is an important study of anti-Semitism with broad, controversial implications. Ralph Linton, "Nativistic Movements," *American Anthropologist*, XLV (1943), 230-40, makes some stimulating generalizations from the comparative point of view of anthropology.

The only general history of American nativism is Gustavus Myers, *History of Bigotry in the United States* (New York, 1943), a superficial, indignant, rambling, and episodic book. For an introduction to nativism in American history one should turn first to books of a broader character. David F. Bowers, ed., *Foreign Influences in American Life: Essays and Critical Bibliographies* (Princeton, 1944) includes exploratory essays and some excellent guides to further reading. Another collection of essays, Marcus Lee Hansen's *The Immigrant in American History* (Cambridge, 1942) is the best single book on its subject. Although conceived along conventional lines and outdated in important ways, Carl Wittke, *We Who Built America: The Saga of the*

Immigrant (New York, 1939) is a major work packed with useful information.

Like most historians in this field, Hansen and Wittke have done most of their research on the old immigration. Their books, therefore, reflect the patterns of a frontier society more than those of an urban one. Oscar Handlin, *The Uprooted: The Epic Story of the Great Migrations that Made the American People* (Boston, 1951) subtly reverses the emphasis. An imaginative blend of psychology, history, and personal sympathy, *The Uprooted* is always challenging if not at every point convincing. A succeeding volume, *The American People in the Twentieth Century* (Cambridge, 1954), carries further Handlin's central theme, the story of group-consciousness. This book appeared after my own manuscript was substantially complete; but see my review in the *Mississippi Valley Historical Review*, XLI (1954), 544-45.

On the related subject of American nationalism, Merle Curti has written the pioneering synthesis, *The Roots of American Loyalty* (New York, 1946), suggestive and informative in spite of a somewhat mechanical organization. It should be supplemented by Hans Kohn, *The Idea of Nationalism: A Study in Its Origins and Background* (New York, 1944), Chapter VI, and Albert K. Weinberg, *Manifest Destiny: A Study of Nationalist Expansionism in American History* (Baltimore, 1935).

EARLY AMERICAN NATIVISM

The best account of the anti-radical hysteria of the 1790's is John C. Miller, *Crisis in Freedom: The Alien and Sedition Acts* (Boston, 1951). James Morton Smith provides further detail in a number of scattered articles, such as "The Enforcement of the Alien Friends Act of 1798," *Mississippi Valley Historical Review*, XLI (1954), 85-104. A substantial and discerning monograph by Vernon Stauffer, *New England and the Bavarian Illuminati* (New York, 1918) shows how the political anxieties of the period interacted with the Puritan tradition.

In studying the anti-Catholic tradition one may begin with Sister Mary Augustina Ray's ponderous *American Opinion of Roman Catholicism in the Eighteenth Century* (New York, 1936). Ray Allen Billington, *The Protestant Crusade, 1800-1860: A Study of the Origins of American Nativism* (New York, 1938) does not fully justify its subtitle but remains the outstanding history of anti-Catholic propaganda. Of the many studies of mid-nineteenth century nativism in individual states perhaps the best is Louis Dow Scisco, *Political Nativism in New York State* (New York, 1901). On nativist politics see also W. Darrell Overdyke, *The Know-Nothing Party in the South* (Baton Rouge, 1950), and Harry J. Carman and Reinhard H. Luthin, "Some Aspects of the Know-Nothing Movement Reconsidered," *South Atlantic Quarterly*, XXXIX (1940), 213-34. Oscar Handlin, *Boston's Immigrants 1790-1865: A Study in Acculturation* (Cambridge, 1941) puts the issue in the perspective of a conflict between Yankee and Irish cultures. In this connection see also William G. Bean, "An Aspect of Know Nothingism—The Immigrant and Slavery," *South Atlantic Quarterly*, XXIII (1924), 319-34, and "Puritan Versus Celt, 1850-1860," *New England Quarterly*, VII (1934), 70-89. Robert Ernst, "Economic Nativism in New York City during the 1840's," *New York History*, XXIX (1948), 170-86, treats a generally neglected aspect, and John Lardner recaptures the rowdy flavor of the Know-Nothings in "The Martyrdom of Bill the Butcher," *New Yorker*, XXX (March 20 and 27, 1954), 41-53, 38-59.

LATE NINETEENTH CENTURY

The main theme of Chapter Three is argued more schematically in my article, "Origins of Immigration Restriction, 1882-1897: A Social Analysis," *Mississippi Valley Historical Review*, XXXIX (1952), 77-88. Morrell Heald carefully reviews "Business Attitudes Toward European Immigration, 1880-1900" in *Journal of Economic History*, XIII (1953), 291-304. No comparable investigation of labor attitudes has been made; but there is an essay by Arthur Mann on the leader of the American Federation of Labor, "Gompers and the Irony of Racism," *Antioch Review*, XIII (1953), 203-14, which presents an interpretation different from my own. Among the leading studies of the economic aspect of immigration in the late nineteenth and early twentieth centuries are Harry Jerome, *Migration and Business Cycles* (New York, 1926), and Isaac Aaronovich Hourwich, *Immigration and Labor: The Economic Aspects of European Immigration to the United States* (2nd ed., New York, 1922). The latter, secretly subsidized by the American Jewish Committee, constituted a statistical attack on the forty-one volume *Reports of the Immigration Commission* (61 Cong., 2 and 3 Sess., Washington, 1911).

The best general account of anti-Catholicism as a cultural force in the late nineteenth century is hidden in Robert H. Lord and others, *History of the Archdiocese of Boston in the Various Stages of Its Development 1604 to 1943* (New York, 1944), Vol. III. Alvin Packer Stauffer, Jr., "Anti-Catholicism in American Politics 1865-1900" (Ph.D. thesis, Harvard University, 1933) has a broad scope but little perspective. The most careful and detailed account of the A.P.A. is Donald L. Kinzer, "The American Protective Association: A Study of Anti-Catholicism" (Ph.D. thesis, University of Washington, 1954). Reacting against the pro-Catholic bias of earlier studies, Kinzer leans over backward in depreciating the importance of his subject. A slighter sketch by Humphrey J. Desmond, *The A.P.A. Movement* (Washington, 1912), remains of value. John Higham, "The Mind of a Nativist: Henry F. Bowers and the A.P.A.," *American Quarterly*, IV (1952), 16-24, is a psychological interpretation.

For a case study of the political tactics of nativists see my article, "The American Party, 1886-1891," *Pacific Historical Review*, XIX (1950), 37-46.

RACE-THINKING

Europe was the seedbed of modern race-thinking, and a rounded view of the race idea in America must await a better knowledge of European intellectual history than is yet available. To a surprising degree the history of race-thinking on both sides of the Atlantic has been neglected, perhaps partly because our sense of guilt makes detachment difficult to achieve, and partly because the subject requires a grasp of both scientific and social thought. For an introduction to the scientific phase of the story one should turn to Earl W. Count, ed., *This Is Race: An Anthology Selected from the International Literature on the Races of Man* (New York, 1950), and to the same author's essay, "The Evolution of the Race Idea in Modern Western Culture During the Period of the pre-Darwinian Nineteenth Century," *Transactions of the New York Academy of Sciences*, VIII (1946), 139-65. John C. Greene adds some illuminating comments on eighteenth century anthropology in "Some Early Speculations on the Origin of Human Races," *American Anthropologist*, LVI (1954), 31-41. Perhaps the most suggestive sketch of the rise of race-thinking in its social and literary aspects is in Hannah Arendt, *The Origins of Totalitarianism* (New York, 1951). I believe that the book errs, however, in stressing the philosophical incompatibility of nationalism and racism rather than their psychological affinity. Jacques Barzun, *Race: A Study in Modern Superstition* (New York, 1937) is heavily polemical.

Richard Hofstadter, *Social Darwinism in American Thought, 1860-1915* (Philadelphia, 1944) provides a good starting point for studying race ideas in America; it deals more sharply with the social than with the Darwinian side of the matter. Edward A. Saveth describes the various race attitudes of a number of historians, notably Henry Adams, in *American Historians and European Immigrants, 1875-1925* (New York, 1948). Barbara Miller Solomon, "The Intellectual Background of the Immigration Restriction Movement in New England," *New England Quarterly*, XXV (1952), 47-59, is an analytical critique of the Boston intelligentsia in the Gilded Age; it interprets the drift toward race-thinking as part of an inner decline in the regional culture. Several scattered studies of individuals are also available. See Edward Lurie, "Louis Agassiz and the Races of Man," *Isis*, XLV (1954), 227-42; Edward McNall Burns, *David Starr Jordan: Prophet of Freedom* (Stanford, 1953); Carl Bode, "Cappy Ricks and the Monk in the Garden," *PMLA*, LXIV (1949), 59-69, which discusses Peter B. Kyne; and, for England, Frederic E. Faverty, *Matthew Arnold the Ethnologist* (Evanston, Ill., 1951).

ANTI-SEMITISM

Moses Rischin, *An Inventory of American Jewish History* (Cambridge, 1954) supplies a general bibliographical orientation. The only extensive treatment is Carey McWilliams, *A Mask for Privilege: Anti-Semitism in America* (Boston, 1948), which generalizes loosely on scant research. Bertram Wallace Korn, *American Jewry and the Civil War* (Philadelphia, 1951), valuable as an intensive study of a limited period, lacks subtlety and discrimination. Oscar Handlin has written two provocative essays: *Danger in Discord: Origins of Anti-Semitism in the United States*

(New York, 1948), and "American Views of the Jew at the Opening of the Twentieth Century," *Publications of the American Jewish Historical Society,* XL (1951), 323-44. The latter, breaking sharply with conventional exaggerations, seems to underestimate the extent and character of anti-Semitism in nineteenth century America. Rudolph Glanz has also made some pertinent comments on the early period in "Jew and Yankee: A Historic Comparison," *Jewish Social Studies,* VI (1944), 3-30, and *Jews in Relation to the Cultural Milieu of the Germans in America up to the Eighteen Eighties* (New York, 1947). Lee M. Friedman, *Jewish Pioneers and Patriots* (New York, 1943) contains a brief sketch of the Seligman Affair. On Henry Ford see Keith Sward's severely critical *The Legend of Henry Ford* (New York, 1948); William C. Richards, *The Last Billionaire: Henry Ford* (New York, 1949), a reporter's reminiscences; and Allan Nevins, "Henry Ford—A Complex Man," *American Heritage,* VI (1954), 54-59.

WORLD WAR I

Two complementary studies treat the ordeal of the leading minority of the war years. Carl F. Wittke, *German-Americans and the World War (with Special Emphasis on Ohio's German-Language Press)* (Columbus, 1936) is good on public opinion, and Clifton James Child, *The German-Americans in Politics, 1914-1917* (Madison, 1939) further clarifies the political and diplomatic context. James R. Mock, *Censorship 1917* (Princeton, 1941) is a hotchpotch of information on official and unofficial curtailment of free speech during 1917 and 1918, while Zechariah Chafee, Jr., *Free Speech in the United States* (Cambridge, 1941) remains the classic analysis of the constitutional issues. A detailed treatment of repression and public opinion in a local setting may be found in Franklin F. Holbrook and Livia Appel, *Minnesota in the War with Germany* (St. Paul, 1928-1932), Vol. II. Ray H. Abrams recounts the hysteria of a significant group of opinion-makers in *Preachers Present Arms: A Study of Wartime Attitudes and Activities of the Churches and the Clergy in the United States, 1914-1918* (Philadelphia, 1933). For important nationalist agencies see James R. Mock and Cedric Larson, *Words That Won the War: The Story of the Committee on Public Information 1917-1919* (Princeton, 1939), and Emerson Hough, *The Web*

(Chicago, 1919), a lurid, authorized history of the American Protective League.

On Americanization the standard monograph is Edward George Hartmann, *The Movement to Americanize the Immigrant* (New York, 1948), which chronicles the activities of the principal voluntary organizations and of state and federal governments. Unfortunately Hartmann does not draw upon the brilliant interpretive essay on the Americanization movement included in Horace M. Kallen, *Culture and Democracy in the United States: Studies in the Group Psychology of the American Peoples* (New York, 1924). A first attempt at synthesis—Howard C. Hill, "The Americanization Movement," *American Journal of Sociology*, XXIV (1919), 609-42—still has some value.

BIG RED SCARE

The first over-all treatment of the Big Red Scare appeared after this book went to the publisher. Robert K. Murray, *Red Scare: A Study in National Hysteria, 1919-1920* (Minneapolis, 1955) is a sound and readable evaluation. Strongest on public opinion and on labor unrest, it still leaves important questions about federal policies unanswered. The book largely supersedes Robert D. Warth's good essay, "The Palmer Raids," *South Atlantic Quarterly*, XLVIII (1949), 1-23, and Frederick Lewis Allen's engaging appraisal in *Only Yesterday: An Informal History of the Nineteen-Twenties* (New York, 1931). All historians, however, have strangely neglected the searching analysis of the deportations of this period in Kate Holladay Claghorn, *The Immigrant's Day in Court* (New York, 1923), an extensive review of the legal difficulties that aliens faced during and after the war. Chafee, *Free Speech in the United States* continues to be useful.

Several immediate post-mortems on the Red Scare make further contributions: Constantine M. Panunzio, *The Deportation Cases of 1919-1920* (New York, 1921), a study of individual experiences; Louis F. Post, *The Deportations Delirium of Nineteen-Twenty: A Personal Narrative of an Historic Official Experience* (Chicago, 1923); Interchurch World Movement of North America, *Report on the Steel Strike of 1919* (New York, 1920), and *Public Opinion and the Steel Strike* (New York, 1921).

KU KLUX KLAN

This dramatic subject has attracted a good deal of popular writing but little historical research. The most trustworthy studies to date are local ones. Emerson H. Loucks, *The Ku Klux Klan in Pennsylvania* (Harrisburg, 1936), a solid Ph.D. thesis based largely on oral testimony, illuminates the general character of the organization. A vivid re-creation of the Klan crusade in Herrin, Illinois, is contained in Paul M. Angle, *Bloody Williamson: A Chapter in American Lawlessness* (New York, 1952). Norman F. Weaver's "The Knights of the Ku Klux Klan in Wisconsin, Indiana, Ohio and Michigan" (Ph.D. thesis, University of Wisconsin, 1954) is not yet open to inspection.

John Moffatt Mecklin, *The Ku Klux Klan: A Study of the American Mind* (New York, 1924) is a vapid sociological interpretation, but an extremely perceptive one appears in Frank Tannenbaum, *Darker Phases of the South* (New York, 1924). Frank Bohn, "The Ku Klux Klan Interpreted," *American Journal of Sociology*, XXX (1925), 385-407, offers some interesting data on Marion County, Ohio. A Catholic journalist, Michael Williams, discusses the Klan's influence on the Democratic national convention in 1924, and the anti-Catholic issue in 1928, in *The Shadow of the Pope* (New York, 1932). In a strange, privately printed book, *The Mad Mullah of America* (Columbus, 1927), a former Klan official, Edgar Allen Booth, gives his own chaotic revelations of internal intrigue and chicanery within the organization from 1922 to 1926; the book centers on the career of D. C. Stephenson.

Winfield Jones, *Knights of the Ku Klux Klan* (New York, 1941) is propaganda faintly disguised with information. Stanley Frost is reported to have written *The Challenge of the Klan* (Indianapolis, 1924) in conjunction with Milton Elrod, the general editor of the Klan's newspapers in the Middle West. William J. Simmons presented his own romantic version of the ideals of the organization he founded in *The Klan Unmasked* (Atlanta, 1924). In contrast to most contemporary reports, a series of articles that R. L. Duffus wrote for *World's Work*, XLVI (1923) is soberly informative on the Klan's career up to that time.

IMMIGRATION RESTRICTION

Roy L. Garis, *Immigration Restriction: A Study of the Opposition to and Regulation of Immigration into the United States* (New York, 1927) records successive legislative provisions and court decisions throughout American history. As a scholarly nativist, Garis' purpose is to show that the quota laws of the 1920's were "not a thing of the moment but the product of almost two hundred years of study and thought by the American people." Joseph Henry Taylor, "The Restriction of European Immigration 1890-1924" (Ph.D. thesis, University of California, Berkeley, 1936), though attempting little interpretation or explanation, gave me a better introduction to Congressional action. A good concise history of restriction legislation is buried in Charles P. Howland, ed., *Survey of American Foreign Relations, 1929* (New Haven, 1929), Section III. Rowland T. Berthoff provides copious information on "Southern Attitudes Toward Immigration, 1865-1914" in *Journal of Southern History*, XVII (1951), 328-60. An intimate view of legislation and administrative problems around the turn of the century is available in Victor Safford, *Immigration Problems: Personal Experiences of an Official* (New York, 1925). John A. Garraty, *Henry Cabot Lodge: A Biography* (New York, 1953) is unsatisfactory on this phase of Lodge's career, but Blair Bolles, *Tyrant from Illinois: Uncle Joe Cannon's Experiment with Personal Power* (New York, 1951) casts light on the political background of the law of 1907.

Index

Abercrombie, Thomas, 168
Adams, Henry, 68, 93, 139
Adams, Samuel Hopkins, 214
Addams, Jane, 121, 251
Alabama, anti-Catholic law, 292
Alien and Sedition Acts, 8, 19, 97, 210
Aliens: excluded from unions, 72; federal policy, 210, 217; role in wartime, 213-15; wartime sympathy for, 215-17; military service, 216; N.A.C. plan to control, 249; registration of, 249, 260, 325. *See also* Discrimination, legal
Alien suffrage: persistence, 98; passing of, 214; Wilson on, 376
Alpine race, 154, 156, 276
Amalgamated Association of Iron and Steel Workers, 49
Amendment, Fourteenth, 73, 183
Amendment on public education, proposed, 29, 60
American Association of Foreign Language Newspapers, 126, 188, 258
American Breeders' Association, 151, 152
American Constitutional Association, 232
American Defense Society: character, 199, 208; anti-German propaganda, 209; Americaniza-

tion, 245; anti-Semitism, 280; immigration restriction, 306
American Economic Association, 41, 95
American Federation of Labor: internationalism of, 50; debates restriction in 1890's, 71-72; restrictionist trend (1902-1907), 112, 163; and Arizona alien law, 183; attacks distribution, 189; drive for suspending immigration, 305-306, 313; fears action in 1923, 316; adopts race argument, 321; mentioned, 49, 106
American Iron and Steel Association, 51, 70, 187
Americanism, 100 per cent: origin, 204-207; wartime restraints on, 215-16; and anti-radicalism, 219; postwar version, 222-23, 268-70; in Americanization, 247-50, 255-56, 259, 260-63; relation to prohibition, 267-68; and anti-Semitism, 278; in Ku Klux Klan, 286, 289, 294; and fundamentalism, 293; and immigration restriction, 301, 305-306; immigrant reaction against, 304; decline, 325-30
Americanization, 234-63, 269, 308
Americanization Fund of Los Angeles, 261
American Jewish Committee, 188, 192, 280, 327